Not What I Thought I Wanted Nevertheless Everything I Needed

Discovering Love's Truth, Marriage as Purposed by God

TONY SCOTT

FIRST EDITION.
Durham, North Carolina

eBook: ISBN: 979-8-9885933-5-5
Paperback Print Book: ISBN: 979-8-9885933-0-0
Hardcover Print Book ISBN: 979-8-9885933-1-7

For more information, please contact: redeemedwriter718@gmail.com

DEDICATION

To my wife, Lisa M. L. Scott, and my gift from God. Thank you for being everything I need. I celebrate you! My sons, Desmond and Mario. Being your father and me Shepherding my home while you lived there was a joy. You two are also a gift from God. My sons, I promise you that reading this book will give you the tools to Shepherd your home. To my grandchildren: You are growing up in a world that does not love the God I share with you. I pray that you may come to know Jesus as your Lord and Savior. He loves you, and so do I!

Contents

Preface

This book is not intended to be a quick read or a typical self-help book, far from it. Nevertheless, you will receive invaluable information to aid you in righteous living unto God. And even bring healing for your soul so that you may live in victory over this present evil world through God, our Father, and Creator. This book deals with the often-difficult relational challenges experienced while dating and even within a marriage. However, this book offers so much more than ... boy meets girl; they marry and live happily ever after! This book contains a vast amount of information regarding relational dynamics and their nuances. Dividing this book into two books was suggested. However, I was not compelled to do so. The various topics addressed herein will doubtless cause the reader to ponder much about his or herself, one's past, current situation, and future.

From this book, you will also gain Scriptural (Biblical) and spiritual insight that I wish I could have received when I was a child, teenager, and even a young man. Within the first half of this book, you will understand or see the broader relationship of the created order. And how we are dependent, one upon the other. As well as our dependency along with creation. And of most importance, our dependence upon our Creator and God.

The content contained within the book's first half also interweaves aspects of my back story and that of my wife. You, the reader, will be enabled to assess how your past influences your; here and now. And the *good, bad, and the ugly,* of who you are. Also presented are various relational joinings. And their interdependence, which will evolve, either for good or contrariwise.

I bring you along with me in the second half of this book as I invite you into my home. Therein I will provide a more in-depth look into my marriage and what shaped this book's author – yours truly. My readers will be shown the spiritual challenges my wife and I encountered. Undoubtedly, this will make you more aware of your spiritual reality and the force of evil that opposes humanity and godly marriages.

I decided to write this book due to hearing and observing the many relational challenges accompanying good relationships, even when it was clear that a couple was good for one another. However, the couple's inability to get in sync, establish order, and work through relational differences and various life challenges caused the dating relationship to dissolve and what appeared to be a promising marriage to end in divorce.

Having overcome a challenging season within my marriage, I said to my wife, *You Were Not What I Thought I Wanted, Nevertheless Everything I Need.* Reflecting on what we had accomplished and our victories, I now had a far better viewpoint on what it takes to have a successful marriage. Now, I could better help other couples or those desiring to have a healthy and victorious marriage.

As a result of my spiritual maturity (not perfection), I began to understand God's will and purpose for my life. And better discernment and knowledge for the needs of fallen humanity, not the least of which, myself.

As a result of my forthrightness and transparency throughout this book, I pray that you will become disarmed and that you may come to see and understand some things about yourself. And even things about others that perhaps you had not considered. Such reflection brings about understanding and even healing for the soul as one learns to trust and rely on God.

As you come to know God in His love for you, you cannot help but see your true self or spiritual reality fashioned in God's image.

This book is ultimately a love story of these tales. Love extended its betrayal and its suffering. But eventually, love is restored. Resulting from these related and inseparable stories; my wife and me (our marriage) with God. He will be highlighted as the One who has ordained weddings and enables us to sustain our marriages and be victors over this evil world.

The readers of this book will be faced with more than a few choices by which to make. It will be up to you to decide for yourself to choose God's love, love some other, and be willing to put in the necessary work to remain in and sustain a loving marriage.

Supposing you have not given up on love. If you desire a healthy and victorious relationship and marriage, this book is for you! This book will assist you in identifying situations or trappings that work against relationships and marriages. And too from this book, you will gain invaluable information or tools regarding living a healthy and victorious relationship and marriage. This is accomplished with God and through God the indwelling Spirit.

I have written this book from my perspective, life experiences, others', and even a Biblical and secular worldview. Throughout this book, I have attempted to be conscious of engaging all who uncover its pages, who are desiring to know relationships in *True Love* and intimacy. I pray that this book may be of assistance in helping you to meet both your spiritual needs and physical desires found only in True Love - the very love of God.

Introduction

We are alike in that we are imperfect creatures, flawed and broken individuals attempting to figure this thing out - called life. We desire order in our lives and meaning and purpose for our living. For many, this seems to be an elusive pursuit.

However, If one would dare take a critical self-analysis, going back as far as one can in memory, then work forward, identifying those vital happenings or those essential things of want or lack in your life. Who you've become and why many things have occurred over your life will begin to make sense regarding your good, bad, and ugly experiences. And too, why you possess the attributes that make you – you.

For you, my readers, this is what I have laid out on several pages to make this book. I have opened myself up, becoming transparent in sharing that you may walk relationally along with me. And perhaps, even relating with me in some manner or another in my sins and as an Overcomer! If you have not yet become an Overcomer, this book is surely for you!

You will see while journeying with me through the various phases or seasons of my life - from boyhood to becoming a husband and my pilgrimage to spiritual maturity. Although I was an adult when I gave my life to Christ, I was merely a babe regarding the spiritual matters of God. In desperate need of growing up or maturing spiritually, you will know me in my failings and see in them how God did not forsake me. But instead, He was mercifully watching over me until such time I would see, through a gradual process, my great need for a *personal relationship* with the Father, to the saving of my soul, my family, and marriage.

I want to point out that the first two chapters, in particular, did not originate from my initial thoughts as I set out to write this book. What will be shared over these chapters and in more than a few pages throughout this book is what can be understood as inspired, illumination, or revelatory writing.

As for what I mean by inspired, illumination, and revelatory: Simply, God brings forth an understanding of His mysteries or hidden truths, not considered or originating in the minds of man, this understanding or illumination from Scripture occurs only as one who has been regenerated by the Holy Spirit spends intimate time with God through His Word and prayer while seeking to know God and His will for their life. It is in *Relationship* that we receive revelation. God will reveal Himself and even His will and purpose for you if only you are willing to enter into a *personal relationship* with your Father and Creator.

As I wrote this book, *The Author of Life* - God Himself revealed aspects of His personhood which I had not considered. Even so, things about myself that I may share with you this insight regarding His personhood as a relational Being and not some far-off unknowable deity. But instead, a lovingly relational God and Father, who can even love, one such as me - terribly flawed and broken. And yet a wonderful work in progress at the hands of my Maker, to whom I've learned to continually submit and surrender myself.

This book is about relationships, one thing with another—a man with his co-equal woman. And also the relationship between the earth and its inhabitants. And the entire created order in relationship or being connected with our Creator and Father. He is *The Giver and Sustainer* of life as we know it. The Father will also have us consider the interrelatedness of our physical being, as we, in our fleshly nature, are from the earth and even one with the earth. And too, our spirits being one or becoming once again united with God, who is Spirit.

From the created things, we can learn a tremendous amount about our Creator and God. Such wonderfully marvelous and transcending understanding about our Creator is not conceived within man's finite minds but from God alone. Yet it is to greater depths of knowledge that God desires to take all. Those who have willing ears to hear and a heart that seeks after the One and only True

God. The only True and Living God who can be intimately known through His Word. Or this *love letter* presented to all via the Judeo-Christian Bible.

God's truth and His purpose are what He wants humanity to come to understand. Whereby coming to the truth, wisdom, and knowledge found in Him, one willingly and obediently enters this lively relationship with the Father and Creator. Entering this relationship, we then discover what our soul longs for - a purposeful, orderly, and meaningful life.

This book will help you understand your spiritual identity or reality, as it also directs you toward an *intimate relationship with God*. Additionally, this book will candidly take on various matters regarding sexuality, dating, marriage, family, and factors that affect the vitality of each.

Here too, you will see how my personal experiences perverted my view on sex and females and how these things affected me relationally. And of most importance, how my flawed and broken ways jeopardized the relationship I had hoped to build with Lisa, the woman I dated and who is a gift from God, became my wife. Despite my flaws and brokenness, or aptly called my sinful nature. The grace of God would overshadow me! As a result, those of my home and I would stand in victory.

Now, being married or engaged in a meaningful relationship is not without its unique challenges, as two people are growing and teaching one another, even learning to become one. Becoming the ultimate and consummate teammate, winning on every level, this binding and building of you two will not be without its trials. And so, a perfect relationship is not about being perfect in your relationship. Instead, you two together, overcoming every challenge or obstacle that comes your way! While learning and growing together as a championship team in marriage, operating in sync so that you two may reach the team's end goal(s) successfully and victoriously.

This book will provide for you why you and your significant other are no longer to be two unilaterally thinking individuals, operating autonomously or without considering the other. But should be one in a cooperative effort to build your relationship and/or marriage.

One in this sense, consciously considering the other in decision making, never excluding your spouse - where choices or decisions are made that significantly affect the home. Where you are dating, choices or decisions made, not to work against the trust, or the building process that promotes oneness, leading to unity, brought to perfection through marriage.

A godly couple is no longer independent of the other but co-dependent upon one another as you work together. As a dating relationship builds towards marriage, this co-dependency should also be practiced within boundaries or limitations.

To that end, and now for a question. Upon what foundation are you building your understanding regarding dating and marriage? This matter of your foundation is what I will address in detail throughout this book. There is a sure and solid foundation to build upon. This foundation upon which to build requires work, which is part of the process of building and sustaining a vibrant relationship. But it does not have to be complicated and grievous work! It is critical to establish a healthy, strong, and well-supported relationship.

However, this is not a task to be undertaken alone. In trying to do so, you will be ill-equipped to perform the task … it takes three – yes, three! Though work is necessary, it is not to be seen or judged as a burdensome undertaking.

Here love is not an understanding of love as heard in today's music or portrayed in cinema. Instead, this building project between you and your Beloved is to be eagerly embraced as an awesome opportunity awaiting you two. Why the eagerness, and why awesome? Because this superstructure that you two will be constructing will be built and held up upon the foundation of Love - God Himself.

Instead, upon God, His love – Truth's Love because it is the principal thing upon which all godly relationships must be established. Understanding His love and acting accordingly because of it – that is, one toward the other, your relationship will thrive, and your marriage will be a success!

Understanding God's transcending love is the foundation and the Power or Supernatural Force that will see you through your building project and sustain it. No matter what snares await you or any prey lurking in the darkness to overtake your marriage – you two holding fast to Love, to God Himself – will prevail! You will be victorious in your godly union!

If you allow Him, God will be the Great Architect, that Master Builder, of the brilliant and masterful piece of work – erected and orchestrated in each of you! You and your spouse – the house that God built! God binding together two as one, and He as that Mortar, and that Sealant which tightly bonds and holds that which He has fashioned and fastened together, with superior and unfailing substance – Love. The remaining fruits of the Spirit or attributes of God that holds fast a godly marriage are peace, longsuffering, kindness, goodness, faithfulness, gentleness, and self-control (Galatians 5: 22, 23).

We are the workmanship of God, created by His very Breath and Power. We belong to Him and are to be in an unbroken and undefiled relationship with the Father. When we enter into a covenant relationship with God, He will see that our ways are prosperous. This blessedness speaks toward our spiritual benefit. And, subsequently, our Father's glory!

Regarding our spiritual and physical needs, consider these words of Jesus. "Look at the lilies and how they grow. They do not work or make their clothing, yet Solomon, in all his glory, was not dressed as beautifully as they are. And if God cares so wonderfully for flowers that are here today and thrown into the fire tomorrow, He will certainly care for you" (Luke 12: 27, 31). In other words, seek you first, the *kingdom of God,* and all our (spiritual) needs will be added unto us.

On the other hand, apart from God, those who work or contrive alone in this building endeavor. They unknowingly establish a weak and faulty foundation for their union upon a false premise or understanding. Their building project, based or built on inferior substances - one's reasoning alone, shaky and shifting, will be the foundation upon which they hope to develop their relationship. Therefore, neither can such a union be holy or sanctified before God because

He has not been invited into or become intimately one with the union as the Master Builder. Yes – it takes three!

It must be upon *Love - The Unifier*, that common ground, even that *Solid Foundation*, as purposed or laid out by God. That the building project, beginning with godly dating, wherein a marriage and ultimately a family is established and will be able to stand firm and victorious - especially in troubling times, as are before us.

My prayer is that this book will enlighten your understanding. And that it will take you deeper into God's Truth, His Light being for you, life unto righteous living. For my Christian reader … it will be the Spirit of God who will lead you into all Truth. Surrender (and also my non-Christian brothers and sisters) yourself over to Him that you may hear Him speak to your heart on all matters of His Truth unto righteous or holy living.

Not until one establishes that vertical relationship with God will they be able to effectively engage in those horizontal relationships with others. Specifically, the person with whom they have chosen as their Beloved in holy matrimony.

Some may say my approach in this book is bold or risky. My response: To be a Christian, one must be bold! What may be viewed here on earth as a risk, but for the sake of establishing the truth and destroying strongholds, will work towards my (our) reward when we see our Savior's face. And that for our good while we yet sojourn here on earth.

So, let it be that the God I serve be glorified through this book! Those seeking His will, be encouraged and edified. Many people are needlessly, even desperately, struggling and suffering in silence! And isolation! We are seeing this in the destructive patterns of people's lives. Even so, in how people are settling for and doing all sorts of foolish things that, they may find a false sense of purpose, belonging, and what they have reasoned as love.

For Christians, our relationship and life of relational growth with God is presented or characterized as a walk of faith. And walk by faith we must, as relationship building is experiential, enduring by faith, and through faith every unpleasant thing that comes our way. Over time a relationship is to mature. It is to grow stronger as love and care are given and proven by those relationally involved. Nevertheless, this loving relationship we are extended from God is not based upon blind faith. We come to have faith in God when we see His love for us and His power, as revealed in Scripture. While this is occurring, we will also experience and come to know Him intimately.

For many, the thought of a Supreme, Loving, and Just God. This One, who will hold all accountable for their actions, has been dismissed. Or God, so grossly misunderstood that there is no reverence or godly fear of Him. As a society - we have become faithless and foolish through our own reasoning.

And so we have it. The moral compass of God that once guided the lives of many has been trampled underfoot! Therefore, people are living in ways based on their understanding or reasoning. And are consequently going after that which satisfies their lust and sinful passions. Where this occurs, mankind or humanity has become a god unto himself.

As you forage through this book, ruminate or chew upon what you read. May the longing and hunger of your soul begin to be satisfied as you engage in prayer with your newfound hope and relationship with Jesus.

While some of the material in this book will immediately appeal to your liking, perhaps other portions of it you will later acquire a taste or appreciation, like that of vegetables to a growing child. But in due time, all of it will certainly be good for your spiritual diet and enlightenment or enrichment.

Chapters one thru three, I believe, will be rather tasteful for my inquisitive or spiritually hungry readers; this meal (writing) has been prepared for you. I think it will provide you a little something that perhaps you had not given thought to or even gleaned from the title of this book. Nevertheless, the content remains focused on relationships howbeit from a broader perspective. Perhaps not something that you thought you may have wanted, just the same; it will benefit towards your Christian maturity, therefore, something you need.

Though it would be beneficial to read the book in sequential order, some of you may desire to get to more practical aspects of the book. You may prefer to skim through the first three chapters or so and begin your focused reading after that. After completing the book, you can then give more attention to the chapters skimmed through.

Unquestionably there is no replacement for the Book of books - the Bible or the Holy Word of God, to satisfy and answer all our soul's questions and longings. God says to those who will seek to know Him. "For I know the plans I have for you, says the Lord. They are plans for good and not for disaster, to give you a future and hope. In those days, when you pray, I will listen. If you look for me wholeheartedly, you will find me. You will find me," says the Lord. "I will end your captivity (for this age, from sin) and restore your fortunes (eternal salvation)" (Jeremiah 29:11-14).

From another of God's words, consider the following. "Taste and see that the Lord is good " (Psalms 34: 8). And from Psalms 119:103, we have the following. "How sweet your words taste to me; they are sweeter than honey." There is nothing to be added to God's Word; it is fully and completely satisfying - a four-course meal that will hit the very spot of your soul's longing.

Nevertheless, God allows and needs servants such as me to bring something to the table for his people, even spiritual refreshment, as we expound upon God's words in light of our personal experiences. Embrace this sharing as complementary spiritual nourishment for those who hunger for understanding in righteousness through the experiences of others.

In this book, I have prepared a meal for you. If you now have your dining essentials - your pad, pen, highlighter, and of course, your Bible. Then ask for God's blessings on this food. And as my youngest son, Desmond, used to say, when he was a toddler, it's time to "eat-eat."

You have chosen to read a book written and edited by an unskilled writer... the author of this book. However, God impregnated me with this book and brought forth its deliverance. Whatever grammatical errors you may encounter, they are mine alone. However, if you focus on the content on these pages and not my grammatical errors, God will bless you real good!

I welcome the editing skills of the one whom God may have placed upon your heart to refine this great work. If you embrace this task, your labor and acknowledgment of your work will be noted in edition # 2. The cost of a professional edit is too expensive! This book is needed by someone right now! It has already been in its incubator too long.

CHAPTER I

A Garden Home -
Established Therein God's Holy Union

Now let us feast on the Truth of God! It is fitting that the opening chapter of this book would have our attention directed toward the Bible, *the Book of Life* – and the first book of the Bible, Genesis. The title Genesis has as its meaning – *Beginning*, hence the first book of the Bible. For Christians, the Bible's teachings bring *Life (Zoe)*; it is spiritually nourishing, and its truths are the foundation upon which we build our *kingdom* understanding as children and ambassadors of God.

This truth is the very *Light of God* that instructs the child of God, as *it* guides us out of spiritual darkness and directs the child of Light in every matter for which we are to live our sojourn and kingdom mandate while here on earth. These mandates prepare the child of God for their entrance into their eternal dwelling – the new earth and heavenly home prepared for them through Christ. When we get there, we will rejoice in the presence of our Lord and Savior forever!

Let us consider the following Scriptures, Genesis 2: 4 - 25; I believe it to be essential reading and upon which I will lay the foundation for this book and construct it. Much of what will be presented throughout this book will have you occasionally reflecting on this text, as will be the case with other Scripture shared throughout the pages of this book.

The account of the creation of the heavens and the earth:

The Man and Woman in their garden home called Eden

"When the LORD God made the earth and the heavens, neither wild plants nor grains were growing on the earth. For the LORD God had not yet sent rain to water the earth, and there were no people to cultivate the soil. Instead, springs came up from the ground and watered all the land. Then the LORD God formed the man from the dust of the ground. He breathed the breath of life into the man's nostrils, and the man became a living soul.

Then the LORD God planted a garden in Eden in the east, and there he placed the man he had made. The LORD God made all sorts of trees grow up from the ground—trees that were beautiful and that produced delicious fruit. In the middle of the garden, he placed the tree of life and the tree of the knowledge of good and evil.

A river flowed from the land of Eden, watering the garden, and then dividing into four branches. The first branch, called the Pishon, flowed around the entire land of Havilah, where gold is found. The gold of that land is exceptionally pure; aromatic resin and onyx stone are also found there. The second branch, called the Gihon, flowed around the entire land of Cush. The third branch, called the Tigris, flowed east of the land of Asshur. The fourth branch is called the Euphrates.

The LORD God placed the man in the Garden of Eden to tend and watch over it. But the LORD God warned him, "You may freely eat the fruit of every tree in the garden —except the tree of the knowledge of good and evil. If you eat its fruit, you are sure to die."

Then the LORD God said, "It is not good for the man to be alone. I will make a helper who is just right for him." So, the LORD God formed from the ground all the wild animals and all the birds of the sky. He brought them to the man to see what he would call them, and the man chose a name for each one. He gave names to all the livestock, all the birds of the sky, and all the wild animals. But still there was no helper just right for him.

So, the LORD God caused the man to fall into a deep sleep. While the man slept, the LORD God took out one of the man's ribs and closed up the opening. Then the LORD God made a woman from the rib, and he brought her to the man.

"At last!" the man exclaimed. This one is bone from my bone,

and flesh from my flesh! She will be called woman (The Hebrew word for woman is ish-shah, which literally means a female man) because she was taken from man."

This explains why a man leaves his father and mother and is joined to his wife, and the two are united into one.

Now the man and his wife were both naked, but they felt no shame" (Genesis 2: 4 - 25).

Unearthing Divine Truth from Within the Garden

Presented in the text, God has given the account and the institution of the first nuptial, mankind's only perfect union. However, this union soon came under spiritual attack. Stained became that union that had been established in harmonious perfection by God. Adam and Eve were perfect in that they were without sin. Perfect, whereas their marriage was complete in holiness, as they were intimately connected to and in right fellowship or *relationship* with one another and God ... The very God of the Judean-Christian Bible, who is Holy, and through whom man is or becomes holy when united with God.

We see that Adam and Eve were perfectly made for one another singly and/or exclusively ... God saw to this personally! Eve had been formed (taken) from the rib of Adam but made by God to go back, whereby uniting herself unto her spouse in the most intimate of physical expression – sexual relations. This design of God was that they might share in God's fullness of a sanctified union, this gift from Him, to be shared through marriage while showing forth His glory through the miracle and the gift of childbearing. This union was not just their union or only about these two. And I remind you, neither was this marriage of their making. Rather, as God's created agents and imagers, this marriage was established by and for the ultimate Glory of the only Wise, Perfect, and Holy One – God Himself!

God alone presided over this union of Adam and Eve and was to remain eternally one with them. Marriage is ordained or established by God to make His name glorious! Through our obedience to Him, as we build for Him and with Him, His kingdom, or our families, we magnify God or make His name celebrated or known throughout the earth!

Often mentioned at Christian weddings is the phrase "Holy Matrimony." However, I want you to give careful thought to this truth: A marriage can only be holy - when and where God is brought into the midst of the union to occupy and preside over it. He is the only One who is Supremely Holy – without flaw, and He alone who establishes a marriage to be holy, as a husband and wife willingly become subject to the will of God for their lives.

A holy union does not equate to marriage without challenges. However, those challenges will be worked through and out as God, the Presider over the union, is prayerfully sought after for His infinite wisdom and understanding that a couple may overcome whatever challenges life brings their way.

Therefore, it is not the announcement of these words, "Holy Matrimony" or "Holy Union," by the presiding officiant of the wedding ceremony that makes the marriage holy. Instead, it is God presiding over the union, even dwelling amongst this union as the couple; His very offspring acknowledges Him as Lord over all. Only then do they become one with their Father, set apart or sanctified for and by Him, whereby a marriage is deemed holy. What every child of God must realize is that we are sacred spaces.

It is through God's prescribed institution for marriage, as seen with Adam (man) and Eve (woman), his complementary opposite, that God's favor and blessings will be bestowed upon that union. Even the blessed mandate for them, who are now partnering with God, that they may *be fruitful* ... Or add to God's kingdom, children (Genesis 1: 28). God got it right when He made for Adam - Eve. Any union apart from that of a man with a woman is judged and condemned by nature itself and God. Such a union abnegates God's command to procreate - even still opposing God's supreme design and will, who decreed marriage as that of a heterosexual union.

Looking forward to the New Testament of the Bible. A Spirit-led reading of its pages unfolds the picture of a blessed marriage, which entails greater spiritual and eternal significance. From various Scriptures, we are shown God's love for His children; *The Redeemed Universal Church or Bride of Christ*. Resulting from Jesus's redemption and reclamation of mankind, for those who are now one with Him and God the Father, a glorious wedding is pictured in heaven taking place between the Church - the Bride of Jesus, and He as their Bridegroom. This wedding will reach its zenith when Jesus returns with His Angels for His Church (Bride) (Matthew 5:1-13; Revelation 21:1-27).

Jesus will soon return for His Bride! At His appearing, those who are asleep in the Lord, having died before His return, will be resurrected to new life. Those who are alive at his return - are raptured. Therein, we, the Church, Jesus's Bride, being rescued from this present evil world, forever to be with the Lord (1 Thessalonians 4: 13-17).

Whoredom In The Garden _ The Fall And Consequence

Resulting from Adam and Eve's willful rebellion and spiritual adultery against God, mankind was given over unto an unholy alliance with "Satan" - that *Man of Sin*. Subsequently, death became man's inheritance. Here meaning … Our sinful disposition or inclinations toward evil, including physical and spiritual death. Beguiled by Satan, our Adversary – *Adversary* is the meaning of the name Satan, which is better or more accurately understood. Adam and Eve, rejecting God's rule, tragically - underestimated the consequences of their rebellion and interaction with Satan, became defiled, and were rendered unholy before God, their Creator, Who is Holy (Romans 5: 12-19).

In their disregard for the command and wisdom of God to refrain from eating of the forbidden tree, they forced God's hand to release them from the holy union they once enjoyed. Though His love for them was unceasing, they, in a sense, forced God to divorce Himself from them. A Holy God and a defiled people cannot dwell together in unison. Adam and Eve's actions – spiritual whoredom in the garden, now defiled caused them to become unevenly yoked or unmatched with their Creator, undoubtedly this being to the grief of their loving God and Father. *"Can two walk together, except they be agreed"* (Amos 3:3)? Mankind and God were no longer in spiritual agreement or relational oneness. Adam and Eve's betrayal or unfaithfulness has proven to be to humanity's detriment. What tragedies and atrocities the world has known because of the rebellion of Adam and Eve!

A single act of disobedience, a moment of fleshly pleasure, and selfish gratification, they became one or yoked together with death - Satan himself, in this newly formed triad or family of rebels. Having been beguiled by Satan, Adam, and Eve, breaking their covenant (agreement) relationship with God, willfully and woefully entered into a covenant relationship with that great *Deceiver of humanity* – the enemy of God and every soul – Death or Satan Himself.

Humanity, now one with that *Domestic Abuser of their souls* - most miserable and without hope, was now in need of a *Redeemer, Deliverer,* and *Defender.* They needed a *Savior,* that One who would come to their rescue and attend to their needs (Genesis 3:15; Romans 16:20; Hebrews 2:14).

Suppose humanity's first representatives – Adam and Eve, were present with us. If this was the case, I am sure they would amen and even echo my expression, saying, "Father, my God, and Creator ... *"You Were Not What I thought I wanted - Nevertheless Everything I Need!"*

Using my imagination, I will share with you how Adam and Eve got caught up with Satan: Eve, who had been in her home and garden paradise, may have initially been by herself, minding her own business, but not far from the sight of her man, as she tended to her responsibilities and Adam his. I will imagine that out of curiosity, she and Adam, too, may have occasionally glanced in wonder at their only prohibition - *the forbidden tree.*

Let me say it is one thing to wonder or be curious about something - so have we been made - to be curious. However, no matter how amused we are or full of wonder about something God has restricted us from ... they must remain off-limits! Certain things have been prohibited, whether we understand why or not – must be understood as being for our good! This is the heart of God ... to protect us! But seeing from the story of Adam and Eve, and perhaps your own story, we know that going against the will of God is not without consequences.

Now Satan, observing Eve's (the Bible describing a woman as the weaker of man, but is yet his equal,1 Peter 3:7) curiosity regarding the forbidden tree, set his wicked eyes on Eve to tempt her. Seizing upon the right opportunity, with all the swag he had in his steps and silky-smooth speech, he moved in and enticed Eve to go against the will of God; she thereby became one with him in an unholy union.

Eve would succumb to Satan's seduction and ever-so-flattering and persuasive mind (rap) game. It certainly appears that it did not require much effort for Satan to pervert Eve's thinking and persuade her to give in to his desire that he may have or seduce her emotionally. Satan knew the right words to plant in Eve's thoughts,

whereby shifting her thinking toward that which serves his purpose – that was and is man's rebellion against God and, too, man becoming self-reliant and one with him.

Mankind now, in subjection to, and one with Satan, their Adversary. With power and authority over man, Satan rightly unleashed his fury and vengeance upon humanity while using and abusing powerless mankind as his accomplices to war against themselves and God while bringing about mayhem and destruction in the world.

My friends – saved or not, sin's lure and call for us is all around; through *his people agents*, he whispers in our ears and subtly beckons us to play his games of death. At other times, he shouts at us, even while drawing uncomfortably close to us, as they - his human agents, make plain their sinful intentions with us or their desire for us. Regardless of sin's approach, when it is all said and done, what is important is how we rightly respond to the voice of evil or the consequences of the guilt resulting from having given in to the tempter. This is man's dilemma ... how will we respond to sin or temptation? Our choice(s) will determine our end – either for better or worse.

Eve ended up giving herself over to that determined and seductive *Tempter.* Having yielded her unstable and deluded mind to his will surrendered the battleground of her mind. Through his cunningness and flattery, Satan was able to seduce and lure Eve from her mind's place of peace, innocence, and contentment. But that was not all! He, too, enticed her away from her purpose and destiny, which God foreordained before she had life breathed into her earthen body.

The metastasis of sin is far-reaching! Eve was also to be *seduced* away from the comfort and security of her garden home as Satan showed up unannounced. Satan's plan was intentional; he would first go after Eve, the weaker vessel, so that he may then usurp Adam's authority over creation and his lordship as Eve's covering and husband.

Satan audaciously and persuasively tempted Eve! In a sense, He led her away, *captive mentally* from her home. And also from the comfort and security that her man was supposed to provide for her. Of most importance, Satan led Eve away from *Life – God Himself, her Creator, and Sustainer unto Life.*

On that day, two homes became divided and destroyed! Their earthen tabernacles became corrupt, meaning their bodily dwelling place for their spirits began to die from a fatal spiritually transmitted disease. And then the garden domain that they shared with God, which He prepared for their physical habitation. Even so, from it, they were evicted because of the rejection of their God.

It is mankind's spirit that is formed in God's *likeness. Our spiritual essence makes man one or relational with our Creator and not our clay bodies through which we express or live out the will of God here on earth.*

God had breathed His essence – *Life* itself and eternity into clay or earthen bodies that are merely dirt – those bodies of Adam and Eve as well as that of their progeny. That which was and is Celestial/Divine (God) was one with man, who was and is terrestrial or bodily but who also has a spirit. Man had been created and animated by the *Breath* or Spirit of God to express bodily, here on earth, the nature or glory of God. Even so, we are spirit *beings* without divinity, humans/flesh who were created to walk and live under the authority of the Almighty God.

But now, Adam and Eve were separated (given over to Death) by God, who is *Life*. Where there was once peace and unity with their Creator within their home of paradise or heaven on earth. Now there was and continues to be hostility between unregenerated man and God (Romans 8:7). And dysfunction throughout the human race as well, within man due to the sin of disobedience. Resulting of this rift, this disunity, and the brokenness that sin creates, conflict would find its way into the union of Adam and Eve -and all of humanity.

This cancerous effect of sin is ever-present in marriages and families today. Only by the intervention of God, the Conqueror, and Unifier – one, or a couple seeking the will of God for their lives, can endure or be victors over the debilitating effects of sin. However, not without challenges! Some challenges will be from without, while others will be from within, as the Apostle Paul reminds us in Romans 7:21-25; 1Corithians 7:28. Nevertheless, with the Spirit of God dwelling in us and working on us, we can be *Overcomers* and *Victors* in our marriages and as children of God!

Until Christ returns for His Bride – the Church, this contention or striving within our souls, in some measure, will persist to have its way in order to work against that which God has purposed for those who are His. Therefore, through watchful prayer, we must be on guard against all uprisings that attempt to dethrone the child of God or work against the holy union shared with the one we love and the One who first loved us - God.

Satan is a clever schemer! Getting in the head of Eve, thereby winning the battle over her mind through his enticement of her, he was essentially suggesting to

Eve that God was, in fact, selfish. He caused her to think that God was holding out on her by denying them access to the *Tree of the Knowledge of Good and Evil.* Satan became the victor through his use of the art of manipulation to overtake Eve's thinking. He has also been successful with ensnaring many of you, not the least of which - me.

This relentless, deceitful, and deadly game of our Adversary continues to be played out by him. Through various mediums, Satan is twisting the minds of many to get anyone - saved and unsaved alike, to do what he desires. Through Satan's assault against our thoughts, he aims to keep us away from the truth(s) of God. To turn us away from God or have us in doubt regarding our faith, thereby rendering many spiritually ineffective and powerless.

What Satan fed Eve, through lies and deception, caused her to believe that there was much more for her to have and enjoy apart from what God had provided – that the grass would be greener on the other side, was the lie Satan was selling to Eve. He successfully put forth his sales pitch to her; that he could offer her something far better than what she already had. And Satan was strategically reeling her in that she may partake of it! The bait was hanging near them and on the forbidden tree. I know all too well what it's like to have bait dangled before me! You will see what I'm talking about a few chapters later.

I imagine he urged Eve from the mere curious glance of the prohibited tree to now gaze upon the beauty of it and its fruit. Enticing her, he said, "How satisfying it will be. Eve, how convenient it is right there; God has placed it at your grasp; just reach out and take hold of it. Eve, just taste and see that the fruit is indeed good."

Satan was meticulously reeling Eve in. Once Eve's feet were set on the lustful path toward the forbidden fruit, Satan was undoubtedly full of sinister delight as he was about to get what he desired … Eve! Eve with arms outstretched and raised, with hands open to receive the fruit, had unknowingly been outwitted. Eve was now assuming the posture of surrender and praise unto Satan and self-satisfaction. Eve was unknowingly enthusiastically raising her arms in defeat and surrender through her action. Eve's ill-advised curiosity, resulting from entertaining wrong thinking planted in her mind from the mouth of that Seducer - Satan, caused her to fall from grace and that perfect union she had with God and her man, Adam. Grabbing hold of that fallen or alternative life and lie - this fruit represents as much. Eve would now be fully dedicating her life and her posterity over to Satan and their own unrestrained passions. There would be no escaping the rule that Satan now had over her.

It is that same seducing spirit, Satan, who is presently at work, weakening and disintegrating what could be victorious relationships. The influence of Satan is even gaining entrance into Christian homes, destroying marriages, and demolishing families. And he is also wreaking havoc in Churches.

Because of the schemes of Satan, the ruler of this world, spiritual indifference, apathy, and even apostasy have also gained much ground in this country. Not to mention, resulting in the United States slowly and steadily foregoing its Judean-Christian morals, many have become confused and delusional. More than a few are no longer concerned for or aware of what God has deemed inappropriate and prohibited or what is biblically or what some may call fundamental rights and wrongs. People's minds have been seduced and misguided that in multitudes, they are being led astray by the cunning lies of Satan and those who belong to him.

So it is, as a people, we have become disjointed and spiritually disengaged; believe me, matters are only worsening. Our only hope will be in turning back to God. We are powerless to make the world a better place, let alone deal with our personal sins and brokenness. We only fool ourselves as we pursue our selfish wants. God alone has what we need: a right or restored relationship with Him!

More can be learned from Satan's assault upon Adam's home: Having gotten mind control over Eve, Satan also suggested to her that God was being unreasonable in forbidding her to have what she wanted - the tree's fruit. And I will add that out of the corner of his eye, Satan was also throwing a well-aimed and intended jab at Adam, undermining his authority while getting him to begin thinking double-minded about what God had told him about the forbidden tree.

Satan now has Eve looking at her man sideways. While she was eyeing him, Satan said to her, look at your man; neither will he provide for you what you want and deserve. Sadly, Adam knew what was happening to his wife. From his silence, he was complicit and, worst yet, consenting to Satan's seduction of his wife! He also was undoubtedly feeling the pressure from without and from within.

Satan, pouring on the pressure as he appealed to Eve's mental and fleshly longings, probably said, as I continue to read into this unfolding drama. "Eve, all that I'm saying is - trust me! Just believe in me; a world of opportunity and possibilities awaits you! Just take one bite – what harm is there in doing so?"

A deceiver and the father of lies is Satan! As well as anyone who will attempt to lead you away from God's truth as presented in the Word of God.

Before Satan showed up, Eve had a great thing going on! The grass was not greener on the other side, as Satan would lead her to believe. A perfect situation was before her! And alongside her, the man God had designed for her to become one with.

This belief that something is better than what God offers is the main tactic of those who oppose God. They will argue that there is a better way and that God's way is antiquated or restricting. And so, Eve would fail to realize that everything she could ever need or desire was already before her and ready to flourish if only she continued in reliance upon God and obedience to Him.

Instead, she was led by her mind, which she allowed to be infiltrated by Satan. Through self-will and reasoning, she went after what she now lusted for. She pursued after the forbidden rather than that which would keep her undefiled and holy. She shunned what her soul desired and needed – *Life, God Himself*. Having been persuaded by Satan, she instead went after the way of *Death*.

Eve was strategically removed along with her husband, mentally away from the strategic position she held with her man while in their garden paradise. Both had been in perfect harmony and relationship with God; this, too, was now disrupted. The correct perspective she had known that positioned her to be victorious in life was defiled and now overshadowed by her new distorted and disoriented worldview.

A read of this domestic failure is found in chapter three of Genesis. There, we discover that Eve also added to God's Word regarding "touching" the fruit. In this distortion of what God had actually said, we see her suggesting that God was unfair and overbearing. In one wrongly arguing against God and distorting God's Word, this clears a path in one's thinking to embrace the lies of their telling or to pursue that which has been deemed prohibited.

The temptation was presented, the trap was set, and Satan ensnared Eve. This deception resulted in her forfeiting that which she had, God and the benefits of being His subject and His responsibility. Sadly, there are times when we fail to see and appreciate the blessings that are already before us. Subsequently, we mess things up while pursuing so-called greener pastures or fleeting pleasures found in someone or something forbidden.

Poor choices will inevitably have or perhaps have produced far-reaching consequences, even long-lasting fallout, seen or understood as we look back over our lives, reviewing our individual stories of sinfulness and bad choices.

I imagine Eve's reach to obtain the forbidden fruit from its branch was a meager distance from her outstretched arms. And Adam's reach to receive the fruit from Eve, his wife's hand - shorter. Yes, he drew closer to Eve, not correcting her but rather being one with her and Satan in their act of rebellion and disloyalty toward God. The order of headship was now reversed; Adam had chosen to follow Eve's lead instead of maintaining his position of authority.

The result of the two taking hold of what was off-limits had historical and eternal ramifications. Such is the very nature of sin's payoff. How much? Oftentimes it is grossly underestimated, but there is always a cost to be paid! Indeed, we will pay to play in the sandbox of sin.

Eve, eyed by Satan, became his target of choice. The fall or deconsecration of humanity began with her. However, make no mistake about it; Adam was not without blame by no stretch of the imagination. No! He is not off the hook in the slightest!

Earlier, I implied that perhaps Adam was doing his thing in the garden when Satan eyed Eve. When the timing was right, Satan then pursued her so that he may have his way by seducing and manipulating the mind of Adam's wife.

Men, are you helping to spiritually guard the minds of those in your care through godly edification, prayer, and your active presence?

Whatever Adam may have been doing, no doubt he was close enough to the situation that he knew what Satan was up to. He knew Satan was messing with his woman; Scripture affirms as much. Adam "was present with Eve;" however, a spiritual breach was underway between him and God, causing Adam to fail to act as the guardian and steward over what he had been entrusted under his watchful care ... foremost his wife. But also his earthly domain.

Adam failed to protect and correct his wife; he failed to defend their home. It could be said that Eve had Adam's *head* and his heart; therefore, he bowed his head to Eve in surrender to the *fruit she possessed* and the fruit she also held in her hands.

Adam, now assuming the role of the subordinate, clearly failed - in that he did not offer lovingly yet firm corrective words of wisdom and rebuke of his wife. Neither did he operate strongly and forcefully in God's authority ordained upon him to thwart the plans of Satan's advances and assault upon his home and woman!

From Scripture, it is evident that Adam had been led astray by the influence of his wife. As mentioned, Adam was present when Eve lustfully ate the forbidden fruit. Emboldened by Eve's act of defiance and there being no immediate consequences of her wrongdoing, Eve then offered the forbidden fruit to Adam. Surprisingly or not, Adam willfully and wrongly submitted to his wife by eating the fruit. Their act of rebellion was a parting or defecting from God, even though they did not see their action as being so at that moment. Subsequently, they formed an unholy alliance with Satan.

Adam and Eve are both personally accountable for their act of whoredom. However, the greater responsibility is to be shouldered by Adam! He, Adam (man), was first created, the one to whom God had given the prohibitive decree and designated by God the Federal-head of his home and the earth.

Here is a look at and an understanding of the rule of first mention as observed throughout the Bible. After Adam and Eve's rebellion, God called out to Adam, "Where are you" (Genesis 3:9)? His calling out to Adam clearly implies that Adam is held responsible for their deconsecration and even his headship over Eve and what was supposed to be their God-honoring home. Throughout Scripture, this ordering for a godly home is shown. It is clearly and undeniably expressed in 1 Corinthians 11:3, Ephesians 5:22-24, and Colossians 3:18. Adam had a duty to act against whatever threatened him and all given to his care. However, he failed to execute his God-given authority when most needed when he chose to listen to his wife instead of God (Genesis 3:17).

Adam and Eve's woeful choice to disregard God's one prohibition has caused severe consequences throughout the ages. In varying degrees, lawlessness, lewdness, and death – both physically and spiritually, experienced by all are the reaping or result of them having disobeyed God. However, *death does not have the final say*! If you are a Christian, you already know this.

The evil seen and heard about that is occurring daily throughout this world; the destruction it brings about us is never ceasing. The breakup of marriages and dysfunction within families is de facto, Death or Satan's hallmark or calling card, and fallen man's inheritance.

But in God rest our hope, salvation, and victory over *death*. Before I came to know God, I saw no need for Him. The fact of the matter, He was not even a thought as being something, let alone the One I truly needed. When I began to hear about Him - in my mind, He was just out there somewhere. Now that I have come to know Him for myself. I can say of my God, Creator, and Father: *You were not what I thought I wanted - Nevertheless, everything I need.*

If you do not know my Father, I encourage you to get to know Him for yourself. You may not realize it now, but He is the One your soul longs after and the very One you need!

Creation - Its Order, Its Covenant

Here is merely a vague illustration to make my point that creation has laws through which it is ordered. Creation's arrangement can be understood as a cooperative agreement or a covenant that has bound creation together. Or, some may describe creation's interrelatedness and operation as the *laws of nature*. As seen with Adam and Eve, there is a reliance and interdependence of all things within creation's ordering. God, the Creator of all things, has established this joining or alliance and even reliance within and throughout creation. Through Him, life is given, and by our Creator, all things are sustained (Colossians 1: 15-17). This ordering and interrelationship are evident within our world. For example, our dependency on the air we breathe and the food and water we consume makes the created things' dependence and alliance apparent.

All creation is in a relationship. God gave man His agents, stewards, and crowning glory charge over the created things. God said to Adam, subdue the earth and have dominion over it (Genesis 1:28). Man was supposed to be the earth's caretakers or stewards, while God the Creator provided oversight and rule. If we take care of the earth, it will take care of us!

God is eternal – in Him and through Him is *Life* or *Zoe*. *Zoe* speaks to the *Self-existence of God*. In Him, there is neither beginning nor end – He is Eternal! Our Eternal One is our Creator, Animator, or *the giver* of *life – bios*. Bios speaks to life that is given to the created order. This life is temporal and temporary. So, life, whether that of man, beast, or whatever the sort, as designed and intended by God, should emanate from itself, life after its likeness. We are agents of God to not only care for or be good stewards over the created order but likened to God; we are also to bring forth life through the institution of marriage – a man with a woman. This joining of a male and female is a gift from God! Through this union, a man with a woman and the human life brought forth by the two, who are complimentary opposites, speaks to the omniscience, intelligence, and magnificent ordering and design of God, who is Zoe.

Again, *Zoe* speaks to the *Self-existence of God* or the *Eternal-existence of God* our Father - the Eternal Spirit. In comparison, the giving of *bios* is the prerogative of God. As it were, man's life or existence is shown or expressed by three different Greek words. You have been introduced to two of them, *Zoe* and *Bios*; the other word is *psuche*. Each means life but with different functions, activations, or operations.

Their concise meaning:

Zoe: Divine life which is possessed in and provided by God alone. *Zoe* is God who was, who is, and who will ever be *Life* - The Eternal One – God the Supreme Spirit Being or Deity!

Bios: physical life and is the root word of biology.

Psuche: Means the psychological life of the human soul, the seat of our emotions and intellect – hence soulish. We get the word psychology from psuche.

Man consists of a mind, body, and spirit. However, those belonging to God, their spirits have been born again. Therefore, man is identified as a living soul, in either case, those who are born again or those who remain dead in their sin. Within our earthly realm or place of habitation, bodily, we experience the external world. Internally we experience the activation of our emotions, which is soulish or with our minds or psuche. Within our bodies, we experience our world through our senses and are, in essence, one with the world. Bodily, we express or live outwardly, either our soulish, inward-man or spiritual self and reality, as one with this world and Satan. Or one with the Triune God through the indwelling Holy Spirit. As spirit beings or sons of God, we are in the likeness or image of God, the Father of spirits - *Elohim* or *sons of God*. However, He has chosen to clothe us/man in flesh to image Him and represent His heavenly domain here on earth (1 Corinthians 15: 39 – 41).

And so, bodily, we experience the world and are one with it. Through the mysterious and extraordinary functioning of our minds, which is the Central Command Center System of the body, we are enabled to know or become aware of our terrestrial reality in which we manage our bodies to express ourselves. Also, through our transformed minds, this extraordinary member of the body, we who are born again and/or children of God come to know the Mind of our Father – God our Creator. Whereby we become relationally acquainted with our Father as we hear about Him and learn more about our *Loving Father* through His Word – the Holy Bible and the help of His indwelling Spirit.

The Word of God is Spirit (John 1: 1- 4, 14; John 6: 63; 1 John 5:7). Mankind are spirit beings who are clothed in flesh – hence we are living souls. As it is, with our bodies, we relate to this world. With our bodies, we are one with this world; with our regenerated spirits, we become one with the Father of Spirits, with whom we have been restored to right relations through Jesus so that we may come to know God our Father. And also to one day become like Him, even Jesus, His unique Son, wherein we are clothed in our glorified bodies that we may live in our renovated earthen home in glory - a world without end (1 Corinthians 15: 42-53; Isaiah 60:20; Revelation 21:1).

So, we hear or learn about God from His written Word. Scripture thusly says, "Faith comes by hearing the Word of God." When we accept the Word of God by faith, which is accorded to man through the function or Power of the Holy Spirit, this activation of one's faith signals our rebirth. Having been born-again by the Holy Spirit, we then can come to know God more perfectly wherein we have intimate or personal relations with God our Father (Romans 10: 8-11,17). Even so, through His Word, God empowers our spirits or inner man and transforms our minds so that we may overcome or have victory over our sinful nature (flesh) and the evil of this world (Romans 12:2)!

All who are born of a woman have received bios – physical existence. This is also the case with animals. However, all who have accepted Jesus as Lord and Savior have had added to their *bios* or restored to them *Zoe* or eternal life through our renewed spirit resulting from the *Life-Giving* and indwelling Spirit.

Herein, our spirits have been born again, and we are reunited to and/or revived by Life - Zoe (John 3:6,7).

God desired that Adam and Eve would remain one or freely partake of Him - *Life* (*Zoe*), by continuing in right relations or covenant union with Him through their loving and willful submission and loyalty and thereby dwell before and with their *Loving* God and Father forever. Although man rejected *Life* – their Father and Creator and has since faced the consequences – spiritual death or separation from *Life*, our loving and merciful God again made *Life* (*Zoe*) possible through Jesus. Christians who now have new or eternal life - those born again spiritually. Are required to share with fallen humanity - *the walking dead* - those who remain one with this world and Satan the "Good News," this renewed spiritual reality and eternal life given through Jesus - the second Adam to all who will only believe in *the saving grace of the Son of God* (1 Corinthians 15:45-49).

Through creation's ordering, here, meaning our terrestrial world, this oneness, and co-dependency of all things therein are designed in one way or another to support and strengthen the living, preserve, and propagate life. However, we must also consider this ugly truth. Death's intrusion into our earthen realm is now one with Earth's "lifecycle" as we currently know it. And that which we often experience through lawlessness, wickedness, and destruction of every sort!

Nevertheless, "Natural law," as referred to by many, continues to function as purposed by Jesus, even though nature itself has been negatively impacted by Adam's rebellion (Colossians 1:16). All that is within our earthen realm that shapes and forms and works in concert to establish our world's ordering – such things seen as well as unseen. They all function environmentally or relationally within and throughout our domain despite the disruption and intrusion of Death.

The entrance of Death into our world has temporarily caused the created order to be out of sorts from the perfect way God intended before the Edenic desecration or fall (Romans 8:22). In spite of this invasion from the Evil one, God's restoration of man and their new place of habitation has been set back in order through Jesus' death and resurrection! This reordering will be inaugurated at our Father's appointed time. Things have already been set in order. However, they are not yet but will come to pass soon enough (Hebrews 2:9; 10:9; 2 Peter 3:9; Revelation 22:20).

Although Death invaded the home of Adam, know with assurance that nothing, absolutely nothing, has caught God off guard! He is *Sovereign* and *Omniscient* (all-knowing)! Everything that Satan is allowed to do. Yes, allowed to do … Has done and will continue to do is a part of God's grand plan to restore His Edenic promise and plan for mankind's Savior-Redeemer and Evil's destruction as foretold in Genesis 3:15, 12:2, 18:18; Romans 16:20).

Man is the highest order of the created things here on earth - in that, we alone are made in the image and likeness of God. Only mankind who is created within this earthen realm can have a personal, intellectual, and intimate relationship with God our Father. Man was created for this very reason – we are relational beings just like our Loving Father. As partners with God, He instructed Adam to rule over the lower order – earth, and not for man to rule over one another. That was and is God's place and His alone! God desires and deserves our complete loyalty. However, Adam and Eve rejected His rule; now, look at this world and the troubled state of humanity!

Man was purposed to be God's stewards and caretakers of earth's resources. From these very things that He gave us to manage, we were not only to recognize our co-dependency upon these things. But also from observing creation, though in part, to comprehend the nature or the mind of the only Living and Loving God.

Scripture tells us that from the very things God has created, so has He made himself known. From or through the things created, we can behold, though dimly, the nature and mind of our loving God and Father (Romans 1:20; Psalms 19:1-6).

God is Divine and Deity; He is eternal, having no beginning or end! He reigns *Supreme* and is the Life-giving Spirit! He is the *Source* and the *Sustainer* of all that is! Everything that exists … with or without the breath of life, seen or unseen, upon the earth and below. And such things in the unseen heavenly realm are - because God spoke them into existence (Psalms 24).

However, it is when God meets with redeemed man through Scripture, His Holy Word, that we grow spiritually. And are enabled to see or discern the profound mysteries or spiritual reality regarding the things of God, *The Most High God -Elohim,* over the spirit (elohim) world and all of creation. From His Word and spiritual enlightenment, we can then see beyond the mere writing of the Holy Word of God, not contradicting Scripture but instead affirming it, as we are taken deeper by the Spirit of God and Truth into our Creator's heart or mind. Intellectually we read or deposit the Word in our minds. Humbling ourselves before God and relying upon the Spirit to teach and reveal the Truth of God. Our minds, having received this spiritual enrichment, or Truth and Life, as children of God. Our minds or ways of thinking are then transformed or renewed by God's Word and/or Spirit (Romans 12:2; Ephesians 4:23). Therefore, through our new way of thinking, we become less and less carnal or worldly or soulish, or even animal-like in our thinking and behavior resulting from been born-again and our thinking renewed!

The Tree Speaks

I will now share insight that I have gleaned from the lesson from the *Tree of Life.* In the book of Genesis, we learn that there were two unique trees within the garden home belonging to Adam and Eve. These trees are symbolic, as they foreshadow the many choices or covenants in life, where we will have to decide to either be one with something or oppose some matter we are faced with. We make these decisions through verbal consent and even implicitly. Through our choices, we, in one sense, become one with that with which we agree.

One of the trees was called the Tree of Life. I will submit that this tree is representative of the abundance or blessing from God Himself. If its fruit had been eaten, man would have remained perfect in their likeness of God and completely satisfied - spiritually and physically. In contrast, The Tree of the Knowledge of Good and Evil. It can be thought that this tree represented man apart from God, man's emancipation from God - and Go it alone, Do it myself, and My way defiled identity.

I found it interesting, as I considered further the reason for the Tree of Life. Adam and Eve were alive and well. Sin had not separated them from God; besides, they had the perfect home in their garden of paradise. Surely there was no lack in their lives?

Man's cup was full; however, it was to overflow in God's abundance, beyond which they could imagine or think. If only they had chosen to partake from the Tree of Life (Ephesians 3:20).

It is the goodness and nature of God to bless His children. He is a loving Father and *Provider*. He desires to provide for all, and even at this very moment, our spiritual needs. May this outpouring of God's spiritual resources upon man be understood as being first and foremost regarding the gifts of God to be bestowed upon all who belong to Him.

Our Father knows our physical wants or creature comforts, I call them. However, we often miserably lack in identifying our spiritual needs. The reason behind this lies within our fallen nature, or as immature Christians, we are spiritually deficient and therefore fail to see this lack. This results in man, from our void within, pursuing creature comforts or temporary gratification from the world. But in truth, only that which God can offer will thoroughly satisfy our soul's longing (Matthew 6:33).

With regard to our creature comforts, how God chooses to bless us in exceptional manners will be at His discretion. He will determine how, how much, and when heaven is to open and shower our material or physical necessities upon us. He sets the measure when pouring out and extending His blessings.

Now, let me add a word of caution: Be slow in your assessment, that you do not pridefully equate all that you possess or your perceived blessings as correlating with your supposed uprightness before God.

How we are blessed is determined by God. Again I am primarily speaking of those unique occurrences or God's favor that's extended our way that we recognize as being extraordinary or supernaturally acquired! That said ... God causes the heavens to open unto the just and unjust alike (Matthew 5:45). In other words, He will bless whomever He wills to be blessed. Regarding spiritual blessings ... unceasing is the outpouring our Father desires to shower on all who earnestly seek after Him or such things that pertain to heaven (Matthew 6:33; 7:7; James 1:5)!

As splendid as things were before the fall of Adam and Eve, I maintain that they were only experiencing a foretaste and not a full taste of what our Father had to offer. I believe that all that God had purposed for them, that full taste to be experienced by them and brought forth through them, whereby fulfilling God's full intention for man was interrupted, disrupted, and temporarily delayed by Death.

Consequently, all of creation suffers – it is ever-present; even so, we wait for God's deliverance and restoration of all things. Consider the following Scripture:

"Yet what we suffer now is nothing compared to the glory he will reveal to us later. For all creation is waiting eagerly for that future day when God will reveal who his children really are. Against its will, all creation was subjected to God's curse. But with eager hope, the creation looks forward to the day when it will join God's children in glorious freedom from death and decay. We know that all creation has been groaning as in the pains of childbirth right up to the present time. And we believers also groan, even though we have the Holy Spirit within us as a foretaste of future glory, for we long for our bodies to be released from sin and suffering. We, too, wait with eager hope for the day when God will give us our full rights as his adopted children, including the new bodies he has promised us. We were given this hope when we were saved" (Romans 8:18-24).

Though pronouncing judgment upon Adam and Eve, God allowed them to continue to be fruitful - to bring forth man or children of their likeness. Creation was also permitted to continue to yield its fruit. Nature's fruit was and is for man's benefit – a gift from God. Nevertheless, both courses of life – mankind and all other life forms would inevitably meet with death.

Satan's intrusion established a *New World Order,* with his rule or influence being over all the earth, including man. Even so, fallen man, the offspring of Adam and Eve, was understood as a gift from God. As such, they were to raise their children to know and revere their God and Creator (Psalm 127:3; Malachi 2:15). The foundation for a family was established through the union of Adam and Eve. The *Blessed One* - the Messiah, who will come from their offspring, will restore all things from our current fallen or corrupt state (Genesis 3:15).

However, this union of Adam and Eve and every marriage that follows thereafter will not be without their unique challenges. Just the same, through man and the establishment and structure of the family, God would make His ways known upon the earth.

Creation Is Wedded

More is to be learned from the Tree of Life: Like seeds planted throughout the soil, my thoughts on the matter will be spread over the next few pages.

Let us look at a Christian Marriage ceremony and its attendees. First, looking at the attendees: All invited are special guests; they are significant to the bride and groom. They are in attendance for that sacred moment to witness this most honorable and hallowed celebratory occasion. However, the point of their attendance is missed if they are merely seen as seat fillers and spectators. Or are there for the after-party and are mere gift bearers.

Those in attendance are not just acquaintances, friends, and family members looking to be entertained. But instead, they should be activated as prayer warriors; we saw how Satan came against the first family; his tactics have not changed; he wants every Christian marriage to fail – this is his end game! By any means necessary, he will seek to destroy marriages and families! And so, prayerfully, there are in attendance those who understand the spiritual battle that has been waged against godly unions and are therefore praying for the couple. This Christian community – all attending the wedding is a rallying of sorts of individuals who are to be spiritually prepared and armed for battle! And who are therefore on standby - capable individuals who can offer support and godly counsel for the newlyweds if the need should arise.

It is customary for a Christian couple to state their wedding vows during the wedding ceremony. There is also the presentation of wedding rings to both the bride and groom. These rings symbolically seal the marriage covenant, which is not to be broken or defiled.

The man and woman having dawned their rings - the couple's public salutes or kiss is then extended and received by one another. Now a most significant and often underappreciated and understood change occurs; the husband's name is given and assumed by the bride. In most cases, the bride excitedly accepts and is ready to be called by her husband's name. With increased anticipation, the couple faces the assembly, and the officiating minister announces Mr., and Ms. ___, his last name, for the first time, which therefore recognizes this union.

In a Christian marriage, it is the husband's name that the wife is to assume or carry and be recognized by. Adam's wife is called woman (Genesis 2: 23, 24). Adam's name is representative and symbolic of him - man, with whom Eve now becomes one with – hence woman. Adam - the man, is appointed head over the home as Christ is over the Church (Ephesians 5:23). The man is his wife, covering protector and provider as much as he is able. The Christian husband is to be under or subject to God, even so, the spiritual leader of his home as he learns from God, his Head and Covering-protector (1 Corinthians 11:3).

Concluding the wedding ceremony, and not until then, is the married couple permitted by God to withdraw to their secret chambers to consummate their holy union. Through the beautiful relational expression of sexually joining together, the two unite more intimately - emotionally and physically. As approved and even celebrated by God. The husband is permitted to plant himself and his seed within his wife lawfully – and, if I may, his cherished territory, to plow, protect, and carefully attend to for the duration of his life.

Consider this illustration. It is simple and perhaps insightful: Within my yard, I have various trees that have been planted. This is my lawful property. I went under a contract with another to become the legal possessor of my territory. Therefore, I can plant as many trees as I desire and enjoy their fruit or the pleasure they provide. However, suppose I plow another man's soil and plant my seed in his yard. In this case, I should expect legal consequences. This will probably not be the worst outcome because I chose to plow and plant my seed within another's property or possession.

My wife, whom God has granted me the right and privilege to alone, will provide for me what He has intended and purpose for her to render. Through the marriage covenant established with my wife, I can now legally and lawfully plant my seed; she alone has become my territory, and I hers ... Yes, we belong to one another! It has also become my responsibility to be forever mindful of her intrinsic worth and value. I must protect and care for her as I recognize that she is a most valued property – one who actually belongs to God, her Creator, and her Father. Let me make something abundantly clear: Men, our wives or ladies are not our property, over whom we are dictators. We all belong to God! Secondly, through marriage, a husband and wife belong to one another (1 Corinthians 7: 1-7).

Regarding the marriage covenant, a couple is to be understood as ratifying or sealing their marriage through the sexual act of holy consummating their union. Scripture states that when we become one with God, we are sealed by the Spirit entering or dwelling within us (Ephesians 1:13; 4:30). Resulting from this union, God with man, there is restoration and even a consummation of sorts. An individual is, in fact, impregnated by the Spirit or, as often and more correctly stated, *born again*. As a result of being *born again* or *regenerated*, one may very well experience a spiritual connection or change within. It may be spiritual peace that overcomes you, joy, perhaps some other deep emotional-stirring, or sensational experience when your spirit is revived and unites with the Spirit of God. Or it may be that you experience no sensation at all; I didn't. And this is perfectly okay.

Nevertheless, having received Jesus as your Lord and Savior, know with unwavering assurance that you have been born again! And, yes, indeed … you can now testify to the change in your life. As a result of this union with God, you are then enabled to bear the fruit of the Spirit (Galatians 5:22, 23).

Much can be said regarding the godly wife, who understands her role and willingly surrenders, submits, and gives herself completely to her husband, even so that she may receive him in the most intimate way of physical expression. Where sexual union is comprehended in sanctified sacredness, it transcends mere selfish physical gratification experienced through forbidden sexual relations. Instead, the godly marriage between a sanctified husband and a sanctified wife is both spiritually and physically satisfying (Matthew 19:6; Malachi 2:15).

Sadly, to the dishonoring of our bodies, sexual expression, which is to be held as consecrated and sanctified for marriage as ordained of God, has been perverted, demeaned, and reduced to a mere bodily passion that is to be satisfied whenever and with whomever, one chooses (1Corinthians 6:9,18; Ephesian5:3; Colossians 3:5; Hebrews 13:4).

Sadly, in our morally depraved time, "having sex" can be likened to a casual greeting and transient as a handshake. And in many cases, the sexual encounter lasting only moments longer than a handshake or the interaction held while setting the course for the prohibited agreement of sexual relations to occur.

There is something to be said; it is diabolical regarding the ease with which two people can come together for "casual sex." Such behavior is no longer viewed as profane, perverse, or sinful. Instead, "casual sex" is presented by those of the world and even carnal Christians as the "harmless activity" of two consenting individuals. "Where is the harm they will argue?"

However, in the sight of God, the purpose for which sexual intercourse was gifted to only a husband and wife from such individuals differs from His intent and design. Those holding the view that "casual sex" is a "harmless activity" between two consenting people are certainly not what our Creator calls it: *He calls it corruption and even an abomination.* Sin is not just the breaking of abstract law; it is a violation of a person - the Person is God and even sinning or a violation against our very bodies! We are created in the image of God; therefore, we are to honor and glorify God in and through our bodies; we all belong to Him as His imagers and are, thus, to conduct ourselves accordingly or to our Father's will (Romans 12: 1, 2).

* * *

Nonetheless, the aberrance of mankind, in their pursuit to satisfy their longings, does not just stop here with sexual sin. Great is the debasement of which humanity has fallen … to the defilement of their bodies. Even so, the violation of others!

A read through Leviticus 20:10-20, and Deuteronomy 27:20-23 will give an unmistakable look into the sordid condition of fallen humanity. A cautionary word: Even those who have accepted Jesus as Savior, if not careful, watchful, and prayerful, can undoubtedly be derailed from the course of God by falling into sexual sin and other activities to the defilement of their bodies, the sins against some other to include God!

When we sin and misuse and abuse our bodies, the emphasis here on sexual sin, we grieve our Father. He despises our conduct. His love for us never ceases; however, He hates our misconduct in how we misuse and give our bodies over to abuse, where damage is done mentally and spiritually. This damage works against what God desires to accomplish through man. Such behavior can altogether derail God's initial plan(s) for you or delay His purpose intended for your good. Many have no idea this has occurred or even the psychological or spiritual harm incurred through sexual inappropriateness.

Through marriage, spouses giving of themselves sexually to one another truly is a gift to each other and a gift from God, which is to be protected, honored, and valued! It allows the couple to procreate and enjoy one another through physical pleasure, comfort, and strengthening of the bond when they are joined sexually, emotionally, and/or spiritually.

You see, whether understood or not, the act of sexual intercourse goes beyond the mere physical! Sex cannot be seen as just a "hookup," a moment lost in time for mere pleasure seekers. As the union matures, the bonding or growing together of the two who have chosen to become one will become stronger, where the marriage is embraced as God's undertaking and gift.

And so, it should go without saying: The position I maintain is that sexual relations are never "just" physical… to the contrary. Therefore, the notion of "no harm, no foul," where "casual sex" is practiced, is illusory and delusional for any who maintains this lie. The sex act may be absent of authentic feelings, emotional attachment, or care for the one(s) involved. Still, injury has been inflicted on some level, causing conflict and contradictions within one's soul. The short: one does not merely walk away from having so-called "casual sex" and be not unscathed.

One is undoubtedly affected adversely – physically, the violation of the body has occurred, and so one's well-being has been compromised. The effects of the misappropriation of sex can be immediate or surface later. It may be the whisper within of regret and shame after one carelessly and frivolously gives their body over to sexual sin. Or it can torment another's mind! It could be from carrying a load of guilt or from one becoming trapped in sex's destructive and addictive grasp. Without going into specifics – make no mistake about sex's powerful and destructive addictive trappings! One's sexual past affects or influences one's thoughts or actions, whether mindful of this or not, when one decides to settle down. Like a drug habit or less damaging habit, you cannot necessarily or easily shut down something you found pleasure in! People, there is a tremendous cost to pay when you covenant with the forbidden … sin is a deadly serious matter that will not let you go as easily as you may think!

In marriage, a man with a woman, his complementary opposite, is the will, even the perfect plan God has laid before man to follow. It is the agreement or covenant through marriage that a man and a woman enter before God, bringing forth the blessings and peace of God upon that union!.

For sure, we are destined to reap that which we sow within or through the flesh - either unto life or death. Our harvest is determined by our foundation and the seeds we plant and allow to take root within our souls. It is our choice whether to sow seeds unto life eternal. Or choose to remain in cahoots and as cohorts with death as one who sinfully sows to the flesh, thereby resulting in death (Romans 6:23; 8:6; Galatians 6:8).

With all this elucidation of sowing and reaping, prayerfully, my point is made clear. If not, here it is again: a seed inherently has life within itself. Where planted according to the will or Word of God, the seed brings forth life. It will therefore bring forth life of its kind. For mankind - the reborn, who is implanted with and by the Spirit - the fruit of the Spirit and as determined by God – springing forth unto eternal life. Or, if the seed one plants or allows to be planted or remain within themselves is a sinful or corrupt seed, destruction will be their reward, and they will remain as one among the walking dead in this fallen world (1 Timothy 5:6; Revelation 3:1).

The Bible declares that those who have rejected Christ or who have not accepted his saving work are *twice dead* - physically and spiritually or utterly dead (Jude 1:12). And that God's judgment awaits all who refuse the redemptive work of His Son. Such ones are described as sowing unto the flesh: that is, they do what Death demands or what the carnal mind and flesh lusts after, and so, they bring forth of their kind – death!

If one desires to get things in order relationally. What must occur to fallen man or that carnal or fleshly driven Christian - this being the first order of business: One must get things in order with themselves. Meaning: one's hardened heart or head must be fallowed or softened (Jeremiah 4:3; Hosea 10:12). The Spirit of God, through His Word, brings this about in the one who surrenders their life to God.

There has to be a tilling or breaking up of one's hardened heart or the mind of stone within fallen mankind. God, the indwelling Spirit, is the plow or force that transforms our hard hearts and minds into fertile or receptive soil. The Word of God is the Seed that can now be received or planted into our hearts, bringing about transformation toward our eternal way of thinking (Job 32:8; Mark 4:3-20; Ezekiel 36:26).

Indeed There Is Much That Can Be Learned From God's Creation

Let us now consider how marriage and the family can be understood and strengthened from the lessons of a tree. I am not skilled in the science of Botany nor trained in the field of an Arborist. Nonetheless, if one slows him or herself from the grind of life, escapes the confines of the concrete jungle, and pays attention to that which God has created. Where done, we can learn lessons from God's natural Botanical Gardens and Arboretums that surround us.

Likening man to a tree. Where both are planted within a healthy environment and not hindered by toxins and other pathogens that work against their development, being free from destructive agents and adequately nourished and cared for will mature to their productive purpose and end. And that is producing fruit of its kind or *namesake. Even so, displaying its strength and full glory when matured.*

A tree is inseparably one with nature or the created order. It is a significant factor or agent for life here on earth. The air we breathe is produced by trees and other plant life; as a result, we live. Scripture even declares this process is the breath (life) of God (Job 12:10; 27:3). Even so, from the tree, not only do we eat its fruit for physical nourishment, but we also inhale its breath so that our souls may be sustained unto life.

Both the tree and man are agents of life. And both have been created to bear fruit of their kind for the furtherance of life. Through and from the tree's breath and the fruit it produces, man's earthen bodies have life and are sustained. As Christians, issuing from the *new life* within our earthen bodies, we also bring forth life – a child, after our likeness. However, as we speak or breathe forth the Word of God to our offspring and all others, we exhale *Life* (Zoe), the very breath (Word) of God which has been given that they too may come to receive *Life* eternal.

We can share and demonstrate our new life and love for Christ only as we abide in the Spirit or remain one with Him. And so, as the tree produces fruit of its kind. God has purposed that a man and a woman should join together through marriage to produce fruit of their kind and for His glory and praise. This is God's law or decree – God's anatomical and biological design and perfect work to be performed by man.

God's decree went forth, establishing that the operation of creation should be in a covenant. This pairing and partnering serve God's purpose that life (bios) in the created order may propagate. Amongst mammals, it's a male with a female. Once again, by that which is living, life is brought forth, and life is sustained. So it is; the created order can be viewed as married for the purpose of bringing forth life. This partnership of life bearers shows forth the magnificence and mind of our Creator! Although in our fallen world order, death soon follows that which brings forth life. However, the restarting, rebirthing, or beginning of new life is ironically initiated in death and through death.

Jesus put it this way, drawing a comparison to His life and the death or sacrifice that He would undergo so that man may have eternal life. "Unless a kernel of wheat (an illustration representing Jesus' death and burial) is planted in the soil and dies, it remains alone. But its death will produce many new kernels, a plentiful harvest of new lives" (John 12:24). Jesus died, and we who believe in Him have died with Him. Through His suffering and His sacrifice for humanity, He conquered death and now lives! Even so, we now live and have eternal life because of Him and His sacrifice for you and me (Galatians 2:20).

Codependency is intrinsic to the Divine design and order of creation so that life may continue or propagate. We are repeatedly shown this through the things that God created. We know that a healthy tree can thrive for hundreds of years, providing its continuous byproduct to sustain the cycle of life. Breathing on creation, trees, or plants provides earth dwellers with breath for life and food for our nourishment so that we may live out God's plan for us.

What a marriage of sorts we see throughout creation. This covenant arrangement within the created order was to remain constant. However, death showed up - Satan himself, disrupting and corrupting the world!

Before the fall of man, Death did not reign over the earth … *Life* did! God, Adam and Eve, and the world were in perfect harmony. How glorious things were; there was no end, corruption, or brokenness. All things pertaining to *Life* were sustained by God! Though we now live in a corrupt and broken world, we can still see the hand of God graciously holding things together. Until God brings judgment and an end to this world, creations' relational ties will persist; life and its unions and even death that breaks these relations will be this world's norm. And so, as long as this world exists, life will go on, and these marriages continue until death, through whatever means, dissolve and break the unions established throughout creation.

If you need reminding, God established marriages to be perpetual, ending only through the death of one's spouse. The exception is marital unfaithfulness (Matthew 5: 31,32; Mark 10: 2-12; 1 Corinthians 7: 39). However, if a spouse abandons or abuses their wife or husband, I will submit that this, too, may be grounds for divorce.

The trees and nature have revealed to us the mind of God. We have been taught God's intended permanence and relational bond or marriage of all things. Resulting from Death's takeover, we have also gained insight into the cycle of life and even death that now sustains our fallen way of life. Though death continues to be a part of this world's order, those of us who are new creatures through Christ Jesus have been awarded a letter of divorce from Death. We are now eternally one with Jesus - *Zoe*! Read Romans chapter 6.

Life Givers Unto Perpetual Harmony Are We Created

Permanence and relational harmony within - and throughout God's creation - was and continues to be His end; this shall ultimately come to pass. Meanwhile, as Christians, we strive for harmony and unification, particularly among other Believers. But in love, relate to all, even those who may hate us. Within Christian marriages, we have learned from creation and the very Word of God that this union is to also operate in harmony and is to be a permanent covenant between a man and his wife.

When a couple is wedded under God, the officiant over the marriage ceremony shares their thought on what the wedding rings represent. The officiant reminds some and informs others that the rings exchanged between the man and the woman represent the unbroken and harmonious life they have chosen to share until death parts the two.

In His infinite wisdom - God has revealed to us through nature, life's cycle, and creation's interdependence. He has also given mankind insight into our bipartite and tripartite formation. In the likeness of God, we are spirit beings. Having been clothed in flesh, we become living souls. Of both the Celestial and the Terrestrial, mankind was created to be one with both the Earth and God. God, our Father, was to reign over the earth and mankind, but Adam and Eve abnegated their position as stewards or co-agent with God over the earth and handed it over to Satan.

God had purposed for there to be perfect unity; man with God, man with himself, man with one another, and man with the rest of God's creation (Isaiah 11:6 - 9). However, this perfect unity is yet in the future. Meanwhile, God wants man to work towards this high calling found for the moment only in Jesus. Each of us needs first to have work done within. In varying degrees, we are out of sorts; we are broken people. When we become one with the Father, the Spirit of God begins to show us our brokenness and the mess that needs sorting out. Once we begin to understand ourselves and subsequently experience the harmony and inner peace that God intended for humanity to have, only then can that forever bond that God purposed between a husband and wife be achieved. Operating in harmony, a couple is enabled to secure the longevity and stability of their union and family. Such a family dynamic works toward the good of all people and the glory and praise of God.

Like a tree firmly rooted within a nurturing foundation of soil, a family must be firmly rooted and nurtured within the rich foundation of spiritual understanding so that it may grow heavenward. And so, as a tree grows by the sun and reaches toward the sun, so is man to grow spiritually by the Son, too, with raised hand reach toward Jesus - *The Son*. Having been spiritually grounded by the Spirit, a marriage and family can truly flourish, producing spiritual fruit for the furtherance of life eternal in abundance following the plan of God to build His kingdom (Ephesians 2).

Through their unification, a man and woman, uniting in holy and unbreakable marriage, are permitted by God, as His under-agents, to perpetuate the cause of life, as His life-bearers.

Where children are not given through a marital union. The Spirit-filled couple or Christian who is single ... in obedience to God is to just the same, bring forth spiritual life through sharing with others the new life enjoyed with their God and Father. As one lovingly and passionately imparts or plants *life* into others – they, having been made alive through the Spirit, and one with the Spirit, is, in fact, sowing *Seed or The Word of Life* as life-bearers and under-agents of God.

If you are single and desirous to be in a relationship, I understand that your longing for companionship presents challenges. Make no mistake about it; God knows the desires of your heart (Psalms 38:9; Matthew 6:8). While you are single, I emphasize the importance of you seeking or remaining in the will of God. Your prayers are heard by God, but you may have to include within your prayer ... "Father, give me peace and even contentment in the state that I am in" (Philippians 4:12).

As for God knowing the desires of your heart and answering your prayer, more is to be said in chapter three, subtitle ... *You Are Not Alone – The Helper Awaits You.*

In light of what we have come to understand about our blessed hope and eternal salvation. *The Good News* of the Bible is that our spiritual heritage and (or) marriage is sure; it can never be broken, neither by death or the grave ... nothing can separate us from the Love of God and the Life (Zoe) that belongs to true Believers (Romans 8:35-39).

An invitation to eternal life has been extended to all by merely embracing Life, even so, the love and sacrifice that Jesus has offered. Adam broke the covenant with his God and Father, but we are restored to the Father through the renewed covenant in Jesus. The Father's invitation to be one with Him will not be withdrawn. However, if you meet with death before saying I will and do to God, the door to come to Him will forever be closed. You will have literally and truly missed out on the opportunity of a lifetime (Matthew 22:1-14).

Because God is Life, His invitation is extended to all to be one with Him in *Life* and to thereby be fruitful and multiply. Being granted by God the opportunity to bring forth children displays God's grace, blessing, and very mind toward establishing His Eternal Kingdom first within the hearts of man and then eternally (Luke 7:21).

Therefore, a woman's womb ... where life (Bios) begins ... for her to bring forth a child into the world is a marvelous privilege and even a gracious gift from God! This is no trivial matter! Children born of a woman are to be embraced as a miraculous gift from our Creator. However, many parents have failed to recognize this miracle and appreciate the blessing that a child truly is ... Children are God's imagers too!

Without God, man is in gross spiritual darkness! I will now give an example of such spiritual darkness or one who is spiritually blind: A child can be living – (*bios*) this occurs at conception and developing within its mother's womb. And yet the child can be readily and tragically discarded as holding no worth. People, I am talking about a child – an imager of God that has been aborted! By the hands of death, *their own parent(s)*, and those performing the execution. Or it may be that after a child is born into this world, they are so neglected or abused that the humanity of the ones entrusted to the child's care, this intended guardian's sanity, is called into question. Diabolical is the nature of such things, as man, God's creation, has become Satan's agents of death (John 8:44)!

Relationships desired by God are under attack; shifted from God's natural course of harmony and *Life* due to sin, man has committed evil against one another of all sorts! Violence and destruction are the ways of this world! Neither has the mother's womb nor the life (child) within been able to escape this violence! Pause for a moment ... give thought to what I just said. Such disregard for life is a direct affront and attack on God – *the Giver of Life*. We were created in His image; therefore, man is sacred and endowed with intrinsic worth because of whose image we are made in – and to who we ultimately belong.

To partner with God was the reason He created man. In the beginning, God spoke the world and every living thing into existence. But as for *Man* (Adam or mankind), He said … "Let us make *man* in our *image*, after our *likeness*" (Genesis 1:26; 2:7,18, 21-24). The body of *Man* (Adam) was created *from* the earth, then God breathed *Zoe* into him. Eve, however, was taken and/or made from Adam. We see from the beginning they were *one* with the earth, flesh– man, animated by the Spirit of Life; they then became one with the *Father of Spirits.*

By God's will and intended purpose, from the life or seed within Adam and the egg or life within Eve, from their union, was life conceived of their kind. Their progeny, the human race or mankind, began through and from Eve by the Power or Spirit. Hence from that day forth, the cycle of life (not without death) continues like a fruit-bearing tree.

By nature, we are life-bearers and life-givers created in our Father's image and likeness. Although death intrudes upon physical life, we are yet to enjoy a covenant and a vital relationship with the Father, unto life eternal. We are now one with our Creator as spirit beings clothed in flesh through our restored relationship with or in Jesus. As it is said, "flesh and blood cannot enter the Kingdom of God" (1 Corinthians 15:50); we must be born again by the Spirit (John 3:1-7).

Through our spiritual rebirth and reunification, we are to bear children, not just unto or for ourselves, but for the *One* who made childbearing possible. You see, our offspring are destined for a more extraordinary inheritance than anything we can provide for them through our natural order or earthly realm. Kingdom kids are the redeemed of the Lord; we must raise our children to be heavenly-minded as they foresee or keep in mind their heavenly destination. So, we must ever be mindful of this reality and therefore bring up our children to understand who they really are and who they belong to – God their Creator.

Our responsibility as Christian parents is to rear our offspring and put them in the best possible position to become one with and blessed of God! They must understand that they, in turn, are also to be a blessing to others as they wait to attain their eternal spiritual inheritance.

The children we bear are not ours … "The earth is the LORD's and everything in it. The world and all its people belong to Him" (Psalm 24: 1). Having been commanded to have dominion over the earth and to bear children. We are to see ourselves as stewards over what has been entrusted to us to care for.

Humanity's destiny does not have to have death as its inheritance – it is a choice. Choose Life (Jesus), and live – this is our intended inheritance. The perpetuation of life is shown as children are gifted to us, who are to be dedicated or commended over to God (Luke 2:22; Proverbs 22:6; Deuteronomy 6:5-7; Psalm 127:3).

It is a Christian parent's responsibility to raise their offspring with reverence for God. And the knowledge of their Father and Creator. They are to be guided until such time that our children may choose to enter into a *personal relationship* with God, becoming Spirit born and one with Him.

The Tree Continues To Teach Us - You Are What Our Creator Made You To Be

The tree has further to say regarding its relatedness to marriage, in particular on the matter and order of reproduction and the growth of its seedling. If you did not know, biologically, a tree is neither male nor female. It is asexual, yet it bears fruit through the unique pollination process – either through cross-pollination or self-pollination. In some ways, this life-cycle process is similar to human reproduction, who, as we know, were created and are born male and female, co-agents for or with God unto life.

As for the identity of a tree, having no gender is identified by its given name, species, or kind. The designation assigned to a tree is based upon such factors as the tree's shape, color, size, leaves, or the fruit it produces. Perpetually, the tree is called by its given designation. If the tree is uprooted and planted elsewhere, the given name for the tree is unchanged, and its essence is not altered. Perhaps you can see where I am headed with this.

Regarding an apple tree. Each apple that falls to the ground or is plucked from the tree; its fruit or essence is unchanging neither becomes modified because it's detached from the tree. Hence, the designation of the fruit is to remain - apple. Calling the fruit by some other name of one's choosing, yet it is clearly an apple, will be thought irrational and even deranged; it is what it is - an apple, no matter one's rationalization.

If an alternative name is suggested, reinforced, or forced into acceptance, it does not negate or change the tree or fruit's nature. Instead, it will lend to confusion, where one attempts to redefine, reorder, after their liking, what God has already defined and ordered. He called it good when God completed His creative work of the lower animal species and plant life. However, after God's crowning glory - man was created, He called His finished work - *very good* (Genesis 1:12; 31)! Any man seeking to edit, rewrite, or delete God's design and plan for His creation cannot be in his right mind. A right mind is aligned or allied with God (Romans 8:6; 12:2; Ephesians 4:17-24).

With respect to the law of nature, from a tree that bears fruit as its outgrowth, the fruit is predetermined within its essence or the tree's genetic code. There is no editing needed to the tree's blueprint; it is already perfected … God has stated it to be so!

No matter where an apple seed is planted, an apple tree will bear apples if the ground is fertile. To that end, the apple tree shall have no alternative essence. It is what it is! What is written within the tree's genetic code will come forth of its kind. Peel the apple, crush, and mince it into applesauce; cut the apple into multiple sections; it yet remains an apple; squeeze its juice from it, and what do you get. Apple juice.

Even if the soil lacks vitality, a tree may still grow. It may be feeble in size, perhaps producing little to no fruit, and yet, it perpetually remains an apple tree. The changing environment nor anything else changes this fact. Add some life to the soil, and the tree's outcome will certainly change toward a good outcome - fruit.

Giving thought to soil or the earth. A foundation of good or fertile soil is indispensable! It can be regarded as an incubator, even a womb for life and from which life emerges. The seed here, an Apple Tree's seed planted in good soil, will sprout and maturate from the ground.

Although the soil's contents are vital for the tree to grow and thrive, it is not the earth that determines the nature of the tree. Even though the tree sprouts forth from the earth, the tree's nature or essence has been predetermined by God, written with the construct of the seed's DNA.

Perhaps you are thinking: which is more significant – the soil or the tree? Neither the tree nor the soil holds any greater value or importance than the other ... as pertaining to their life-giving properties. It can be said that they are ontological equals in their intrinsic usefulness or significance, as it is with man and woman. Each maintains distinct roles or functions within the earth's economy. They are essentially married together, soil and tree. Even as it is with a husband and his wife, agents of God, for the furtherance of life (Bios).

And so, a seed from a tree falling to the ground, or sown therein, will produce a like tree. As with the husband's seed ... it will create a man-child in his likeness when implanted into his wife.

Here, the term *man-child* or man is not associated with gender; it is gender-neutral, as commonly expressed within the Bible. The use of the term holds a deeper meaning as it transcends the physical identification of the human race. Instead, by using this term, I am emphasizing our earthly existence as living souls – hence, neither male nor female, instead *man*. Or even sons of God.

As spirit-beings, we are *Man* and not given to gender (1 Corinthians 12: 12, 13; Galatians 3:28). However, as living souls, we have exclusively verifiable (in most cases), clearly, identifiable genitalia, distinguishing our unique sexual individuality and explicit purpose for which God created males and females.

How is the gender of an individual determined? You probably learned this in middle school ... I did. A quick refresher: Simply, it is determined by the father's chromosome. The Y-sperm (Chromosome) of a husband planted into his wife will produce a male child, and his X-sperm (Chromosome) will produce a female child. As ordered in God's perfect design within man, the gender of a child born of a woman is determined by the seed of the Father. In this sense, the father can be likened to the Apple Tree - in that there is no changing in God's design of the man and his seed. A man-child will come forth, biologically identified as either male or female - *man*. This is the natural order of God's design unless a husband and wife choose not to have children. Or being unable to have them.

The rare exception is that a child born with a birth flaw identifies them as hermaphrodites. In simple terms, these birth defects occur because of hormonal imbalances, producing a child born with male and female internal sex organs. Or the more common occurrence is the external appearance where a child has what appears to be both male and female genitalia. The sickness or effect of sin and mankind's doings have far-reaching consequences. Thereby causing disruptions and breakdowns throughout the natural or perfect order of God's design. Otherwise, there is no disputing a man and woman's purpose and sexual identity for the exception given.

Now, let me clarify: This birth abnormality must not be viewed as the fault or sin of the parent(s). And the erroneous assumption that God is now punishing the parent(s) for some transgression they committed.

* * *

Here are a few things I want you to consider when such unfortunate situations, whatever they may be, affect a fetus (unborn child) or child: Prenatal care or the lack thereof will influence the child's development or health. Also, a parent who may have abused their bodies through drugs and other harmful chemicals or pollutants entering their bodies, and such toxins or chemicals they were unaware of. As far as I am concerned, the most significant thing that we must bear in mind is that all creation has been affected by sin! Sin equates to death and brokenness of whatever sort, be it of the mind, the body, or the spirit of man.

Death or its counterpart, corruption or decay, must be seen as the destructive culprit at work in this world, affecting all of creation (Romans 8:21-23).

Therefore, brokenness; whenever it is seen, in whatever form it takes or wherever it manifests itself, whether through natural disasters, dysfunction, pain, and suffering and the world's chaos, such abnormalities have as their root cause sin, which is akin to Death. For this very reason, we need a Savior to deliver us from this present evil and broken world! Listen, people, Jesus is our Deliverer from this evil and sin-sick world (Genesis 3:15; Luke: 2:11; 1 John 4:14)!

As for the woman who lovingly submits to receive her husband's seed so that it may fertilize her ovum, she becomes the incubator for life (bios) upon conception. Though she is seen as submitting to her husband, she remains an equal co-agent in this process of procreation, as she becomes one through sexual intercourse with her spouse and the child conceived by and born to them, becoming one with them. A family they are, a *trinity* – the making of *one*.

Intercourse or marriage - the tree with soil, the husband with his wife, neither incubators – the earth or the wife have input or are the factors as to the gender or fruit which will come forth from their womb. The new life or fruit has been predetermined within the *seed* of the man and that from within the tree by the foreknowledge and will of the Creator.

This ordering of God lends to an additional observation and lesson to be pointed out by the tree: I will submit that it concerns the precedence of the husband's surname establishing and identifying his family lineage for generations to come. There is great importance and historical significance in one knowing their family history. Matthew and Luke's gospel presented Jesus' lineage; elsewhere in the Bible, we find the family's lineage through men to be significant.

Suffice it to say, God has established the Husband as His designated head of the home. And the one who will be primarily held accountable for the management of his household, which is to be ordered under God. The husband's namesake should distinguish his home from God's home structuring. Therefore, his name is to be joyfully received by his wife, this here indicating their oneness. And she consequently lovingly submitting to her husband as her appointed Shepherd of their home.

This name recognition is not inconsequential; it speaks to the unity of the family and a wife, under God also coming under the headship of her husband as she formally takes upon herself his name (1Peter 3:6; Genesis 18:12; 1Corithians 11:3).

As offspring are given through the union, they carry their father's name. The male offspring perpetually represent their earthly father through his name. However, it is the father's daughter who, at the appointed time, is given away by her father to marry. That she may assume her new name arrived from her husband, with whom she has become one until death parts them.

And so it is, in a Christian Family, the father's name is to be given to his descendants and should be eagerly received by his spouse. And not the other way around, a husband assuming his wife's name upon himself or the wife refusing her husband's surname.

Relationally, this is another area where we are perverting things. I am convinced that this is another of the enemy's methods that work against the unity of the family. This misnaming has a way of operating deceptively that undermines the integrity and structuring of a God-centered or His ordained family.

As African Americans, I recognize that this idea of establishing or naming our families, where many have Euro-names, presents somewhat of a conundrum for some. Through the evil ideology and practice of slavery, African families were broken, ripped apart, and stripped of their native names, amongst other things. The significance held within those names and heritage has since been long lost by countless African Americans. Nonetheless, the underlying point within the husband's name establishing his family remains of most importance, no matter the name's origin, for the sake of his posterity and maintaining family union and history. That said, I clearly recognize that we who are born-again Christians are part of an eternal family that supersedes our biological lineage and heritage! Even still, we all are descendants of Adam and Eve.

God has clearly established His purpose and order amongst creation; man must simply be willing to submit to His way and will for their life. It is God's standards and mandates that we who confess Christ are to surrender if we hope for our marriages and families to be blessed by God in accordance with the plans He has for us.

A husband and wife under God are to be codependent one upon the other, working together to accomplish their goals and the intended purpose of God as life-bearers. I cannot overstate the necessity of the co-dependency and harmony needed within our world so that life may emerge; God has spoken to us through His Word and even through nature. May we respond accordingly.

* * *

The tree's summation:

"You people ... Life is in me because it was placed within me by my Creator. From me comes life, which satisfies your fleshly appetites for sustaining your body. This process or activity represents my glory, to my Creator's praise! There is no changing of His character and nature, neither is there any changing in my design and purpose."

"Even so, the breath which comes from me, which sustains your soul, represents my glory to the praise and glory of my Creator. As life is in me and through me, so life has been given to you that you also may bring forth life, representing your unchanging glory as predetermined by God. This too is for the praise and glory of your Creator and God."

"You are who you are. If you came forth from your mother a male - a man, you are! If you came forth from your mother a female ... a female, you are! You are who God fashioned you to be while you were yet in the womb of your mother. Life-bearers and underagents of God. You were created to be - a man and a woman ontological equals joined together in marriage, for life, that there may be life brought forth through you, even spiritual life, to the praise and the glory of your Creator and mine, Who is to be praised forever! Amen!"

God Requires Order - Fine Tuning The Family

God got it right! He has made no error in his ordering of creation nor the purpose for which he has created all things. His decree that there be life is unmistakable! Only a fool will dispute with God or reject His truth (Psalm 14:1).

The lower order of creation adheres to "natural law" or instincts determined by God, their Creator. Even from animals, we should take note and be as intentional as the beast to live, in many cases, in harmony together as they procreate. However, man is not to live as mindless beasts as many are! But rather to live purposefully after the Spirit of God unto eternal life! Not possessing human intelligence and rationale, the lower order of life nevertheless gets it right and, I dare say, lives more honorable than some of humanity.

However, those seeking God's will and mind are being conformed to the likeness of His son Jesus. This is done through the transforming work of the Spirit of God as we remain in fellowship with Him.

It is worth repeating men and women; boys and girls, are ontological equals. A man is not held superior to a woman; neither is the husband superior to his wife. Nonetheless, God has established instructions for structure and order amongst His family and followers within a God-honoring home. The home is to be regulated and the rules enforced by the father. Maintaining a God-ordered home is his primary charge, but not to the exclusion of his wife and helper.

A look at a father's build: In general, the father's towering and masculine statue, in part, is evidence of this assertion of his loving rule, but not authoritarian dominance over the home. Even when his offspring hears the sound of his voice, a difference is made regarding how the child responds to him, as opposed to their mother. In the case of my sons, when they were boys - the youngest one, in particular ... at times had problems following his mother's instructions. She was so loving, meek, and mild, and her sweet disposition has remained intact for over three decades.

I would witness or hear my wife, who is petite and was just over a hundred pounds, attempting to bring order and compliance with my sons. Her effort was countered with some resistance and, at times noncompliance. However, when I stepped into my sons presence, the correct behavior or response my wife was not entirely successful getting … when I showed up or spoke, my sons became compliant and fell in line.

I am not suggesting that a mother cannot bring order to her offspring… not in the slightest. Some mothers are more effective than the child's father regarding bringing order and compliance with their child – sadly, this is true.

Nonetheless, from that incredible mother, there are times that more effort is required and exerted to get the desired result. Where that father is standing in his rightful place, understanding his godly and guardian role, the mother's responsibility for bringing or maintaining order amongst her offspring is or should be minimized. This is God's intended order for the family, and in no manner is to be seen as a slight on the mother – simply, this is not God's intended role for her as an enforcer or the home's primary protector.

So it is … the father's responsibility to administer stewardship or leadership within his home. Along with that responsibility, he is to be the family's spiritual overseer. This does not preclude nor diminish a wife's active involvement, as she is the co-leader of the home.

The point to be emphasized is that each parent should understand their God-given roles and then effectively execute their responsibilities as husband and wife and parents. Let me also add this: A wife, for whatever reason, may have to assume the lead role, if only in a particular area of governance, for the home's wellbeing. Yet, at the same time. She must be mindful not to overstep her scope of authority in the home or exert her will over her husband.

A wife may very well have better leadership qualities than her husband, even having a closer walk with God. She may be wiser, more competent, or even making more money than her husband. These are great gifts, attributes, or assets for her to possess and be utilized to strengthen and maximize their family's development and even blessings. However, the wife must honor her husband's position as the rightful head of the home.

The wife is not to be just galivanting or doing whatever she chooses because she brings "more" to the relationship – no! But neither is the husband! Things are to be discussed with her husband, after which a prayerful decision is made, then moving in the direction that works for the family's good, bringing honor to God. Where children are involved, all the more critical that this family structure is clearly established as God prescribed. God is One of order.

As children of God, our Father does not expect us to be perfect; He knows that we cannot, but rather display exemplary living as belonging to and representing Him in this fallen world. This is God's perfect structuring for imperfect people so that harmony and abundance of love may be displayed within the home. Though we are imperfect people, recognizing our shortcomings, we are to all the more seek to know the counsel of God, thereby governing our lives after His wisdom and order so that there may be peace and harmony amongst all.

Understanding God's will or mind enables the child of God to be considerate and respectful to others and not be excessively self-centered. Where there may be genuine disagreement between spouses, even after prayerful consideration, the wife must willingly yield and lovingly submit to her husband's final say or authority on the matter or decision he felt compelled to take.

If it becomes apparent that a better choice could have been made or the choice made by the husband, it proved to be flat-out wrong. Seeing this, the husband should acknowledge the fact and extend an apology.

The loving wife should willingly accept her husband's apology. If there is something to be learned from the experience, be sure to do so and then move on, leaving that situation behind, never to be brought up and spitefully used. To do otherwise divides and works against the family and the will of God.

You are to always be mindful of building and not tear down one another and even your relationship. What we say and do will either strengthen and raise our relations to a level of success and blessings or weaken and raze our relationships to despair or defeat.

I recognize there are unique family dynamics (blended families) where the child is not the biological child through marriage. This situation has created much grief for many homes. As for how is one to address this sensitive and, in some cases, exceedingly difficult or even hostile matter?

I realize this can be a rather complicated situation to navigate; as for my simplistic response: the structure and operation within a godly home should not change. The couple must agree to do things according to the will of God. Under the parent's guardianship, that child must respect and learn to submit to the parental authority over it. This transition is made less complicated when the biological parent within a blended family informs the child beforehand of their expected behavior and consequences if they fail to meet them ... again, not after the marriage, but beforehand.

From the parent figure, ruling under *Love* must be demonstrated within this family dynamic! It will be love that tears down the walls of resistance that may come from the child. Depending upon the child's age and the influence of the other parent or their family, it may take some time for resistance or even apprehension toward the new family dynamic to be eliminated. Nonetheless, respect for the adult of the home and order must be maintained, and corrective loving discipline administered to check inappropriate behavior by the child when needed.

Initially, such corrective measures will be that of the biological parent, but not excluding the guardian-parent, if and when such actions of correction are required. Depending upon the age or gender of the child, it may be solely the biological parent's responsibility to correct inappropriate behavior by their child. This situation can make for a difficult time for all involved. Therefore, love, patience, and understanding will be the families' practice as order and peace are sought.

In the home of Adam, he was the designated federal head and God's first representative on earth, while Eve was the co-federal head, his helper, and second in command of their home. Their offspring, including you and me, who are born again, are also God's representatives through relationships, the organization, and ordering of this organism called a family of Believers. Even within the structure of the Church, Lead-Pastors are to be men (not women) who are approved by God.

Let me clearly point out that the first family served and lived under a command structure where God was their Ruler and King. Adam and Eve had different roles and responsibilities, yet were equals before and under God, as His under-agents and/or co-agents and ambassadors on earth (Luke 2:49; John 5:36; John 17:21).

Even so, the Divine ordering has a hierarchy or chain of command. We see this - in that Jesus came from heaven or was sent by His Father to perform His Father's will and to be a witness of Him. Likewise, the Holy Spirit was sent and came to fulfill the will of Jesus and to be His witness, indwelling the bodies of all who receive Jesus as the Father's Savior. We are now one with the Creator. Children of and ambassadors of the Father. We, the Redeemed, having been brought back and restored within His rank and file through the redemptive blood of Jesus ... who is over, or the Head of every Believer, is to live under our Father in an orderly and harmonious manner (John 4:34; John 5:30; John 6:38; John 15:26 and John 16:13-15).

As set in order by our Creator, our Commander, and Chief. The human family - a godly home, is also in the likeness of the Tri-unity of the Divine and His command structure as seen in the earthly father, mother, and offspring. The family structure is to operate and mirror or reflect the image of the Celestial Bodies or Trinity – God the Father, Son, and Holy Spirit. They are one and yet have Their distinct personage. The tri-unity of God is completely one, while the children of God are to establish a resemblance of this oneness within the home as displayed through the life we live as our Father's children and ambassadors here on earth.

As Christians, enabled by the Spirit, we embrace and live out through obedience God's will, representing and reflecting the Holy and Heavenly One. We do this anticipating the return of Christ for us ... as well to be taken away by Him from this evil world. Jesus has made all things new! He has spoken ... saying that He is one with the Father and that we are one with Him. We now, with patience, wait for His return while reflecting the image of Christ through our new lives orderly and with proper conduct (John 17:20 - 23).

While you wait, you must maintain prayerful vigilance against the enemy of our souls – Satan. He works through those who cause division. Even so, with the help of the Spirit of Jesus, we must identify our shortcomings and weaknesses and diligently work them out so that we may become builders of a healthy self-image as children of God. Only then will we be able to build a healthy relationship with others and, most importantly, the one we desire to spend a lifetime with – our spouse.

Satan and his evil horde of demons (Elohim, lesser spiritual beings) have been mentioned a time or two. I, therefore, dare not leave out mention of God's Angelic host, His servant soldiers, and ministers for our good. As for the Angels (messengers) of heaven: though they are not a part of the Divine Trinity – not possessing deity or equality with Yahweh (Jehovah God), they are God's agents or *Angelic Host* who serve Him in diverse capacities within their ranking. Last but not the least of which are the *Sons of God* (Elohim), who are also created beings. They are ranked just above the angels. These *Sons of God* require a study of their own (Deuteronomy 32:8; Job 1:6; 38:7; Psalm 82:1; 89: 5 - 8).

However, regarding the subject matters of Angelology and Demonology and their operation and relationship with both heaven and earth, God and man, there is so much more to be understood about these lesser elohim (gods), or spirit beings than I have provided. Or the traditions taught in most churches. Just the same. As freewill agents, even so, imagers of God, as noted, they too can rebel against God, their Creator, as seen in the Edenic garden fall when the one we call Satan led Adam into rebellion against God.

Under the command of God, their Creator, these gods (elohim, spirit beings, or angels) serve at His pleasure, in heaven and even occasionally upon the earth (Genesis chapter 18; Hebrew 13:2). As for these spirit being who are loyal to Him; God has also established a command structure or hierarchy within their ordering. Our God is one of order! And so, He requires it for His subjects or all who are to be loyal to Him.

As with humanity, they worship God and show loyalty to Him by conforming to and performing His will. Or, like mankind who has free will, they can reject God's authority and rule over their life. This is what Satan chose to do … He broke rank with *Eternity*, or relationship with God, and persuaded others of the angelic host to follow his lead.

Death or Satan's marching order is clear: break rank with God so that he (Satan) may establish and maintain his kingdom reign over the earth, his subjects or offspring being all who reject Jesus as Lord and Savior. These rebellious and ousted ones are the evil spirits behind all that is anti-Christ (God) and contrary to His will. And the cause for the upheaval and confusion in the world. Through their influence, these dark spiritual forces keep man from returning to God (Ephesians 6:12). Satan's command structure mimics the heavenly; he has also established a counterfeit trinity. More can be learned about this in the book of Revelation.

Do not be deceived; the influence of Satan's evil empire is flourishing, and his sinister efforts continue against man and God with every keystroke I have taken to write this book! And after this book is done, his evil influence will continue! He does not want you to become one with God. This is his ultimate objective … to keep man from returning to their Creator and loving Father!

To be a Christian, Jesus must be understood as Deity, the very Son of God – and not merely some righteous man. He is equal to His Father, was yet subject and obedient to the will of His Father that we may become one with the Eternal One – God our Creator. Under His Father's order, Jesus willingly came from heaven and clothed Himself in flesh.

Hear what the Scripture actually says about Jesus' obedience to His Father:

"Though he was God, he did not think of equality with God as something to cling to. Instead, he gave up his divine privileges; he took the humble position of a slave and was born as a human being. When he appeared in human form, he humbled

himself in obedience to God and died a criminal's death on a cross. Therefore, God elevated him to the place of highest honor and gave him the name above all other names, that at the name of Jesus every knee should bow, in heaven and on earth and under the earth, and every tongue confess that Jesus Christ is Lord, to the glory of God the Father" (Philippians 2:6-11).

Reiterating the subject of God's order that there may be peace and harmony among his people: The husband is the head of the house as Christ is the head of the Church. The husband is the final authority within his home, and Jesus is the final authority over the husband. And too, as Christ is subject to His Father, the husband must also be in submission and obedient to his Lord - Jesus. To that end, God will hold man (husband or father) primarily accountable for how he orders and leads his household ... just the same, all will have to answer to our Lord regarding how we lived our life here on earth.

I am thoroughly convinced that where the gravity of man's responsibility is understood as head of the home, a lovingly obedient relationship will be pursued with God and the man establishing a God reverencing home. Where this occurs, the matter of a man who would treat his wife with disrespect, who neglects, abandon or defects from his family, will be eradicated. Even so, will a wife render unto her man the love and respect due him when she is in a right relationship with the Father. When she fully comprehends from the Word of God that she is the glory of her husband and also a representative of God, people, relationally, things will begin to be ordered aright within the home. I am telling you what I know to be true ... not what I think.

When Adam and Eve disobeyed God, what they did was likened to committing adultery as they broke rank with *Eternity*! They became covenant breakers in choosing Satan's words over God.

As for the forbidden tree, I believe that the tree did not inherently possess the essence of sin or death, neither the knowledge of good nor evil. My reasoning: God created it – and it was good, among all that God had created. In God, there is no evil nor ill intent - only that which is *holy, loving, just,* and *good*; that which brings out the best for man unto life eternal.

Because the tree was forbidden, Adam and Eve choosing to take from it broke their commitment and loving relationship with God. They thereby forfeited *Life* and all of their divine privileges.

The choice of *Life* or Death was represented by the two trees. They could take from the tree of their choice; however, one tree had clearly been deemed off limits! They opted for the forbidden – whereby receiving death by uniting with and becoming unevenly yoked with the wrong man – Satan, the Man of Sin. It was not purposed for them to partake of the forbidden. Therefore, it was off-limit, not theirs, from which they could freely experience its pleasure, not without dire consequences.

What we saw played out in the garden was the test of love, faithfulness, and commitment of Adam and Eve toward their God. God had perfectly displayed His Love toward Adam and Eve. True love is expressed through loyalty and faithfully gives of itself to meet the needs of their Beloved ... this God had done! However, recipients of love, in turn, have to choose to return love as freely as it was given. And to remain faithful to the covenant and principles upon which the loving union was established. Herein is the test for the strength of any relationship or marriage: One's continued love, faithfulness, and commitment towards the one with whom they entered a covenant ... forsaken all that has been prohibited through their covenant agreement.

The union Adam and Eve shared with their creator and God was now broken and violated. Even so, with one another. A hard bed they made, now they must lay upon it while being repeatedly violated by Satan – the Abuser and Destroyer of souls. Satan could and would now do unto man, and through man, as he well pleased, and man being powerless within himself, to ward off his evil. This truly is a grim and horrible depiction of what Satan has done to man and is continuing to do. This is, in fact, humanity's reality, but it does not have to remain so.

Adam and Eve were lured away from God and were now led and even taken advantage of by Satan; they subsequently forfeited their earthly kingdom dominion over to him – Death. Unto the world, and its inhabitants, now reigned a new world order - Death (Romans 5:14)! However, our loving and merciful Father had a plan! At His appointed time, He displayed the *highest* act of love ... He sent *Love*! He sent Jesus His own Son to die for mankind's sins so that we could be delivered from our abuser, that destroyer of souls, Satan (Galatians 4: 4-7; 2 Timothy 1:10; Hebrews 2:14-15)!

Adam and Eve also had before them the Tree of Life. If they had only taken for themselves from this tree, I am convinced the Father would have brought forth blessing unto them unimaginable!

Tragic was and is the circumstances resulting from their decision. Great trouble and sorrow have their decision meant for all creation. Many of you and I, as well, have experienced these troubles at one time or another. But Jesus has delivered and continues to deliver from sin and death all who will choose Him.

I have chosen *Life*! Contrasting those days of my boyhood or when I was a young man. And even a babe and fool in Christ! Because I chose *Life*, Who had first chosen me, I matured as a godly and exemplary man, howbeit not a perfect man. I am, therefore, more in tune and aware of my shortcomings and the fiery temptations of the Evil One. Take my word for it; he remains active in this fallen world. In these *last days*, his treachery is picking up momentum! Look around! He earnestly desires to destroy you and me, along with any relationship that we hope to establish that has the potential of bringing praise and glory to God! Satan wants you; make no mistake about it! Many he still holds in his grips and control!

Joyfully, I know how the story will end for Satan and those belonging to Jesus. Victorious, it will be for those who have chosen to enter into a *personal relationship* with God through – Jesus our Savior and Deliverer!

God says to you, as He speaks through nature, this book, and His Word, "I have set before you this day, *Life* or Death" (Deuteronomy 30:15). He continues, "At this very moment, as was the case for Adam and Eve, you have a choice to make. Choose *Life*, choose Me as your Lord and Ruler, and eternal life is yours!

In this opening chapter, I have attempted to present a perfect picture of the right relationship to be held with God and the right relationship to be established in marriage through Him. Not that I have presented it before you perfectly, but rather, presenting before you that *Perfect One* and the perfect way of God. Now let us always be mindful to look to Him, the One that we *need*, that we may receive His ordering and direction for our lives.

CHAPTER 2

From the Ground Up - Groundwork (Psalm 127: 1)

In the first chapter of Genesis, we are informed that our Creator spoke from heaven, mysteriously instructing and constructing atoms... building cells upon cells to form this world. From the mind of God. And the command of His Word. He established the foundation of our world and all that dwells within and upon it. From the earth, the ground up, He created man and brought forth every living terrestrial thing to partake in life and perpetuate it. Even so, at the Creator's appointed time, every living thing that has been corrupted by sin (*death*) will return to the earth from which it came.

So it is, an encounter with death, all life as we know it will be confronted, apart from the rapture of man occurring beforehand (1 Thessalonians 4:1-17). Until such time, all living things will continue to be fostered upward from the earth, reaching outward and heavenward to attain its fullness from its life source - the sun. However, it is of greater importance for man to recognize the need to reach outward from within our bodies of clay, and spiritually or with our *inner-man*, reach upward unto the *Son* who grants Eternal Life; through whom and by whom all things have its existence and are sustained (John 1:3; Colossian 1:15 -17).

Regarding sin and death, which resulted from Adam and Eve's unholy alliance or hookup with Satan. God, in His permissive will, while knowing His plan of Redemption to follow, watched as a heartbroken Parent while the drama unfolded between this threesome in an unholy union of spiritual whoredom leading unto death. Lest we have forgotten, God had forewarned Adam of His judgment that would befall him if he disobeyed and ate from the forbidden tree. God has, therefore, permitted this unnatural occurrence, Death, throughout the ages to reign and seize hold of creation because of the first man, Adam, his sin of unfaithfulness, rebellion, and unholy union with Satan.

And so, it was ordained through God's righteous judgment that Satan (Death) would have power over the earth. Therefore, man meets with death. And our bodies are summoned back to their origin - the *ground* pending their restoration or renewal. This renewal of one's body is unto all who have been Redeemed by the *blood* of Jesus. And our spirits, therefore, returns to God's resting place until judgment, either to reward or eternal damnation (Matthew 3:12; 13:24-30; Matthew 16:24-28). Thanks be to God, death for the Christian is not the end; it is only a point of transition or rest from the terrestrial while we wait to be awakened to dwell eternally in the presence of Jesus.

Relative to eternity, short is the sleep of death and this repetitious unnatural cycle of life and death. However, this needed abnormality is the union of life and death, that life may be sustained here on earth. Even so, the promise of life eternal, and our dead spirits receiving regeneration, comes but through death and our new life through the death and sacrifice of Jesus. In the meantime, the terrestrial story, the drama, and connectedness or relationship of life and death continues until the set time of the climactic end of *death* - Satan himself, when *Life* will then swallow up death forever and reign eternally as Victor (Isaiah 25: 8; 1 Corinthians 15: 54)!

All the sadness and suffering we witness and experience as temporary earth-dwellers is the process leading unto that excellent and joyful end awaiting the child of God. This will be when all things are made new (2 Corinthians 5:17; Revelation 21:5 Romans 8:17)!

This paradoxical union of life and death. If we are not consumed by the sorrows death brings. Nor distracted and defeated by its pernicious pervasiveness and ravaging of this world. But instead ... we as Christians are focused on living (*Life*) even as non-believers. Who, however, simply do not want to die ... who are merely *bios* and who are without hope. Then we who have hope, with patience, wait on the Lord (James 5: 7,8). We find this agreement within our souls for the Believer and even the non-believer alike ... that death is problematic. We all want to live! However, our aims toward living and how we view life are different.

For Believers who are not overcome by the thought of death, we view death as the end or means to our new hope and beginning ... And not just - *the end!* In the souls of both Believers and non-believers, we innately experience the will to live. The will to live is because eternity is in us ... meaning we still have within our souls – though corrupted by sin, the image of the Eternal God. Eternity, or our souls, therefore, cries out from within us ... I want to live (Ecclesiastes 3: 11)! However, for the Saved and unsaved alike, many put up a relentless effort to live or prolong life (bios) in our dying bodies in excessive and extraordinary measures, although our corrupt bodies are dying with every breath we take.

However, as proven through Scripture and even secular history, death had no hold nor rule over Jesus! Rather, *Life* seized hold of Death and overcame him! The "Good News" of the Bible is that Christ has been resurrected (Romans 6: 1-14)! From the ground up, He rose from the grave. From the sleep of death, He sprouted forth from within the earth, proving His Preeminence over Death and the grave ... neither did His body experience corruption because He was without sin! Jesus living or bodily resurrection was evidenced when He manifested Himself to His disciples and many others over forty days before ascending back to His Father in victory, now holding all power and glory (Matthew 28:18; Acts 1: 2-3, 9; Romans 14:9; Revelation 1:18).

In Jesus and through Him, we have all we need to be spiritually satisfied and complete in this life. If we would only remain in an unbroken relationship with Him, spiritually rooting ourselves and/or being rooted deeply within our *Foundation* and *Wellspring* of *Life*. In this rooting and being rooted, our souls will be satisfied, and our faith strengthened. We can then face this life accompanied by death confidently as overcoming this world.

Remaining one in the Spirit, rooting ourselves, and being rooted deeper into the truth of God, we connect to an endless source of spiritual nourishment for the development of our spirit-man. That we may thrive in this sin-sick world; reaching full maturity, having been called home to be with the Lord, we suffer no more at the hands of Death's abuse and tyranny (1 Corinthians 15:50 – 55).

Just as Jesus is the *Source* or *Foundation* for our inner man's *life* and spiritual well-being, the composition and elements of earth's soil contain within itself the essentials to bring forth and sustain the life of our physical self. We see then that all things, seen – the natural and unseen – preternatural, have a starting point, a foundation or beginning from which it originates.

In other words, from the ground up, we view all things as coming into existence and developing. In the world we live in, success or achievement is considered as upward mobility. Regarding living things, accomplishment or the health of such things is gauged by the strength of its reaching outward and upward as it matures, thereby developing or fulfilling its intended end or purpose.

This is the natural way of our thinking and is displayed through the course of nature or life itself. Therefore, it is then reasonable to suggest: That the growth, strength, and longevity of a thing will be determined by its *foundation*. Although I am referencing various kinds of relationships within the created order. The relationship of mankind with one another, particularly the relations between a man and woman, is where I want you to maintain your focus. From the *ground* up, strong relationships are built.

That said, the foundation and the necessary work required to establish a healthy union to bring forth and maintain an organism (couple) that it may accomplish its intended end is indispensable. Therefore, a firm foundation for a developing relationship of whatever sort - having from its start sure footing or underpinning, is critical to its sustainability and success!

Here's a look at a different kind of relationship to make my point. Life as we know it is relational or a marriage of sorts. Some people do well relationally, while others are challenged in this area. Humanity, in our creativity, for the most part, does a decent job with building, producing, and administering the necessary care for their various inventive endeavors to enhance the quality of life for their fellow man ... this is an aspect of relationship building. The stability, functionality, and soundness of their product, especially when it comes to making a profit, are essential.

However, for others, monetary profit may not be the primary motivator when rendering goods and services to their consumers. Sometimes, there is simply personal delight in seeing a satisfied customer ... I'll call this personal, relational care that concerns this provider. However, some may provide customer service; nevertheless, it is only under the watchful eye of the consumer Watchdogs that the service provider may render a worthy product or service. In this case, proper relational care is given over to oversight – the Watchdog, to safeguard the consumer from such people's misdoings or unscrupulous dealings.

Man, whom God endowed with various gifts and talents, but being apart from God, carnal, uncaring, and selfish, unfortunately, does fall short in the area of personal, relational care, as sometimes seen in bad business practices or business dealings. Some again are self-seeking, concerned with only their benefit or profit; others have *within themselves* - to do good or perform *good works,* while the latter mentioned will take advantage of customers until they are called out. The earlier mentioned are regarded by and delight in their self-achievement.

In these two illustrations, the motivation or foundation of their action was about themselves. For one, it was about their profit; for the others, which is not altogether wrong, but for the purpose of this illustration, their product or service rendered was about their adulation ... "Look at what I did." God's oversight and undergirding are needed; that focus is turned from self to God and the service rendered to others. Only then can one achieve their higher calling, which is found in the delight of knowing that God is well-pleased with our interaction with or service to others (Matthew 25: 34 - 40; Ephesians 6: 7 - 8; Colossians 3: 23 - 24).

For sure, mankind, in large part, has fallen short in establishing our sure foundation and maturing in the manner or ways of God concerning relationships; our deficiency and failings in this area go without saying ... It is clearly visible! Man, not embracing or being unaware of their higher calling, or lacking in spiritual maturity toward their spiritual profit or good, are incapable of displaying the best God has intended for them ... this also being for the benefit of their fellow man.

Many who identify as Christians have failed to achieve *the mind of Christ.* Stunted or delayed in spiritual growth, not knowing the purpose for which they have been called and created, are therefore spiritually immature. However, some Christians are on the verge of breaking emotionally, if not already broken. Such individuals can be called babes in Christ, carnal Christians, or Christians needing spiritual healing.

The state of creation or where one may be in life did not occur incidentally. Things do not just happen by chance or in a vacuum; there is cause and effect. And so, there is God who sets in order the purpose, operation, and intent of His creation. Evidence of this is seen in the unity, the dependency, and the relationship of creation. Behind these relationships and the order seen within these partnerships; results from there being an *Intelligent Designer* and *Overseer* and even a God who *watches* over everything. There would be no other way for relational harmony or order as displayed throughout creation. And even the desire for order in our lives if there was no *Intelligent Designer ...* that *One* laying the incontrovertible *true* and *sure* foundation upon which all things have their beginnings or origin.

Developing anything meaningful, a relationship or otherwise, must be engendered or engineered through intelligent consideration and design before the subject can function satisfactorily or orderly. Only from or through the constructive and ordered work of the *designer* or *creator* of a thing, that thing reaching completion and now ready for production, can the words be spoken ... *It is good or very good!* This was God's proclamation when He formed and outfitted the earth. However, after Adam and Eve were created, God declared that creation was very good or perfect (Genesis 1:31).

I often hear people when asked, "How are they doing?" Respond by saying, "Good." However, from God's point of view, are you truly good? Meaning … Are you walking in God's good and perfect will and the purpose for which He has called you? If you are … well, you are, in fact, "Good," no matter what may be occurring in your life or what may be going on around you.

Nevertheless, to the contrary is your "good." If you are merely going through the motions of living (*bios*). If you are not one with God, you are simply existing … He even says, "You are dead in your sins." For others … though, you may be saved. However, if you are unproductive for the kingdom of God, if you are not in fellowship with God and living according to His will, you are not as good as you would lead yourself to believe. For such individuals, danger looms nearer than you may think, as the enemy of your soul has enlisted his minions to come at you all the more in the hope of destroying you because you are not in a right relationship with God and the Believers of God. Therefore, you are most vulnerable (Luke 11:24-26).

I want you to take from this that causality is always in play. What we do or do not do, our actions, choices, and words, will always determine some outcome. The outcome may work toward our good or the good of some other. Or toward our detriment or the detriment of some other. For sure, we help to create our outcomes. Even so, influence in some measure the condition or outcome of others.

Where meaningful purpose is behind the design of a thing, it goes without saying that the thing has been predetermined to bring meaningful results and even positive effects with that it was purposed to interact. As for the unregenerate person, the immature in the Lord, and even the mature in the Lord, there is conflict within our souls, keeping or attempting to keep us from fulfilling God's meaningful purpose and original design for our lives – to love and be in harmony with one another! And first and foremost, to love and be one with our Creator!

Although created in perfection. Man became corrupted through their rebellion and defection. So, in becoming intimately one with Satan … Adam and Eve contracted a spiritually transmissible disease, which has affected and/or infected all of humanity like a virus. Though man can do good, sin also beckons us to do its bidding. And for many, the ability or the strength to resist sin is beyond themselves. This inability or weakness has to do with one's foundation ... it is our foundation that we choose to build upon that will determine the good we will do or the evil that will be manifested through us (Matthew 7:24-27).

God purposed for humanity - good works, a people of excellence in love, who would worship Him. Due to Satan's intrusion and our spiritual death, the good we would do, the love we would express, and our worship of God were upset. Therefore, we find a different operation within our souls ... Satan's evil influence and plans that war against our design and purpose (Romans 7:14-25).

Because of this ongoing conflict, we are to daily work out our salvation ... we must purpose in our hearts to be about our Father's business. Indeed, it is work, and even hard work, and a battle for many. Nevertheless, this work must be embraced and understood as an invitation and enlistment unto labor for life and oneness with *Love*. The very presence and *Spirit of God* who indwells all Believers; enables us to overcome evil practices – those influences from without and our personal struggles (virus or fallen nature) from within.

A Labor of Love - A Labor for Love

The amount of effort or labor required to maintain a healthy, properly functioning relationship will be determined by the foundation upon which we build our understanding ... that makes for a healthy and productive relationship. And too, a conscious effort, accompanied by effective preventive maintenance, is a must to preserve the stability and duration of the relationship, of whatever the sort: That is, man with his environment, himself, and without question, with one another, those in a heterosexual relationship or platonic unions.

Certainly, the development of a healthy relationship will be determined by the foundation from which it was built – the groundwork. Over time, how it is superintended will determine its sturdiness, effectiveness, and longevity.

The principal concern is the reliability and sureness of the relationship's underpinning. If its footing is steadfast and unmovable, then the relationship will withstand the test of time. And those inevitable disruptions, distractions, and diversions that will accompany life's journey; even so, those disruptions that seek to break us, thereby creating a breach in a meaningful relationship.

I have drawn this conclusion having spoken to various individuals, some who are currently in a relationship that has been met with challenges and others who have not had success with relationships. That far too many, some of my generation – born in the sixties, and particularly those younger; do not understand what goes into making a healthy relationship and sustaining it, which I call a victorious marriage.

It does not take long to discover why this is so. After a brief conversation and a few questions later, it became apparent that the required groundwork for building a healthy relationship was beyond their ability to understand. Most of those struggling relationally, and those who are no longer in a relationship, not having sure footing from the beginning, came to ruin. For those who are yet holding on … things can be described as shaky at best. Though they could not see that there were problems early on or chose not to acknowledge this reality, just the same, the proverbial – "handwriting was, or perhaps is, presently on the wall." This writing indicated that challenging days were/are ahead because their foundation was insufficient to build and maintain a healthy, vibrant, and victorious relationship.

For any relationship to weather the storms or challenges that life brings, a conscious effort toward stabilization or shoring up the relationship's footing is a must! Figuratively, the joints that hold fast the relationship that it may endure whatever obstacles or challenges encountered from time to time will have to be checked for soundness. After some situation or crisis, it could be as simple as one in the relationship saying to the other, "Bae, are we good?" or Bae, are you good?" If their response is … "Yes," you know it is ok to move forward.

Before erecting a brilliant and sound structure, any good builder will have set aside time for strategic planning, incorporating a blueprint and the course of action before undertaking their project – *the groundwork.* This kind of thoughtfulness should also hold true before one enters into a relationship.

The challenge behind building relationships today is that people's understanding, opinions, or views on dating and marriage are all over the place! There must be a coming together or unification of ideas and beliefs ... There must be *One Blueprint* before you two and an *Architect* who *Superintend* the building project!

When you decide to date someone as a Christian, the relationship must be established upon Christian principles or beliefs. As well as coming into agreement as best possible on other essential views. Thereby establishing and securing a solid foundation as you consider building a future together.

Because principled Christian reasoning is greatly lacking in many regarding the *truths* that establish and foster a healthy relationship. This within itself establishes as its foundation uncertainty moving forward relationally. Then add in the baggage brought by either of you, if not you both, complicating matters all the more. I tell you ... *The handwriting is on the wall.*

Not having common, basic core values and understanding regarding relationship construction makes it extremely important. That you work toward developing commonality or unity within yourself and with each other as you lose yourself to the will of God. In the preliminary stages of dating and throughout the courtship. During this development period, you two will learn to compromise and cooperate – here, giving of self, growing together, and binding and bonding as reasonably possible in unity of thought and action so that you may be able to fulfill God's blueprint and building plan for marriage.

Understand something - there will be situations that will assist you two in growing together. And there will be situations that can drive the two of you apart if you fail to establish a foundation that has you two on one accord. That you two may be firm and settled ... knowing and embracing the love of God and the true love shared between one another, being the most consequential (Amos 3:3)! You two need to become like-minded or be in agreement on substantial matters.

Unfortunately, many regretfully pressed the matter of remaining in a relationship or situation, even though they saw the handwriting on the wall. Because time had been invested, money spent, and even perhaps a child or children brought into the union, etc., they chose to stay the course, not following their better judgment. However, relationships and even married couples can reach a breaking point where the foundation is insufficient or the necessary maintenance is not performed. After the rise of tension and stress in a relationship, all things considered, one or both parties can decide to call it quits, having determined that they just cannot get along or cooperate any longer. Unfortunately, this scenario plays out amongst too many married and unmarried couples, but it is tragic and of tremendous consequence for children. However, where God is the foundation of the union, or He becomes the *New Project Manager,* or is reestablished over the union, love can find a way to prevail in what may have been thought to be a lifeless and hopeless situation. I personally know what God can do when His will is sought for the restoration of a God-ordained marriage!

I do not know of any relationship, mind included, which you will read about later that does not encounter in the developmental phase, or perhaps into the marriage, experiences that stressed or challenged the relationship in some degree and one way or another.

***

But less likely, the effects of the related tension and stress causing instability, a teetering of the relationship to the point of snapping – literally, or the falling apart of a relationship whose foundation is solidly supported by Christ. Where the footing is sure, necessary maintenance is provided, and even well after the - *I dos, and I wills.* The marriage or a developing dating relationship will stand true and grow stronger due to the challenges encountered.

As for the maintenance and preventive care that I have mentioned, relationships need; it is not intended for that couple, married or not, who is just together or tolerating one another; perhaps for the sake of the kids, the financial benefit, or other benefits. Or who are cohabitating and maintaining some front, a manufactured reality to appease others, when the union - loosely speaking- was never in good standing.

I suppose one could argue that those reasons for remaining together are a better option than divorcing, certainly where children are involved. However, how about a better choice than just cohabitating? How about finding or rediscovering love as it was meant to be. How about taking on a renovation project of your heart. Strip away that old foundation of understanding and rebuild your marriage or relationship from the ground up upon that *Sure Foundation*. How about seeking the will of God for your life, upon W*hom* we are called to stand. Jesus, the Word of God, is our Solid Rock and Sure Foundation!

Do not merely exist or coexist. Instead, build upon that new and better foundation and way of *living* ... that surefire groundwork - *Love* Himself, Jesus as your *Chief Cornerstone*. You may not be able to see this happening. However, if the two of you – again, I say, the two of you stand in agreement, truly desiring better for your lives. The very *One* who was resurrected from the dead with *all power* can resurrect a new life and loving relationship that you may have thought impossible. Two willing and submitted people plus *The One* equals the impossible being accomplished. With God, all things pertaining to spiritual regeneration are possible (Matthew 19:26).

God's love is freely given. Nonetheless, God's *agape* or unconditional love is something we must learn to embrace and actuate in our lives. It is the Holy Spirit who teaches agape's operation in those who receive Him in His abundant and gracious love. And it is He – the Spirt, who wills within man, even giving us the ability to exercise or put into effect true love, the very love of God.

On our part ... We must be willing to surrender to *Love – Jesus, the Bridegroom*, as a wife who surrenders or submits to her husband. Then begins the labor of and for love or maintaining love as expressed towards others. You see, exercising or expressing love unconditionally, intentionally, and consistently does not always come easy or naturally. Gaining a cerebral understanding of love is one thing. However, agape has to be quickened within our souls by the Spirit before we can embrace and appreciate the labor, attention, and effort required by Love and appropriate love to others and maintain it at all costs.

Effort or One's righteous actions have to be observed working through them – and rightfully so, for others to believe and then accept the love one may say they have. To say you love another can only be evidenced by your action or display of love. One now seeing and experiencing the other's change, the Spirit's indwelling love in them, can now freely and without trepidation, offer and open themselves freely and with security over to the person expressing love and desiring love in return.

Agape is to be recognized as that intangible experience that transcends mere fleeting feelings or some "second-hand emotion." Agape just is! Agape is God – God is love intrinsically. Therefore, He cannot help but love us; even so, His love He desires to impart and input within those who belong to Him. Or all who will freely receive or give themselves to Him.

God's love is selfless; it is unconditional, always giving, and affectionate, yet without sexual expression, even though it works towards life for the born again. God's love gives us life and has a way of maturing within us or causing us to grow spiritually because of His love. This kind of love is sacrificial. It is proven in the crucible of let-downs, and opposition, even under circumstances where you must love the unlovable, those not wanting our love, or those in our carnal reasoning - not deserving it. As shown in Jesus' life and His death (self-sacrifice) for the world, this love is also to be expressed through Believers. So it is; all who belong to Him are called to live out love unconditionally and sacrificially!

In the natural, man struggles with expressing agape toward others. But with and through God's Spirit, we can learn to love as God loves. Suffice it to say love must first be worked within us before it can be worked out through us. Love has to transform our thinking and renew our hearts. There has to be an inward renewal of our spirit before there can be that outward expression of agape's influence and radiance toward and before others.

Christians should not be difficult to get along with. A non-believer may find it challenging to get to the place of surrender and acceptance of God. And even though many Christians have accepted Jesus as Savoir. Some can be as mean as the Devil (the Slanderer) … so I have heard. I will leave it at that. For a Christian, even after rebirth has taken place, expressing agape for many will not be automatic or easy – hence the progressive work required, whereby one learns to surrender to God's transforming process. This is of utmost importance and necessity that the Believers may learn to truly live out love while being aided by God (John 13:35; 1 John 4:21; John 3:16).

After accepting Christ, some will discover that they find themselves struggling against their old nature to reframe from what they know is wrong. Regardless of the pull to do wrong, you are victorious by not yielding to the wrong. A spiritual war is at hand; therefore, remain faithful in your battle for righteousness.

For sure, in some measure, with regards to relationship building or its restoration, there has to be a deliberate, attentive, and collaborative effort with both parties to achieve their desired outcome of having a successful relationship. The required work must be put in; it is inescapable in order to achieve victory in relational agape with the one you have chosen to be with and that which is acceptable unto God.

Anyone important to you or someone with whom you are affectionately interested. You should expect and embrace the necessary work or preparation required of you to acquire the desired results from the relationship. This is a two-way street where couples often fall short; in their lack and neglect of preparation or failure to see the need – to put in the work. The saying is true, failure to plan is a plan to fail. This begins with us individually – we must first get our thinking ordered.

In our day and time, the effort required in this area of sustaining a meaningful relationship is proven to be sorely inadequate. Another way this is made apparent is in the multiple sexual relationships that one has been in over a short span of living or a lifetime. This can also hold true if one has experienced numerous failures in platonic relationships.

Many of you are likely holding down a job. At the end of your workweek, or at some point, you expect what? ... To get paid a return on your efforts! Yes, you expect to reap the benefits of your labor. My point ... there must be work put into the relationship you are in so that you may reap the benefits. Payday is not a given; it is earned after the necessary work required is consistently put in. And the work does not stop when you get married.

Living life productively is all about the effort we put in and the right choices we make along the way. Therefore, we must live with a proper understanding directing us and choose 'wisely' our effort given and to whom they will be rendered, instead of "carefully," which is often the expression. Now, this is not to suggest that care is not important.

Why the distinction? Care alone... in this sense, suggests that the carnal mind and our feelings alone are at work in our decision-making. And that the wisdom, counsel, conviction, and guidance of the Holy Spirit are absent. The careful-minded one is self-reliant and self-confident. The Bible is clear regarding our deficiency in self-reliance ... that we cannot please God. And, for that matter, others. Glory and honor and spiritual victories alone belong to God. Therefore, we must seek the wisdom or counsel of God in all that we do so that our efforts honor Him, resulting in His sufficiency and not our care or carefulness alone (Psalms 37:5; Proverbs 3:5-8; Proverbs 16:3).

To choose wisely as the Christian alternative is to embrace the Wisdom that is not of this world. Our ultimate objective is recognizing that we do not have the answers to please God or accomplish the ultimate good or plans that He has for us within ourselves. If you think that you do have a viable answer or solution to an important matter, you should want to confirm through Scripture, prayer, and perhaps godly counsel that it is what God will have you to do. Receiving confirmation on a life-changing situation. Or that of some other is to walk in God's counsel, will, and wisdom.

The Christian man or woman is not to be self-reliant. Our absolute reliance must be upon God, our Architect, our Superintendent, and even Foundation. We have seen what happened to Adam's house ... it was conquered and laid in ruins.

One's spirit being at peace, having trusted the wisdom and counsel of God: be it known… you are a victor no matter what life throws at you (Psalms 23).

Rules of Engagement

It is necessary to clarify for times such as these, even though some insight has been shared. To sharpen the distinction between Rules of Engagement. Or Codes of Conduct between a couple dating and those who are married. As a Christian, it should not come as a surprise for those reading this book that I accept the *Word of God,* the Bible, as supremely authoritative, inerrant, the very Breath of God that inspired His writers. We have the Word as our counsel, guide, and operational manual. God's Word enables Christians to see clearly into His mind that we may be granted understanding on all matters of morality or righteous living. That we may learn to be watchful of Evil's lurking within the darkness of this world and the Evil that attempts to keep our understanding shrouded in darkness. Quickly read 2 Timothy 3, in particular verses 16, 17.

There have been and will continue to be reoccurring themes throughout this book. As for now, I want to deal directly with sexual relations while dating. In the following chapter, under the subchapter - The Experience vs. The Experiment, Dating and Dating Disciplines, I will go into greater detail regarding this matter of Christian conduct while dating.

It goes without saying… many unwed couples have chosen to cohabitate, with more than a few not considering marriage in the slightest. Though they may have provided "good reasons" for not doing so, thinking relationally, things are seemingly going well. Nevertheless, understand this truth: That which may seem right in our eyes may not be right in the sight of God. And so, it is… this living condition is unacceptable, especially for those confessing Christ as their Lord and Leader.

Where there is cohabitating, the proper assumption is that the two are sleeping together … ok, having sex as though they were one in marriage. People, in case you do not know, this is committing fornication. It is a sin against your very body! Our bodies are to be held in honor before man and God. Sexual sin is also a violation against God, who created you for His glory. No, I do not know what is going on in your house, but God does; this should matter to you and certainly if you are a Christian. Consider this … if you are a Christian, then your living is an example to others. Therefore, as followers of Jesus … What we do or how we live must be done with decency and His ordering, even so, that your "good intentions" "are not evil spoken of." Cohabitating, even if by chance, sex is not occurring, can very well be evil spoken of and the wrong message conveyed to others. Not to mention the ever-present temptation to commit the sin of fornication.

It is not my intention to provoke you, nor am I condemning anyone for your actions. I am simply sharing with you what the Bible expresses. If you feel rubbed, this can be considered a positive; now, you must take the matter up with God, as His Word has passed judgment on you and your situation (1 Corinthians 7: 3). God's Holy Word holds absolute authority! It clearly speaks against this matter, specifically to those who claim to be a child of God, those who no longer practice sin or conform to the ways of this world.

Look. I speak to you as one who has been there and done that! Yes, practicing sin (fornication) in ignorance and getting caught up in sin (adultery) when I knew the righteous ways of God. Just keep reading; my story will unfold on these pages soon enough. And so, it is God's calling on my life to point you to that better way; God's holy way unto right living, which honors Him and brings His blessings upon you and your family. Even so, that you may avoid heartache and other consequences for living outside God's will.

Understand that the prohibited exercise of free-will works contrary to what God desires for you – again, I call your attention to Adam and his wife. Where God's prohibitions are willfully practiced, this wanton act of sin and rebellion against Him undermines the unity and integrity of a relationship and works against the blessings God desires to show through family, marriage, and each of us individually.

The union of Marriage is the most meaningful way that the glory and favor of God are shown operating in and through man. As established and blessed by

God, the institution of a Holy Marriage subsequently becomes a channel of blessings unto all humanity. God's blessings flow best or freely where His eternal ordering and purpose are established and expressed through the individual, couple, and family who seek to honor Him.

We who are one with Christ are not to conduct or order our living after the dictates or the wisdom of this world. Instead, we govern our lives, looking forward to that eternal hope and our heavenly expectation. As Christians, we are to live out heaven or God's mandate here upon this earth. Jesus expressed our form of living when He taught His disciples to pray, "*Your (God's) kingdom come, Your will be done, on earth as it is in Heaven*" (Matthew 6:10).

Satan is in the business of presenting "alternative choices and even alternative lifestyles!" Where we choose to do things apart from God, society suffers, by and large, evidenced by society's dysfunction and brokenness. Some may see such living (cohabitating) as the easy, less risky, or safe way to engage in a relationship. But I want you to know what it truly is: it is a lie that Satan has fed this world, a counterfeit option or simulated structure for a relationship or family that opposes the perfect will of our Creator and Father. Satan will have you believe otherwise – this is what he does ... remember Eve?

If our choices are not God's way, not leading to a life according to His righteousness for us, our actions are then the antithesis of what should be - hence lifeless and/or dead. Simply... living our way is missing the mark or sinning before and against God; there is no negotiating, compromise, or justification of wrong of whatever the sort before Him. Arguing or resisting His truth is equivalent to rebelling and even fighting against God. Is this the stance you really want to take toward a loving and merciful Father... who simply wants the best for you? Or will you recognize the error of your way(s)? And therefore, submit to Him, to that which He knows is best for you and those He has entrusted to your care.

It should be understood and accepted that looking for or moving toward a serious dating relationship is not without risk. And for this reason, my book is to aid its readers with minimizing the risk and inevitable hurt that comes from those bad relational decisions that are too often made and the problematic situations many find themselves in. I call this *guarding your heart* - herein minimizing as much as possible bad decisions leading to unnecessary hurt and pain that could have been avoided.

Embracing God's practical guide to right living. Significant disappointment or risk and altogether avoidable hurt and pain while dating can be minimized if the proper steps or approaches to dating are applied by one who is ordering their actions unto sanctification. Or simply following God's plans for their lives and honoring themselves as sacred space. You two who are dating, staying the course of fidelity or sexual abstinence; with the common bond towards a maturing love, holding true unto right living, working toward your ultimate objective – a holy marriage, life will be far better.

If one takes to heart what they glean from this reading and applies this knowledge and wisdom of God to their living, the heart-wrenching doubts and feared *what-ifs* regarding dating and marriage that you may have will be significantly diminished. Even so, the struggle of compromising right living will become less burdensome because you have made a choice unto God's plan for your life.

Before there can be a productive and healthy marriage, the seriousness of dating and what should occur and not occur during courtship should be understood. Christian dating must be thought through, wisely talked out, and prayerfully navigated if there is to be the blessed hope of moving toward the blissful destination of an enduring marriage, where peace and love are enjoyed within a home and the unnecessary drama altogether eliminated.

People, life is not always smooth sailing … Far from it! Unfortunately, many well-intended courtships do not make it through the shallow challenges, those expected or not, before calling it quits and abandoning what appeared to be a promising journey. The problem for some. Again they are either lacking in understanding regarding the process of navigating a relationship. Or simply do not want to put in the work to make it through the turbulent times. And more than a few people are ill-equipped to successfully manage life, let alone a relationship, in mere times of rain … yep, I said mere rainy days … And not those stormy times!

For others, perhaps they thought they understood how to embark upon a relationship and how to navigate it successfully. However, because their compass reading was sorely lacking in finding *True North* and their *Depth Finder* could not search out the approaching hidden dangers below, their relationship was a shipwreck waiting to happen. However, they could not see this for themselves nor the looming dangers that awaited them. But soon enough, they found themselves in troubled waters. Directed by their lack of navigational relational insight, they steered into the imminent threats of the jagged rocks beneath them, to be sunk and/or run aground, whereby their relationship capsized!

While dating and even in marriage, there will be challenging seas, changing winds, and other known and unknown threats. Therefore, setting in order proper preparations so that there may be smooth sailing or knowing how to make the right adjustments during the rough times of sailing is a must! When two seek to engage relationally, *the rules of engagement* must clearly be established and understood before lifting anchor to set sail.

Would you be surprised if I told you that one of the primary causes of boating disasters is when an inexperienced boater encounters unfamiliar or dangerous conditions? Living life and facing the varying aspects of life ill-prepared and inexperienced is no different. For this reason, God has provided for His people, His navigational manual – the Bible, to guide and safeguard us while we sojourn and traverse life here on earth. Why must we insist on learning things the hard way … why must we continue to make our beds hard?

A dating couple choosing to express themselves sexually instead of abstinence can wreak devastating emotional turmoil when one's hopes have been dashed as the relationship has been called off or overturned. Especially when mistreated by the person you gave yourself over to sexually. And you did them no wrong.

Where choosing the ill-advised route to sex before it became apparent that you two really could not get on par with one another intellectually or otherwise.

Now, sex added to the questionable, if not the lousy relational situation, and "the sex was good," ignoring or disregarding the warnings, choosing to remain in place because you were on par sexually, will only complicate things. Do we ever have things turned upside down and backward! People. Where sex is involved ... a deeper connection occurs! Either fondness for the person you are "just having sex" with deepens. Or one's sexual appetite increases for what God has forbidden! Enough said ... at least for now!

CHAPTER 3

Not By Chance

I believe that for those *searching for truth and meaning in life*, the child of God in particular, but not exclusively, occurrences that unfolds in your life that significantly affects you are not by happenstance. Rather, God has/had His part in directing your course in life, although the matter may seem coincidental in one's natural reasoning. Read 1Samuel 2:9; Psalm 37:23; Proverbs 16:9; Proverbs 20:24).

Perhaps God, through these experiences you encountered, is not only making life's meaning clearer for you. But maybe He is also attempting to draw you closer to Himself or into a better understanding of His ways and Truth for you! When encountering unique situations, there is a benefit in lending prayerful consideration to the matter. God may be trying to get you to perceive how He is working on your behalf. Sometimes it takes looking back over our lives to see just how God has directed our steps.

While we carry on with volition, seemingly charting our own course in life, God, our concerned, merciful, and gracious Father, sits in heaven, from there watching our every step, as does any loving parent who carefully watches over their child. When we misstep or are headed in the wrong direction, He, at times, divinely intervenes, redirecting our course. Often, we are unaware of His involvement as He keeps or sets us on the right path (Romans 8:28).

However, there are times when our Father allows us to stumble. It is not that He willed our stumbling or approved of our wrongdoing, but rather, He permits such things to happen that we may learn from the situation, we got ourselves in. If we listen, turning our hearts to Him ... He, in turn, shows us His better way for our lives so that we may grow from the experiences and learn all the more to put our trust in Him for guidance.

Have you found yourself questioning ... why this or that happened to me? It is especially hard to grapple with or understand where untimely, unfortunate, and unwelcomed situations come our way ... as if there really is a good time for such occurrences.

However, you must remember ... such events or situations can be the very thing by which God enables His child to grow spiritually. In such times be mindful of this maturation process that a child of God will experience. Instead of dreading these moments and labeling them as bad outcomes. Or perhaps suggesting, "the Devil (the Slanderer) is messing with me." Instead, consider how such things can strengthen and mold your character. God allows such things for the good of building up and encouraging His child (Romans 5: 3-5; 2 Corinthians 1: 4-6; Romans 4: 8-12).

For just a moment, give thought to how your past, the situation you were born into, the wrong choices you made, or the hurt experienced by some other that has affected you. As I am currently working on my first edit of this book, a phenomenon called "Me Too," like a massive wave, is moving across this nation.

If you were awake, you remember this tsunami that caused many perpetrators of sexual misconduct to fall. And others to become quite uneasy as twenty-seventeen was ending. I will highlight regarding this moment how those who were taken advantage of felt at the time of their violations and even how they remained affected years later.

Sadly, many of these violators of women never identify with or acknowledge empathy for the harm caused to those they victimized. Neither are they aware of the emotional distress these women have to live with. As these victims recounted their stories, their hurt remains; others are visibly shaken as they relive what they went through. The emotional wound for some of these women may never completely heal. While for others, there has been progress toward their recovery. Because of the "Me Too" movement, many of these victims have disclosed their painful suffering. This is the beginning of closure, even a time for healing and renewal.

Recognizing and understanding the nature of cause and effect can be liberating while empowering one to make the necessary steps to move upward from a low point or season in their life and towards their healing and betterment. And so, as one looks back to address issues of their past (cause), it is for the purpose of moving forward and upward. Now unhindered by your hurtful or shameful past. One can begin to excel unto spiritual growth and that for which God has purposed for you. This makes the final outcome of your future much brighter or more favorable ... surely this is what you desire for yourself?

Though sensitive or emotional memories may be recalled and relived, I leave with you: "Vengeance is mine, says the Lord" (Romans 12:19). A heart of love and forgiveness is the way of God, bringing about healing and even reconciliation. For the child of God, we should not needlessly expose the weakness of some other (Romans 15:1). However, justice must roll on when one is unrepentant and remains in the bondage of corruption toward evil practices and criminality. Where there is the need for exposure and accountability, darkness must be brought to the light and justice rightly rendered (Psalms 11:7; Proverbs 21:15; Jeremiah 22:3).

I have this book to share because God performed a spiritual work and awakening within me. God worked or birthed this blessing and gift through me for your benefit – this book. Despite my past and its hindrances because of others and those of my making. Scripture says, "Therefore, if anyone is in Christ, he is a new creation; old things have passed away; behold, all things are made new" (2 Corinthians 5:17; Isaiah 43: 25; John 1:7-9; Hebrews 8:12). If you belong to Christ, you are no longer imprisoned to your past; neither are you defined by it.

Through His Spirit, God's inner working within my soul enables me to clearly understand this matter of cause (sin) and effect (the evils and disasters in this world) and, most importantly, understand the spiritual nature of man's being. We are told and shown through Scripture. That our acts of obedience towards God result in His blessings. Not being one or remaining in relationship with Him, we can commit acts of evil of all sorts, thereby reaping curses or harm unto ourselves, which is the judgment of our wrongdoing.

Even though Christians are born again by the Spirit of God. I have come to understand that through the continual work (sanctification) of the Spirit in us and one's desire to be obedient to our Father, we remain faithful to God and live righteously (Philippians 2:13).

I … my born-again spirit dwells within a broken or sin-desiring body. In varying degrees and manners, if we lose focus of our spiritual calling and heavenly identity, we can conduct ourselves in the way of those in this world whose evil influence is from Satan.

Although the Spirit of God continues to operate in and even through me and all Believers. To sinless perfection I've yet to attain. Neither I nor any man will attain sinless perfection while we are clothed within these earthen vessels … For this reason, Scripture declares: "Flesh and blood cannot inherit the kingdom of God" … our bodies yet remain corrupted by sin (John 3:6; Romans 2:7; 1 Corinthians 15:50).

However, it is upon nonbelievers and not the Spirit's indwelling that He moves or prompts them so that they might come to know Truth, turn from a life of sin, and turn to Jesus for deliverance and Salvation.

For Christians, herein lies the vital subject of spiritual maturity that we are to attain. Our growth and understanding of the spiritual or eternal matters are what cause us to further desire and seek after those things above or that which is eternal. Otherwise, our energy, attention, and focus are fixated on worldly longings or one's aspirations and passions rather than God.

When we learn that living after the flesh does not please God. We then learn by the help of the Spirit the necessity of bringing our bodies under subjection to the will of our Father ... this too is by the Spirit's empowering (Colossian 3:15; Mark 7:21; Romans 6:13).

I have experienced my confidence and hope in God, my Father, becoming stronger over the years in my personal growth as I come to trust God as my *Hope* and *Help.* Even so, I am learning to trust my Father daily and welcome His *Guidance* and *Strength* for my life! And so should you!

Giving myself over or submitting to Jesus. Having the same mind as Christ when Jesus said ... *"Father, not my will but Yours be done."* Maturing in my oneness towards or with my Lord, there is a growing assurance within me; that as I go through this life of uncertainty, nevertheless, nothing that happens to me of consequence is by chance. Rather, my Father's will is being worked out in and through my life and is for my good.

I do not embrace the doctrine of predestination regarding the notion that in everything I do, God is in heaven pulling each string or that He has willed or foreordained every aspect of my life. No, we are not God's puppets, nor are we automatons. Love cannot be expressed or understood absent free will.

However, God has and can place an extraordinary call and purpose upon an individual, even while the child is yet in their mother's womb. This has been shown throughout the entirety of Scripture. That person will fulfill that particular purpose of God despite their shortcomings or whatever the situation. Such a calling is designed to bring God's divinely directed objective and Kingdom purpose for man to be worked through that person. I give you three such people from a long list ... Abraham, Jesus, and Mary, the mother of our Christ.

Furthermore, I firmly believe that God has called forth every child born of a woman and has impregnated each of us with purpose. That purpose will not be fully realized or birthed until a relationship is established with God. After this relationship has been established, one will begin to realize their reason or purpose for *being.* Then choosing to live by the Spirit, within their purpose, that which is to be delivered through them will meet its fulfillment or divine destiny (Psalm 139:16; Isaiah 49:1, 5; Jeremiah 1:5; Galatians 1:15).

As a free-will under-agent of God, I determine my path in life, and so do you. However, having chosen to freely give my life over to God, I now ask Him and even permit Him to order my steps according to His will and that which He knows to be best for His Kingdom and me.

Bear in mind that His transcending ways, His thoughts, and His timetable are not as my finite view of things. God's scope or His view of things is always based upon His eternal and Kingdom perspective and what He deems best for His sons and daughters. We can only remotely, at best, wrap our puny minds around His divine prerogatives. Therefore, in faith, our souls in total surrender, we are to embrace and trust our Father while expressing to Him ... "Not my will; but Father, your will be done."

Our Father gets excited when we ... His little children put our trust entirely in Him (Luke 18:17). Even as mere men, we delight in doing good for our children and for them to have confidence in us. Our learning to trust and surrender to the Father brings Him immense joy. And with this, He is well pleased! However, whether willfully or in ignorance as free moral under-agents, we can also elect to go in a direction that seems right unto ourselves ... God's love, patience, and permissive will allow us to choose. We can choose God or say no to Him.

We can and often do ... make decisions apart from God's perfect plan for us that will determine or significantly affect our destination or outcome. And so, it is ... we run a grave risk when God's direction for our lives is neither petitioned nor followed. Of a certainty, not knowing or following God can have adverse effects as we fashion or perceive within our reasoning what is best for ourselves, whereby determining our own outcome ... remember Adam and Eve?

One's reasoning shaped, by perspectives and understanding, not aligned with God, produces results that do not serve us best or our good. We must not try to go it alone!

Life presents many occasions, at our making or otherwise, that give us reason to pause from time to time. We may think about certain things that happened to us during or after those occasions. Looking for the seemingly elusive answer to the questions ... why this, why that, or why me. And even why now for the reasons we experienced or are currently going through what we are. Especially those situations or circumstances that inconvenience or bring us significant discomfort and displeasure.

Such moments can be called troubling times. In order to receive new or better insight, we may present our thoughts to others for feedback or a fresh perspective. Human nature begs the answer to our question(s) of why.

Perhaps after researching the matter or seeking counsel, your questions yet remain as to the ... Whys? Seemingly your questions were not answered through prayer neither the Word of God to bring you satisfaction. All measures sought after, now exhausted ... your dilemma of unanswered questions - yet before you; now you are at a standstill and standoff. How is one to move from this stuck position and mental disposition; when one needs answers - and there seem to be none.

I cannot stress enough that your faith must be put into action; it alone is the key to going on with your life. For it is by faith that the children of God are called to walk and live when the uncertainties and unexpected situations of life, for which we seemingly have no answers, press in on us. We are not primarily to live through what is seen, understood, or perceived with our minds and *our orientation with time*. Instead, it is that maturing trust and faith we are to learn to activate and have in God: Knowing that He is ordering our steps, that He has got us and will keep us! We place our hope, even grow in belief or faith that all things will be worked out for our good." This is in accordance with the plan God has for our lives. And, if not on this side of glory, for certain when all things are made new. Therefore, we must live with our renewed minds *orientated with eternity* (Romans 8: 18-28).

Many questions and ideas are emerging from Bible skeptics. Or those lacking understanding and faith. Or those who even question the existence of God, and to the other extreme, there being many gods. For instance: "How much of my destiny do I have control over?" "What part does God have in me reaching my destiny or fulfilling my purpose?" How about: "Is it not through the influence of astrology that charts my destiny and brings good or bad to me and others?"

Here is a dangerous conclusion that others draw: We are just living ... meaning, life simply unfolding, playing itself out, even playing with us at times. Therefore, one has no or little to say about their outcome – we just exist. So, "Live your best life now!"

Considering the latter: Humanity is here without purpose. We are merely existing and are being directed by the unpredictable winds of time, the changing seasons, and one's whims and passions. Therefore, what is the point of life? Some maintain that the deck has been stacked either for or against them. Therefore, let the chips fall where they may. As a result, do you, for "You only live once," aka, "YOLO."

Life and its outcome holding no real or true meaning or value. Some have all but concluded by reducing human life to merely an intelligent life form. As another put it, "Sophisticated primates participating in the drama of the survival of the fittest."

Is man simply; time plus matter plus chance? The result of some "cosmic big-bang mishap from which we emerged from the slime of some cosmic soup as the magnificent reasoning self-conscious being to which we have evolved?" [Myles Munroe; *Rediscovering the Kingdom,* pages 23-24]

Me adding: Man, therefore, having no greater importance than wild beasts and creatures that roam the earth; the birds soaring the vast wonders of the backdrop of the great blue canopy of sky. Or life that makes its dwelling in the waters of the majestic depths of the seas and oceans.

Is man to be reduced and reckoned to meager creatures of intelligence with no God? All of which whose outcomes are merely influenced by "the laws of nature," their environment, and mere *animal instinct* ... But of course not!

As held and beholding in its grandeur and order, creation certainly could not have come into existence from mere happenstance. Neither is man of intelligent design and worth to be deduced to no greater worth of their cohabitors, a mere animal existing to eat or be eaten, poop, procreate and die.

Come on now! A transcending difference must be made between man and beast or other lesser animals. Unlike earth's creatures, man, through his intelligent reasoning, embraces the need for truth, justice, and answers to his questions. However, due to free will, mankind may choose to cast aside what is true, just, or contrary to their liking and even lifestyle choices. For man to be thought of as creatures of evolution resulting from some big-bang idea or random occurrence. For me ... it simply does not make for intelligible sense - it is an unreasonable conclusion.

A cosmic accident or evolutionary idea falls short! Better yet, it offers no explanation as to why we are here, our purpose, where we are headed, who and what man truly is, which are intelligent spirit beings, likened to our Abba (Daddy) who clothed man in bodies of clay. And not creatures of chance, accident, and/or evolution.

The Bible makes it abundantly clear that man was created by our Supreme Intelligent Designer; in our Father's likeness and image, we were shaped – and *very good* at that! Even after the Edenic fall, man is expressed as being "fearfully and wonderfully made" (Psalm 139:14). We are, in fact, God's crowning glory, created to be one with Him no matter our back story!

This means that in God's great and glorious design of man, we exist as the highest order of the created things! You are indeed someone truly magnificent and special to your God and Father, so much so you were worth dying for! Ask Jesus (1 John 4:9,10; Revelation 1:5).

We are saved by grace; though flawed structurally, some greater than others, we all remain a work in progress, regardless of our flaws in past practices of sinning. God knows our potential and the purpose we have been created. He has made provisions for man to excel and abound beyond our frailties and flaws. While relying on the help of the Spirit of Christ, our responsibility is to measure up to

God's reasonable expectations of us ... to follow and put out trust in Him! He will then do the rest.

For the child of God, we live out our salvation daily, pressing onward to reach the end of the race so that we may receive our heavenly reward. With our eyes fixed on the prize of our eternal calling, every intent for which God has purposed in us to fulfill will surely come to pass! As you read this book, God is making way for you to partake of this moment right now and commit to a better life for yourself. What this is to look like is between you and God. Although you may have squandered opportunities for bettering your situation, or perhaps conditions were working against you ... nevertheless, your time is now! God still has a plan and a purpose for you for such a time as this. Seize it!

It doesn't matter when one accepts Jesus or decides to commit to living for Him. There is a work that the Spirit of God desires to perform in and through you ... Right now! Regardless of the season you are in. It is our physical bodies that age and ceases to bring forth life. However, unto spiritual life or sharing the Good News of Jesus, we remain fertile and vibrant as long as we have a sound mind.

God's work is finished, yet He is always working behind the scene on humanity's behalf. However, He will never impose or force His will upon us; it is against His nature. Furthermore, it will be a violation of our free will. Love is never forced, nor can it be demanded from another ... freely it is given, and love must be received freely.

God working behind the scene and being in control can be challenging for some to grasp. While they try to make sense in their minds of God having absolute authority, and yet they see the evil and suffering in this world. Nevertheless, He is in control and reigns Supreme (Psalms 135:6; Daniel 4:35; Isaiah 14: 24). As for God working behind the scene, it may appear contradictory to suggest that God is working things out for us if we have not asked Him to do so. In doing so, one can argue that He is operating against their will. And definitely, if things are not going as they prefer. How is it then possible that He is at work behind the scene?

Look at it this way: Assuming that you are in good health, you therefore give little to no thought about your well-being. You then go about your daily business of enjoying a relatively good quality of life. Though you may do all the right things to maintain your health, or maybe not, nevertheless, your body functions to restore itself without your input. This restorative work is God behind the scenes operating on your behalf. Even though our bodies will inevitably meet with death. Daily, within His prerogative, God extends His grace and mercy toward you to prolong your life.

Another way we experience God working behind the scene: Without your input, the sun shines, the rain falls, seasons come and go, and you are allowed to enjoy the benefits of the earth's fruit and other pleasures because of these events. These occurrences are considered as good things, even blessings ... Right? This is possible because God controls and works behind the scenes for you and me. Therefore, we are experiencing God's general providence at work.

God has decreed these things to be as they are for creation's benefit. The good that comes our way is from the grace of God. The Bible declares that ... "Every good and perfect gift comes from the Lord" (James1:17).

However, in His benevolence and as our loving Father, God desires very much, to participate intimately in our affairs; He wants us to freely embrace Him and celebrate Him as our *Leading-Man* and *Benefactor*! He wants to be upfront with us, sharing the center stage of life with us as an *Active* and *celebrated Participant* in our lives!

For the child of God, God brings to pass that which He desires for our life so that we may mature spiritually. Therefore, we see nothing as chance happenings (Psalms 34:1; 1 Thessalonians 5:18; Ephesians 5:20). God either did it or directed a thing. Or we or some other, acting apart from God through free will, brought forth the result - be it good or even evil. Just the same God permits whatever occurs in this world to happen. He is in control! All things will eventually be worked out toward His end and purpose. He will see to it!

You Are Not Alone - The Helper Awaits You

"Though one may be overpowered, two can defend themselves. A cord of three strands is not quickly broken" (Ecclesiastes 4:12).

By entering into that perfect union with the Father, learning the mind or will of our God, and being enabled by His Spirit, you will be prepared when you meet your potential spouse, ready to live as victors in and over this world, married or not.

I will now briefly address a matter which is, for some, a delicate, dicey, and debatable subject ... the topic of interracial relationships. Ladies, I want you to understand something; your "Boaz" may not be what you may have imagined for yourselves. In case you have no idea what I mean regarding "Boaz." It has to do with a Christian book regarding the Biblical account of Ruth and Boaz. Ruth is one of the Old Testament books found in the Bible. By the way, this was one; there being other interracial/intercultural marriages and unions shown in the Bible. Though I have not read the book "God Where Is My Boaz," I understand that it shares with women how to get a husband, their man – their Boaz.

I dare not attempt to present some formula guaranteeing that you will get a man, or men, your woman ... there is no such thing! However, possessing the character of God is another matter and a sure starter for meeting a potential compatible spouse, no matter the color of their skin! We are all one under God and are made in the image of God.

I am convinced, for those who are single and desire companionship, that God also desires the same for you, even before you wanted companionship for yourself. This is evidenced in what we learned in Genesis ... Eve was brought before Adam, her husband, that they may be fruitful and multiply. On the other hand, considering the current climate, serious societal problems are catastrophically working against this natural longing – companionship or Biblical marriage. Resulting from moral decadence ... an individual's spiritual deficiency, a crisis of magnificent proportion has worked against the institution of the family. This moral decline is visible everywhere! It is Satan's tactics to keep us blind and broken as individuals. Thereby keeping us divided as a people and separated from God! What happens as a result? Many seek after their selfish wants and passions and not the good of others. Relationally we are broken people! To ourselves, selfish desires, we are brought into captivity (Isaiah 58:6; John 8:34; 2; Peter 2:19; Galatians 5:1,13)!

Satan initially came at Eve (woman). Now it's immoral men (Adam) with selfish intentions who are coming after Eve's daughters. Men with unchecked sexual and sinful desires, the saved and unsaved alike, are taken advantage of needy or vulnerable women. By needy … I mean women who desperately want to be in a meaningful relationship. The ease with which some compromising women give of themselves sexually and the unbridled sexual passion of countless men lead many men into sexual bondage. And increasingly, women are also trapped by sexual sin and are led astray by their emotional longings. Tremendous harm has been done to women who have been taken advantage of sexually! As for women who have made it exceptionally easy for men to indulge their sexual appetites - more becomes the sexual pleasure they desire! And even deeper into their dungeon of sexual debauchery, many have ventured and remain trapped! With their minds perverted and sexual passions unregulated, this is the dilemma that godly women face – hence there is a shortage of godly or worthy men (Boaz) to consider for healthy godly relationships.

Let me further address this dilemma that is also before God. It is a fact that God is a miracle worker and that nothing is too hard for Him. Though He may choose at times to work supernaturally, it is within the natural order or the ordering according to His Word that He has already established how all things are to come together and work collectively for the common or relational good of all.

If only God's order for man relationally as laid out in the Bible was adhered to, there would not be this man (Boaz) shortage and spiritual shortfall that has overtaken humanity. Therefore, we cannot reasonably expect God to perform a supernatural feat when He has already established within His plan for us that which we are to follow. We must return to His blueprint for our lives, which is given through His Word – the Bible. If I may word it as so …The dilemma before our God and Father - is that, in the natural order of this now-fallen world, His children will experience disappointments and hurts – such experiences are inescapable. No parent wants their child to experience such things; however, they can be minimized by following their parents' godly counsel, who are to be led by the counsel of God!

Here is a way to look at the godly man shortage: Though many fish (men) can be caught, many must be thrown back for various reasons. Some fishing locations are forbidden altogether because the fish have been contaminated by toxins or impurities. Which was either spilled intentionally and/or allowed to seep throughout their environment. These fish are therefore deemed hazardous!

So, my sisters in particular, but not to exclude my brothers ... take heed! Everything that may look good to you is not necessarily good for you! Though the waters are teeming with fish, few are to be desired! Though many men look good and seem to be a good catch ... ladies, many of them are straight-out lethal and contaminated with toxins and impurities! Ladies, therefore, understand something; your prayer for companionship is heard by God, but His hands are tied; the picking of godly and worthy men is disappointingly few! And so, God will not send your way an undesirable catch. Therefore, you should be careful where you choose to cast your line or who you present yourself before! A good catch or spouse is one that meets God's Federal or Spiritual Guidelines and FDA approval!

If you experience a lousy catch, man or woman. It was certainly not God's provision for you. Instead, your lack of spiritual discernment, maturity, or you wanting what you wanted caused you to settle for a poor catch that likely had every indicator that it should have been thrown back. Or perhaps the person, who was a Christian or not, started out honorably and caring, and for that Christian, became a fish of a different color or a character change occurring. Such ones can be difficult to detect and safeguard against. The key to making sure that you have a good catch. Or to be kept from being thrown back yourself. Both of you need to remain within the River of Living Waters (John 4:10-14; John 7:37-39; Ezekiel 47:9).

But, for the non-Christian you choose to hold on to, you can never be confident about what you are getting. For this reason, the Bible warns Believers, "Be not unevenly yoked with a non-believer" (2 Corinthians 6:14). Just the same. Where one has confessed Christ as Lord, and if they are babes in Christ, or have broken fellowship with Him and the Church, the exact outcome of that which can be experienced with a nonbeliever can undoubtedly come your way – heartache and disappointment! You will see what I mean when I begin unpacking my story later in this book.

As for the matter of not wanting to date outside of "your race." I am going to be blunt but also understanding … I get the position that some have with not wanting to date outside of their race. However, you need to work on getting over yourself! I see this as closed-mindedness, even so, a worldly way of thinking, and therefore certainly keeping shut or limiting the doors that God may otherwise usher His blessing(s) your way.

Racially and in other ways, we are relationally divided as a people. This prevents God's plans from effectively working through man for the good of humanity. If you are an Afro-American woman, there is such a shortage of compatible, godly, or worthy black men. You cannot afford to envision your life partner from the narrow lens of desiring a husband only from your race. Instead becoming globally minded, your Christian worldview radically changed; you must see God at work through the human race. This transformation in thinking just might be where the extended blessings of God await you.

I must make something perfectly clear. I am by no means knocking nor dissing my African-American brothers … I am you! Though we all are to be held accountable for our actions or choices. I certainly recognize that factors, forces, and systems – spiritual or otherwise- have worked and continue to work against people of color for our betterment.

In addition to spiritual blindness, which has overrun many Afro-American families and this country. There has also been the bondage and torture of systemic racism here in the United States against "Blacks." The powers-to-be, knowingly or otherwise, has worked feverishly against the well-being of men of color and African American Family for decades. I get it! As a Christian, I dare not close my eyes to the injustices that deny the inalienable rights and equality endowed by God to people of color. One's race is what it is by birth. Before God, we are all one – our race does not matter, nor should it matter to those who are one with Christ. If I am not mistaken, "Race" is a construct of fallen man. I am not mistaken, so did W.E.B. Du Bois maintain this view.

Naturally, or resulting from sin, we are a broken and divided people. But we do not have to remain broken nor divided. Jesus came to make us whole - one in and with Him and one with another. This must be the aim of all who are one with Christ Jesus; to be one in *Love* (John 17:21; Galatians 3:26 - 28)!

As for our transformed minds and new Christian worldview, having put on the mind of Christ, we become desirable, dateable, and even marriage ready ... I am convinced of this! This new or restored mind of ours is a gift from God! We are not alone in this process of being transformed into the image of Christ (Romans 8: 5,6; Romans 12:2; Galatians 3:27). Jesus told us when He returned to the Father that He would send us a *Helper,* the very Spirit of Christ, who is our *Comforter* - God in us! Who is remaking us through right or renewed thinking (John 14:16 – 21; John 16:7).

As you earnestly seek God to know Him intimately through His Word and the indwelling Spirit, He will begin to reveal some things to you about Himself and some not-so-good things about yourself that perhaps you had not realized. This is a good thing, and not unto condemnation or for you to feel bad about yourself, but rather to begin your transformational process, which is underway at the moment of your flawed realization or being born again. Embrace the discovery; a new you is being shaped and conformed into the image of Christ only if you submit to His Word and/or Spirit.

Coming to recognize the flaws of your fallen condition, being helpless to do anything to bring about the needed reset of your ways, you cry out to God ... "I need your Help!" This does His heart good ... He has been waiting to hear from you!

Surrendering to God, being fully transparent, and trusting Him; through such openness or intimate relationship with God, your walk becomes pleasing to the Father, thereby bringing honor to Him as His light shines through us. For the Christian, this is the meaning of being a light in this world – we reflect or illuminate the truth of God's Word in our conduct.

Where *transparency* is understood and *practiced* before God, this same action will or should be displayed and embraced with the one with whom you are married. And, as a dating relationship matures, so should this be the practice – *complete transparency or honesty!* The attitude of surrender and openness goes both ways. In our society, with the increased belief or thinking … "It is all about me," these concepts can be challenging to embrace. However, in a healthy relationship … *It has to be about us!* It is about giving and taking, finding balance, and being open and transparent. What affects one; affects all within the family … for the family's good or contrariwise.

Learn to put your guard down so that the person you are in love with may see you and genuinely get to know you. Where you two have learned to freely express yourselves to God, in praying together and for one another, you become confident and secure in each other. Your mutual confidence in God allows you to develop confidence in one another. God is indeed making a new people for Himself, and you two, one for another – not perfect people, but rather, perfect in the love and assurance you have for each other, resulting from the transforming work of the Spirit.

Real Talk Brings Liberation

Real talk or meaningful conversation cannot be undervalued or taken for granted, especially in these times. Your new attitude or posture toward freely letting go, yielding, or surrendering to one another produces a newfound freedom of expression that aids in developing and strengthening your relationship. This openness, sharing through unfettered self-expression, is the much-needed new norm for the health of a relationship.

Transparency or self-disclosure encourages and welcomes vulnerability. This leads to greater bonding and sustained trust that will even positively affect your sexual relations with your spouse. Developing this deep trust through uninhibited expression. Gives way to a couple freely and fully expressing themselves sexually, freely, unabashedly, and unconditionally.

Where a couple is unfiltered and even defenseless, surrendering or giving of themselves to each other. Each is, in fact, offering themselves to one another as a valued treasure, a gift from God! That is to be cherished and cared for by one another! The relationship can only flourish where such awareness, openness, attention, and care are given to one another.

Now, that enduring and forever-lasting relationship that you hoped for is inevitable. No longer guarded or fearful, now your hands and arms are lowered or stretched wide before your lover; you have become trusted protectors and defenders, one for the other. Guards that were once up for self-preservation lowered - you are now free to express yourself as one who has surrendered to their Beloved.

Where this is accomplished, the total giving and yielding of self, without having to say it, you are asserting to each other that you are in this thing called "I thee wed" until separated by death. In what has been said, I am not inferring that you will have a fairytale marriage or that you will not have some obstacles and rough places to make it over or traverse through – but true love finds a way; true love looks to *The Way* ... true love perseveres unto victory.

Suppose difficult times are encountered, no matter the making. In that case, because the two of you would have invested and given so much of yourselves and other things in building your relationship, you will have or should have a solid resolve or foundation to make things work. Remember ... Do not attempt to go it alone – you have a *Helper*! Surely your Helper will enable you to see your way through, whatever the challenge. Be sure to seek God and put your trust in Him and His process. Where God is for you – nothing can come against you ... remain in Him, and victory for your marriage is yours!

I often express this truth ... Marriage is work. If the proper steps and precautions are made in the beginning phases of a relationship, the work does not have to be hard. If you apply appropriate and godly care through the Word of God. Provide spiritual maintenance as needed throughout a marriage; hard work will be nonexistent.

When concerns are noted or recognized within the relationship, they should be dealt with promptly and in love. This may also be where new and uncertain situations arise within the home. Or from the result of a condition that happened beyond your control. Or even in situations that were expected yet brought forth difficulties, open and sincere dialogue must take place for the relationship's health.

The Apostle Paul said that within a marriage, one can expect difficulties. However, the severity of the challenges will be determined by how quickly the matter is dealt with. Even the necessary wisdom and love applied in working the issue through (1 Corinthians 7:28).

And Jesus has said ... those who abide in Him (the Vine), so will He abide in them (the branches). And so, will you be fruitful, thereby prospering in all things, not the least of which, your marriage (John 15: 1-5).

The Experience vs. The Experiment
Dating and Dating Disciplines

Innumerable wrongs and evils have been born, resulting from the unholy union - of mankind with Satan. Marriages and the family, as God intended, as a result, are under siege. And the enemy's assault is being mounted and explicitly aimed at the godly - those who have confessed Christ, but also at the unsaved alike, are the forces of evil set up to ruin the plans that God has for you, if not outright causing your utter destruction! Therefore, cautiously, you must be watchful and prayerful regarding every aspect of life – not the least while dating.

If you hope to be victorious while dating, triumphant in your marriage, or even have the hope of bringing forth God-fearing children, you must consider first things first. It must be understood that a dating relationship must be disciplined towards honoring self, and commitment and loyalty shown towards the mandates of God your Father for your life.

When restraining disciplines regarding sexual relations are practiced before and while dating. More often than not, marriage is less likely to be defiled through adultery or other inappropriate sexual conduct. When a child is born into this blessed and holy union. The baby is recognized by such God-fearing parents as an extraordinary gift from God! And therefore, the baby at the appointed time is to be presented or dedicated back to God. And the child is nurtured to reverence their God and Creator. At an early age, the child must be taught that God is real and that He desires the child to return to Him. Having a child believe in some make-believe or fairytale character is tantamount to feeding their soul's lies … This is destructive! Satan is the one who is behind such deception … this is this fallen world's system at work to distort one's perception and the reality of God!

My brothers and sisters, this matter of our Christian life and earthly sojourn is to build God's Kingdom, which is first established within the hearts or minds of man and is later inaugurated and established by Jesus when all things will be made new! And so. It is about the *personal relationship* God wants with each of us as He orders the affairs of His children in every aspect of our lives. People! This is real talk I'm presenting before you and serious business! This conversation really is a matter of life and death – victory or defeat! Satan wants to destroy you! Or keep you, one with him!

The lost holy union between Adam and Eve must be restored within our homes. It can only occur as man and woman get back into right standing with God. Adam and Eve, our fore-parents, have long passed from the scene; their damage has been done and is clearly visible! Therefore, I call out to you, my brothers and descendants of the second Adam (1 Corinthians 15:45- 49). You *new creatures* and descendants of Christ … godly men, Adam, rise up to your rightful place and rule your home in reverence unto God! My sisters and daughters of Eve … I call out to you too; you *new creatures* and descendants of Christ … godly-women, Eve, rise up to rule your homes alongside your husband!

Brothers, hear me … My sisters, I am also appealing to you! Those who have backslidden you are needed to stand boldly for Christ; return to Christ and reign with Him as His ambassador here on earth! And even you who do not know Jesus personally, I invite you to come to *The Only True and Wise God* who loves you and who died for you to free you from sin and death. It is through a renewed covenant and a right relationship with your God and Father that you will become the best men and women, husbands and wives, fathers and mothers that God has called you to be!

As for dating, I have discovered that many find it quite daunting, a draining endeavor, just to begin dating, let alone engaging in that extended and committed process of actually seeing someone to get to know them better. There are several reasons for this, many of which have been noted.

With its modern technology, the Twenty-first Century ushered in a change in the likes of which many were unprepared! The pace of the changing times has been astonishing, overwhelming, and even ever-changing and/or evolving! The worldwide effects of technology have significantly impacted many facets of life, and relationships and families are taking a direct hit!

Technology has changed the "game" and the rules regarding social engagement. Even the *dating experiment and experience* are very much within play or are affected whether you want it to be … like it or not! This being the case. It necessitates more discussion on technology, which I will touch on later, and its play or influence on relationships. As for now, let's look at this matter of *the dating experience* and its companion topic; I'm calling, *The dating experiment.*

For many, courting can certainly be seen as a *dating experiment:* unpredictable, uncertainties with blowups, and messiness! And no longer just a *dating experience:* minimum unpredictabilities and uncertainties, minus the blowups and messiness! I have chosen to call the first dating encounter mentioned *dating experiment* because of the many societal variances that now shape many people's thinking and belief system. This merging of two people with their varying ideas, viewpoints, and ways of thinking makes for a potentially dangerous concoction.

What were once common threads of core values and/or ways of thinking in the Twentieth Century that directed one's reasoning and choices for dating now consists of a rainbow of threads that direct our worldview on various matters. Things are not as simple as they used to be!

These varying ideas about life have brought about relational confusion! Adding to this confusion, the baggage and emotional instability accompany many dating experiments.

Therefore, I submit that dating has become an experiment because the couple has no idea what they are doing or getting themselves into. This can also be said of many marriages that are rushed into or not thought through. For these reasons, the *dating experiment* is the dating situation having come together based upon many unknowns and uncertainties. This uncertain mixture brought together by these two people will need neutralizing, or things will likely get messy. However, God, the *Neutralizer* and *Equalizer*, is the *Main Element* that has not been considered by those engaged in the *dating experiment*.

These *dating experiments* have proven to be costly, dangerous, and also a lethal mixing! On the other hand, the *dating experience* can be thought about in these terms: You are going into the dating situation with your eyes wide open. You know what to look for ... you are informed.

Though you may not have all the answers about the person you have chosen to date or get to know. Nevertheless, you know how to effectively navigate the dating world without things becoming explosive or injurious to you. And where warning indicators arise, you can readily identify them and, therefore, quickly place the person in confinement while isolating and/or insulating yourself from the potential danger.

With these *dating experiments*, from those looking at the situation from without ... one would think that common sense would override whatever reasoning went into the *dating experiment* involving the couple. It could be assumed from the onlooker that at least one of the people in this dangerous mix should realize this is a bad situation and choose to abort the experiment! Where this is not the case, those observing what is brewing say to themselves ... "Get out! You are in a toxic relationship ... try someone different!

However, many remain in such experiments or continue with others in the cycle of failed experimental relationships with their accompanying heartaches, messiness, and blowups. They continue in the same mode of operation, even dealing with the same kind of life-draining people, and in some cases, even after being forewarned!

For some, hard is their head, and hard will be the beds they make for themselves. Where this type of repeated cycle of instability and dysfunction is observed, one may begin to question the person's mental stability. For sure, their spiritual well-being is off ... No question about this! Sadly, and more common for these times, common sense is not that common. And why? Because of our once common denominator – the guidance of the Judean-Christian belief system – the Bible, which had directed and even indirectly influenced many, has been abandoned. Our *Neutralizer and Equalizer*, the God of the Judean-Christian Bible, has been discarded or forgotten by so many.

Unfortunately, we are seeing these experiments disastrously lived out before us and with frequency, repeated time and time again! Needless to say, we see that many of these ... on-again-off-again, cyclonic cycles of toxic *dating experiments* somehow make their way to marriage. However, if this unstable mix of an improbable couple persists, it will be short-lived. The couple unable and ill-equipped to coexist harmoniously, the outcome is all but predictable – that is, costly, volatile, and perhaps even lethality, being its end!

This has to be considered in some measure insanity... surely it is! The non-medical definition of insanity is ... "Doing the same thing over and over again and expecting different results."

Different will be the outcome when one (fallen man or that carnal Christian) acquires the mind of God and/or when things are done His way. And sure to be good, if not a great experience, yielding the desired results as purposed of God unto man. This does not mean that while dating or married, there will not be things to iron out, matters to negotiate, or difficulties to overcome. Neither does it mean that if a person you dated and things did not work out, it amounts to failure or that you necessarily did something wrong. Life happens, is what I call it, when things may not go as planned; nevertheless, you are to keep it moving while taking away from the experience whatever lessons there are to be learned. All the while giving God thanks and trusting His continued guidance.

Even though a relationship may have seemed to end unexpectedly, perhaps there were some good, if not great, times together and maybe even a time of personal growth. After the disappointment of a breakup, hindsight can take you back over the time shared and perhaps reveal to you and teach you some things you otherwise may not have gleaned about yourself. Though you may have been good to each other, you were simply not suitable for one another. Nevertheless, the appreciation and respect you gained for each other were invaluable. Though you may not be a couple, a friendship hopefully was developed that will endure; this can be considered a good thing.

This latter scenario and outcome have a greater chance of materializing when dating is conducted in a godly and respectful fashion. Agony becomes the norm when God's moral safety boundaries are crossed, which have been put in place to safeguard one's heart from significant problems and avoidable hurt, not only while dating but also after the relationship ceases.

Many are emotionally devastated when a break-up occurs because they did not guard their heart! In choosing to cross the boundaries, whatever they were, to include giving of themselves sexually - their treasure, and yet not theirs to give, but only until such time as deemed appropriate to one (their spouse) who is worthy of such a gift, avoidable grief is now a part of their experience! Marriage is the time for the gift of self and sex to be given and received; the recipients only now are worthy to receive and appreciate it or you!

In the wake of these many societal changes, we face the good, bad, and the questionable of these social changes. And more is to come, and I dare say, more bad and questionable changes than the good! As Christians, we must hold fast to the fact that God's principles are unchanging, no matter what the world says (John 17:14 -16; Philippians 3:20; Colossians 3:1).

How society can influence you or not have sway over you while dating will be in relation to what you hold and know to be true according to the Bible's teachings. I now ask ... "How well have you established your Biblical foundation? Has your understanding of the Word of God been firmly constructed in your heart or mind, thereby enabling you to steadfastly counter the lies of this world (John 8:44; 2 Corinthians 11:14; Revelation 12:9)?

To merely assume the person you have chosen to date is on the same page regarding dating norms or expectations is unwise, to say the least. In doing so, you have made yourself vulnerable to hurt. So, what measures can one take to safeguard their hearts during this period of courtship? And what do I mean by dating? I will now present what I believe to be a reasonably safe and healthy approach to dating and what dating looks like for me.

My approach should be simple enough to follow. Many begin dating this way – at least for my generation, and I believe more so for my predecessors. I am not suggesting that all stayed the righteous course while dating ... I am not naive to believe this in the slightest. However, I think far more knew of my generation and those before me, morally speaking, unlike many today, of the righteous way of God, though they (myself included) may have chosen otherwise.

My view on dating: Where one has considered dating, this implies that you would like to get to *know* the person of interest better. Within the context of Biblical interpretation, the word "know" can denote a sexual encounter ... This is not what I am talking about!

Knowing what I now know. I have regrets for my past sinful sexual practices and am troubled by what I now see occurring between our children and adults alike ... sex has become a free-for-all! While considering my past sexual indiscretions and the lack of self-restraint seen amongst many today, dating or relationships hold different meanings.

As my Biblical understanding became enlightened on sexual propriety or appropriateness. I recall giving thought to sexual relations in a manner I found at the time to be both profound, bewildering, and saddening: How is it that two strangers or mere acquaintances can *know* one another or come together sexually. And the name of the person with whom they are having sexual relations may very well not be known? Or is shortly forgotten after that, in the mere time it took to fulfill their decision to come together and complete their sexual union.

As I grew spiritually, for the first time, I could see beyond the physical aspect of sex and begin to see things as I now do. However, I get it ... I understand the appetite of the flesh and the flesh wanting what it wants! But consider this; our flesh cannot crave what it never had! There is something powerfully special to be held within the discipline of sexual abstinence! I can see that it is actually liberating for those who have chosen to remain a virgin! I now know this as a result of having been in sexual bondage. Sex had a hold on me even though I did not perceive this to be the case as a young man and young husband of approximately 25 years of age. And when I recognized sex's grip upon me ... not until I got married and was tempted by a *seductress*, I felt the real struggle to withstand my sexual longings. I lost the battle, but I would win the war! By the Spirit of God within me, I became a Conqueror and Man of God!

Let me now make something clear. Naturally, we experience bodily arousal because we are physical and sexual beings. The problem arises when one chooses to entertain the body's whispering or urges. And when the body's whisperings are met, it then screams for more and more!

Sexual stimulation or arousal apart from marriage is not only inappropriate; it, too, is a sin! We are not to succumb to our fleshly or sinful passions. Therefore, if any purposeful act is put forth to satisfy the flesh – here, sexual desires outside of marriage, you yet sin against your body (yourself) and God! Our bodies are to be temples for the Holy Spirit. In and through our bodies, we are to glorify God and offer praise to Him and not conduct ourselves as those of the world who lack self-discipline and are void of the Spirit of God (Romans 12:1,2; 1 Corinthians 6:18 - 20).

The following is for those who would do better if you knew better! For those who need a reminder, this, too, is for you! And for those who have not given thought to dating guidelines, this is also intended for you.

As you begin dating, allow these simple steps to be your guide. You may choose to add to what I am sharing. However, I will argue that disregarding this counsel displays a lack of wisdom and sound judgment on your part (Proverbs 1: 5-7; 4:7). Therefore, get wisdom ... like a meal, I have spread it out before you throughout this book. And the Bible is to be your main *Dish* (Proverb 3:13; Proverbs chapter 4)!

Steps towards disciplined dating:

1) Remember that a child of God is not to be unevenly yoked with a non-Christian. That said, communicate the interest that you have toward the other. It can be initiated by either of you; obviously, the interest must be mutual. You then begin evaluating or getting to know each other before allowing emotions or your heart to get involved. This evaluation period should result in quality time shared while getting to know one another and not communicating excessively through your devices. Date: sharing time together, not actually dating one another exclusively in a committed relationship. There is no intimacy, as a commitment has not yet been acknowledged.

Following the initial steps and having become better acquainted.

2) It has been determined that you are not compatible, and therefore you amicably decide to go in opposite directions or just be friends.

a) You agree to be just friends – need I say, with no "benefits!"

3) Dating has been going along splendidly. If you are beginning to feel a connection and something more is developing between you two, some stipulations may need to be implemented. This is to guard your heart as well, for the sake of the health of your friendship. This new direction of the relationship must be approached cautiously. And more so, for the one whose feelings are developing faster toward their friend. There being no commitment, expectations are minimal. This can be considered a feeling-out period as you consider whether or not this relationship should be pursued. Be sure to guard your heart by keeping your emotions in check. Unless it is mutually determined that a connection is developing between you two.

a) While determining where the relationship is headed, you should also get to know the person through their friends and, most importantly, their family. Do not hesitate to ask these individuals questions so that you may get to know the person you are dating better.

4) After spending quality time together, you two have recognized just how compatible you are, not the least of which on Christian views.

a) It is agreed upon that you desire to further build the relationship.

b) Feelings are more involved – so beware! You should exercise much caution as your feelings are beginning to be heightened towards one another. This may or may not be sexual in nature. However, emotions are becoming involved; therefore, boundaries must be clearly established, or they may become blurred. Caution cannot be thrown to the wind!

c) Now that you have decided to date one another exclusively, there should be reasonable and agreed-upon expectations that the relationship may continue to grow in every area.

d) No harm in holding hands. Where kept honorable, a welcoming or goodbye embrace is allowable … know your limitations! (Young people, this is to be decided by your parents, what the boundaries are.) Perhaps, even a slight kiss, not one leading to the point of arousal. Here I am speaking to grown folk on the matter of kissing … May your conscience be your guide.

5) This is a repeat of step 4. However, you are now speaking about spending a lifetime together and making the necessary provisions to do so. Confident that this is whom God would have you spend your life with. Convinced that this person compliments and brings out the best in you. A team of three you are indeed becoming. Now comes the engagement!

a) Pastoral counseling should be offered and received, even though you may be or think you are already spiritually prepared for marriage.

5) You are now married! Congratulations!

I am confident that if these basic measures are followed, a great deal of heartache and disappointment will be avoided while dating and in marriages.

You and your Beloved, led by the Spirit of God, can expect a healthy and enduring courtship and marriage! Keep in mind that you both are a work in progress - who will not attain perfection. Work will be required throughout your relationship as you daily put on Christ. However, your courtship and marriage and you two achieving your desires therein don't have to be overly difficult work! Do not expect perfection in your union; instead, be perfect in expressing unfailing love toward your Beloved.

ONE LAST REMINDER BEFORE WE MOVE ON – SATAN WANTS YOU AND YOUR MARRIAGE! THEREFORE, ABIDE IN JESUS, AND HE WILL ABIDE IN YOU, PRESERVING YOU AND YOUR HOLY MARRIAGE (John 15:1-11).

CHAPTER 4

God the Matchmaker – Two Becoming One

It has been over three decades since my Beloved, Lisa, and I made the excellent decision to share our lives together as husband and wife. March 20, 1988, marks the date of our union – she and I were only 23 years of age. We became one through Holy Matrimony following a memorable Sunday's worship service. One of the things that I appreciate about my wife is that she is through and through – good at heart and caring. She, in part, is the inspiration behind this book.

Lisa is a jewel as she represents the kingdom of God. Other women will undoubtedly benefit by modeling themselves after her character. My sisters, I say this about your sister and my wife because of these glaring attributes: She has a disposition that is relatively quiet in spirit; she is not given to arguing or foolish talking; she is a peacemaker and keeper at heart. My wife is hospitable, unselfish, caring, and loving. She truly exemplifies what an honorable and godly woman should be! Ladies, my Beloved Lisa, your sister in Christ, is indeed a virtuous woman to pattern your life after (Proverbs 31:10-31)!

Her attributes are displayed not so much in what she says. Instead, are readily observed in how she lives her life, conducting herself not to be seen, but nonetheless, for all to take notice. Few are the words that she speaks. However, when she does, even if angered, which is extremely rare, her words are few; they are thoughtful, not hurtful, and reckless. My wife is no "spiritual giant." She is not one who you will hear quoting Scripture or readily engaged in conversation about the goodness of the Lord… nevertheless, she is a Believer and woman of integrity! Lisa is a living testimony as she represents the character of our God.

There is much that the women and girls of this generation can learn from the admirable life that Lisa radiates as a kingdom child and daughter of our *Most high God*. Throughout this book, there will be occasions that I will illustrate what I have said about this woman; mother, your sister, and my wife.

We all need, at times, a role model who can inspire us; my wife has been just that for me! I am not trying to present my wife as someone perfect who is without shortcomings. However, I find that her flaws are few and likely to go unnoticed by others. Nonetheless, what I have witnessed from her. And have learned through observing my wife - she is applauded by me and, again, one to be emulated. Not just from other women, but my brothers can also learn from such a woman, even as I have.

Believe me when I say this: It is not because Lisa is my spouse that I praise her and say such kind things. Instead, through her living and her actions, I have learned much! Therefore, I praise God for partnering her with me to do life together. This woman - *Who Was Not What I thought I wanted - Nevertheless Everything I Needed!* And so, I give her due praise as a godly woman. Her exemplary example as a wife, in part, is the reason for sharing her with you through this book. Her life is a life that God has blessed. I have been blessed because of her; she has been blessed because of me! We together have been blessed because of our God! Because I have witnessed what God will do through a marriage that has Him as its Head. I am compelled to share with you the marvelous work God did in my marriage and in me. As Christians, we are called to be examples and lights in this world – for various reasons, many fall short as God's ambassadors in this fallen world.

These sorts of people – Lisa types, who mirror such commendable godly lives are rarely seen and are not celebrated enough. So, I gladly share our story so you may learn from her and me. That prayerfully, you will thereby strive to also have a relationship and eventual marriage that will endure the test of time, withstanding those forces that threaten the institution of a God-ordained marriage.

Lisa and I represent those couples who are somewhat opposites. And yet, we uniquely, wonderfully, and lovingly work together, which has allowed our union to grow and thrive! I rejoice in saying that hard work was not how we found harmony in our marriage. However, work, maintenance, and preventive care were performed as needed, bringing us this far.

As I considered Lisa's and my upbringing, I noticed that Lisa and I held one significant and unifying influence in common. There were other similarities and even dissimilarities woven into our rearing and now our union. I will not share them, but rather the *influence* or *thread* that I realize to be the key to our bond of longevity and marital victory.

No doubt you know where I am going … Yes, toward Jesus and our Christ-centered home, even though it was in the early phase of spiritual construction, yet, He was the Head of our home. Let me clarify what I mean by a Christ-centered home. I will slightly differ from what is generally understood when this expression is heard. This is not to take away or dismiss what is commonly thought; I simply wish to make a point.

Before doing so, the following information, in my opinion, supports my belief for one of the most significant challenges regarding sustaining a healthy family and forever marriage.

What Statistics Tell Us

This quest started in 1992 as a *Fuller Institute* project picked up by *FASICLD* (Francis A. Schaeffer Institute of Church Leadership Development) in 1998, seeking to find out what had happened and why the bride of Christ was in decline. God's marvelous Church has become culturally irrelevant and even distant from its prime purpose of knowing Him, growing in Him, and worshipping Him by making disciples! This is evidenced by what is going on in our communities and churches. Most statistics show that nearly 50% of Americans have no church home. In the 1980s, membership in the church had dropped by almost 10%. Then, in the 1990s, it worsened by another 12% drop - some denominations reporting a 40% drop in their membership. And now, over halfway through the first decade of the 21ˢᵗ century, we see the figures drop even more!

[Statistics and Reason for Church Decline; By Dr. Richard J. Krejeir. Church Leadership.org the Francis A. Schaeffer Institute of Church Leadership Development]

This ddecline in Church attendance is noticeable. No doubt, this directly correlates with society's moral decay. Numerous reasons can be given why there has been an exodus from churches. And the Jesus who I love is not one of them. Although some so-called churches rarely, if ever, mention His name or recognize Him as I *Deliverer and Redeemer. Deliverer and Redeemer* from what … sin, and Death!

Believers and nonbelievers alike, in varying degrees, were influenced or governed by Judean-Christian values. When the Church was more vibrant and effective towards the mission of God, her influence was experienced widely by many. Even among non-believers, the practice of decency, self-respect, and respect for others was relatively commonplace. The moral standards of God, Biblical truth, and His justice were woven into the fabric of daily living.

Even apart from embracing the Christian faith, there was a societal standard for right living. Many called or referred to this standard as the "Golden Rule:" "Treat people the way you want to be treated." And where one's indiscretions or willful disregard for the norms (morality) of that time were practiced, it was conducted mainly in secrecy, veiled or done with discretion – not on display for all to see and hear as it is today.

And so, many have turned from the Church or the faith. This has resulted in impotence in such ones who are to be for the cause of Christ. Such living for the *cause* is evidenced in power through the Holy Spirit. And producing the fruit of the Spirit in all who are down for the cause of the *Cross*! And the greatest fruit is evidenced in *love* toward our fellowman. As for the non-believer, those "dead" in the world, and those powerless Christians … Should we expect anything other than a greater turning away from the influence of Biblical morality and *Truth*? But for lifeless or impotent Christians, this is shameful. We are indeed experiencing the results of our weakness. The force of death is wreaking havoc! Even so, within many Churches.

This falling away from and/or denouncing the Christian faith has led to the population growth of spiritually dead people with poisonous fruit. As a result of increased Biblical apostasy, there abounds spiritual ineptness, immature and weak Christians, and a people lacking moral fitness and integrity.

After God created Adam, let me remind you what He said: "… it was not good for man to be alone." Adam was then presented with Eve – a match made from heaven! This woman was bone of his bone and flesh of his flesh, completing and perfectly complementing Adam for the service they were to render unto their God and one another. God, our Creator, knows what we need and even who we need. However, we need to see our need for Him! And then learn to trust His decrees and plan for our lives!

She Was Destined for Me

In March, I first laid eyes upon my bride-to-be – Lisa, in the spring of 1986. I believe it was my second day home, returning from Germany, where my service in the US Army was completed. I now realize this was no chance or random occurrence, our becoming acquainted. Lisa was a single mother of a two-year-old son; I did not know this at the time. She was employed by a local fast-food restaurant when and where I met her, this being one of the three jobs she was holding down. Lisa was a co-worker with my younger brother, Dexter, God's agent, who introduced me to her and several of his coworkers.

Our introduction was cordial and brief, a simple – hello. Little did I know that God was presenting my Eve, my bride-to-be. Through what I have called, *The Divine Set-up*, Lisa would be the answer to my sincere petition to God that I had prayed a year or so earlier. In this prayer, I shared with God my desire to have a wife. As a youthful teenager, marriage was something I had desired. But this was the first time I prayed for a wife ... I was no more than twenty years of age.

We all exchanged greetings at my brother's workplace; the introduction was brief because they were working. As it would be, the vibrant and robust twenty-one-year-old that, admittedly, I gave Lisa a look over. Although she was cute, she didn't pass my grading at that time. Do not hold this against me; hear me out.

In her and my defense, the unattractive uniform and brown polyester work pants she had on ... well, provided absolutely no complimentary value to show me what she was working with - her assets. I'm just being real! I, therefore, dismissed her as someone not to pursue; shallow thinking ... I know! However, this turned out to be a good thing, even a blessing, as I was certainly not ready for her, and she, perhaps not ready for me, but God's timing is always right-on-time!

Nonetheless, God's setup had been initiated that I was obviously oblivious to. Truly God's ways are not like our ways, and neither are his thoughts likened to those of man. God holds the plan for those who are His. And He knows the good that He has purposed for those who call on His name. We must learn to call on Him; He alone knows our hearts and what we need, and He will direct our path accordingly if we allow Him.

Engagement Beyond The Superficial
There Is More Than The Eye Can See

As a younger man, I must confess - I was most definitely visually motivated and still am when it comes to the ladies who attract my attention; again, why Lisa did not measure up to my standards at our initial meeting. But later, God would allow me to see what I desired in her aesthetically and even beyond the physical. In my defense - what male is not highly motivated by the sight of a woman who appeals to his standard of attractiveness? As it was, my first interest in a female, someone beyond mere self-indulgence, had to do with how she appealed to me ... did she capture my attention visually? Some men would refer to such a woman as having passed the eye test. Having done so, she may be endeared with such titles as: "Eye Candy," "Trophy," "Dime," or some other catchphrase, descriptor, or designation signifying an appreciation of her God-given attributes or "Fine." As I see it, these names or phrases are not intended to be disrespectful, even though some may take exception to such referencing.

This attraction, of which I am speaking, is motivated simply by her external features – the visual stimuli and natural appeal she presents and nothing more. However, where the natural visual appeal toward a person becomes inordinate or lustful, this presents a spiritual problem (sin), and trouble could follow. Mere unregulated fleshly appetite, even when entertained in thought, is to be understood as unnatural! Such passions or lust ... we must guard against (Matthew 5:28; James 1:14,15)! Now ... there is nothing wrong with the natural attraction one may have toward another, married or not. My wife would help me come to this conclusion. You will read about our story a few pages from now under the subtitle *"You May Look at the Menu – How Liberating."* Nevertheless, if there should be interaction, boundaries must clearly be established when you or the other person is married or in a committed relationship.

Man and woman being sensory and/or sensual creatures who share similar responses to various stimuli is how our Creator has fashioned us. However, I have observed that there are also unique differences within our similarities. I am not talking simply about our preferential or reasoning variances, but rather our difference as male and female and that which stimulates our sensory gateways as men and women. Or which captures or draws our attention towards the opposite sex. Though there are exceptions, I believe my findings to be the norm: that men are more motivated by external sensory engagement - meaning that female who has caught his eye! This alone, a woman's sheer physical attraction, can drive a male toward an interest in her at a moment's notice! And without him even considering anything about the woman, that really matters. This may be a healthy physical attraction, or the appeal can be sexually motivated.

On the other hand, a woman's physical attraction toward their male counterparts is important. However, it is not the single most important thing to capture a godly or self-respecting woman's attention towards their male interest. Her appeal goes beyond that which she beholds with her eyes or that which she desires physically. The guy has to appeal to her beyond the superficial or flesh. And instead, meet her at that subsurface level, the non-physical her. He has to be able to engage her in the secret and protected place - the seat of her emotions and intellect, her heart or mind.

My brothers, for this virtuous or honorable woman - within the chambers of her heart, you must be able to reach and enter, therein bringing her satisfaction, peace, and comfort inwardly. I am aware that there are other factors to be considered. Nevertheless, appealing to a woman's heart, to arouse her emotionally, is to reach that place that makes her who she is ... Woman. The more emotional or feeling being, our equal and complimentary opposite.

Having thereby awakened or reached her on that deeper level, she sees you beyond what is merely seen. She then becomes interested or attracted to you by the unseen you (non-physical) that she feels or senses or experiences within her soul that you aroused, thereby awakening her interest toward you. And so, our complementary differences understood ... men, you, therefore, bringing out from yourselves the effort and intellect to bring a measure of satisfaction and reassurance to the woman. In turn ... She is willing to respond accordingly or favorably toward your advance.

This engagement occurring through different means or motivations indicates the uniqueness of the male and female relational interaction or dynamic. Hence, these complementary differences as a relationship develops must be realized on all levels regarding our differences. Be continually worked out that there may be relational understanding in order to bring about balance and/or harmony and knowledge of what one another *needs relationally.*

Physiology Gives Insight
Into Gender Complimentary Uniqueness

I have put forward, but not insisting, there are exceptions, that men have to be more than physically attractive to win over a virtuous or self-respecting woman. He must be able to engage or connect with her on a deeper and non-sexual intimate level. That said ... I will infer a correlation between a woman's psychology and her physiology or physical makeup. Though a man may approach a woman of interest, along with the best, he has to offer. And yet, she must be willing or open to *receive* him. I then surmise that women, by design, are *Receptors*. Therefore, a man is to present to a woman or his woman and complementary opposite. That which she needs and/or desires within. She, in turn, freely opens or receives that which he has to offer. This results in a fruitful or favorable return for her male benefactor simply because he could present what she requires and/or needs. A woman, therefore, receiving or allowing a man into her *secret places* ... he has to be deemed worthy and capable of entering therein. Qualifying to gain entrance, the virtuous woman will then welcome him into her secret chambers – her heart and, when married, her vagina. From one source I read, the woman's ovum even selects or permits which sperm it will become fertilized by. [Source, Dr. Ananya Mandal, MD. The Egg Decides Which Sperm Fertilize It]

In contrast to the female genitalia (*receiver, receptor*), which in part is concealed and/or protected, the male sex organ (*penetrator and planter*) is not so fashioned and is designed for external stimulation. And so, this ordering of our genitalia is that which makes us male and female ... We are not "nonbinary!" Being male or female is not what you are "assigned" at birth – it is what you are! Resulting from our sexual anatomical design and purpose as ordered by God our Creator. And our psychological making ... to me, speaks to how we, as male and female, approach and even receive one another. Therefore, men are designed to be externally activated, are not overly emotional, and at times not emotionally aware enough regarding expressing heart matters or being more empathetic toward their partner ... There are exceptions. I fall in the category. Whereas women are internally motivated, with emotional deepness and sensitivity – but too, not all women. Through our uniqueness and complimentary differences, we are to therefore learn from one another. Whereby growing together, with this better understanding of our design, we can effectively operate in the roles assigned by God to us as husband and wife - who are one, physically, emotionally, and/or spiritually.

* * *

From the created order, we learn about ourselves and, in measure, the mind and will of God. We now, and from a unique perspective, understand that the wife who receives her husband sexually submits or willingly yields herself as designed. However, her husband has to yet prove himself worthy of such submission from his wife. And still, she yet extends an invitation that he may enter *their* secret place for mutual enjoyment and bonding (1 Corinthians 7:3-6).

The sexual experience between a husband and wife is physical, psychological, or mental. Although the wife receives gratification from her husband's touch upon her *womanhood* or his touch upon her bodily. However, it is the experience of granting him access - within her internally or her *womanhood* ... thereby consummating the union far exceeding the external pleasure of caressing, hugging, and/or kissing alone can bring. She, being receptive to his entrance, he now moves her inwardly – physically or sexually. And going deeper - here, nonsexual, he mysteriously stirs his wife emotionally as he (they) reinforce and deepen their emotional connection through the stroke of their powerful words of affirmation and appreciation toward each other ... This, too, is relational intimacy!

It is that which a wife receives from her husband that occurs to bring satisfaction within her that she experiences the greatest fulfillment! Thereby causing her to be fruitful or lively, bringing out from her life and/or the best she has to offer - physically and emotionally. Simple enough, what care and love the husband imparts or inputs into his wife, he also gets back in return. This manner of giving and receiving is teamwork at its best! When done right, it makes for a Win, Win! Go, team!

Regarding men, I have concluded that we are designed to be externally or visually prompted toward a woman of interest ... some more than others.

Therefore, we are primarily visually motivated, so when a woman catches our attention, we move in toward the woman of interest in hopes of acquiring her! Even though her immaterial attributes are important. I will say that most men do not prioritize this as they should or know to do so, especially in our time when multitudes are lost to self-indulgence and sexual gratification.

The most extreme case of such sexual craving and debauchery, and perhaps a person is spiritually damaged elsewhere leading to this horror ... is in the case of the atrocious act of rape! I mention this appalling act for this reason; to contrast the loving bond of a husband and his wife. Rape: A woman so *violated* ... does not bodily or emotionally *receive* or *invite* such an intrusion! No! ... She didn't want it! No! ... She did not ask for it! No! ... She does not benefit from such an egregious act! Instead, bodily and emotionally, she experienced an assault ... she experienced hell! As she was overtaken, or her *secrets* invaded by the ultimate violation - rape! Therefore, she is so traumatized that bodily and emotionally, she may shut down or become lifeless! Unlike the unifying, satisfying, and full of life and loving bond of a husband and wife, a woman victimized in this manner receives no such pleasure bodily nor emotionally! Rather, bodily and emotionally, she suffers significant loss and torment ... instead, she experiences a deadening of her soul!

Although tragic is the experience of one so violated! God is, nevertheless, the One who can heal the hurt from such a trauma! And bring back to life a soul rendered lifeless by such brutality! This is what He came to do! (Psalms 55:22; 147: 3; Matthew 10: 8; Luke 4:18; Romans 12:19; Philippians 4: 4 - 9)!

Continuing to be transparent in an attempt to lead by godly character and understanding. Here's my preference for a woman – apart from the obvious, my wife. Well ... she must be natural: meaning adding nothing to or taking away from what she was given at birth. Through and through, God-given from top to bottom! Nothing purchased, implanted, added on, or permanently altered to so-call enhance what God has already provided her with. To do otherwise – these add-ons is to again say that God got it wrong when He made you the way you are! I understand there will be objections – but hear me out. It is not just about my preference, but rather how God sees you and you then being enabled to see yourself from His perspective and the love for you. Until then, you will continue to define yourself, mold your thinking and alter or remake who you are from the dictates and influences of this ever-changing fallen world that you are trying to fit in with or be accepted by. God, who created you and brought you into this world, is well pleased with your appearance. And so should you be.

Grab hold of this truth: This world in which we currently live emphasizes the importance of the temporal and the temporary; that which is perceived bodily or sensory ... to the dust of the ground will these things and our bodies - soon enough return. However, God our Creator is concerned with that which is imperishable and eternal, our inner man or spirit self. Meanwhile, as we yet remain on this earth and in our bodies. It will be through the teachings and empowerment of the Spirit of God. That we will be able to bring our bodies along with our carnal or unnatural longings or thinking under subjection to the will of God. We are called to be Spirit-led and not carnally or by our flesh (1 Corinthians 6:19,20; Romans 12:1,2).

As free-will agents, we can choose what we will. The historical problem with man is that we take free will and exercise our liberty too far - beyond what God intended for us ... it is in our fallen nature to do so! We then seek to justify what our conscious and others may have spoken against ... why – because we want what we want! Our mind or consciousness directs our decisions, even though we may not know directly or precisely what the Bible says on a matter. Operating therein is man's guide and a warning beacon from our consciousness or psyche. But too often, what we hear or feel from within is disregarded. Hence our slant toward sin; the severity of our evil will vary from person to person. And such sin(s), their variances and severity are often dictated by our upbringing and environment raised within.

In addition to our consciousness (reasoning) serving as our guides, we as Christians need to know what God our Father says on all matters toward right living. His guiding truth to be directed by; then there will be little to no doubt regarding the can or can not(s) or boundaries we are to abide within or the limitations of our free will.

Those desiring to please God by knowing and performing His will, though not perfect people, do not readily go against their conscience or the will of God. They neither attempt to justify their uncertainty through *worldly reasoning* or *standards* regarding acceptable or unacceptable behavior and practices.

On the contrary – a maturing child of God will be the one whose heart is set on knowing and doing what is acceptable and orderly before their Father and God. They have come to know the love and grace of God and therefore have chosen to be loyal to Him. Their love for their Father and his moral standards is the motivation behind such obedience and self-denial or those boundaries they choose not to cross.

I challenge you. Before deciding to do something doubtful, prayerfully ask yourself two questions: "What is the true motivation behind what you're considering?" And, "Does the matter you are considering fall outside God's boundaries or His will?" If you are unsure, ask someone wise and mature in the truths of God. And not someone who will tell you what you want to hear but their prayerful thought on the matter or what Scripture has to say on the subject to be your guide.

Listen, it is better to be still on a matter you are not clear on than to go with the flow, thereby bringing dishonor to your body or sinning against God. Here is a standard you can also apply that can help you with God-honoring decision-making: No, it is not the question, "What Would Jesus Do," though this could work for some. Rather, ask yourself, "Does my free will choice honor or dishonor God?" "Is the decision I'm considering hindering or working against my witness to build up others within or for the Kingdom of God?" Even, "Does or can my free will choice lead others astray, call into question my faith or cast doubt on the credibility of the God, who I confess?"

In our humanity and the weakness of our flesh, powerless is one to subdue sin apart from the Spirit of God or to follow His guiding truth. Now I want you to get what I am about to share. Being stirred by the flesh and its desires, even the enticements of this world are to be expected. In varying degrees and manners, sin's lure will pull at us to manipulate us and cause harm to and through us.

The problem arises for mankind when the visually appealing, intellectually alluring, or otherwise wrongfully enticing is presented before us. And we consequently give in to that which is off-limits or sinful. Sin, now having gained leverage over a person, it may not be easy to break free from its grasp. This is what we must be prayerful about! And guard ourselves against; that we do not give in to temptation!

* * *

My brothers, as well as my sisters ... pertaining to an intense or shallow lustful attraction you may have toward someone, and thereby deciding to partner with them ... through marriage or otherwise is sinful in that you were motivated by your flesh! If such a connection is only physical. Or, from the person's visual appeal, you have become spelled-bound. Or it's about how they make you feel, sexually or emotionally. This is not a natural attraction or affection; this is merely lust or the passions of your flesh becoming your guide and a sure recipe for problems relationally once the appeal diminishes and your feelings or excitement fades. A union of this sort is superficial and driven simply by one's fleshly appetite. There being nothing of substance bonding you two together nor a solid relational foundation to build upon ... if this is a dating situation, you can expect, sooner or later, for there to be drama. Or within a marriage, in the unlikely event that one should occur, a marriage that will become strained or brought to an end because the union's establishment was superficial with no underpinning!

Know this: A lustful eye is never satisfied ... it is always gazing! A voracious appetite is never contented ... it will constantly seek to have its fill! We cannot allow our flesh or sensual appetites to run and ruin our lives! We are all, therefore, in need of the Spirit of God so that we may be able to put up a defense against our sinful self – the evil within or our corrupt flesh.

My sisters. Now, those of you who know or have convinced yourselves that you are to be desired; you, thereby appealing to my brother's fleshly longings and failings, not that which they need from a God-honoring woman. By you dangling yourself as bait and flaunting what you are working with – your bodies, as a meal ticket to get what you want from a man or maintain what you have. Some of you have put in place an open-door policy that they may "get at you" through your quid pro quo arrangement. In this, you are praying on sexually weak or vulnerable men … yes, weak or vulnerable! However, ladies understand your truth … you are equally weak and vulnerable - in that your passions or lust of whatever the sort have also seized hold of you! My brothers and sisters … Only God can help us get it together and to rid ourselves of the madness!

I think I have made it plain; therefore, there is no longer a mystery regarding how most men and some women are wired related to visual or physical attraction. As for men administering the eye test before considering giving a woman, attention is more common than not. For our time, I am convinced that more women are becoming like men with the ease of engaging in sexual relations. Some say that women have become more expressive or sexually liberated – so says and is promoted by this sinful world. I have come to understand that though God has wired men and women with inherent differences and similarities, our environments play a significant role in how we view things and express ourselves. Question: What environment dominates your life? The things of this world? Or that which pertains to the Kingdom of God?

This World's System Seeks To Hi Jack Hack And Reprogram Your Thinking

My thoughts on women becoming like men have not been based solely on what I have observed. But also on what a few women have shared with me. Perhaps there is hard data to support my position … I'm sure there is. However, empirical data is observable all around us. I understand that increased accounts of "sexting" are also occurring between our youth and the older population. And even a growing number of women are taking to or, better yet, are being overtaken by pornography. God has designed males and females as complementary opposites. However, this world's system or programming, overseen by Satan, is always at work through its/his many platforms and mediums, hi-jacking or hacking and attempting to hi-jack or hack into our reasoning to takeover, rewrite or override God's programming within us and

His plans for us. *We can only counter Satan's hi-jacking or hack of our minds through our reprogramming of God's Word* (Romans 12: 2; Ephesians 4: 22 - 25).

Just look at the absurdity, the brokenness of many who are trapped in darkness and ensnared by the agenda, propaganda, and programming of LGBTQ. Their incursion or resurgence is occurring throughout the world! And don't be fooled; "Black Lives Matter" and other so-called "social justice groups" is being used as their cover-up and partner! No doubt, the playing field is also leveling and lowering in moral decay for women. *Where the men go or are led, so will women follow … And so will our children!*

The consequences for godly relationships and the family will be dreadful as this decline in women toward sexual immorality increases. Where men are emasculated, have become effeminate, and their God-given roles disregarded, devalued, or redefined … what are we to expect?! But relational dysfunction and gender identity crisis, and confusion! There are some Christians who have bought into the lies and deception of this world's programming … they greatly need a *Hard Reboot!* While Mankind at large most assuredly is out of sync and sort resulting from the virus of sin … *They need Rebirth!*

And so, as things are, women are attempting to become as unto men … and men as unto women! There is confusion and gross darkness in the land! I will point out a couple more things indicating or diagnosing eye problems that have been generally associated with men. However, females are becoming more readily diagnosed with the same ailment – lustful gazing! An eye problem: if the looking is lustful or done disrespectfully by either gender. Otherwise, being visually attracted to someone is natural, as I've mentioned.

To hear some men talk about women's attributes: well, it is one thing to compliment or appreciate their *fine.* It is another thing to undress her in your mind and there engage her sexually. Or to share with someone what you would like to do to some woman or vice versa (Matthew 5:27-29). We who are Christians. We must be mindful of what we give our thoughts and conversation to (Ephesians 4: 29; Philippians 4:8; Colossians 4: 6; Psalm 19:14).

Ladies … simply observe a male that locks on and tracks that woman who has provoked him from visual slumber into acute awareness as she walks by, barely wearing any clothing; clothing that is provocative or so tight that her attributes are overly accentuated. This can be observed anywhere … Even in church! My Christian sisters, this is one of the reasons that the Word of God instructs godly women on the matter of modesty and decency concerning how you are to dress or adorn yourselves … It is towards your honor to dress in a godly and self-respecting manner. And, too, to help your Christian brothers who may be weak or struggling in this area of lust (1 Corinthians 8:9; Galatians 5:13; Ephesians 5:21.

On the other hand, and in times past, women generally have not been as apparent regarding their attraction toward men. Again, the tide has begun to shift. And so it is with some women; their curiosity toward a person of interest is becoming more noticeable. Some are even bold enough to let it be known, to include what they want from the man and what they intend to do for him if the occasion should arise.

As for most men in a respectful relationship, for sure, and for obvious reasons, are more subtle with their look upon another woman. This is because of the consequences some brothers and those few women will encounter from their significant other, whose eyes have been caught wandering upon some other to peep out her attributes or to check out his fine. And fitting to say for others, rendering a sneak peek is what they will do when their partner is not paying attention. Again, my point, being attracted to the opposite sex is natural. However, there is the extreme toward our appeal for someone that we must not go mentally or otherwise!

Because I believe men are more *lookers* than women, my Christian sisters let me speak to you. Ladies, those of you who see this as an issue of trust, perhaps the problem is you are insecure … this is what many men do; our eyes are prone to wander. This may have absolutely nothing to do with you … so try not to make it about you or your shortcomings and/or insecurities. I have more to say about this shortly under the subtopic "Don't Tip Your Hand."

For some men, this matter of scanning occurs as naturally as breathing … it may even happen subconsciously. Trust me on this, if you have a good man: Meaning his heart is in the right place regarding you and toward God, nor has he given you any reason to question his faithfulness to you … although he may look, understand something, this is by no means a negative reflection upon you or some lack on your part. He is not comparing you with her nor desiring her; he was or maybe is, simply visually attracted toward her, as we all are attracted to one thing or another or some other(s).

Ladies keep this in mind: It is one thing for your man's eyes to wander upon another woman. And a totally different matter for your man's eyes to wonder upon or about another woman! As for the difference … you will not likely know between the two. So just let it be unless he clearly goes overboard with a wanton stare, thereby showing a disregard for your presence and even disrespect towards you. Where his lack of concern about your feeling or disrespect is shown. Your relationship is either in trouble or headed that way.

Hopefully, you will know how to address the matter if this should occur. Throughout this book, I hope to assist you in handling other issues besides the subject before us that you may encounter within your relationship.

Assuming you are and always have been heterosexual. If by chance, you find your eyes wandering and suddenly you are taken by the attractiveness of the same sex, there is no reason for alarm … no, not at all! A same-sex longing is not necessarily stirring within you. To think otherwise is the influence of this world/Satan, hacking into your thinking to rewrite or override what you know to be true … that same-sex infatuation or desire is wrong! Nor is it that something is wrong or off with you if you find a person of the same sex attractive. It is perfectly natural to recognize the external and even the inner attractiveness of another, even if the person is of the same sex. The problem arises when you begin to *entertain*, yet again, unnatural thoughts towards the person. If this is your current situation, the enemy of your soul has already started to corrupt your programming. You must give yourself to earnest prayer, even as you immerse yourself in the Word of God, thereby defragging your thoughts and removing the corruption from your programming.

Where such unnatural thoughts towards the same sex (or evil of whatever sort) are not willfully entertained by you; they have just entered your thinking from out of nowhere. What is likely to have occurred or is taking place; Satan, through the influence of his demonic agents (unclean spirits or elohim), have shot their fiery darts at you (Ephesians 6: 16)! It is, for this reason, we must remain suited up with the *armor of God!*

Our world has become so inundated with sexual immorality and sins of other sorts … it is virtually impossible to escape hearing about sin or observing depravity almost everywhere we turn! Even though you may not be giving active thought to these sinful practices when heard or seen, you are being subliminally affected as your minds are fed the filth and garbage of this world! This is another method of being demonically influenced or spiritually hacked. Or an attempt to bring you under the influence of spiritual darkness. Both actions are of the wicked spiritual order, whether active thought is given to sin or messages received subliminally. Therefore, it is imperative that you recognize that there is a spiritual war that has ensued, and the battle is for your mind. *Are you suited up?*

Where one has willfully given way to sinful thoughts, this one has been overtaken by that evil one – Satan or his demonic hackers. Next to occur, unless the person repents and reclaims their thoughts, is to give their bodies over to sexual sin or whatever evil they have been entertaining (James 1:13-15). If this is your current situation, pray, I tell you; immerse yourself in the Word of God; confess to Him that you are struggling. Our Father has promised to deliver us from the present evils of this world … allow Him to be your strength; He is waiting to hear from you. One final thought: separate yourself from whatever or whoever may be causing you to have these thoughts. Take control of your mind as you give it to the things or focus thoughts on that which is eternal and righteous (Philippians 4:8).

If you have given yourself over to homosexuality or any other sinful practice. Know that God loves you and wants you to be free. However, for you to remain in a relationship or bondage to sexual sin and perversion is not the will of God. It was for sin, its *trappings* and *stronghold* of all sorts, that God, in His love for us, sent Jesus so that all held captive to the evils of this world may be set free! Set free not only from sin. But also from God's righteous condemnation of eternal suffering in Hell with all who choose to remain one with Satan and sin!

Don't Tip your Hand

My sisters, with insecurities, do not get so bent out of shape if you should happen to see your man simply looking at another appealing woman. He cannot help himself ... he is not blind! But he is faithful – right? For faithful men, I believe it to be an innocent look – but too, you know your man ... I don't. Again, keep in mind that his looking – for the faithful man has nothing or little to do with you. Therefore, do not feel threatened, nor allow the insecurities that you may possess to cause you to go stir the hornet's nest and strain your relationship needlessly. And whatever you do, in particular, if you or your man know the woman – or not, do not allow the other woman to see that you were bothered that your man took notice of her.

When you allow this to happen, you have done what I call - *tipping your hand*. I liken this to playing a card game. You see ... in a card game, you are to protect the cards in your hand at all times. They are not to be seen by your opponent. As for your cards, they will either work for you or perhaps against you during the card game. And certainly against you if they are exposed and seen by your opponent(s).

Stay with me on this: If you unknowingly or carelessly expose your hand in a card game, the opponent will use what they have discovered against you without question. And will therefore be able to manipulate you, even use you to their advantage so that they may gain the edge in the game because they now know what you are holding ... you tipped your hand.

This kind of dangerous gamesmanship or manipulation plays out in "the game of life" and certainly within relationship dynamics. If you expose your emotional insecurity, even if done unintentionally, there will be someone who will exploit the matter to gain an advantage over you or your relationship, and certainly, if your relationship is not strong.

Some self-serving women will play games with you, working you up, manipulating you just to get a rise out of you emotionally because you exposed your feelings or tipped your hand. This is their only purpose ... as in their twisted mind, they have just beaten or bested you in this game of life because they made you squirm or caused you to become uneasy.

Then there are those sinister women ... again, if your relationship is not rock-solid. They will seize such an occasion as an opportunity to disrespectfully step up to your man. Their goal and only objective is to see if they can triumph over what is off-limits to them – your man! Here, meaning sexually – solely a sexual conquest is what they are after! This is the ultimate endgame and a game-changer if they manage to have their way, all because you exposed or tipped your hand before them. You did not guard and keep your emotions in check, thereby opening the door for such a foolish woman to seduce your man.

For some women, who may not even be seeking your man sexually but rather for twisted emotional reasons or to feed their egos - they come at him. They simply want to see if they can get in his head and near to his heart. It is all a game to them – just a challenge. They are thrill-seekers who get a rise from messing with your man emotionally and manipulating the situation. It is not about pursuing him physically but yet to just lead him on, or win him over emotionally, even to further expose the kink in your relationship. What a ruthless game! Men play these games too!

Now, I am not saying that your man is off the hook or that he does not bear responsibility for dealing with such a woman – by no means! If your man, at any time, is confronted by such a woman. Regardless of what you did or did not do, what you said or did not say. Occurring in your presence or not, he needs to bring that chick in check ... quick, fast, and in a hurry - unmistakably shutting her down! Your man must protect you always and certainly in your weakest moments – no exceptions, even when you are in the wrong; he is to defend you! He is not defending your improper behavior or wrong, but rather protecting you from being disrespected or insults or attacks that may come against you and from anyone or anything which undermines the relationship you two have established.

I am mindful that though I may address a specific gender to share my thoughts, the genders can be reversed.

You May Look at the Menu - How Liberating!

My dilemma and oppression of being physically attractive to the opposite sex will be shared through this section of your reading, played out a short time – perhaps a year or so into my marriage. I would have been perhaps 23 or 24 years old. This matter – my attraction to other females hit home; I would have to come forward to my wife regarding my dilemma! As a result, of sharing with my wife my struggle, I would be liberated from my perceived problem of looking, scanning, or wandering eyes. I am confident that what I've shared thus far. And now, my story from 3 decades ago can further benefit you and your relationship; if the issue of wondering eyes is the source of disturbance within your relationship.

I can recall the anxiety I felt when my wife was with me as I observed a woman who was appealing to me. In the early stages of my marriage, at some point, I found it torturous … a strong word I know, as a young husband, to refrain from looking at another woman who appealed to me. As a married man, this became my first recognizable spiritual and/or fleshly battle and bondage I encountered, though I did not understand the nature of things at the time.

What did not help was that I had never been in a longstanding and meaningful relationship. The kind of relationship of substance that required meaningful dialogue, reasoning, and even vulnerability. I could hold a conversation and maintain purposeful discourse; however, the matter of transparency and vulnerability within a relationship was something that I was unfamiliar with and apprehensive about approaching.

Now married, newly wedded - my first real and substantial relationship. And I did not know how to approach my wife with what I thought to be a delicate and potentially dicey situation regarding my struggle, feelings, and attraction to some other woman. This was my thinking … "I am married; I should not be attracted to another woman!" And because I had this attraction, it created conflict within my soul, which I had never experienced ... the battle or oppression was real! Demonic influences were behind the oppression I was undergoing ... this I now know.

In contrast, the short-term relational situations I had been in before marriage occurred primarily due to my flesh's desires; therefore, I had no real sense of commitment or sincere or loving care for the female I was with. Therefore, there was no pressure because of my selfish or sensual state of mind. Now that I am married, this experience presented a unique challenge. Somehow I knew that I had to face my wife about what I was experiencing so that I may regain peace of mind. However, my concern about her response was also before me! I felt as if I was in between a rock and a hard place!

Now allow me to briefly digress. I will share something I had not contemplated until now as I write this section of my book. Considering my distorted state of mind as a teenage boy and all boys of like mind regarding sex and females, this mind or thinking can and highly likely will be carried over to adulthood, which is "No commitment, care, or pressure ... just pleasure!" Sadly a female is merely viewed as the object of our desires where there is such thinking!

What I am about to say here results from a boy's mind, aka that of an irresponsible man. This may be difficult for a single mother to hear and accept and perhaps even more so for a fatherless child. I believe the reason why some fathers leaving their responsibility or never take responsibility or care for their child: There was no care for the mother of their child. So, why would they care for a child conceived in the heat of self-gratifying passion and sin? When a child is conceived through this kind of unholy union, the father feels little to no pressure or obligation to do right by the mother of his child, let alone the child. As a result, he can just abandon or never acknowledge his responsibility or child. Sex was all that was wanted from the female. A child was not a part of the plan! Having gotten what he wanted – sex; however, more than what he bargained for – a child, he now ghosts the situation or becomes "MIA" *Missing In Action* or perhaps better stated "MAA" *Missing After Action!* Daily this tragic drama is played out time and time again ... And who suffers the most – the fatherless child!

This is the very reason and the great need for a book like this … for me to share my story. To address and show the patterns and problems to which improper sexual relations and perverted thinking and behavior lead. And therefore, a dire need to desperately break those patterns or practices as we submit to a better way of living through Christ our Savior and Deliverer!

That said, maybe a year or two into my marriage and while in my early twenties. I thought that I should not be having an attraction to another woman. It did not seem right that I could be attracted to and lured visually by the physical attributes of another woman. "I am married, so this should not be," so was my thinking; "the only person who should have my undivided attention is my wife." However, this was not the case. I needed to be rescued from my troubling and this struggle within my mind!

As I have given thought to this matter, I find it somewhat astounding that this situation caused me to struggle as I had. It was not like I wanted these women sexually – it was not a matter of lust. However, the compulsion to simply look or keep from looking created a battle from within.

Years later, I would grow to understand this spiritual battle. Satan's tactic is psychological warfare. Whereby creating conflict in one's mind - oppression, doubt, and fear. He also causes there to be uncertainty about right and wrong. Overcome by such emotions or thoughts, he renders his targets helpless and useless regarding the things of God. Satan wants to trap our minds. He puts a stronghold on them through the methods I mentioned and many more. From his trappings, we must always be alert. Satan wants our minds … When he seizes them, the body is sure to follow.

In our fallen or sinful nature, even after being saved. Where we yet remain babes in Christ. Not only are we susceptible to evil's influence from without. But are also predisposed to the evil that works within our bodies and through our thinking. Due to the lack of understanding of my sinful nature and the spiritual nature of my situation, I was weak and vulnerable (Hosea 4:6).

God will not have us be ignorant of these things or Satan's tactics. The Spirit of God will reveal to us our true nature, and through His help, we learn and are strengthened to put or bring our flesh and minds under subjection and unto the will of God. However, like a spoiled child, when the flesh is told no to something it wants, having been denied after already experiencing pleasure from it. The flesh screams and rants all the more because it has been told no or denied the pleasures it craves.

However, even though the flesh may "cut up" or "act the fool," what must be realized: as long as one does not give in to its demands, they are Victors. Each time you refuse the quibbling of your flesh, for many, the easier it becomes, perhaps over time for others, to resist its yearnings, ultimately muting or quieting the screaming altogether. If the struggle persists or tantrums return, you are yet triumphant, where you stand strong and do not give in to sin! Therefore, do not bring yourself under condemnation or guilt because you are battling. Do battle with yourself, and stay in the fight; this is the road for many of the faith … just do not give up, throw in the towel, or surrender to your flesh. Stand firm! Stand strong! Then sin will not rule over you!

With the Spirit of God strengthening you, the righteous supporting you, and their prayers covering you, you will be a flesh and world Overcomer ... you will be victorious (2 Corinthians 12:8-10; Romans 7:15 thru chapter 8)!

Again, as a young husband, I did not understand the spiritual assault or oppression raging within my mind or my body's sinful passions and inclinations. As it was for me. Many of my brothers have yet to understand this opposing enemy of their souls. And the evil of their flesh and therefore find it challenging to be faithful to the one they are with. In their twisted reasoning, their flesh screaming, they give in when they should be faithfully fighting to remain true to the one they are with, the one with whom they need, the one with whom they were so in love, when they said, "I do" and "I will until death do us part!"

Why do some males do what they do sexually? Innocently, a man may be drawn in by the attractiveness or the words of some woman. Then she becomes a temptation as wrong thoughts are being entertained by him. This was the situation that led to my fall. My brothers, you need to run from this situation, less you to fall! Initially, I ran – But! You will read about my failure later in this book. However, some men give this reason for committing sexual sin; "I am just attracted to women. I cannot help it; therefore, I pursue what I naturally desire … it is only natural."

Then others have chosen not to marry because they do not believe they can be satisfied by and/or faithful to just one woman. The problem is; some simply enjoy giving in to their insatiable sexual desires. They cannot help themselves … there is truth in this. They can't help or, better yet, fix themselves. And neither can a good and honorable woman cause such a man to get it together. So ladies, do not even try! God is who they need! Then there is another group of brothers who know they need to stop running the streets. They know they need to get it together, but the fear of relationship failure and other factors or uncertainties regarding starting a relationship prevents them from doing so. They, too, need the guidance and the confidence that comes from being in a relationship with God.

This issue with our flesh, one learning and being strengthened to bring it into subjection, cannot be overstated! The casual and careless encounters of sexual excursions and exploits that many are involved in have and will continue to pave the way for problematic relations and even problems manifesting after the "I do`s" and "I wills" of matrimony. Look! Improper sexual relations are nothing to toy with! The cost is too great to play! Its effects are far-reaching and devastating! My parent's homes met with this! My home met with this! And far too many homes have met with devastation due to careless regard for sexual relations! Perhaps even your home?

As for my struggle, it was not a matter of lust or my wanting some woman sexually. Instead, It was the attraction I had for certain women that I didn't think I should have as a married man. Now for my path to liberation and victor, I can take no credit; I owe my release from a captive and struggling mind to my wife! The battle ensued while at Walmart, which at the time was located on Roxboro Road near Old Oxford Highway; my wife and I were there shopping. There is not much to say about that day. However, I was in the store struggling to keep my eyes faithful!

I simply remember some woman passing my way; maybe I had looked, or I was trying not to look. Just the same ... the thought of my wife saying something to me if I was seen looking was unbearable! I felt I needed to attach to my head - horse Blinders or Blinkers, which are designed for racehorses. They serve as eye guards to keep the horse focused on the race ahead and not be distracted. And lured off course from their race, thereby gaining the prize that awaited them, resulting from a strong finish and free from distractions and diversions. I thought I needed this safeguard. There would be no looking to the left or right, no wandering eyes if I had them! Only straight ahead would be my focus, and I would then be okay. This *no-looking* was the self-imposed restriction that I had attempted to place upon myself but to no avail!

Returning to the car, I asked Lisa to drive ... I needed to think through what I had to say. I needed to talk to my wife even though I was apprehensive about how she might feel and the outcome of things. Exactly how the conversation began is unclear. Nevertheless, I was internally pressed and had to get this weight off me - I needed peace.

I can remember crafting my words as I contemplated what to say to her, although I do not remember precisely what I said. I just remember needing to lift this burden as I nervously pondered my wording. After approximately 15 minutes or so, I finally mustered up the courage to address my wife, saying - only what God now knows. However, it was Lisa's response that I had not forgotten. My wife's words liberated me from my burden and struggle.

Surprisingly, I remember we were in downtown Durham, on Ramseur Street, nearing the parking deck as we approached Blackwell Street. Now stands America Tobacco Campus, erected upon one of the buildings, the image of the iconic Durham Bull, directly across the street and railroad tracks from the parking deck where we now were.

It was here that my wife responded to what I had said to her regarding my struggle. Her reply was with few words, yet they were simplistically profound and liberating; I could not have imagined such an outcome. Without reservation, caringly and confidently, she responded to what I shared with her,

"You can look at the menu; you just can't have what's on it." She continued, "You are a man; you are going to look; however, it's how you look." My thinking: What?! ... is that all?! I am speechless and relieved! Neither was there a need for anything more to be said. If there was more said … I cannot recall. What I needed … man, did my wife ever deliver, freeing me from this unnecessary turmoil and battle to which I had been engaged and even in bondage.

However, sometime later, perhaps a year or so in passing, I sadly and regretfully did wrong my wife. I would be seduced to partake of the forbidden fruit, to take from the menu that which was prohibited, hazardous to my spiritual well-being and my family's health.

Ladies, your sister, my wife, who was also only 23 or 24 years of age at the time, did not take offense or become defensive about what I needed to share with her. There was no change in her body language or tone when she addressed my concern. I was in awe and stilled by her calm demeanor; her response put me at ease from the words of wisdom and insight she offered ... Wow!

Her words were profound, and why I have been able to hold this moment in my memory. I had never heard what she had lovingly spoken to me. Her response - the simplicity of those words amazed me and eased my trouble. I did not know what her comeback would be to address my concern. However, my wife's response would prove to be indicative of the faithful and enduring character she possesses. And whom, over the years, I have grown deeper in love with.

There you have it, me simply looking at another woman was neither a concern nor a bother to my wife. However, for me to graze – figuratively speaking, upon or partake of another woman was clearly forbidden and off-limits. My wife made this clear by saying that I could not have what was on the menu. From the heart, Lisa said what she meant and meant what she said. We must never take for granted such frankness when spoken by those whose hearts are open and given to us. I will come face to face with the menu's forbidden item in a matter of a year or so later – just keep reading; I will get you there.

What I have shared, I think it is clear and straightforward. Nonetheless, I want to highlight something; it is the matter of real talk or upfront conversation. Listen carefully. If you hope to build a stable relationship, such discussions cannot be ignored or taken for granted when needed – hence *performing preventive maintenance care.*

Preventive maintenance talks must be administered as needed when you care about a person. Or perhaps you should talk to avoid ending up in the doghouse! But really, let your care for one another be the motivation for effective communication. There is power in your words, either to life or to the death of your relationship. If care for your companion guides you, you will also be careful if angered not to let the first things you think part your lips (Proverbs 18:21: James 3:6).

Therefore, give thought to your words so that you do not offend or needlessly cause discomfort to another. Do not take for granted the effect you have upon another and how you can make them feel through your words. Is it asking too much, child of God, to be considerate of others' feelings? Of course not ... such care is required of the child of God.

Additionally, if a matter is important to the one you are with ... it is a heart concern; they need to be able to express themselves to you. You must then lend yourself to be attentive when their concern is brought to your attention. This is caring and even compromise, a part of relationship building ... love in action as you give care and consideration to the one you are with.

To minimize their concern(s) or brush them off. Such an attitude from you will have a way of working against your union. This is unacceptable. This behavior or disinterest can create a bad relational situation where unresolved issues are suppressed or the person's thoughts devalued. Where repressed speech is not given a voice. Or the concerns they spoke about are not heeded. Over time, erosion of the relationship is highly likely to occur. Then the opportunity to fix and resolve any issues arising afterward may be too late for some relationships or issues to be worked through when one finally decides they want to listen.

During this time of real talk, much about the relationship and one another can and needs to be revealed. There are many who are carrying things/hurts within. And, in some cases, suppressed or held inwardly for years! Therefore, they need to be able to release, find relief, and be released from their inner turmoil of whatever sort. And this release is without one feeling condemned or thought less of by the one with whom they are hoping to spend a lifetime; they need to be able to be transparent and vulnerable before their Beloved. So, the more concerns or issues that can be addressed and sorted out before the nuptials, the better, even greater, the chance of a healthy union. And after marriage, providing preventive maintenance care or talks when necessary will lead to a victorious and enduring marriage!

Your Secret Is Safe with Me - Love Finds Away

Every couple needs to be able to comfortably talk to their significant other about anything and be heard. My brothers, this is an area in which many of you significantly need to improve. Yes, giving an attentive ear to your ladies, but it is equally vital that you also learn to open up and become transparent or vulnerable, whereby sharing your hidden or suppressed feelings and concerns with your Beloved. Ladies, however, before your man can freely open up, he needs security or protective custody from the woman who is to care for him – that is you! Knowing and with certainty that his secrets are safe with you, he will be put at ease. He knows his secrets can be entrusted to your care for safekeeping and never used against him; he will, therefore, have peace of mind and freedom to open his heart of treasures and secrets to you.

Although I believe the numbers are growing amongst females, fewer ladies than men are unwilling or incapable of genuinely expressing their heartfelt thoughts. However, for many men, this is nothing new. Look, fellows, learning to talk openly with your beloved can be highly beneficial, even therapeutic.

This machismo nonsense from the world needs to be overhauled. I get it - there is a time to "man up!" However, when you are with the one you love and trust, this should be a time of complete surrender as you are allowed and even welcomed by your lady to express your vulnerability where there is a need to do so … at least, this should be the case. We, too … strong men, must be able to exhale and decompress from the cares of this world. Is there any wonder why women outlive their spouses and males in general? They do a far better job of talking and decompressing than we do.

Your secret is safe with me is the message we must get our significant others to see and trust. Over time, we accomplish this as we learn to be good listeners and hold positive and encouraging conversations with our Beloved. As our inner character is manifested through sharing our life experiences, hurt, shortcomings, and needs, this will show our beloved who we indeed are. But one may have to work or perhaps be patient while arriving at this place of free expression. However, where a person's integrity is revealed, and their character of faithfulness is lived out daily, your partner will become more at ease and apt to open up and freely share the secrets of their hearts.

For some, freely expressing matters of their heart is so out of their character. Therefore, one must guard against being pushy because this, too, can work against the relationship. Where heartfelt communication may not be the strength of your partner. If you love them and care is active in your relationship, love will find a way to work around or through this.

Early in my marriage, it was apparent that I was the affectionately expressive one. I identify my personality as verbally expressive and touchy-touchy, feely-feely, although this was far from my wife's personality or method of expressing affection. This became somewhat of a problem early in our marriage because this form of expression was foreign to my wife's disposition and upbringing. My need for my wife to respond in kind … affirm me, and even confirm her love and affection for me - she fell short in this manner of expression.

As newlyweds, perhaps on three occasions and over a period of a year or so, I expressed to my wife my need for her to show me affection. The irony here, regarding sexual intimacy … All was well! However, I did not feel, see, or get what I expected love to be like from my wife daily.

After the first two or so conversations with Lisa regarding what I perceived as a lack of attention and affection from her, she always put forth the effort to meet me at my point of need. However, it would not be long until she returned to herself, and over time, I again felt unloved and even unappreciated. Then there was our final sit-down regarding this matter.

My wife truly has and has always had the heart to please me! Early in our marriage, this was beyond my complete comprehension and appreciation that I now have. As I once again brought my concern before her on needing more attention and affection, call me needy; I am cool with it. On this occasion, her emotions came forth due to feeling inadequate; she all but said this ... Frustrated, she teared up. My wife was clearly upset! More this time because she, yet again, failed to meet my needs in what I considered to be reasonable expectations from my wife. I was surprised by Lisa's outpouring of emotions and inability to consistently meet me with what I believed to be a realistic rendering of a wife. After observing Lisa's outpouring of emotions and her heartfelt disappointment, I was led to ask my wife questions about her upbringing.

Her response began to shed light on the situation before us. What I desired from my wife, I saw it displayed between my mom and dad before he divorced the family. On the other hand, Lisa saw little to no affection expressed between her mom and dad. For her, reciprocating the attention I gave her was difficult to express with regularity – but love would find a way.

The insight that I received or that shined forth while probing my wife's past. I will say it was the love of God directing or opening my eyes to see what had always been present – My wife's unfailing and unquestionable love for me! It was visible through her actions but not the actions or interactions I desired to be expressed toward me. Before, there was a book on love languages - by the way, I have not read it. God opened my eyes to see how my wife expressed or spoke her love for me in a multitude of ways: I was shown her care for our son and me, the care she gave in the upkeep of her home, and her selfless nature, to name a few and most important things. She was and is, to this very day, *love in action*. I told her that I would not, and never again did I mention to my wife that I needed more attention and affection from her. The funny thing now is when she attempts to express these things towards me, most times it catches me off-guard and sometimes even feels awkward – but it is all good. She does not know this - but soon will.

Because of this life and love lesson shared between my wife and me, I was brought to understand the pressure upon her. She had now been liberated! I continued to be me, touchy-touchy, feely-feely, and Lisa continued to be her. From that time forward, things have moved along rather fine. I have shared with young couples, or those who are babes in Christ, that if they can successfully make it through the first three to five years while growing together should not have much difficulty staying the course and being victorious in marriage. I describe the first couple of years as feeling things out and finding your way, even securing their foundation. If God and love toward one another guide and motivate each of you, you will grow together ... you will succeed as a couple!

Again, communication is an essential element of this process. For me, this came naturally. As I grew in confidence and trust toward my wife, it became easier for me to share sensitive matters with her. This brings me to one evening and the experience of that night, a time shared with my wife that I will never forget. I describe that middle-of-the-night disclosure as one of the most intimate nights I had ever shared with my wife, if not the most intimate moment ... I affectionately call - *Pillow Talk.*

While in our bed, my wife and I were blanketed by the dark of the night. I began to pour out my heart and secrets to my wife. I do not remember what brought this about. However, on that night, I became highly vulnerable before my wife in a way I had never imagined. I had never been this transparent as I shared some of my deepest secrets with her. I could unequivocally trust my wife! It was not much for her to say. As best as I can recall, she just listened.

As I reflect on that moment occurring over three decades ago. I now understand that I was revealing to Lisa my personal demons or internal struggles and why I was the way I was, even why I reasoned things through in the manner I did. My secrets were and remain safe in the care of my wife! What I shared with her, she has never again mentioned. No doubt those secrets, we will both take to our graves.

CHAPTER 5

From Whom Do You Take Your Cues

The role of parents is consequential … they shape their child's future! Much, if not all, that shapes a person's perception about marriage will come from their home – what is learned from one's parents, provided one is brought up in such a setting. This knowledge may be information that parents shared about marriage. Or knowledge acquired through observation as the parents lived before their child as mom and dad or husband and wife. There we have it, a child's parents will be their child's teachers or from the parent whom a child takes their cues on marriage and much more.

As for our day and time from this practical experience and teaching, parents live before their children; sadly, there are little to no filters in many homes. Or safeguards whereby protecting the child from things they should not see or hear. In this, the child has no input regarding the information they are forced to receive. That said - in whatever manner parents live before their successors, the information received by them, whether good, bad, or – the ugly, the child inherits it all, takes its cues, or is influenced by their parent's actions or what the parents have taught them.

Likening this outcome to an inheritance bequeathed to a child from a parent, whatever possessions a parent bestowed upon their child … it is what it is – no exception … the good, the bad, and the ugly!

After a parent's demise, perhaps they passed on to their child riches or little to nothing of any real value or significance. Or possibly leaving unto their offspring things holding no earthly worth but tremendous sentimental or spiritual value - to that extent, priceless! Gone but not forgotten; perhaps a parent or parents only left their progeny with memories that will forever consciously and subconsciously influence the child.

I can imagine that some memories are likely to be funny or entertaining, while others are perhaps emotional, even profound, as they leave the child with invaluable knowledge or words of wisdom. These memories as they come to the mind of the parent's offspring. This impartation of knowledge and understanding, when considered. They realize how this information assisted them in their decisions, in this case bringing forth positive results. These are indeed good memories – for them, the offspring is grateful!

And yet, there may be those memories that one would rather forget, as they may have left scars emotionally or even physically. Or maybe, leaving one debilitated to some degree or another, socially and conceivably in ways that have not been considered.

Such are the effects of memories – good or bad and even those forgotten. They will forever have an influence on us to some degree or another. The tragedy. When bad memories are attempted to be hidden away or suppressed. This can lead to all sorts of problems as one tries to live their life with a past they want kept behind them. However, it can be, and one is not aware, that their history is operating in their right now, as evidenced in one's brokenness and/or lack of peace. These troubles or struggles are manifesting before the eyes of others - although the one broken or troubled by their past cannot or is unwilling to see this. For Christians who have discerning spirits, these maladies speak to us that there are unresolved issues from one's past from which they need healing and/or deliverance.

A person who is oblivious or unwilling to acknowledge that these unfavorable outcomes result from bad memories suppressed or forgotten. Does not dismiss the fact that one's past is causing the difficulties one faces in relationships and is very likely the cause of the challenges in other areas of their life. In this case, one must come to terms with the bad and ugly of their past! And then deal with it through the power and presence of God that they may be made whole or restored to spiritual health!

One's painful past, left to themselves alone and unresolved, will play a substantial role and the outcome of their quality of life. The measure of satisfaction with one's quality of life will depend upon their steps and the direction one take to confront their past. If they dare to cast aside their fears and apprehension; confront their past head-on, their *healing,* and *deliverance* will undoubtedly begin. It was for this reason that Jesus was sent or came to us; that all who are held captive *to whatever* may be set free from that which troubles us (Isaiah 61:1; Luke 4:18)!

Make the matter personal; because it is! There has to be a deliberate effort on your part to loosen and break free from the grip that has held you back from effectively walking or moving into God's purpose for you ... Your right now! And your tomorrow and days to follow, that healthy and productive future in the Lord that awaits you will be determined by you ... even right now! This is the word of God, for the people of God ... will you heed His cue to, *Come unto Him and find rest for your soul* (Jeremiah 31: 25; Matthew 11:28). Will you receive His *better* for you? Will you trust Him for your deliverance - the One who desires to give you Life (Zoe) and Shepherd you through this life (bios) – even right now? He is your Liberation, your *Help,* and yours for the choosing (Psalm 9:9; 46: 1)!

If you choose to do nothing regarding your past and its adverse effects on you ... take heed! I will therefore liken your life, howbeit spiritually, to a rip-current with the ocean's deadly and stealthy undercurrent, unnoticed by the untrained eye. And yet dangerously churning away as it exhausts you of strength leading to your downfall! Or perhaps the turbulence is felt within your soul. However, you are putting on a front, living under the false pretense that all is well. Needless to say, there is within you that ever-present churning and pulling resulting from you not confronting the tide/trouble(s) that you have been taken captive and are being swept away with.

As with an ocean's rip current, howbeit, spiritually, you are being pulled further from the safety of the shore. The safe shore? ... your peace and soundness of mind. Even so, that peace that God gives to those He has rescued and delivered from trouble. Where the mind is at ease, this is the hallmark of a healthy relationship found as one dwells securely in the arms of God.

Scripture informs us that God will keep safe those whose minds are freed and stayed on Him ... In perfect peace, we shall be kept, even though storms and dangers may oftentimes swirl and churn around and about us (Isaiah 26:3; Philippians 4:7).

No doubt, there are countless people who are desperately trying to keep their heads above the waters and stay afloat in this thing we call life (bios)! But are being taken or swept away by their tides of troublings (Mark 4:19; Luke 21: 34). Subsequently, their energy is depleted while they struggle to fight against life's wearisome currents, the riptide of a shameful past or the hurts and cares of their right now, unable to comprehend or accept the means by which to overcome this cascade of overwhelming cares racing through and troubling their minds; from a past of inundating and precarious predicaments holding them within their rip current, they are therefore drowning! They are lost to their struggles or overcome by their rip current! They are consequently overtaken by this world! Their breath stolen by the inhalation of the suffocating waters, this being their cares and concerns of this world.

They were not taught how to swim or effectively tread life's turbulent waters by their parents. But neither from their past experiences nor that of their parents were they provided lessons on life, given a life jacket or thrown a lifeline to grab hold of, that they are not overcome by the unpredictable rising and turbulent waters of life. And what a desperate predicament many are trying to tread in. Or strong currents they are attempting to swim against! They are overwhelmed and are drowning because of their broken past and desperate lives of uncertainties! And so it is, what it is! ... daily a struggle to survive!

Under such circumstances, how long is one expected to be able to hang in there? How much fight will one have within themselves before giving in to the forces or turbulence at work against them? Applying maximum effort - fighting and struggling to hold out and to hold on, even to whatever relational situation they are in. Where one has experienced failed relationship after failed relationship, having no precise understanding of why. What will be their breaking point? What will it be as described herein, which will cause such a one to throw in the towel and yield to defeat – if not give up (commit suicide) on life altogether? What is missing – what is going on? What is the answer to such despair?

Is the answer to be found alone in a two-parent home? ... This is undoubtedly a good start – but is the solution found merely in a two-parent home alone, as some will argue, being the answer? If so, what is to be said when one is or was raised in this setting. Yet, they venture on their own and are met with challenges of their own making. Particularly regarding failing to establish a healthy relationship and a well-adjusted and functioning family?

If challenges and problems, again of one's own making, are experienced amongst those reared in a two-parent home, what is to be said about a child raised within a single-parent home? Is it really ... all but expected that they are destined for troubled waters. I, too, am from a single-parent home. I am aware that life happens. Therefore, one must make the best of the situation before them. And so, kudos to you single parents – not of your own choosing, but instead through a divorce or the loss of a spouse, and you are yet holding things down righteously. My point. The argument for a two-parent home is not the elixir or fix-all of society's ills.

Now for real talk and not condemnation: For those of you who chose to be sexually active but not married, resulting in birthing your child into a single-parent home. You have, in fact, created for yourself and your child a more uncertain and challenging future. Consequently, more significant and unique challenges will be before your child ... even so regarding their mental or emotional well-being. Period! What is to be understood is that an absent parent leaves a void in the child's social rounding and grounding. However, where there is no relational balance - both parents being one with their child as a unified family, all hope is not lost.

It is the unity of the family – both parents operating as one in which God has purposed for the family. And yet, this arrangement alone is not the solution for avoiding relational dysfunction or rearing well-adjusted children. Even still, the same sorts of problems can manifest within a two-parent home as within a single-parent home. And likewise, a single-parent home can experience the blessings of God even beyond that of a two-parent home.

Nevertheless, the perfect will of God is a two-parent home. However, those of a worldly viewpoint will suggest otherwise, arguing that a single-parent home seemingly faring well - and perhaps so, should not be shunned or thought to be less favorable. Seemingly doing well? … maybe or maybe not. Where all seems well, are things really well? … Or as well as things could be? And where all seem well by man's standards, this is the exception – not the norm nor what God intended for His family from the beginning as being *well* or *spiritually healthy*. Regarding a single-family home, and without going into the specifics, I will share a relational challenge that is often played out in front of a child when the parent chooses to date. And also, how the child may be affected must be considered. But too often, this is not the case. As a result, a child becomes collateral damage.

For you, single parents, those desiring companionship, did you beforehand, or have you now considered just how much more the challenge of being in a healthy relationship will be because of your status? And of more importance and even consequences, regarding your child growing up in this hit-and-miss, revolving door, uncertain dating environment to which you have exposed them. Have you given thought to what they are learning? Or the messages or cues you are sending them? And too, how they may be affected and challenged when they come of age, desiring companionship for themselves? I am sure that many children who reach adulthood are not even considering marriage because of the failures and dysfunction they experienced and learned from their parent(s). This cannot be what you want for your child.

No doubt some of you will take exception to what I will now share. Nevertheless, I must speak! Hear me on this … Dysfunction can only beget dysfunction, and confusion can only beget confusion! In other words, "We reap what we sow!" Or another way to see things, The rooster will come home to roost! I am convinced. That the confusion and dysfunction many children and young adults are having with "gender identity." Or that of choosing a same-sex relationship instead of a heterosexual union. Essentially is the result of a child being reared in an imbalanced, dysfunctional, and confused home. Such homes: no matter how well things may appear, the home is not directed nor ordered by God. And so whatever exceptions you have with my statement, it's that which God has spoken. Your argument is then with Him and not me.

Understand something. Relational dysfunction manifests itself in a variety of ways, however, regarding gender identity and homosexual relationships. They have more significant and far-reaching consequences, as gross spiritual blindness has overtaken those who have been taken captive by these lifestyles. Such ones have come under deceptive demonic influence, and maybe even demonic possession (demonized) as this spiritual attack against the person of God's imagers is taken captive and led astray. I say this not to condemn anyone. Rather I am speaking God's truth, that God and His deliverance may be sought so that such ones are no longer held in bondage to sin. And that godly families may become or be more effectively spiritually weaponized to thwart Satan's attacks on God's ordering and purpose for the family – the husband (man), the wife (woman), and their offspring.

Parents, listen to me! Your children are watching you! You are their polestar; they take their cues on living life from you. So, the question for those of you who are parents ... From whom are you taking your cues? The solution and help for the family; the remedy for the brokenness and problems we face societally. It is to be found in men returning to God their Father! That we may learn to lead our homes as godly men. And women returning to God also! And with both parents through marriage, raising their children in the adoration and admiration of God (Proverbs 22:6; Deuteronomy 6: 20-25).

Technological Trappings

From my experiences and while observing the lives of others, I have gained insight or understanding from God to write this book. This spiritual insight and wisdom have enabled me to better understand relational cause and effect. I, therefore, clearly understand what a child or any of us experienced during our youth, whether from within their home or societally, will significantly affect the child's mental and social well-being or development. Psychiatrists and others within the mental health field can undoubtedly corroborate my position regarding how dysfunction within one's family, particularly for a child, profoundly affects their decision-making as they mature. And even how they develop or adjust socially and relationally.

As if being raised in a dysfunctional family is not problematic enough – we must also consider those negative influences presented daily through technology that is being forced upon us all … Now more than ever! We must also consider the various forms of dark and destructive media, their messaging, and our access to them. As a result of these mediums, varying spiritual assaults are constantly coming at us; often, and even tragically, we are opening the doors and welcoming these attacks against our mental and spiritual well-being. A child's protective borders, even with dad and mom standing watch, let alone a single parent standing guard, are no longer as impenetrable and secure as they once were. Therefore, our children, if any of us, for that matter, will never be as safe as we were before this technological age.

If relationship building and establishing a healthy family were not challenging before these times. The difficulties of building and sustaining a productive and healthy relationship or family today are outright frightening for many. If not frightening … for sure, a great deal of apprehension arrests the minds of many. Instead of marrying, resulting from the fear of failure or the thought of material loss and other discouraging scenarios that could unfold if things were to go bad, alternative arrangements are being agreed upon or tolerated within relationships instead of marriage.

However, there is another perspective from which we must learn to look at things; *He* is no secret or mystery. Tragically this *Way* is either misunderstood, His practices abused and misrepresented, or even considered antiquated by others. Meanwhile, an increasing number are oblivious to the *Alternative* to what they know or believe. And are therefore listening to the pundits and talking heads of this world.

From *The Alternative,* the cues or influence He provides are infallible as they are from none other and the very *One* who holds the blueprint and outline for humanity's existence and living. We must take our cues from Him, our God and Creator.

As the Father, Son, and Spirit are *one* - inseparable and everlasting, this union must be understood as it puts the bond of a holy marriage in view. Marriage, therefore, is not to be entered into lightly or without careful consideration. Even so, the two, being joined together under God, are to receive godly counsel beforehand. Much hurt, heartache, and disappointment could be averted if this attitude and approach to marriage were understood and esteemed as sacred.

The sacredness of marriage has been made a mockery by the faithless and some Christians alike. We clearly see this betrayed through the media. Marriage seems to have less value or honor and meaning than the paper, which certifies the union governmentally to be legally binding. This is seen in those who trivialize marriage and subsequently annul their union or covenant agreement. The nonchalant attitude toward disbanding a marriage is observed in the ease and readiness many have toward ending their union for little to nothing. This is also evidenced as a number of high-profile people embrace marriage, but it lasts only days, a few months, and, at best, a couple of years. This disregard for the holiness and covenant of marriage significantly undermines the integrity and sanctity of marriage as intended by God. And subsequently has a profound negative effect on those with whom such people influence.

Some of these high-profile unions seem to be staged - self-serving and only for the purpose of attempting to hold on to fame or relevance. Their lust to keep their name, or brand, trending or alive through various platforms is insatiable! With many of these celebrities or Hollywood marriages that are done away with ease, it appears that some of these individuals have no shame or regret in abruptly ending their marriages or, perhaps better stated - their contractual arrangements.

Mainstream television and radio, with their irreverent depictions of marriage and scandalous content in their portrayal of marriage, even take jabs at the "traditional Christian marriage," leading to further disregard and even desecration of the institution of that of a holy union. The glorification of media's corruption and even attacks upon traditional marriage stands in *contrast and opposition* to the very ways of The Most Holy God. Meanwhile, mainstream media - those of this world, attack and attract man, taking captive the weak, the gullible, and unlearned by seducing man through so-called entertainment are doing the will of the very god of this age, their father – The most unholy, Satan!

If one's heart is not totally - desensitized, blinded, or removed from the moral truths of God and understanding of the holiness of marriage, in this case, you can very well see this and, now perhaps, better understand why things are as they are.

What must be realized. Is that all activity, no matter the source, great or small, for adult consumption or rated for a child. Where presented for so-called entertainment or otherwise. If this information or activity is contrary to what is taught through God's Holy Word, it is, in fact, an insult and assault even against God. And even an attack against His imagers – mankind … you and me!

Look … one may be susceptible to being led into wrongdoing and not even be aware of the industry's influences over them. Before you realize what has happened, Satan's seductive and often subtle and subversive ways, operating through media, have you hooked and locked into perverted living, not to mention our innocent and ever-so-vulnerable children! Today's Satanic influence through media has lured and entangled a generation of our youth. Make no mistake about it; while in Satan's grasp, he intends to literally destroy our children and keep all he can in his grasp and under his lifeless influence until we take our last breath! Then comes God's judgment and sentencing to eternal damnation for the enemies of God - all who have chosen to remain one with this world and Satan.

Beloved of God. Satan wants you to himself, through any and all means to keep or capture you, that we may suffer as he has. And as he knows he will on his day of eternal confinement and suffering (Revelation 20:10)! He, therefore, longs to destroy you, whereby withholding from you, through lies and deception, the healthy, vibrant, and victorious relationship that is yours in Christ. Satan cannot stand that God has you back in His family or desires to have you back to Himself and not him!

Evil's media blitz, sensory overload, incitement, and even enticement is to be comprehended as the very activity of the *seducing or evil spirits* (Ephesians 2: 2; 1 Timothy 4:1)!

Make no mistake about what I am presenting to you: This is demonic activity cloaked in so-called entertainment labeled as – "For fun and laughter, artistry, mere acting, harmless and exciting media, and/or just gaming;" the entertainment industry will argue and deceive you with. People, the dangers of these seducing spirits are ever-present; it is witnessed by spiritual wickedness and debilitating consequences that are all around: sexual crimes, murder, hatred, theft, pride, delusion, overindulgence, addictions, chaos, and immorality of all sorts! A heavy dose of this is injected into our psyche as we daily tune in to our media and technological options.

A television show momentarily caught my attention. It was/is called "Marriage at First Sight. This show undermines the sanctity and seriousness that should be given to marriages. If you are not familiar with this "reality show," its focus is on pairing random couples for pre-arranged marriages. Unlike those arranged marriages occurring in other cultures and at the hands of thoughtful and caring parents. Rather, there are so-called dating and personality experts who partner these willing participants together based on their profiles alone for the purpose of "marriage." Wedding planners, the build-up, and all the hoopla that comes with such an event are played out on television. Parents and friends are even a part of the show. The way family or friends of the groom and bride feel, or their opinions about this arrangement vary from person to person. Christians, other faiths, and those of no particular faith are shown expressing and sharing their thoughts on this sort of arrangement.

What is troublesome for me is watching a professing Christian considering this betrothal. And other Christians who are in favor of such an arrangement. And where there may be reservation or concern for a friend or family member moving forward with the "marriage," they nonetheless go along with this proceeding to show "support" for their friend or loved one. Is this how God intended for marriages to occur among Christians? A resounding - No!

During this spectacle, one can choose to forego the proceedings at any point leading to the wedding or while at the altar ... How wise! However, if the "marriage" is seen through to its completion, then there is the matter and awkwardness of considering having sexual relations - among other things, with their - *stranger spouse*. Though "legally" married, if one or both parties decide to no longer continue in this arrangement, they can walk away from their contractual agreement faster than it took to arrange the event and wedding. The tragedy, some see no problem with this "reality" failure. Such ones are spiritually blind and desperately need to be brought to the light and truth of marriage and what it represents before God.

It is this sort of foolishness that is working against the sacredness of marriages, families, and those with hopes of someday marrying. This show is being witnessed by many who are entertained and influenced by this nonsense. Its influence and other, like, perverted media of persuasion, are pervasive in our society; again, it is clear evidence of this nation's moral decline. As we consider this one situation, is it any wonder why we are not seeing sustainable marriages and relationships built upon common, understandable, and healthy principles that many once valued and held before the 21st Century and this technological age?

Those behind the "entertainment" industry who know very well immorality sells (*the love of money is the root of all evil, 1 Timothy 6:10*) who push and promote perversion can certainly be criticized. Their lust for the "all mighty dollar," they being spiritually bankrupt, put out these images, movies, etcetera, which subsequently affect many, as seen in the havoc wreaked within marriages, families, and society!

Two truths: This is nothing new regarding the entertainment industry. However, its corruption via media and other electronics is astonishingly more prolific and easily accessible today. *Secondly*, the industry's defense is, "We are not forcing any to watch or purchase our products. Besides, We are Federally regulated; therefore, we rate movies, shows, and products as the laws require." The fight, nonetheless, must be continued by the faithful, those few who are attempting to keep Hollywood and others in check … an uphill battle for sure, where this world's system holds an edge.

Here is something else that is very important and must be understood; morality can never be held in check by rules and regulations! There has to be the regeneration of man's heart, motivated by the love shown to them by God, and one being regulated by the Spirit of Righteousness unto sanctification or right living.

What happened to the virtuous notion of being one another's keeper? As a people, we are struggling more and more with keeping this noble concept and holding one another accountable. Is there any wonder … we are like our brother Cain; before we are *saved* - agents of evil and destruction? Before we became one with Christ, we were about the business of Satan. But now, accounted as the Redeemed of the Lord. How is it, then … some Christians still act as if they belong to this world? We must get it together! We must learn the will of our Father to do His bidding as Kingdom builders and caretakers, one for another!

Those holding strong moral convictions want these industries that negatively influence our society to provide moral restraint as they ought to consider the greater good of their fellow man. However, those who have elected to self-rule hold no true moral compass, conviction, or consciousness other than what they have established to be acceptable and that which benefits them. Such ones not acquiring a relationship with their Creator nor having concern or care for their fellow man. They will do what they do … commit evil, and destroy others, even themselves, though they may or may not be directly involved in such corruption nor see things as I've described. However, this does not let those behind these industries off the hook. Nor should it deter the righteous efforts of those opposing the media industry to persist in wanting change and bringing a stop to the media's continued corruption of the weak and vulnerable through their sinister messaging.

Now, to those of you who are carnal Christians, I will strongly add: you cannot be party or bedfellows with the industry, as are those actors and actresses who may have moral convictions, yet for fame and getting paid, are choosing to play roles that go against their loose moral views and their Christian belief system. Such ones compromise or seek to justify their acting or actions by suggesting what they do as an "art form" or a "creative way of expression." And other such assertions to deflect from the concerns or sin at hand to ease or appease their conscious from what they know to be the truth regarding reprehensible and deplorable characters played on the screens of the theaters or other viewing means. Some have, in fact, sold their souls to the Devil! The Bible is never wrong; indeed, the love of money is the root of all evil! My Christian brothers and sisters, are your dollars, or are you personally contributing to the industry's immoral messaging? Are your logins and attention given to such programming driving up their ratings and followers?

Music And Media's Trappings

What is there to be said regarding the music industry? The same as previously mentioned regarding the movie industry. Neither can this industry be found guiltless regarding some of the songs, vulgar and immoral content that is sold for profit. As I give thought to music from my childhood. Since I've become an adult, I can discern hidden within the lyrics the sexual overtures, liaison, and suggestions added to music in poetic and rhythmic blending that, as a child, went over the heads or was unintelligible to my youthful ears.

I will describe that era's music as thoughtful, beautiful, soulful, and holding a beat that caused one to move. For me, it was always about the beat while at times latching on to the hook or some catchy saying. However, hidden within many of those songs were lyrical messages for grown folk which younger people did not readily understand. I am confident this was intentional by some within the industry. Why was this the case … To protect the innocent or the most vulnerable – the children. Certainly, this was the industry's conscious decision regarding how adult content was cleverly eased within, or them blending words and phrases to a song that did not jolt one's sensibilities. Or arouse a youth's attention to the sexual nature and content expressed in and through a song.

So, it would seem moral standards governed the people of that era that would not allow just anything to be said or sung over the airways or sold by businesses. It would appear that there was something to be said about being decent and in order. And not being offensive to your neighbor, and even protecting the innocence of our children. This is unlike the music produced by this permissive and unrestrained generation of the age. Where many readily give an ear to such sexualized, authority-undermining, degrading, and even violence-promoting songs.

If I recall correctly, around the mid - 80s to early 90s, the language expressed in music began to become abrasive and more explicit. My sons were relatively young at the time; the oldest was six years old when my youngest son was born in 1990. Much of the music played over the radio did not appeal to me. But neither did I give thought to the potential influence of the musical revolt and takeover that was taking shape and advancing before me. The music industry began embracing and capitalizing on songs that flirted with the boundary of acceptable language until the boundaries were virtually erased.

The conversation for the mature was no longer hidden within the music; discretion was no longer used in the expressed lyrics. It was clear and beyond question what the "artist" was conveying and suggesting through song. This vulgarity, sexually suggestive lyrics, and verbiage that degraded women were found offensive to many and shocked the sensibilities of more than a few.

For many of the "Hip-Hop" era, some who had not heard one lyrical stanza of a particular song were simply turned off by the thumping beat of this musical movement. But many who dared to listen out of pressure to do so or curiosity. The lyrics of a particular song were not always apparent or evident with its offensive content. However, when the words became clear, they were taken aback to have discovered hidden (loosely speaking) within the base-thumping beats and, at times, hard-to-understand linguistically musical ingenuity and genius of the entertainer and song's producer. But after lending a careful ear and perhaps receiving some help to clarify what they were hearing. It became apparent that the songwriters and artists were telling a generation of young people, sexually speaking ... "Who to do!" "Where to do them!" "How to do them!" "How often to do them!" And even "How it would make them feel when done!" Among other shocking things, suggested or presented to a magnetic and magnificent beat to gain the attention of their listeners or consumers of sordid songwriting!

Appealing to and exciting the imagination of a youthful group of people. Presenting imagery with words of the most graphic encounter, setting the mood, accompanied by the smoothness of a funky, fresh, or fly beat. The experience from the storytelling through song is now played out in one's mind, even to the point of ecstasy of its listeners! All for what? ... The purpose of sales ... One getting paid - that *almighty dollar*! This perversion through songwriting is not limited to sex. But also the use of drugs, alcohol, and even disregard for authority. Clearly... at least for me, it says something has gone wrong within our society when such perversity is freely carried through the airways or whatever the method of transport before our viewing and hearing.

If you do not watch much television or listen to the radio. Let me suggest that you just tune in to a radio station or turn to a local television station - and BAM! You will see that explicit messages, or immorality, are part of the regular programming! No, to minimal filtering; this is what our children are being subjected to and exposed to! And if we would be honest with ourselves. Many adults cannot handle this onslaught of soft porn and tantalizing music that they are being "entertained" by - through so-called regular television and radio. What are we to expect from our innocent and vulnerable youth who are being exposed to and indoctrinated into a world of filth? What do we hope to get in return? Can you even begin to imagine what is occurring to their innocent and fragile minds? Yes, you can ... they are being twisted – just look around! Ask any teacher in our local or public schools if you are unsure what's going on with our kids and what they, as teachers, have to deal with daily!

As I give thought to my young adult life, as well as my early teens, the years ranging from the late '70s into the early '80s, I recall the first wave of my exposure to unprecedented "PG" and "R" rated material landing in our home by way of cable television: HBO, Cinemax, and Showtime, thereby permitting for the first-ever "adult-only channels" – YEAH RIGHT! … to be viewed from one's home.

Establishing a timeline of sorts: A few years later, these viewing options became mainstream; following close behind was hardcore, aka "Gangsta" rap music with its explicit lyrics, then the "bumping and grinding" and sexually suggestive lyrics within the R&B genre of music. This sexually charged music may have been taking place in other genres. However, I can only speak to what I heard from the stations I was inclined to listen to.

There is no question; at the close of the Twentieth Century, these immoral influences through television and music played over the airwaves excited, encouraged, and directed a generation's thoughts, including their passions or fleshly desires. Moreover, I believe that television's influence has had the most significant effect on one's mind and its conditioning. Television stimulates and teaches through sight, sound, and words, unlike music, which is sound only. Through two gates: our seeing and hearing, are these unclean influences rushing into our souls as destructive and insidious forces. They are demonic in nature, leading all who are weak and vulnerable to indulge in unbridled, even detestable, lustful passions.

It is my prayerful hope; that you now better understand how the inappropriate use of media and technology is working against the healthy or godly ways in which we should be valuing and protecting one another. And we cannot forget the "Gaming Industry," though this is a community I am not too familiar with. However, I am sure they, too, are profiting from marketing sexual content and other perverted and graphic games for so-called entertainment. Now that you are informed, turn from these practices and be more vigilant towards safeguarding each other and our vulnerable and innocent children.

Innocent No Longer

Giving thought to my childhood, I remember what I will call experiencing bodily or sensual awareness. I had no idea what to make of things at the time other than the unusual and new experience of physical pleasure. This was not self-examination or touching oneself, but rather through playing, where pressure was inadvertently experienced upon my groin. Perhaps you had a similar experience as a child. We are created social and sexual beings and are, therefore, at times in need of a caring or nurturing touch. And whether by accident or not, we are acutely aware of a pleasurable or physically stimulating touch. That said. If you have small children, do yourself and them a favor; make sure to explain to them the changes they will experience with their bodies and for them to know what is appropriate and inappropriate touching or physical interaction.

As a child, my experience with sensual awareness was few ... Just the same, too many! And so, there is something to be said about me and perhaps even yourself, being able to recall some sensual or physical experience encountered as a child. Why is this so? Here is why: These physical encounters or experiences are potent or stimulating, possibly even entrancing, no matter how the feeling was brought about, through accidental means, self-exploration, or one agreeing to engage in such physical activity with someone. Or even not agreed upon. And know this, the agreement does not have to be verbalized ... Actions can speak louder than words!

However, it is unfortunate, sad, and even tragic when the innocent are manipulated and physically taken advantage of. This experience, whether from exploitation or indecent liberties, the victim's flesh been aroused or not, the experience cannot be simply or easily dismissed or just forgotten. Unless the one violated was too young to remember the situation. Or the trauma and/or horror of the experience was so devastating that the mind blocks the event from memory as a result of self-preservation.

Besides arousal, while at play, I could speak to other, such youthful sensual experiences; however, I have made my point for the time being. Thankfully, the encounters of my youth did not badly scar or significantly damage me emotionally. Nonetheless, awakening me physically, I am confident those experiences influenced my behavior regarding sensuality, sexual relations, or even relationships in general, into my adult years, including into my years of marriage. We are, in fact, products of our past experiences and environment. As a result, we all have a story about our childhood experiences and how they affected us later in life. Some memories are no doubt forgotten; nevertheless, they have been a part of shaping your now.

As for the bodily or sensual awareness that I am speaking about, these experiences occurred before I was sexually aware of or had knowledge of the "Birds and the Bees." Nonetheless, they have not been forgotten. I will now share my earliest sensual recollection of what I have chosen to call *The Aftermath*. Though aspects of the event are unclear, what I experienced, and the lingering physical and mental effect is undeniable. You will soon understand why I have chosen to call this matter - *The Aftermath*.

Even though this sexual occurrence did not involve me directly, the encounter's residual or indirect effect did. It is an experience that has remained within my vague memory for over five decades. I was around the ages of three to five when the incident occurred. I seem to recall that my mother was away from home, and she had gotten a sitter, a young female who was a friend of the family.

I had a younger sister; however, I cannot recall her presence. As a matter of fact, the only things that I can remember with clarity are the event that I am going to share and its *aftermath*. I have chosen to share this particular situation, which for some of you, perhaps will be repulsive. However, I want to show how such experiences regarding sex's magnetism in all of its soulish *involvings* and/or expressions do not easily depart from one's mind, even when one is not directly or physically involved or engaged. The act of sexual relations is a total body or soulish experience - and rather potent at that; all of one's sensory receptors are engaged during sexual intercourse. Even where one is not actually or physically involved in sexual relations but is exposed to the act through sensory engagement alone, sexual activity and all that emanates from the act can be powerfully enthralling and seducing.

For many preadolescent boys and girls alike, the nude body alone can be mesmerizing! This can result in an immediate biological stirring or *sexual turn-on* ... for sure, for those who are adolescents. Even so, for many adults as well! Now, add to nudity, sensual and animated visuals, sounds, and even smell(s) natural (pheromone) or otherwise from the sexual encounter, all of which are uniquely powerful and can be intoxicatingly enrapturing when experienced together sexually! This here: the excitement or activation of all our senses provides insight into the addictiveness of illicit sexual relations and the bond developed between a husband and wife. If not the actual act of sexual relations. It may be the allure of those who strip or dance erotically for hire, thereby visually setting on edge or arousing the passions of their consumers as their bodies move in rhythmic concert with the hypnotic beat and lyrics of some song! Herein we are also given a window to behold the powerfully destructive and addictive force behind pornography, even so-called "soft porn" as often viewed on regular television and elsewhere.

Emphasizing the fact: The sexual experience is powerfully stirring and gripping! For this reason, a sexual encounter is not readily dismissed or forgotten; however, there are exceptions. Even where one is not directly or physically involved, let's say they are engaged through their various senses, intentionally or not. In this instance, the stimulating sexual sound(s) heard emanating from within the confines of a bedroom. Then there are visual aspects to heightened sensuality or the sexual experience as shared ... You've heard the saying, "Seeing leaves nothing to the imagination." And therefore, more significant is the stimuli and influence of sex with one visually experiencing the act of sexual relations. I now ask ... What are your children seeing? What are your children hearing? But rarely does a non-participate in sex experience the *aftermath* of a sexual encounter through smell or touch. This was my experience, as a vulnerable child, somewhere around the ages of three to five.

This experience of mine unfolded in the two-story apartment where we lived. Piecing together parts of the vague story: my sister and I were downstairs. Though I cannot remember anyone entering or leaving the apartment, some boy had done both. After the boy departed, I was allowed to go upstairs.

Entering the bedroom, I climbed onto the bed. While on my hands and knees, my left hand rested upon an odd wet, and strange textured substance.

The next thing I did was lift my hand to smell this odd wet substance that my hand rested upon. The odor was unusual but not repulsive – a strange smell that stirred my curiosity. The smell was unlike anything I had encountered … So much so that this experience and the effect of that distinctive scent have remained within my memory for over fifty years!

As a teenager, I came to know the substance my hand and smell had encountered - the *aftermath* of a sexual encounter. What an unfortunate situation for a child to happen upon. But sadly, many of our innocent and vulnerable children are subjected to far worse.

After I brought my experience to the sitter's attention, she washed away the evidence of her sexual escapade, removing from the bedspread their *aftermath*. However, from this experience, my mind and the smell have not been sanitized from my life experience, nor can they be, thereby leaving a permanent blemish of sorts upon my soul that will forever remain with me – *The Aftermath*. As for how this experience later influenced me, I don't have an answer … but surely it did!

* * *

There are studies that have presented how certain fragrances or scents can cause a chemical reaction within the body, even measured sexual arousal. Though this may not be readily observed, the right scent can be an attention-getter or head-turner. As I mentioned, the smell that I encountered was not repulsive. Rather, oddly different, thereby stirring my curiosity, and I will go so far as to say, also stirring me soulishly, a mere child of 3 to 5 years of age. If you have experienced sexual relations, you are likely to have some idea of what I am talking about … that natural intoxicating scent that can emanate from the person with whom you have been sexually intimate. Now that you have given the matter thought. Perhaps your response. "You are right!" And so, subconsciously, the person's natural body scent can affect you, or perhaps the fragrance they put on their body stimulates or appeals to you.

That said, and not being humorous. Perhaps my experience is why I am fond of the fragrance – Musk. Or maybe, naturally, by means of pheromone release, this is a fragrance that appeals to me. Herein, I am showing the connection between sensory receptors and how they are heightened by various stimulants, even though one may not be aware of this during sexual relations or otherwise. Nevertheless, making way for a more rapturous sexual experience and the person partnered with even more desirous, certainly if all of the sensory receptors are stimulated simultaneously.

I cannot emphasize this enough: The matter of sex and sexual sin is nothing to be toyed with! It is not intended for the recreational engagement of the unmarried. But rather for a husband and wife for procreation. Therefore, God has given a husband and wife this wonderfully mysterious and powerful gift of sexual relations to be shared and expressed between the two to strengthen and enjoy their marital bonding. Where sexual relations are misunderstood and misused unto sin, we can call this a malfunction or even a catastrophic failure. And therefore, we are to expect various kinds of personal and relational breakdowns and breakups where sexual relations are sinfully undertaken. And my, my ... we seeing sexual sin's by-product: in broken people, dysfunctional families, fatherless children, and in a growing number - motherless children.

It can take only one pleasurable sexual encounter with one who is naïve – their age not mattering, whereby exciting their hunger or sexual appetite that is never satisfied. One time or moment of sexual indulgence, and like an addictive substance, one can become hooked on sex. Thereby causing that person to seek out various forms or methods to experience bodily pleasure - if not sexual relations, then a high or arousal of other sordid sorts. This begins a disastrous course of bad choices and destructive behavior because of sex's addictiveness!

A moment of sexual pleasure lost in time, innocence given away or taken; now, a Pandora's box of sexual evils can be or has been opened to one who was once innocent. I am now talking about the extreme wickedness that one can be overtaken by ... by toying with sexual sin or being sexually violated! Sin is nothing to play with! This bondage to one's sexual longings or addiction of one sort or another is all too real. With merely one introduction to the pleasure of sin of whatever sort, one can find themselves trapped in sin's grasp.

Presenting the matter in spiritual or Christian vernacular: sexual strongholds or bondage of whatever kind is a predicament that can seize upon anyone if they are not careful. This imprisonment stems from our base nature of licentiousness that can be aroused if one is not watchful.

Now taking the matter of sexual promiscuity to its most base operation: sexual deviance and defilement, with consideration giving to demonic possession, or one possessed (demonized) by an unclean or foul spirit can be the outcome of a non-believer who has given themselves over to Satan, through the practice of sexual sin or as an instrument of some other method of sinning at Satan's bidding, knowingly or not.

I hold the position, as many others; Scripture supports our stance - that a true Believer or Christian cannot be demon-possessed. The simple reason for this ... because of the indwelling Holy Spirit within the child of God. He has taken residence in all who are born again; therefore, AIN'T no demon (unclean spirit or elohim) will have the power to evict Him. However, if not prayerful and watchful, any Believer can be influenced (demonized), ensnared, or oppressed by demonic strongholds of many sorts and held in bondage until they acknowledge their self-induced imprisonment. Repenting from their wrongs, turning to God for forgiveness, their deliverance is sure; one will be released and restored to freedom through Christ.

Where a pattern of sinful living occurs, this lifestyle or life choice points to either emotional and/or spiritual deficiency for those who engage in immorality. Sadly, many involved in harmful or counterproductive lifestyles cannot always grasp the severity or direness of their self-destructive path nor the difficulties awaiting them if they do not change course. Regardless of how this may have come about, they have been overtaken by their passions, emotions, or both. And even sin.

An individual living in this manner, and certainly if raised in such an environment of bondage to sin. Will not grasp why or see that they are living in such a self-defeating manner. And are also not likely to necessarily identify their lifestyle as self-destructive and self-defeating. In their minds, "It is what it is." This is the challenge that is to be overcome by such ones. And for the Christian who is attempting to show such a one a better way of living. Not only is it disheartening for those who care about a person in this situation. But it can also be difficult for those who care to comprehend the reckless nature and disregard that the individual has for their own life or that of others.

Where this is the case. A disastrous end is likely - if the root cause for their disregard for life is not understood and dealt with. But what is of most importance is that person coming to know Jesus as their Savior and Deliverer. They may not be capable of changing their environment, but their minds can be freed from bondage and defeat to victory in Christ.

As we seek to meet the needs of others, especially the troubled or those living in a uniquely challenging situation. Keep in mind that some do not comprehend that there is anything disturbingly wrong with their way of thinking regarding the counter-productive choice(s) they make to *survive*. Their way of thinking is survival by any means necessary. For many, the damage done to them, the sins committed against them. And the deplorable life or practices lived out before them occurred while they were so young and impressionable that their reasoning has been perverted against what is considered correct, logical, and acceptable moral living or norms as understood by the child of God.

These people are, in a sense, victims ... once innocent children who became products of their environment. This is a fast-spreading new norm of our society, whether lived out in the hood or trailer park, raised on the urban streets, some country back road, and even within so-called upscaled communities.

What we must be sensitive to and have an understanding of ... is that we all have a back story, but in and through Jesus, we all have or can have a new story and a new beginning. Our past can no longer be held against us (Romans 6:4; 2 Corinthians 5:17). In Christ, we are victors; we have become a new creation (2 Corinthians 5: 16 - 21)!

Victim - Violator

I am aware that there are times when transparency about one's life can be quite beneficial when attempting to reach or help someone through a difficult life challenge. By disarming yourself or becoming vulnerable or transparent, you show the other person that you are relatable by revealing how you are or were just as they are in some manner or another. In doing so, someone will not only see their dilemma or situation as a sinful person through your sharing as a Christian. But they can also become liberated as new insight is provided through our Liberator – Christ Jesus, as a result of your witness or story being told. And so ... it remains my hope and prayer by keeping things real or being transparent before you. That you may break free from whatever stronghold(s) that's keeping you captive.

I clearly recognize that I was purposed, and thus spiritually, impregnated by God to birth this book. After my book's deliverance into the world ... the first draft now completed, it needed to be cleaned up or edited before being presented to you. I, too, liken my early spiritual disposition and journey to that of this book ... as a newly born babe birthed into this world. Before I was born again, and leading to my new birth, followed by the process of continuing sanctification. Like this book and its developmental editing and release or presentation to others, as a newly-born babe in Christ, not to mention how I was before getting to this point, I was a miserable mess and, too, needed editing (cleaning up)! I had to therefore undergo by *the Spirit of God* a renovation, renewal, or editing of my mind (thinking) through continued sanctification and washing by the *Word of God* that God's holiness or spiritual-inner beauty could emanate and illuminate from within my born-again spirit.

I will now share with you my unregenerated spiritual journey – whereas I was dead in my sin, unto my new birth through Jesus and deliverance from being one with the walking dead. I will reveal myself to you to present my messiness before I was thoroughly cleansed or sanctified (not perfected in the flesh) by the *Blood of Jesus and* presented holy before my God and Father. As a mature Christian - not perfect, who still needs washing by the Word of God, I share my story with the expectation that someone may see themselves in me. As a result, discover that there is no shame for the child of God in being open or naked about one's difficulties, challenges, or mess that covers or had once covered them. From our sin and filth, Jesus came to cleanse us all. In Him, we become a new creation; all things become new (2 Corinthians 5:17-21; John 1:29;1 John 2:2).

Establishing a timeline: I was born in the mid1960s. As best as I can recall, what I am chronologically sharing occurred from this period mentioned and throughout the 1970s. Details of these situations are no longer retained within my memory. Nonetheless, these were pivotal moments for me as a child. Thanks be to God, my life turned out better than ok. However, looking back over my journey, I see how my now-story or current situation could have been easily written much differently – and for the worst ... Oh, for the grace of God and a praying mother! This period of my life was pivotal because I was vulnerable and impressionable, as it is for any child in these preadolescent and early teen years. As things would be, I would meet up with my foe - my fleshly passions or desires, before I would actually meet up with puberty or even know what it was.

Although my bad experiences may be mild compared to the trauma or horrific situations that some have undoubtedly encountered. Nevertheless, these common threads: brokenness, dysfunction, and sin, are woven into man's soul and even life experiences. However, some people are worst off than others. Whether you were the victim or the violator, the stain or psychological blemish resulting from sin and/or sinful behavior of the victimizer upon their victim is not readily forgotten, purged, or washed from one's memory. And thereby forms the tapestry of one's relational makeup or viewpoint that's soiled or darkened because of the dysfunctional or sinful individual only capable of observing life through the lens of their victimization. Or carnality – their sinful or humanistic worldview shaped by their less-than-ideal experiences or environment raised in. This may be of one's own choosing or making. Or perhaps occurrences beyond one's control – hence one being victimized.

Parents, although playtime is a fun time for your child. However, you must be aware of the physical interaction of your child with others. Also, make sure your child is aware of the biological changes that will occur with them as they come of age. You do not want your child to be caught unaware or even frightened due to the natural occurrence of puberty – unfortunately, this happens. As for the instances that I will share, they did not involve child's play or situations involving arousal resulting from puberty's onset. What I will present are situations where I was mindful of and desiring fleshly arousal... my foe, this my flesh, was at work ahead of schedule.

As I share these unfortunate, regretful, and preventable experiences, the identities of others involved will remain safe with me. Each of us were victims requiring protection. And this, from ourselves, or our fallen nature. I am inclined to believe those with whom I was involved experienced something to awaken their sexual curiosity. Could their experience have been avoided through a parent's watchful and careful eye or some other adult? Look, you cannot assume or take things for granted regarding your child's safety – their mind, body, and spirit! You must have real talk with your child about the evils of this world and even their propensity of evil from within that longs to manifest through their flesh.

The experiences I was involved in through early education could have likely been avoided. Many parents, so it seems, rarely sit down with their children and have real or life talks with their child on those crucial subjects that will determine the outcome of their child's well-being.

Parents, it is your responsibility to protect your child from those forces, whatever they may be, that can cause harm to your child. As the child ages or matures in mind and body, continue to arm them with knowledge, *Truth*, and *Wisdom* - the very Word of God.

The way our bodies are designed to function, even how they develop, is God's marvel – indeed, we are "fearfully and wonderfully made" (Psalm 139: 141).

People, need I remind you – that Satan, through his evil *influencers*, wants desperately to destroy you! He wants your bodies to fulfill his will. He wants to destroy marriages; he wants to destroy families. And he is using sex as a weapon to do just this – the earlier he can get one involved in sexual sin or perverted understanding regarding sex or gender identity – all the better for him! Greater will be the harm and devastation one will later suffer relationally and the difficulties encountered while trying to break free from the spiritual prison of mental and physical perversion.

Sex has been purposed by God to strengthen the marital bond and bring forth life. Conversely or contrarywise, unbridled sex, its perversion, is being used by Satan as an instrument and even a diabolical and destructive weapon to further his dark agenda aimed at bringing despair and destruction to humanity.

My experience with *The Aftermath* was just the beginning of situations that a child should not experience. Unprotected and unprepared, I would encounter additional sexual-related occurrences far too young ... Satan's plans and trappings for my destruction like landmines lay before me. These landmines and trappings are forever present in our world for anyone to be brought down or taken out by! This is not unique to me, nor is the age of such experiences rare.

Parents, these stories should cause you to become more alert and prayerful! In the following situation, I may have been around the age of eight. The female in this encounter was perhaps four years my senior. My mother was a friend of this family; we were visiting this child's home. On this occasion, I do not remember if any adults were in the house – not likely; this older female may have been in charge of watching us younger kids. I remember playing and being alone in a bedroom with this female at some point during our visit. There I was, a mere boy of around eight years of age, and I beheld this older girl lying on the bed before me.

However, she was not simply lying on the bed; she had pulled her pants down. I remember looking and being taken aback as I observed her dark black pubic hair. I was captivated at the sight of her body exposed before me. As I looked upon her, she coaxed me to lay on top of her. I do not recall feeling apprehension or reluctance. Neither do I remember if my pants had been lowered. Why was there no sense of alarm? My simple response – she was a trusted friend of the family, and besides, no noticeable threat of harm was evident to me. Here I was, a child of eight years old, but neither had I been educated about the inappropriateness of such behavior, which would have prepared me for this inappropriate contact and conduct.

Interestingly, I was captivated as she lay before me - this I do remember. Puberty was still years away from me; therefore, there was no measure of sexual arousal; even so, I was oblivious, ignorant, and innocent regarding her intentions as well - her sexual or fleshly urges.

I seem to vaguely remember that she had me touch her groin. She had clearly reached puberty and was pursuing physical stimulation – a child herself, merely around the age of twelve. I can recall no further of this drama. However, one thing is sure, this moment undoubtedly had some degree of far-reaching effects upon me, in the likes of which I may never fully comprehend.

The following state of affairs. Although not as alarming, yet troubling and a cause for concern if you are a parent. As I give thought to the matter, I see that consciousness of right and wrong behavior is now developing within me. It is only an assumption and not with a great deal of confidence. That I say something might have been mentioned to me regarding sex and sexual inappropriateness while I was developing as a boy. Or perhaps it was merely that my conscious toward appropriate and inappropriate behavior was manifesting within and directing me? God has indeed equipped us to know or feel from within a measure of right and wrong conduct that must be reinforced and built upon by parents through God's Word.

As for the next episode – and not the last. Again, I was relatively young – a fifth-grader, ten or eleven years old. I remember from this situation that a female classmate and I were alone in the office connecting to the music room. I do not recall whether we were sent to retrieve something from the room or we decided to sneak away from others. I do not remember, but we were likely sent on an errand by the teacher. Parents, nevertheless, we were not carefully monitored! There was a glass window to this office that allowed one to observe the activity in the adjoining classroom. We then knelt down to not be seen if someone came into the room. Conscious of our motives, we moved close enough to one another - face to face that we were touching bodily. As called in those days, what took place between her and I was "grinding" on one another. Clothed, we nevertheless caused our groins to press against one another, thereby experiencing the temporary pleasure that the pressure and close contact brought us. There we were, two fifth-graders (children) carrying on in such an inappropriate manner. Parents, are you listening?!

Now, I am reluctant to call my behavior learned due to the earlier experience encountered some three years prior with the older girl. Or perhaps better wording: That moment from my past had no known or apparent physiological or psychological effect upon me. My mind was not consciously on what I had experienced a few years earlier as I was now engaged with my classmate for the purpose of physical stimulation. Neither had I seen this kind of conduct beforehand ... Or had I? Is it possible that I could be wrong? Maybe the situation involving the older girl had subconsciously influenced me. Or maybe having experienced bodily arousal with another child while playing – the close contact also led to this behavior.

As for these females, the question can be asked ... Was their situation similar to mine? Had they, too, experienced something robbing them of their youthful innocence? Or could it have been for each of us? That we were simply acting or responding to the impulse of our lower nature? Or that each of us had experienced pleasurable sensations upon our bodies at some point? And therefore, merely being urged by our sense of fleshly pleasure (our lower nature), conducted ourselves in such a manner? Perhaps it was a combination of these things. Whatever it may have been, it is more than evident that neither of us was equipped to handle what our bodies were signaling for us to do. Parents must do a better job preparing and protecting their children from others, the influences of this world, as well as from themselves. Our foe - ourselves, that part of us that longs to operate through our corrupt nature residing within our flesh (Jeremiah 17:9).

Each story I shared was pre-puberty, yet they are retained in my mind. These occurrences, solidly fixed as stubborn stains, unmovable reminders of Sin's or Satan's powerful inner workings within and against one's heart and mind toward the destruction of all he can bring down. Nonetheless, such stains remind us of the workings of Satan's evil, our fallen condition, and from which life lessons can be learned unto spiritual awareness, maturity, and victory over sin and Satan.

In the next two situations, I am unsure if I had reached puberty; however, I was aware of my heightened physical sensitivity. The feeling seemed different than the time before as a fifth-grader ... hormonally, a transformation was occurring within me. Of these two stories, I am unsure of the order. I maintain that the situations involving the other girls and me - that each of us were victims. Victims, resulting from the ignorance of our parents on the subjects of spiritual and fleshly warfare ... their carelessness in monitoring us. And by not preparing us for life and therefore our carnal or base nature overtaking each of us.

Regarding the situation of the previous older sitter and the boy, they also fell victim to their sensual passions. Nevertheless, no one's actions are excusable before God. We are all born sinful. However, there is a matter of personal accountability. When we reach a certain age or level of maturity, not only does society hold us accountable for our actions but so does God. He knows our hearts and motives (1 Chronicles 28:9; Psalm 139:1). It is a parent's responsibility to prepare their child, make sure they understand acceptable behavior, administer corrective consequences because of love, and bring about acceptable behavior from their child. (Proverbs 22:6; Ephesians 6:4; Proverbs 19:18; Proverb 23:13; Proverbs 29:17).

Therefore, I submit that we must consider one's behavior and/or actions and the consequences of incorrect behavior against or according to their age, and perhaps even their upbringing ... either behavior learned through mere observation or that which they were taught. Now, I am not attempting to excuse bad conduct, my individual responsibility, and my accountability. I am simply acknowledging that everyone has a back story that needs to be considered before we cast judgment or throw stones (Matthew 23:23; James 2:13).

Me being more transparent: As I thought about sharing my next story, I will admit there was a measure of apprehension, shame, and regret relating to this situation – but not that of condemnation (Romans 8:1-11). The reason behind my feelings - the table had turned. I was now the older person ... I will presume by two years. The thought that kicked at me now as an adult looking back ... I should have known better.

I was the oldest of my siblings. As the elder child, my single mother had expectations of me; this was my responsibility to carry, whether I was truly prepared ... ready, or not. However, her directives had more to do with "do" and "do not," as opposed to Biblical details and explanations as to why this or why not that. I am not being critical of my mother; I am simply stating the reality of our home and many homes today. Nevertheless, this meant that because I was the elder, there was her assumption that I should know better regarding matters of proper conduct, no matter the situation. Should I or any child just know better because we have attained a certain age? How can a child know better regarding life issues if they have not been enlightened or adequately instructed? Read again, Proverb 22:6.

There are great dangers that await a child where parents or adults operate upon the assumption that their child or a child should know certain things or know better. Yet the child has not been instructed nor prepared on life matters nor that which is decent, orderly, or that which is better. If this guidance was needed for my generation – how much more is this to be the case in these current and uncertain times ... we are witnessing a massive failure to train ourselves as parents and to train up our children unto God, unto righteous or holy living.

For various reasons, I realize that many parents are sadly, even tragically, ill-equipped to parent their children intelligently and sufficiently according to the Word of God. If this cycle of relational breakdown is not headed off through Biblical literacy and living, the likelihood of perpetuating dysfunction within a family line is the logical end. Where there is no prevention or intervention through godly development, education, and awareness, bad choices are inevitable ... it is in our nature. Though evil working may not prevail through everyone, this does not dismiss or omit the fact that God is calling all to surrender to his teaching and Lordship - unto life eternal.

As for my actions with this younger female, how I was feeling, and how I later felt, I assume it had to do with the fact that the onset of puberty was at hand. And too, I was now more mindful of my body related to what I will describe as my physical awakening and my progression unto mental development and understanding. My thinking after the fact, which I believe was intuitive, was that I knew better. I felt within that my action was inappropriate. In other words, I experienced God's conviction through my conscious (not that I was personally aware of God), signaling to me my wrong behavior (John 8:9; Romans 2: 14,15). My further thinking on the matter: She was younger – certainly, she was not responsible for what occurred. I had reasoned that it was all on me simply because I was older.

However, sometime later, I recalled learning and hearing and observing the physical evidence that girls reached puberty, in many cases a year or more before males and that girls also matured faster mentally. And so, recalling the female's bodily awareness, her developing or awakening, manifesting before boys, now shared insight on the situation that I had not considered immediately following our encounter.

Though I was older, I could only consider my hormones' stirring and yearning. It was beyond my comprehension that this girl was also experiencing like passions. I could not fully comprehend what later became apparent ... she was equally involved and aroused. Now, the unfolding of this unfortunate, regretful, and what I believe avoidable occurrence. Avoidable when and where proper training and oversight are provided to a child.

As for what occurred, I recall the girl straddling my leg as we sat on the chair. She had been moving and positioning herself upon me to experience sexual stimulation; again, this did not readily register with me at the time. At that moment, it was only about what I was feeling or getting from her – sexual arousal as I sat there welcoming her every move. We then moved to the floor ... we were clothed while she sat on my lap, both of us being mutually stimulated sexually.

At my age, thirteen or thereabouts, I had no concept of the workings of the female body, let alone knowing that of my own. Needless to say, we were experiencing a measure of pleasure from one another. There we were, two kids separated by maybe a year or two of age. This should have never occurred! However, and this is saddening, I have been informed by those working in our middle schools and even elementary schools that kids are more sexually aware and even sexually involved. We clearly have a flesh problem resulting from sin, spiritual deficiency, or better yet, spiritual death, and the lack of or absence of godly home training and rearing.

At that moment, I could not say for sure if it was the girl's intent to arouse me. She could not have possibly known that she was evoking such a response within me – or did she? Surely, she was only attempting to pleasure herself, as I was merely her instrument for sexual stimulation, as she was for me and nothing more – right? We shall see!

There was no noticeable physiological or biological response within me involving the older girl while on the bed with her, no anticipation or knowledgeable participation regarding sexuality. Visually I was captivated because she lay naked before me and had hair down there. That was the extent of things ... I had never seen anything like this. The table is now turned. The difference, however, was there was a conscious consensus I now know between the younger girl and me – she was receiving the satisfaction she desired, and I too was benefitting – a "win-win," so it seemed at the time. However, this is always a losing situation for children.

Nevertheless, our sad and wrong predicament would evolve while dangerously devolving. I knew nothing of this female's upbringing. Nonetheless, considering her participation, knowing what to do and even what to say speaks to her potentially troubling reality that she had already experienced, sexual introduction. Tragically, so many young and the vulnerable have been subjected to sexual content and have been victims of indecent liberties or even sexual molestation.

As for this female and me, somehow, we agreed to escalate our activity; how things came about is beyond my recall. Moving from where we were, we went to a more secluded location. I remember her lying on the floor with her pants and panties partially down. Pulling my pants partially down, I lay on top of her. There was no vaginal penetration. I did not know what I was doing ... Thank God!

Even as I now reflect upon this occurrence, it does not make sense considering my lack of sexual experience or hers, this being my assumption, that we ended up where we were. Where did such an idea come from? Was there an accumulation of wrongful experiences that led to where this girl and I found ourselves? Were there other indirect or direct occurring factors that now escape my memory or the order in which I recall my past? Or was it simply biology doing what it does? Just the same: How did I ... how did we get to such a disturbing place regarding our fleshly and sinful behavior ... while we were just kids?

Neither of us knew what we were doing and certainly not the potential consequences of our actions. However, bodily things felt good; that was all that mattered, even though we knew our behavior was inappropriate ... I certainly did. Our carrying-on did not last long at all. As the girl lay on the floor with me on top of her, she responded, "That's enough." This ended the one and only encounter we shared of this nature. I can only assume that we went back to whatever we were doing beforehand. Other than sharing this story with my wife, sharing it in this book is the only time this situation has been mentioned.

I have documented these disturbing and unfortunate experiences so that you may become a better parent and even more watchful. As well - for you to search within yourself and your past, perhaps discovering why you may think and act the way you do. You might just find some things about yourself and your history that may prove beneficial as you seek to better yourself and those around you.

From this partial look into my past. The vulnerability of the young has been glaringly brought to your attention – and so, we must do better at protecting our children's innocence! There is no doubt that many of you can relate to my story ... Statistics say you can. Prayerfully you are not in bondage to your past; if by chance you are – it is time to come out!

Let me be perfectly clear, I was not raised by uncaring parents, even by the one I called dad before he divorced the family. Neither was I placed in bad situations or raised in a bad environment. My mother was as protective of her children as any good mother regarding recognizable dangers. And yet, I had experiences that I should not have had, an all-too-common occurrence for far too many children.

My formative years were those of the seventies through the eighties. Affectionately called the "good ole days" for those who grew up on the east coast, my hometown - The Bull City, Durham, North Carolina. However, technology and more provocative entertainment began invading our homes during this time. This outside influence competed with parents' conventional wisdom – a new problem was dawning before the family. However, these new forces went unnoticed, or their pull or lure was underestimated. Additionally, although drugs could be found for those involved in that lifestyle ... a new drug - crack cocaine, began to sweep over our nation in the late 1980s – a tremendous force wrecking many lives and families. We must keep in mind this is Satan's primary objective ... to wreck our lives!

These mediums: Media, technology, and drugs, have brought with or through them severe consequences and changes to our culture and way of life. What our children face and what the adults are struggling with is alarming, if not horrifying. And believe me – the worst is yet to come! However, as a Christian, you should not be caught unaware, surprised, or ill-prepared.

We must stand ready to do spiritual battle (Ephesians 6:12; Job 2:2)!

A Time of Self Awareness - A Time of awakening

A walk down memory lane should not only reflect on the good times, but it should also accompany other experiences as well. From these experiences, we become aware of who we are and why we have become who we are. With greater clarity, one can then understand their history and better share their complete story. This is what I have done by giving you a glimpse into my youthful past. Bear in mind: that those experiences early in your life do not define you. However, they can certainly affect your view of others and how you view yourself.

Resulting of my experiences: if not for the grace of God, my life's path could have certainly been much different than how things currently are for me. *Oh, for the grace and mercy of God!* No doubt, many of you can very well shout praises to God as you express the same sentiment.

During our formative and vulnerable years. And also well into adulthood. We are instinctively governed or directed through or from our desire for exploration, which is prompted by our inward driving. This making is by God's design, which ultimately is to stir and steer man to seek after God, our Creator. Hear what King David says in Psalms 42: 2: *"My soul thirsted for God, for the living God: when shall I come and appear before God?"*

This is also the human dilemma apart from God – we are never fulfilled with only what this world offers. Therefore, we often find our lives to be meaningless, empty, and void no matter what we amass or experience in this world during our sojourn and many explorations.

As innate Expeditioners, children constantly explore life around them and collect data through their senses, processing and attempting to understand the information received. Resulting from these bits and pieces of data gathered throughout a day. Their senses and brains are stimulated while their minds develop and shape their worldview based on collected data.

Through this process of discovering and collecting data while performing rudimentary scientific research, they become aware of their surroundings and themselves. Through processing and studying the information gathered, they discover their likes and dislikes - that which bring satisfaction and dissatisfaction, among other things. This is God's design for man and the very way we become aware of ourselves and the environment in which we live.

However, within our fallen nature, we are all prone to overstep the boundaries of our exploration, venturing into areas that can and will be to our detriment. Whether in ignorance of the danger(s) presented or in spite of them, many cross over into forbidden territories and often remain because of seemingly, some measure of pleasure or satisfaction experienced. While others find it difficult to remove from the situation after recognizing the danger(s) because of its stronghold ... the satisfaction provided while there, hence its powerful grip or influence over them. They, therefore, find within themselves insufficient strength to remove themselves from the situation they ventured into. Or to resist the sinful pleasure granted to them while venturing into the forbidden.

My mind just quickly carried me to the story of Sodom and Gomorrah. Read it for yourself, beginning with chapter eighteen of the book of Genesis, with attention given to Lot's wife in chapter nineteen. You will see that the city had a grip on her. One of many such stories provided for us from the Bible by which to learn about sin's stronghold.

Naturally, a child and even adults, who, by the way, should have more common sense than a child. Will do what we are designed to do: explore and discover those things or situations and experiences that bring bodily or sensory awareness and satisfaction. We are constantly in exploration mode, in pursuit of the next happy. Or that which brings us satisfaction or a measure of fulfillment, even if it's fleeting.

Mankind if pushed, prodded, enticed, and incited from within through our sinful nature. If one's urges intensify and one gives themselves over to their passions. The search for self-gratification will become the means to their end. The be-all and end-all. That end?... To seek out and experience self-satisfaction, no matter the cost, while giving little thought to the price to pay when partnering with sin.

During one's explorations, danger awaits us where there are no internal boundaries. Or they are blurred, thereby not providing a clear warning of things off-limits. Or the internal signage threatening prosecution for the trespasser is not signaling properly within the explorer. Or, indicating that danger is ahead ... Enter at your own risk.

We do not have to learn from the experience of becoming a trespasser. Or from making hard beds that we then must lay on. Or from touching the fire to see if we will get burned. The Bible is sufficient to teach us in all matters, directing our steps and conduct to avoid the consequences of overstepping the boundaries or wandering into prohibited sinful territory that will cost us dearly.

Without the guiding principles provided within the Bible, God's established boundaries found therein - given to keep us safe. And without oversight and instruction from our Great and Loving Shepherd ... like sheep, we are prone to wander, unaware, into dangerous territories. This is precisely what occurred with me and the other children I have mentioned. Through our ignorance, having not been adequately shepherded and protected by our parents, we crossed the boundaries and into forbidden territory. Even so, adults committing trespassing, who you would think should know better, can and often do overstep boundaries if they do not remain watchful and within the guiding care and protection of the Good Shepherd - Jesus.

There are times or stages throughout a child's life when they reach a higher level of cognitive development, thereby better recognizing right and wrong or acceptable behavior. This does not mean that the child will choose to do the right thing by knowing or having been instructed on what is right from wrong. We see this with adults as well.

As previously mentioned, approaching puberty, my awareness or consciousness regarding appropriate behavior became more astute and apparent. I can only speculate as to when I actually reached puberty. I will also presume more enlightenment followed post-puberty.

Single mothers with sons and ladies in general. I am now operating under the assumption that you have no idea what I am talking about; I will therefore elaborate on male puberty. Puberty has matured in a boy when he experiences what is commonly referred to as a "wet dream," meaning your son unexpectedly ejaculates semen while asleep. He awakes or not to find his underwear wet from semen that was involuntarily released. It could have also dried during his sleep. Or this experience occurring at other times, with or without an erection. This is not to be associated with masturbation. Your son's body is naturally and simply signaling that your man-child is now capable of reproduction… he is no longer a mere boy, perhaps still your baby, but he is entering into manhood.

It is saddening and unfortunate for adolescent boys to experience ejaculation, or a girl her menstrual, where they have no idea what is happening. Mothers, now this should not occur with you and your son. I have given you something to think about; surely, you will act accordingly regarding your developing son. If you feel ill-equipped or reluctant to engage your son on the topic, get a respected man to get it done for you. If he is not a family member, I encourage you to sit in on the meeting or know what he intends to share with your son beforehand. And if this is not an option. Then my sisters, equip yourself with knowledge on this matter so that your son may know what to expect as his body transitions from boy to adolescence … it is essential that you follow through with informing your son of his status change and this life-changing occurrence.

I do not recall having this conversation with my mom, who was now a single parent at this point in my maturity. Nonetheless, at this point in my young adolescent life, I am aware of the change that has come upon me.

Ladies, as for another takeaway or what I want you to grasp from your male child's bodily transformation: The comparative spiritual parallel… His spiritual transformation, its significance, his status change, and evolution from boy to man. Both aspects of your son, his spiritual and bodily evolution or maturation, should be co-occurring.

Many parents fail to prepare or instruct their children on the subject matter of their physical maturity. However, I'm convinced … far greater is the number of parents who fail most miserably at partnering their child's spiritual and physical development while instructing or leading them. To be intentional about this pairing or the holistic development of your child is to guard them against venturing and veering off into sexual trappings and other lurking and crouching dangers.

And for that child who learns to embrace and love and trust Jesus in preadolescence or when they are younger, their life and your parenting them may not be trouble and carefree. However, because they have chosen to become one with Jesus, they are safe in His arms. And therefore, I am firmly convinced that they are much better off than those who are not one with Jesus!

* * *

Before puberty, I was aware of myself, but only partly. As I could not comprehend, nor was I informed of the internal working within me that was transitioning or transforming me from boy to man. However, subsequent to puberty. I was awakened, but only partly to this mystery or change that I could not comprehend through only being self-aware… That part of me that can be readily seen – my physical self. Nevertheless, this transition would usher me into a new or broader self, even a new position within my earthly existence and ordering …From boy to manhood!

The Bible speaks of the mysteries or hidden or spiritual things of God. They were prophesied or spoken to God's people as things that were to come to fulfillment or maturity at God's appointed time. However, these mysteries' deeper meaning or understanding was hidden from their grasp. The Israelites were aware or only knew their loving God in part. It was vaguely understood that His eternal redemptive plan was unfolding. Or being worked out through them on behalf of all of humanity.

A *personal relationship* with God and the fullness of God's redemptive plan for and through them for humanity could not be understood because of spiritual blindness or spiritual ignorance. They could not conceive their needed new spiritual condition and position as only seen and provided by God. They could not comprehend spiritual renewal – they first had to be awakened or brought to spiritual enlightenment or God's revelation of this truth or reality.

The prophet Isaiah spoke these words regarding God and the Israelites, "For the LORD hath poured out upon you the spirit of deep sleep, and hath closed your eyes: the prophets and your rulers, the seers hath he covered (Isaiah 29:10; Romans chapter 11).

The Apostle Paul, in his writing, expresses the following on God's timing or His providence and prerogative, "But when the fullness of time was come, God sent forth His Son, (Jesus) made of a woman, made under the law, to redeem them that were under the law that they might receive the adoption of son" (spiritual sons and daughters) (Galatians 4: 4, 5; Ephesians 1: 9-14).

Also, hear the prophetic utterance of Simeon, "For mine eyes have seen thy salvation, which thou hast prepared before the face of all people; a light to lighten the Gentiles and the glory of thy people Israel (Luke 2: 30 -32). These were Simeon's words as he beheld the Christ-child – the foretold and promised Messiah. Though obscured from the understanding of many at God's appointed time or in the fullness of time, He broke through the darkness of this world, bringing forth spiritual enlightenment or awakening. He came to open blinded eyes by offering new birth and even spiritual maturity to all who would receive the inward regeneration or transformation that mysteriously and wondrously results from the indwelling of His Spirit (John 1:11).

As it is in the natural, so is it for the spiritual. We are to mature from being babes and mere boys and girls and grow spiritually as adults (Hebrew 5:11-14; 1Peter 2:2). That we may expand our awareness and awaken to the new possibilities and greater potential God has purposed for us all.

Those who are mature in the Lord, we have the incredible responsibility of telling those of this world, and even the babes in Christ, that an extraordinary transformation awaits them. Tell them that through spiritual maturation, they will truly come to know themselves in view of how God sees them and that which He has desired for them. Let them know that their spiritual maturation will reach its fullness, not perfection, as they remain in the care and instructions of that Great Shepherd of the sheep (Psalms 23; Psalms 84:11; Matthew 7: 7-11).

Father - His Designation Alone

Puberty now upon me, my body and its passions were fully shaken from slumber - as to say, "Boy, wake-up, welcome to manhood," of which I knew little about.

Unfortunately, there was no godly male presence in my life to give me guidance during these years. The man whose last name I carry, who I only knew as my dad at the time. Although a good-hearted man had divorced the family that bore his name - Scott. As I was about to enter high school, I was told my dad was not my biological father. My mother thought it was necessary to reveal this information to me, as I would likely encounter family members – females in particular, who I did not know.

[Regarding my biological father, this story takes a twist. I discovered this after completing my writing of this book. However, my book had not been published. Resulting from taking a DNA test, the results provided me a new history that I had not anticipated. This matter will be addressed in a later book.]

It should go without saying: Both parents (husband and wife) are needed to effectively raise a child. Can a single parent raise a child who can be considered a productive citizen? By all means! My mother did! Nonetheless, God's design is for there to be the Father... leading as head of his household. A Mother, although ontologically equal to her husband. However, she must honorably carry out her responsibilities in submission to and subordinate to her husband. Where there are children, they too share in the same ontological equality with mother and father; nonetheless, in their position, subordinate to both parents. This is the order God has established within a Christ-centered home (Ephesians 5:22-33; 6:1- 4).

When a parent, in this case, the father, is absent from their child's life. So is the insight and identity that the father has been purposed by God to impart and imprint within and upon their child. A child's identity ... particularly that of a male child, is established by the father. Additionally, the child has information or understanding to be gleaned as they observe the roles and operations of two parents working together to bring harmony and establish balance in the home. And so, in a godly home. We are to have two biologically different parents ... ontological equals that complement one another and complete God's purpose for the family.

A child's life's lessons are to be established upon the principles of God, which are to be lived out before them, as modeled by their godly, however not perfect, parents. A child is to come to know the character of God. At the same time, parents display godliness through their activity and interaction, one with the other and their child. From such intimacy displayed in the home, the child understands balance or compromise, love, discipline, selflessness, cooperation, and harmony within the marriage as well, for the home.

Where a parent (dad) is out of place, the fulfillment and fullness of such bonding and understanding of family and *team* cannot be wholly grasped. Subsequently, there is left a void, a hole in the soul of a child as they are incomplete where a parent is unaccounted for. How is a child adversely affected, and to what degree? … only time will tell. Make no mistake about it; there will be adverse effects. Where there is single parenting, the child's support system, through family, friends, and other positive outlets, will be essential to their overall well-being. However, this does not eliminate the questions a child will likely have resulting from a parent's absence. Or removing the void or longing a child may have for the parent - daddy.

There are numerous single parents - mothers in particular, who have done a tremendous job raising their child (ren) in the father's absence; however, as for those who argue. And some adamantly that both parents are not needed to raise a child must understand that this is an ungodly and unhealthy viewpoint, no matter how one arrived at that thinking. God has purposed that both parents be united as one through marriage when a child is conceived and reared. As Christians, we must always promote this unity before our children and those of this world, no matter what is occurring all around us. Or even unforeseen occurrences that may later unfold in your life, rendering you a single parent. As for a single Christian parent who may be doing an exceptional job raising their child(ren). Just the same, your child needs to know what God has intended for the structure or order of a family.

Parent and potential parent … it may be that you were hurt by your dad or mom in some way. Maybe you were raised by a single parent, or perhaps your husband (man) left you, or your wife ran out on the marriage. Although you may be bitter because of your hurt or let-down. You cannot neglect your child by instilling in them that single parenting is somehow acceptable or normal.

Yes, life happens; breakups and divorces occur; however, this was not in the plan of God (Matthew 19: 4 – 6).

Relationships that break apart are the result of broken people, resulting from the sin of rebellion committed by Adam and Eve, thereby creating personal abnormalities of all sorts. It can be rightly stated that sin or the *fall* has rendered humanity mentally and emotionally ill. Eve was gifted to Adam that they may be eternally one – this was to be the norm. When we choose to unite or become one with the *New Adam – Jesus*, though we are not perfect, we become renewed or regenerated. Where one remains in Jesus and He in us, we mature as Christians and are strengthened to face and overcome whatever challenges this life brings our way.

As I write this book, my age is fifty-two … even now, there are times I long for the guiding presence of my dad, but not as much. The story I am about to share, I have shared numerous times to help others understand a child's void and longing for daddy when he is missing from his child's life. At various points in my life, stretching from my twenties into my thirties, that longing was greater. I will share more details in the next book I intend to write. I am considering the title, or that of a title for a chapter, 'I Too Want My Daddy.' I will now present the short version of the story or experience.

Sitting alone in my vehicle, I am at the intersection, waiting for the red light to change so I may proceed home to an empty house. As I sat there, coming from within my soul - a loud cry, "I Want My Daddy!" I do not recall what I was actually wrestling or dealing with at the time. Whatever it was, I felt that if my daddy were present, whatever it was that I needed, he would have been able to make everything ok. But I had no such luxury. My dad was absent from my life, and neither did I have a positive male to call on.

I experienced a similar occurrence when I was twenty-one years old. And at that time, I was trying to find my identity and way in life, again without a father. This experience was more intense, and my longing for Dad was greater! This longing brought forth deep anguish within my soul. The agony associated with this profound yearning for my daddy was unbearable. I called the moment, *My Graveyard Experience*. Here again, I will not go into full detail.

This period in my life was one of such loneliness and uncertainty that I found myself amongst the deceased - standing alone in a graveyard. I was alone and even fatherless as I stood there. This was my thinking, not realizing that the one my soul cried out to and truly longed for was nearer than what I could have conceived during this period and uncertain crossroad in my life.

As for my takeaway from this agonizing experience: Ladies, no disrespect or slighting of your efforts. You are adored, greatly appreciated, and given the utmost respect by me. However, hear me, my well-meaning sisters! You being created "Woman" no matter how well you are seemingly getting the job done raising your offspring. Or how well you got the job done as a single parent. You can never stand in the place of a man - a child's father. This should go without saying. But sadly, there is a need to say this for such times as these.

Look, no matter how you arrive at such reasoning … it is nonsensical for a mother to say that she is or was both the mommy and daddy, with some women desiring to be celebrated on both Mother's Day and Father's Day. Though you are or were a strong and determined woman, carrying the load meant for two and handled business and getting things done – for this, I applaud, celebrate you, and even give you a standing ovation! You deserve to be recognized and honored! However, the place of man or a father's title is not yours to claim … God did not give either to you. You are a Woman – maybe even an extraordinary woman! So wear this mantle honorably.

Consider this, my sisters. Such an attitude or position against God's design is unacceptable to our Creator, who created us male and female. Look, I understand where you are coming from – that you put in WORK to raise your child(ren) alone! Nevertheless, you are - Woman. My wife and I did it together; I remember the work we put in together as a team – it was work indeed! I can, therefore, only begin to imagine the effort required of you to get the job done as a single parent – I get it! Much respect and Kudos, but do not pervert God's truth or confuse your children with such an erroneous claim.

It is perfectly fine for you to acknowledge the strength and determination - the grace which God enabled or is enabling you with to make things happen for your household. Call yourself - "Wonder Woman," even "Super Woman," or anything else to associate you with your accomplishments and fortitude if you like. However, attaching the male gender or masculine expression to who you are is to attack and diminish the efficacy of the office or position the male was created to uphold.

When a woman embraces such assertions or assumes such an assumption. Subtle it is, or oblivious you may be. Nevertheless, this ideology or undercurrent of thinking and speech works at undercutting and eroding the God-given status that a man is to inherently hold. Even so, such thinking or wording is working to dismantle God's ordering for the family. Just look at the deception of Satan as he works through such ignorance in thought and, too, one's pride leading to the destruction of God's design for the family.

Ladies. I realize that more than a few men have helped create this hostile atmosphere held within your thinking. Even the intense feelings that many of you may have against my brothers who have fallen short of their charge to be "Real-Men," or better yet, God-honoring and godly fathers. As a woman of God, you are not to perpetuate the already dire, even bleak, predicament of Black men in particular by demeaning them and diminishing their role and authority by seeking to claim their title or position. In doing so, there really is not much difference between what you are doing and what Eve did. She disrespected and disregarded her headship or the man, and so are some of you.

Ladies, your words or the position some bitterly hold toward neglectful men or your child(ren) daddy. Has helped to create an atmosphere in the home and culture within the thinking of our youth, to disregard or think less of men (their dads) and male figures in general and even to disrespect those males who hold authority.

It must be understood that where one is operating against the will or purpose of God, whether in action or through speech, they become agents of death as they perform Satan's task of destruction. Too many Christians, unaware or resulting from ignorance, are guilty of such behavior. Life and death are indeed in the power of the tongue; therefore, we must be mindful of how and what we speak (Proverbs 15: 2; 18: 21; James 3:6).

I believe it is crucial for a single mother when it becomes appropriate or necessary to do so, to share with her child the consequences of a father who is absent from the home or the child's life - no matter the reason for the father not being there for them. I am urging you to do this as it helps the child to understand the challenges before you as a single parent; it gives you the opportunity to assess your child's feelings and views regarding the situation, as well as reassure them that they were not or are not the cause for their father not being there for them. Furthermore, allowing you to better assess how to move forward in this most challenging situation.

Regarding what to say? Consider the matter beforehand. Then compassionately and lovingly share how or why things became as they are for the home with your child. As difficult as it may be - honesty wins out, be faithful and true to your child. The temptation to share the events of what occurred in your favor must be avoided. Where you can shoulder responsibility, be sure to own it. Apologize to your child for your failure by not doing things God's way. I believe this will hold weight with your child. As well - greater respect gained towards you as they learn and grow from this painful and unfortunate situation you have chosen to address.

Share with your child so that they can, in fact, learn and grow. Even so, their healing beginning that they may become productive children of God's Kingdom and thereby breaking the pattern of failed relationships.

CHAPTER 6

The Awakening

Biologically, I had been stirred from the slumber of boyhood. It was time to awaken so that I may be ushered into this new phase of life - adolescence. It cannot be said that this natural occurrence was forced upon me; just the same, it presented itself and required a radical change within me. It gave no consideration as to whether I was mentally ready - or not, for this elevation in biological status. At this point in a boy's life, a dad needs to be actively engaged with their son – no exception! I am not suggesting that the father's role is less important at other stages of a boy's development. But here, in their son's rise to adolescence, the father's involvement is essential. It is his God-given role and responsibility to shepherd his son during this critical season of his life that is bringing his son into biological manhood.

It should go without saying the significance of both parent's active and complementary involvement in a child's life should be ever-present. However, it is readily observed that mothers are generally more hands-on and nurturing during the early years of a child's life. Some will say, even until the child leaves home ... if they ever leave. This will likely serve to be counter-productive for the child's development.

However, when that male child has been awakened by puberty, a single mother may have an extremely difficult time raising her teenage son. She may find herself attempting to fill a dad's role and dealing with her man-child in the likes she was not purposed to handle nor designed by her Creator by which to involve herself.

Because the child is coming into his fuller self or, as often stated, "smelling himself," he will likely begin to flex or challenge his mother's default headship and authority. He will start crossing boundaries she could not have imagined her baby boy would have attempted just a few years earlier. Even while just a toddler, he pushed and crossed the boundaries. However, such activity can be easily overlooked or not understood when the child is so young, cute, and seemingly innocent of all wrongdoing. Yes, he is "just being a boy." But there are profound implications when it is not recognized that the child is actually rebelling against his mother's authority, as he pushes to test the established limitations by his mother before deciding to cross those boundaries.

My mother experienced this with me. Yes, I flexed! However, she knew how to flex back! The belt or a threatening tongue-lashing was her response. One time she felt it necessary to engage me with an extension cord. Although that was excessive, I guess my action on that night and her fear drove her to such an extreme. This is not the case with some mothers, meaning those who will flex. Or who knows how to flex when challenged by their son. But, neither should they willingly enter or allow themselves to be put in this position where they have to become or attempt to be the muscle over their adolescent son. Though a mother may be forced to flex back to counter her son's disregard for her authority, this does not mean she will get the desired results or response from the child of her womb.

Plain and simple … my mother's husband – God's designated head of the home; my daddy should have kept his wife from this unnatural, uncomfortable position of having to flex or attempt to shepherd his son and household. This is what I did for my wife … I shepherded our home. My wife seriously disciplining our sons or having to flex was not her responsibility – it was mine. Where daddy is present, the mother's role as disciplinarian should be minimum. On the other hand, mom, where there needs to be a swift and immediate correction of your child, you should not hesitate to bring order, as you require your child to submit to your authority … you are second in command. And where a child is of the age of understanding, they should also know that they will then have to answer to their daddy as well (Proverbs 13:24; 22:15; 23:13-15; 29:15,17; Ephesians 6:1- 4; Hebrews 12:5-11).

My mother, as a single parent, was raising four other children during my season of awakening. The youngest child, a baby, and me, the oldest, at around fifteen, and I was "smelling myself." The thought of such a predicament for my mom or any single parent is distressing for me. Yet, by the grace of God and much-needed flexing from my mother, she managed to get things done the best way she knew how – my mother was a "Wonder Woman!" She was determined to have obedient and respectful children. This was no easy task! I believe her greatest challenge came with me and then her youngest child because my mother was now an older woman as my youngest sister matured. When my youngest sister was coming of age, times were swiftly changing with the onslaught of media's anti-family, antiauthority, and even antichrist messaging.

By no means did we come through this time of fatherlessness unscathed as a family. I will not attempt to point out issues that I have observed. But each of us was negatively affected in various manners and degrees because the head of the home – that godly man ... daddy, and husband was out of place. When God's ordering for our lives and the family are disregarded, we have absent fathers and mothers. When a husband or his wife doesn't function in their perspective role as assigned and instructed by our Creator, there are such disorders as "Passive male syndrome." For the mother, "Displaced role syndrome" ... because her husband is not leading his home as a strong godly man. Or she is an overly headstrong woman. And for the child, "Confused child syndrome" ... because his or her mother is overbearing and their dad soft. Or even effeminate. And this is not a complete list of the syndromes or mental health ailments.

Look, no parent should willingly and wantonly embrace the idea of becoming a single or unwed parent. It does not mean things will work out favorably for you because things seemingly worked out for my mother's household. Or another single parent with whom you may be acquainted. And neither are you likely to know the half of their story and struggles faced as a single parent.

Take heed to my passionate warning! Do not allow yourself or your baby to be without a godly head – a God-honoring husband and father! The hellish consequence of the godly man's absence is all around us! Therefore heed the warnings!

Resuming with other memories from my adolescent years. During these occurrences, my age was perhaps between eleven and fourteen. This time from 1976 to 1979, there may have been 4 television networks to choose from before the arrival of cable television. Before cable, I will classify television shows and entertainment viewing as either G or PG-rated. PG-rated shows were not graphic but consisted of such shows as soap operas, science-fiction, action, and western flicks. And Friday-night wrestling, which concluded the final hour (12 o'clock pm) of viewing television shows before the networks signed off the air. Leaving viewers with a "snow screen" and an annoying hissing sound until the networks resumed airing the following day.

Then came the buzz and excitement of cable network viewing. This allowed for twenty-four-hour television viewing and shows or "entertainment" to be viewed by "adults only." I say this with reservation. My reason - immorality had not been welcomed into the homes, as now would be the case with cable networks. Many homes were unprepared and incapable of handling such viewing. These shows were and are designed to heighten the emotions and passions of their viewers. It is all about ratings for the industry – and these ratings generate revenue. And yes - getting high ratings at any cost. So the Bible is correct in saying, "For the love of money is the root of all evil" (1 Timothy 6:10). And this evil of all sorts can be viewed twenty-four seven on our televisions!

At a crucial juncture in my adolescent development, I would meet face to face with what I believe is the most effective medium used by Satan in the twentieth century to share mass information, thoughts, and views – cable television. Television through cable viewing was capable of presenting the highest degree and volume of immorality known to our modern age.

My mother shared with me this bit of information as I was preparing to write this piece. She stated that she decided to remove cable networking from our home after seeing material she did not want her children to see. When this actually occurred is unknown. Needless to say, she had moved too late to protect me.

One night I was watching Home Box Office (HBO). I have no idea the name of the movie that I was watching. However, this moment I spent face to face with the television has not escaped my memory. My hormones were awakening from sleep, if not fully alert, by the time I stumbled into this new exposure to visual sensuality and sexual stimulation offered by HBO. Through my eye gates, which were fixated upon the shower scene that was being acted out before me. I absorbed the image of the woman who was intensely stirring my curiosity and fleshly passions.

The scene pictured a blonde hair, white female showering. It was unlike anything I had ever seen on television or anywhere for that matter. It was as if I was inside the shower. Or desired to be, as the camera was situated in such a way to bring me up close and personal with the woman. Water was streaming from the showerhead, and flowing down her naked body, as she bathed herself sensually. I seem to recall that a light mist from the hot steamy water also permeated the shower.

As it was designed to do, the scene began to pull me mentally and physically deeper into the erotic drama, stirring my passions, unlike anything I had previously experienced. Then the instrumentation and precise beats incorporated to further enhance the already passionate scene caused the moment to become more intense! This pulsating beat, accompanying the action of this dazzling woman, aided in this experience being etched or engraved in my mind. However, the drama was yet unfolding, as the moment was about to be sexually heightened, taking me with it to a different level of sensual tension and intensity.

This indecent and prohibited scene was no doubt appealing to my fleshy or lower nature. The operation of sin was at work from without. That from within my body, sin may ensnare me through the lust of my flesh and imagination. I have come to realize this as the primary tactic of Satan, that through demonic influences, whatever the medium, to excite our fleshly appetites so that he may accomplish his mission of entrapping the weak or deepening the pit that one may already be in due to sexual sin or whatever the sinful trappings of our minds and bodies.

The television had presented to me this woman in her naked splendor. She not only was off-limit but inappropriately displayed – just the same, my eyes were captivated, and so was the rest of me. Unexpectedly, entering the shower with the woman was this intruder. He was never seen by the woman – as he had no physical form. I am not sure if he was a so-called ghost, demon, or whatever. How fitting that an evil spirit is presented via television and even influencing me, although I had the slightest idea, as I share this part of my life and the operation of Satan through his demonic forces and their influence upon humanity.

Unknown to the woman, he had entered the shower; however, he was about to make his presence known. This is how sin traps many of us: we are unaware of its lurking about. Or we do not heed the warnings of his nearness, and we find ourselves in sin's enticing and violent grasp.

This formless entity then began to have its way with the woman sexually. The instrumentation reflected the build-up and climax of the scene. This was obvious as the instrumentation and the beat were enhanced, corresponding with the actions and movement, the expressions and sounds made by the woman, clearly indicating that sexual intercourse was occurring. As the encounter was nearing its end, so did the instrumentation.

I do not know how long this scene carried on. Nonetheless, it was long, dramatic, and even climactic enough to excite a boy of my age beyond anything I had ever experienced. From such viewing, children need protection. And beforehand, prepared for their awakening and warned about the spiritual darkness that desires to seduce and keep them in bondage to its dark, deceitful, and destructive ways.

As I considered this experience of the shower scene while writing this book, I noticed how this movie segment presented a striking equivalent to Satan or his demonic agent's encroachment into the lives of many. The similarity is worth taking a closer look at. One may be attending to their own affairs, not caring, or oblivious to the happenings or dangers lurking around. Vulnerable is one to Satan's influences, who is selfishly preoccupied with only their personal or earthly well-being. In one sense, Satan already has this person, as they are unaware of their sinful condition and spiritual reality. One who is unaware of the spiritual realm and its evil operations, that evil realm which is against them or their sin nature within. One then does not realize the need to be prayed up, studied up, churched up, guarded up, and even kept up by God, that they may be able to withstand and guard against the wiles and dangers of the waiting Evil one – Satan (Ephesians 6:10 - 18).

It is easy for demonic influences to seize upon one; infiltrate their mind, thereby violating them as they live under sin's forceful and relenting advances. Therefore, we are to be watchful, prayerful, not forsaking the spiritual disciplines or practices of the Christian faith that enables one to be on guard and aware of the devices and tricks of the Devil, who has waged war against God and mankind whom he longs to destroy!

It should now be more than evident that Satan does not consider the age of those he desires to violate or annihilate ... His thinking is, "The younger, the better!" For a child, their first line of defense is their parents. Sadly many parents are failing miserably in this respect. Fathers, you must rise up; you must fulfill your mandate to be men of God, shepherds, and protectors of your homes!

During my youth, I had no awareness of those matters regarding the spiritual, let alone that of my bodily or biological awakening. It also appears to me that my generation as a whole was not as "churched" or God inclined, in tune, or spiritually mature as the generation of our parents and their parents. Tragically, today's generation is worse off than mine.

As for me, church attendance did not occur until I joined Mt. Level Missionary Baptist Church in 1986. I was twenty-one years of age. Regarding global church attendance, unfortunately, some studies show an increase in those who are falling away from the church or corporate worship here in the west. The light of the church or her influence seems to be dimming. Though darkness is advancing from without and from within man, make no mistake about it – the Light of the church shall never be put out. God is yet in control (John 1:5)!

Awakened Into the Darkness

Puberty, my biological awakening now upon me, accompanied by the experiences of my preadolescent dark past, no doubt I was quite vulnerable to sexual sin and fleshly gratification. This natural or sinful wickedness or perversion residing within my soul was heightened due to the awakening of my also natural or biological changes and its emergence. I was left unprotected, untrained, and my passions unrestrained as a mere boy. This is a recipe for a disastrous outcome for boys! Or even someone's daughter, this being of their own making or by the efforts of such boys! And then these boys grow up to be men – here speaking only in terms of their biological and numerological designation. Something to ponder – right?

The man I knew as my dad, whose occupation was a long-distance truck driver, had now divorced himself from our family and was living his "new life" with his new wife and child born from this union. He would occasionally visit my two siblings he fathered and my other sibling (a sister), whom he also adopted, along with me upon marrying my mother. As a pre-teen or youthful teenager, I traveled and worked with him, I believe, for two consecutive summers. This period in my life was when I needed him most … and more than I realized at the time.

I describe my dad as a "man's – man!" He was caring and loving and a physical specimen not to be challenged. He demanded respect! For one to cross the line or disrespect him, they would immediately be made aware of the fact! Caswell Scott possessed great qualities as a dad and husband. However, looking back, I would say that he had conflict within his soul, as he also was raised without his dad. As I seem to recall, his mother, when I was a child, would occasionally drink. She also sold alcohol from her home and did not take any mess from anyone. She could be called a "hell-raiser," indicative of her struggles and brokenness, her need for healing, and a loving relationship with the Father.

What positives I learned from my dad were from what I observed. Such as the lovingly playful interactions between him and my mother and his interaction with us children before he decided to forsake his family. He truly had a kind and loving disposition, but his soul was in conflict. His departure from the home would come when a father should be grooming his son (me) for manhood, as puberty was knocking at the door and demanding me to wake up.

The only counsel, if I can call it that, which I recall receiving from him as I was transitioning or being biologically awakened, was, "Don't be gay." I did not respond. I was more surprised and puzzled by his comment. The statement was irrelevant to me, as I really did not fully grasp that lifestyle; besides, my interest was only in females – as if there was an alternative.

However, four decades later, many are now openly embracing and accepting this lifestyle. Now I understand the reason he made the comment, "Don't be gay." Should my dad have said more to me on this matter of sexual relations? Emphatically – yes! However, he was not raised in the church; what more could he offer? Before his untimely death, sadly, I cannot say that he had accepted Jesus as his Lord and Savior. This really concerned me following his tragic work-related demise. He was only thirty-five years old. He was survived by five children and at least one other son, who we later discovered after my dad's passing. This child was from another woman.

Before moving on, regarding this homosexual lifestyle choice, it is just that – a sinful choice. It is a learned behavior. Or it can be one's sinful inclinations, as are other immoral practices that one may have a slant or tendency towards, and therefore chooses to engage in such behavior. The blueprint or marking of such sinful behavior can be imprinted within the minds of those as young as I was in the stories I have shared. Or when a child is even younger, giving rise to such improper conduct as they age.

When the roles of godly parenting are not understood or maintained within the home, "innocent" children's proclivities or sinful passions can draw them into the dark and wicked practice of homosexuality. Or some other perversion or individualized dysfunction (Romans 12:2). As previously mentioned, relational dysfunction manifests itself in a variety of ways.

* * *

While accompanying my dad on a summer road trip and work-related excursions, which were unknown lands across the country for me. How ironic – that I would also be going through or transitioning toward my personal journey and uncharted voyage unto my awakening into darkness or ignorance – puberty. I don't know if this time spent with my dad was intentional regarding my maturing. Or was it merely about me earning some money?

Now for what I call my uncharted and unknown destination of self. And these mind-blowing and unexpected experiences while journeying with my dad. During this time with him, I was exposed to what I will term, *The enemy's fiery arrows*. Meaning Satan's evil tactics, or occurrences that are at work within humanity and even worked out through sinful men toward the detriment of one another.

This wickedness is the evil that comes against us. Or that evil we are tempted by and/or engage in willingly. Such temptations, whether in thought or beheld visually, are the fiery arrows of Satan. And guess what? … it was my dad, who unknowingly was used by Satan to put me in *The line of fire* for him to destroy me! Understand something. If we are not prayerful and watchful. Anyone of us can be used as agents of our Adversary – Satan. Many, perhaps even more than one will care to admit, are actively engaged in the will of Satan.

For me, a boy whose hormones were now set on edge. The following two situations should have never occurred under my dad's watch. However, I am inclined to believe that he could not apprehend the nature of the dangers of darkness that I had awakened to, nor the gross darkness he was leading me into – the firing squad of dark spiritual forces that were poised to take me out.

As I reflect on my life. I recognize that it was by the grace of God that I did not gravitate entirely over to the dark, cruel, and calculated lifestyle of a lost soul. Or to be trapped or given over totally into sexual deviance of the worse sorts! O, for a praying mother! I am confident that her praying and her faith contributed to me not being a lost cause and lost soul. Each of my parents had their shortcomings and failings. But God, He kept my mom in her right mind and preserved her children. This Scripture from Romans 6:17 comes to mind: "But God be thanked, that ye were the servants of sin, but ye have obeyed from the heart that form of doctrine which was delivered you." Though far from perfect, I see the heart of my mother in this text.

Ephesian 2:1 also speaks to one's sinful condition. All who were once separated from the grace and mercy of God, Scripture declares. *"And you hath he quickened, who were dead in trespasses and sins; Wherein in time past ye walked according to the course of this world, according to the prince of the power of the air, the spirit that now worketh in the children of disobedience: Among whom also we all had our conversation in times past in the lusts of our flesh, fulfilling the desires of the flesh and of the mind; and were by nature the children of wrath, even as others. But God, who is rich in mercy, for his great love wherewith he loved us, even when we were dead in sins, hath quickened us together with Christ* (by grace ye are saved)!" "But God, who is rich in mercy," That part!

While on our cross-country journey, California was one of our destinations. Arriving in San Bernardino, California, my dad stopped at one of the local beaches, Blackhead Beach, if I remember correctly. We had to traverse down a cliff to gain access to the beach. I cautiously slid down this steep slope with my backside close to the ground while bracing myself on my hands. The cliff's height was so great that I could not clearly distinguish the people on the beach.

When I was finally able to focus on the activity on the beach … as a teenage boy, what I saw was shockingly awesome! This was only my second visit to a beach. My first beach experience was not remotely close to what I encountered on this beach. The closer we got to the beach, it became clear that no one had on clothing – it was a nude beach! Arriving on the beach in total disbelief, I walked down the beach, taking in all of the female nudity, before taking a seat on a bolder. While sitting there, I became enthralled as I watched a group of females playing volleyball. I was transfixed by their naked bodies!

My thoughts were all over the place as my mind was governed by my fleshly appetite. My thinking was unrestrained and unprotected – it had been captured and corrupted by my dark, deadly and sinful thoughts due to being on this nude beach. *Oh, how I remember wanting to play!* All that I remember from my visit to California was this nude beach. No doubt, it had a profound and lasting effect on me! My dad underestimated, did not consider, or could not fathom the danger he had led me into. He was seemingly oblivious to the psychological and spiritual ramifications of such exposure on me. Clearly, he needed the shepherding that only God can provide.

I remember visiting the following two states while also venturing on my personal voyage: Salt Lake City, Utah, and Boise, Idaho. It was a stay in one of these states that my dad would again be used as Satan's agent. Once again, my dad would present me before the firing squad of dark and wicked spiritual forces.

This dark situation was one that no father or adult should ever subject a child to. A reminder: my dad had divorced himself from our family. And a life with his new family had been instituted. Perhaps this was the reason that he thought he could do what he did, whereby subjecting me to his folly and giving little or no thought to his gross dereliction of parental responsibility.

Keep in mind that what I share in this book is not intended to bring shame, guilt, or condemnation. But from my truth shared within this book: We learn or are reminded of what we should do ... What we should not do. As well as the hazards and issues arising when our lives are not lived according to the purpose and will of God.

Since we were staying overnight in this next city, my dad found a hotel for the night. Not long after settling in, I was situated in the living room, on the sofa bed, watching television - my dad had the adjacent room. He said he had to leave the hotel for a minute. However, upon his return, he was not alone! He had brought back a Caucasian female. I do not remember what words either of them said to me. I was stupefied, to say the least, but somehow, I knew what was about to go down. They appeared casual and friendly to one another as they went directly into the adjoining bedroom and closed the door behind them.

Sometime later, my dad opened the door and asked me for a towel; it became apparent of their actions – not that I had any doubt. I knew what was up on the other side of that closed door; the thought of their sexual interaction was profoundly affecting me bodily and psychologically. My dad opened the door and poked his head through. With a smile on his face and a chuckle, he asked me to grab a towel while sweat dripped from his face. Giving him the towel, he closed the door.

Now, for a look at my youthful - dark and fleshly take on the matter. I was disappointed and not for the reason of your thinking – which was his unfaithfulness against his wife. No, I was bothered because he did not have someone for me! Twisted was my thinking ... but natural resulting from my sinful nature; the lack of godly parental guidance on the matter of sex; and their failure to protect me from the exposure of sexual perversion and even to protect me from me!

The father is to establish godly standards for the home and provide protection and direction for his children. As for my father, it was unto great darkness, and danger was his leading for me. And so, it is said: *Like father, like son* – parents, you must grasp the significance of this saying. What role will you assume for your child(ren) ... will it be towards *Life* (Zoe), or will it be unto destruction, death, and *Eternal Hell Fire* (Daniel 12: 2; Matthew 25:46; Revelation 20:14)?

The following day, the only thing I recall my dad saying to me regarding his night of folly was ... "Don't tell your mother." Odd considering, he was no longer married to her. And so, I didn't, until several years later. When I finally shared this matter with my mother, she responded with a smile and a laugh of sorts ..." He probably did this *expletive* when he was with me too."

We, as men and fathers, must do better on all fronts! We will be held accountable before God regarding our care for those we have been entrusted to shepherd and protect – namely, our children, our wives - and our families!

I will share this final experience; I was perhaps a sophomore in high school. Though the situation was not physical in nature, another encounter points to the multiple onslaughts of the enemy's fiery arrows, which came against my mind. Satan, the enemy of God, and our enemy, wants to take us down through any means possible. I will present that Satan's most prolific and first means of assault against both males and, increasingly, females is to ensnare and keep us in bondage to sexual perversion. Just look at Satan's playbook and how he came at me to entrench me in a life of flesh or sinful passion-seeking. While one is pursuing after the lust of their flesh, they forfeit their opportunity to *Life* - God. Flesh or selfish gratification, many have made their god!

I was not raised in the church. I did not know this way of living: unto holiness or a life unto sanctification. And therefore, unaware of the *personal relationship* God desired to have with me, thereby leading to my sanctification and righteous living through Jesus' redemption and His indwelling Spirit.

The loss of virginity as defined for my time and by me. The act of sexual intercourse between a male and female. I am relatively sure that I had been sexually involved – I was no longer a virgin at this point in my life. I realize for this era, one's virginity as being lost may mean something different, hence my reason for stating my definition on the matter. And too, I realize other norms and matters of behavior once thought to be clearly defined are being challenged and redefined by this evil and idolatrous world (2 Peter 2:1-3).

After my dad's divorce from my mother, she did not make it a practice to have men visit our home. However, she did become involved with an individual with whom she bore my youngest sister. Interestingly enough, he too became a trucker. My mother now had five children, and I was the oldest at fifteen or sixteen.

This man with whom my mother took an interest. As I give thought to his short time in my presence while he lived in my mother's home ... He did not display Biblical manhood, even though he attended church. And from what I was told by my mother, he sang in the male choir. But, neither did he add anything beneficial to my understanding of life or my personal development. I would like to think he said something of benefit to me regarding manhood – but this was highly unlikely. That said, my view of this individual was not favorable, not then nor years later. He crossed the line when he disrespected my mother. I was in the Army at the time. I came home from Fort Bragg to pay him a visit at his apartment - to do him great harm! But it was not in me ... O, for a praying mother!

As for the next unfortunate situation that I encountered, it was due to his conduct and thoughtless action. This was before I went into the Army. On this day, after he returned to my mother's house from a road trip, he was outside cleaning his truck. I may have been asked to assist. What I will now share and my unfortunate situation ... had to do with his trash. Yes - trash, as viewed from two literal perspectives.

I could not have imagined what I would stumble upon while looking into his truck ... it was his stash and stack of pornographic magazines. This was my first time seeing such a gripping display of nudity and beauty. However, I must have watched to see what would become of the magazines after the fact. To my excitement, he discarded several of the magazines into the garbage can – trash, I now call these magazines. But at the time, a treasure trove for a boy of about sixteen. *His trash became my treasure!*

[This add-in results from a conversation with my sister Wendy after I had completed writing my book. At the time, I was editing this manuscript. Leaving out the details of our conversation. Wendy mentioned that when she was a child ... My guess is she was certainly less than ten years old. And our youngest sister was with her; this same person had openly displayed on his table in his apartment, pornographic magazines. Wendy stated that she was confused by what she saw.]

Enough said! We must protect our children!

As I now do, I will say some men choose to call this material trash. However, make no mistake about it! Such pictures of denuded women ... these sensational sexual images' power to arrest our eyes and even our fleshy passion is inescapable for many. Even so, such imagery has become or can be a gateway to sexual perversion and other sinful trappings for countless others.

Now, as a result of our devices, there is twenty-four-seven access to such images held in the palms of vulnerable men. Pornography is causing problems for many, women included! Its trappings can be instantaneous, like a highly addictive drug, or this stronghold can creep up on one unaware. The grip of pornography is a destroyer, and it causes major problems within marriages and even their demise. Pornography as well creates various challenges within dating relationships or renders one addicted to pornography incapable of engaging in a meaningful relationship. And even engaging sexually.

After noticing the magazines … not knowing what would become of them, I am sure that I was hoping, if not anticipating, that he would trash his trash. I waited for this to happen and then retrieved the magazines; it would be as if I had struck gold for a boy of my age, around 16. Yes, ma'am, sexual imagery can have this kind of pull and grip on your sons and your man.

When he finally discarded the magazines, I eagerly made his trash - my treasure, as I rescued the magazines from the garbage and their certain destruction. Sadly - there was no man in my life to save and guard me against trashing my mind and redirect me from the dark path I was headed. Or to protect me from the destruction Satan desired to leash upon me through these images.

Removing the magazines from the trash bin, I gave them a new home under the protection of my mattress. Never before had I seen such nudity in the likes of what I encountered in these magazines! Every woman was "drop-dead" gorgeous! Even today, I can still somewhat remember two images four decades later, even the props used. The power and the persuasion of sexual images cannot be underestimated – many have fallen victim to pornography's stronghold.

As a man, I was never overtaken by the *stronghold* of pornography. Sexual relations with my wife had never been an issue. However, I found that at times of immense boredom or a purposeless season in my life, that porn was utilized to feel that void or emptiness I was experiencing at the time. So, ladies, your husband, who was or perhaps is caught up in porn … Understand something; it may have absolutely nothing to do with you.

The issue may only be that of your man … for reasons he must find out. An issue he must address. Men and ladies, what you have chosen to watch or view is sinful. Such pornographic display of sexual perversion. Or the flesh or body utilized to excite the imagination. And the viewing of the denuded flesh of some others goes against the will and purpose for which God created humanity (1 Corinthians 6: 20).

When I told my wife about my occasional viewing of porn ... she did not object. Neither did she object when at some point later, I suggested that we watch together. For some of you, what I am about to say may not matter to you. Or you may not even care to read about it. Just the same, some porn is extremely vulgar, repulsive, and degrading. While other porn viewings are produced with sophistication and overall beauty. This was my preference. Where movies or pictures were created so professionally and tastefully. With care to capture a romantic and seemingly loving sexual engagement. It didn't seem so bad; besides, it's not far removed from what is called soft porn that is shown on regular television. This is the lie we may tell ourselves or be led to believe to justify watching or looking at such material.

It is this setup that, for many, they can excuse or overlook sin because it doesn't seem as sinful. Or, in their minds, it isn't sinful at all. However, I remind you that Satan masquerades as an angel of light – a thing of beauty. But death is his essence or true nature! From such deception, we are protected and guarded only when we abide in the *Light* – the Word and Truth of God!

As for my wife and I watching porn together, this was done twice, so she reminded me ... I was keenly aware of the addictive nature of porn. And how it can rob a husband and wife of the pleasure and satisfaction they were to experience only amongst themselves. Therefore, with a clear conscience, I could not continue to endanger and subject my wife to the sin of pornography and the potential stronghold that awaited her.

Now, there I was, a boy of fifteen or sixteen; I now had these women to gaze upon and fantasize with whenever I wanted to. On at least one occasion, I remember showing my magazines to a couple of friends. These women were there for me ... at such a time to assist me with the self-indulgence of my corrupt mind and fleshly passions. Some will argue. There is "no harm with such experimentation, self-exploration, or self-gratification." However, I vehemently take a stance against such practices, as this is definitely a gateway to engaging in other unchecked sexual inclinations and sins of different sorts. Such practices or activities of self-gratification are not God's will or the purpose for which He created us. Rather, we are created to glorify God and honor Him through our bodies ... for this reason, we are created (Thessalonians 4:1-8).

God's Word, His stance on the subject of sex, sexual purity, and sanctification is clear. Such misconduct and misuse of our bodies – the very temple of God is worldly, fleshly, corrupt, and sinful (1 Corinthians 6: 1-19). And so, it is against the purpose and design for which God created His beloved children. Sensual or sexual gratification is to be expressed and shared between a husband (man) and his wife (woman). We Christians are to abstain from such fleshy gratification apart from marriage. Turn away from the practices of sexual perversion we must. As well as from all things that grieve the Spirit and dishonor Him and our bodies (Ephesians 4:30).

Beloved of God, listen. Where there are children under your care, educate them regarding the proper way to view their bodies. Educate them on how to conduct themselves in their bodies which is a gift from God and His very temple. Having been given these temporary vessels by God and an abode for the Spirit, let us give careful and prayerful attention to honor our bodies through righteous living. In so doing, we bring honor to our Father and God.

Through this book, you have been allowed to take a journey with me from my earliest years as a toddler through my teens. Perhaps you saw yourself in my story. By sharing moments of my bleak, dark, and broken past, I discovered some eye-opening things about myself correlating with my history that I had not considered. Perhaps you cannot relate to my story ... how wonderful! However, if you have children in your care or desire to have a child. You now have a better perspective of what they are faced with and even what can occur to them if you are not vigilant and prayerful as their shepherd and protector.

As I close this chapter, the specifics regarding how such experiences impact our lives are not the point of emphasis. Instead, the point is that many are broken, resulting from things occurring in our past. In order to progress toward healing and establish a secure and stable future, relationally or otherwise ... you may have to look back at your past so that you may move forward to become a better you. If you choose to venture back through your past, you must do so prayerfully. This will ensure that you have invited God to go back with you as well to see you through those hurtful or difficult seasons. He will do it! It is there that you search for answers and, too, seek God's healing for your soul.

CHAPTER 7

Real Love Comes at a Cost

Perhaps one of the most important relationship questions that can be asked today is: What is Love? Some are wondering ... Is there such a thing as "real love?" Can it be obtained? Or is it unattainable, a fictional idea, only to be found in the movies or within the creative and fanciful lyrics of songwriters and storytellers? One vocalist has expressed through her song – "That she's looking for a real love." Another has said - "Love ain't nothing but a second-hand emotion."

Many have described love as elusive or not to be found, whereas some share that it has been the best thing they have experienced. But where is real love .... where is my Beloved? More than a few are wondering and losing sleep over and even stressing about as they see time ticking away.

God is the author of *Love*. His essence is *Love* (1 John 4:8). If one is to have any hope of developing and sustaining a life-long relationship with their Beloved. Well, love ... as God has established and purposed for a godly relationship, has to be comprehended and acted upon. And so, it is to Him we must turn that we may know what *True, Real, Enduring, and Sacrificial Love is* and what godly love is not.

If you are a believer in the God that I am presenting: The God of the Judean-Christian Bible - the One and only God who is Love! The very God and Father who begat Jesus who was fully Divine and fully man; Jesus or Love incarnated as demonstrated through His bodily existence, His sacrificial death, and bodily resurrection. Jesus who is active in the world through the power of His indwelling Spirit. Well then, true Love is already yours. However, one may need to mature spiritually to better understand this remarkable and wonderful Love and Gift from God.

The issue for many lies in they are not seeking after God, His love *with their whole heart.* Therefore, such ones are not growing to understand God's complete, perfect, and sacrificial love. Nor what it means to surrender and submit to His love. It is this *Love*, offered and extended from the Spirit of God, who transforms us inwardly, for and toward the outward working or manifestation of love for God, and one toward another.

It is not a cliché to say, "What the world needs is love." Though some people are kind, good, or even loving, others are none of these. Nevertheless, the love of God, which fallen man needs, transcends the mere goodness, etcetera of people and humanity's character flaws and fickleness. It is an enduring love… a steadfast and unmovable love that God provides! It is unconditional love that is beyond human efforts and comprehension. This is the love the world needs! He – Jesus, is received and made known spiritually through regeneration and the renewal of our hearts. By the Spirit, we come to know His love as we enter into a loving and cultivated relationship with Jesus (1 Corinthians 2:14).

Many wonderful things of God come at a price – even love, yet they can be considered free. I will explain. Love, or being able to love with the love of God, is at odds with our sinful nature. Separated from God due to sin, we no longer naturally possess the ability to effectively express the love of God, though some may be loving. Therefore, because of this condition – that is, sin reigning in our mortal bodies, mankind is consequently lost and found wanting – in need of God and His love. You see, the love of God is a gift from Him to be freely imparted through Jesus into the souls of mankind by the Spirit of God. This impartation of God's grace-love results from the gracious gift of Jesus' sacrificial death. The Love given and shown to born-again Believers came at no cost to us; rather, Jesus paid the price in full for all humanity. And He left to abide within man – Love, His Spirit, the Third Person of the Divine Trinity (Romans 5:8; 6:23; Ephesians 1:7; 1 Corinthians 6:20).

The Love of God - expressed in the action and power of the Spirit of God, spiritually indwells or even implants Himself as a life-giving seed within man's surrendered and submitted hearts or souls. Thereby bringing forth new birth, life, or regeneration unto man's loveless dead spirit due to sin.

For those who are empowered. In-lived, or indwelt by the Spirit of Love. That Man of sin – Satan, and his former reign has been broken over your lives (Romans chapter 7). The spiritual union, man with God, this holy consummation and conception can be likened to a loving husband and a submitted wife who consummates their sacred marital union. Even so, through their union and the seed of man, a child - a new life is conceived. This child conceived in the darkness of its mother's womb is destined to grow to maturity. From its temporary darkness from within its mother's womb, God has purposed that this child be called-out and forth from its temporary abode – its mother's womb into the light of this world. So that he or she may come to know the True Life and Light and, too, become a child of the Day!

Therefore, for one to accept Jesus as Savior, they have been re-born. And they have been called out or forth from spiritual darkness. Consequently, they are now to grow unto spiritual maturity in love by the aide of the Spirit of Life, who is Love. After a person has been born of the Spirit, it is to be understood that any benevolence or expression of love extending from the child of God is not found within themselves or by our own effort. But instead, through our reliance upon the Holy Spirit, we can produce Agape … the fruit of the Spirit – love.

Now the fruit of the Spirit is as follows: love, joy, peace, longsuffering, gentleness, goodness, faith, meekness, and temperance (Galatians 5:22 and 23). By the Spirit, we are being transformed in our character. So that we may represent our Father as children of the Day who are temporarily living in a dark and evil world.

Apart from Jesus, we can do nothing. Neither can we do anything that will please the Father or bring honor and praise to Him if we are not one with Him

– in and through the Spirit. All that mankind seeks to accomplish through the flesh or self-will will be for naught, as we are incapable of bringing forth results unto holiness before our Holy Father.

The cost required that one may be indwelt by the Spirit and reconciled to the Father - Jesus has paid in full! His love and very life, He gave freely as a sacrifice for you and me! We did nothing to deserve or earn such favor from God - it cost mankind nothing. But through faith in Jesus alone, we receive the gift of eternal life from the Father!

One recognizing this grace and gift from God should result in a loving response of grateful praise, submission, and obedience toward God the Father. Jesus, who was compelled by the love He has for lost man, in obedience to His Father, gave up everything He knew while in heaven. That the love of the Father *"may be made known upon the earth, His saving health among all people"* (Philippians 2: 5-11; Psalm 67:2).

From Jesus' example of service, sacrifice, and love, it is seen that He, too, depended upon the Spirit's empowerment to accomplish His Father's will. As we are one with Him, we are to also, through the power of the Spirit of God, seek to have our hearts and minds transformed so that we may also demonstrate the love of God to a loveless and lost world.

* * *

Let me ask this question. As you read this book, has there been a stirring or anxiousness within your soul? If so, what you are experiencing is the Holy Spirit urging you to embrace the Father's love and grace for the saving of your soul. Or perhaps this stirring is to prompt you to return or draw closer to God. See how much the Father Loves you... that He will nudge you in an attempt to get your attention so that you may be one and at peace with Him.

All that is needed for you to do is to say "Yes" to Jesus. Respond, "I accept your gracious sacrifice and immeasurable payment for my sins ... I will submit to your Lordship and will for my life. Help me, Father, to be obedient and to love you more!"

Listen to me, beloved of my Father: Returning to your Creator and Father is as simple as that! Now off into your new life and spiritual journey, you go. From this point on, you are to mature in faith; live sanctified unto God, labor in love with fellow Believers, and make disciples for Christ until such time your labor of love is done. This will not be until our God and Father call you home to be with Him.

Make this your simple heart-felt prayer: "Father, work within me that which is well-pleasing in your sight. Teach me how to love … help me walk in obedience to your will … and convict me when I betrayed your love and faithfulness. Amen."

Love Personified

It could only be through the Son of God and He clothing Himself in flesh – Jesus, becoming the God-man. That the Father's love in its fullness could be demonstrated before humanity. True, it is. "For God so loved the world that He gave His only begotten Son, that whoever shall believe in Him shall not perish but have eternal life (John 3:16). Even so, "Greater love hath no man than this that a man lay down his life for his friends" (John 15:13). Jesus did this for you and for me! He did this for the lost souls of this world!

The Father's love was perfectly personified in the life and death (sacrifice) of His unique son Jesus for humanity. Yet, the reach of Love - Jesus' tremendous influence and outpouring; while excellent and graciously experienced by the people (Jews initially), being displayed through great signs, wonders, and miracles; nevertheless, Love personified was limited in His outreach while He (Jesus) worked and walked upon the earth in fleshly garb.

I will explain: While Jesus – the God-man, remained clothed within His earthen vessel – that is, His physical self as the means and vehicle by which to display His perfect and eternal love to mankind. He was, nevertheless, limited by and within His flesh. It would take Him sacrificing Himself or planting His life bodily, like a seed into the earth, that His influence may sprout and then spread globally – beginning with His apostles and through them and their disciples (John 12:24; John 12:32; 1 Corinthians 15:36).

It was necessary for Jesus to give Himself as a sacrifice upon the cross, thereby becoming cursed for you and me; planted in a tomb (the earth) and raised from the grave as the *Firstfruit* that His love and power over death may become known the world over (1 Corinthians 15: 20).

Our culture is increasingly counter to the notion of seeking the good of others or putting someone before self-interest. It is a world system that promotes … "me, me, me!" It is all about me and what I want … no matter the cost.

This self-seeking attitude is just one of many things that work against family cohesiveness and the development of a balanced and healthy relationship. We must be wise to the evil devices and tactics of the enemy of our souls, who seeks to conquer us by keeping us divided. As Christians, those who are one with God - a family of Believers in Christ. Only as we remain one, through love. And under the authority of God, our Father, can we be kept united. As well as protect our families while temporarily living as God's representatives here on earth. Even so, living through self-sacrifice … this here is love in action (John 13:34,35; John 15:12,13).

CHAPTER 8

Our Covenant Has Been Settled with Blood

Fellowship with God can be understood as occurring within an individual's personal devotional time spent with Him. Or quality time shared with God, within the setting of corporate worship, or any individual or group setting held for the purposes of growing spiritually, drawing closer to God, as adoration is extended toward Him.

The spiritual discipline of studying the Bible and other Christian material, along with the spiritual disciplines of prayer, fasting, meditation on God's Word, and other forms of spiritual disciplines, cannot be neglected! If one desires to grow closer to God and to become fruitful for the purpose of building His Eternal Kingdom, thereby attaining spiritual maturity, we (the branches) must intimately trust and abide within Jesus - The Vine (John 15:5).

Intimately abiding with God allows one to know and experience God's steadfast and inexhaustible love. This relationship or covenant God undertakes and enters into with us individually is only by way of the blood and sacrifice of Jesus. This is the New Covenant in His blood. That was ordained before the world was formed. And spoken of by the prophets of old and proclaimed by the Apostles (Psalms 2; Psalms 22; Isaiah 53; 1 Corinthians 2:7-12; Ephesians 1:1-1; Revelation 13:8).

In the days of Abraham, there was established by God, the Old Covenant. Among other things maintained in this agreement was the important and unceasing practice of animal sacrifice, the shedding of specific animal's blood that only covered the people's sins. This system did not remove sin or the guilt of the Jewish people (Hebrews 10:1-18).

Within the covenantal agreement between God and man (the Israelites) were laws governing the Israelite's daily activity, worship of God, and civic responsibilities. This covenant was only between God and His people - the Israelites. God tells them that within this unique relationship – if His people responded in obedience to Him, He would, in turn, bless them and be their God. However, if they broke their covenant obligations with Him, the dire consequences of their disobedience would follow (Deuteronomy 28:14-68). This covenant was conditional and too one-sided. What is meant by one-sided: Only God can keep His promises; never lie and uphold His end of the arrangement.

On the other hand, Israel would fail time and time again to be faithful to their God – God knew this beforehand. Even so, that which He wanted them and you and me to see, that is, man, cannot work out their own salvation and sanctification. Apart from God, man can do nothing! Therefore, the old covenant served to foreshadow and point to a new and even better covenant that would be established by Jesus. A new covenant that did not merely cover sin. But instead, cleansed man from their sin. Vindicating us from death, even breaking our covenant with Satan and the grave, through Jesus' blood poured out for all who will trust and believe in *The Power of the blood* (Hebrews chapters 8 and 9).

Covenants of old were established (man with man) and known to be sealed or ratified with the shedding of blood. A covenant is also understood as effectuating a marriage when a man and his virgin bride consummate their union. The husband and wife's covenant is demonstrated and confirmed in the breaking of her hymen – there being the shedding of blood. Even so, a covenant can be embraced as occurring when a baby breaks forth in a bloody birth from its mother's womb. The mother thereby innately agrees to render unconditional love to her babe, even as the child grows and learns to respect, and is expected to render obedience unto its mother and father. Herein the covenant of family has been established … this rightly occurs through the shedding of blood.

Covenants were resolute, fixed, and in effect perpetually until satisfied. Or where broken, creating problems of various sorts and never a good outcome for the violator. God's covenant with the Israelites was perpetual. However, He knew they would falter in their obligation to keep them. In their own strength, they were incapable of keeping the righteous requirements of His law.

Listen to just two of God's accusations against His people who were unfaithful to Him on several occasions: He said they were "covenant breakers" even so, "being slow to keep and hold fast to their vows." For this reason, the Old Covenant was given: to show the relational commitment that God had with His people. And the loyalty and relationship they were to demonstrate and have with Him. This covenant was also a foreshadowing of the new and better covenant revealed and established in and through the blood of Jesus. The world needed a Savior; we were given the *Only Unique Son of God* for humanity's redemption!

As for another covenant matter on marriage, one must note and take the seriousness of divorce as God does. Frankly, He hates it! Divorces are destroyers of families and work against social order and communal harmony! With the rise of divorces from those who can be called "covenant/oath breakers." Not condemning anyone, but to make the matter painfully clear to all. God's position on this rising devastation and even devilish matter cannot be danced around or taken lightly. In His sight, such ones are indeed viewed as covenant breakers. God despises divorces (not His creation) because of the far-reaching derailment and destruction caused to families resulting from divorces. That often accompanies painful, emotional/mental, or spiritual effects that divorce has upon an individual.

Christian unions or secular. For a moment, let's consider those failed marriages or on and now off again relationships you are familiar with. Perhaps, regarding a few of these relationships, they were thought to be solid. And the couple united was considered a "good match." However, the relationship comes to an unexpected end. Now things are "off" with the previous person, and barely missing a beat, one or both people move on to the next person of interest, here - sexually speaking. My question is this, "Where is or what happened to one's self-worth, self-control, and dignity? Where is commitment ... where is the respect for oneself and God?

There are those who are able ... like with the ease of changing their socks change their minds regarding the one they are with today. And without missing a beat, move on to the next situation (person) tomorrow. Listen, apart from a committed and *intimate relationship with God,* it is proven time and time again that man cannot live out the purpose, the righteousness, or faithfulness acquired of man by God. Indeed, we are faced with the dilemma of climbing divorce rates. And the concern is not just among the secular but even amongst confessing Christians. We, too, are covenant breakers! Far too many of us are dividing our families, and there is no justifiable reason. God's criterion for divorce is marital unfaithfulness, which is adultery (Matthew 5: 31-32; Mark 10:2-12; 1 Corinthians 7:39; Romans 7:2-3).

There may be other unique and unacceptable situations to consider regarding this serious matter of divorce. Of course, prudence dictates that physical or mental abuse could undoubtedly be a justifiable reason for divorce. But keep in mind the marital union is where two have entered into a covenant agreement, and this union is not to be dissolved haphazardly. That I may further my point ... better yet, God's point. Consider the following text. "What therefore God hath brought together, let no one or anything separate that union" (Mark 10:9). The enemy (Satan) of the God who established marriage wants you to give up on your marriage and family. However, you must fight to keep your marriage and family intact! Fight for your marriage at all costs!

As Christians, our primary weapons are love and forgiveness, as instructed in the Word of God. By the Spirit and through the Word of God ... Where the heart is healed and restored after hurt and brokenness, *Love* can resurrect a dead or dying marriage. Where there has been sorrowful repentance, sincere apology extended, and even forgiveness rendered, a godly family can reign as victors!

Where godly love is truly understood, this matter of rampant and rapid divorce could become a thing of the past or significantly reduced in the lives of those committed to Christ (1 John 4:16).

Here are some nonsensical reasons for divorce: "We grew apart." "I am no longer in love with my spouse." "We were better off as friends." They or their spouse "changed or evolved;" "I should never have married him/her because of this or that." "We are no longer compatible;" "there are financial issues." And lastly, not that the list is complete, "I am no longer physically attracted to my spouse."

Again, the Biblical ground for divorce is unfaithfulness; this includes the abuse of one's spouse. If you are currently considering a divorce, do not be too quick to throw in the towel. There is godly counsel that can assist you and your spouse with marital reconciliation. Where both parties genuinely want their marriage, it can be restored. I know this personally … God can heal and resurrect the dead! My God is in the business of reconciliation and restoration! Are you wondering how I know? … continue reading this book; you shall see.

In a dating situation where there has been a parting of ways, sadly, and too often, it is after the two gave themselves over to sexual intercourse. I am not speaking as one who has not traveled such a forbidden and precarious path. Through my personal involvement, even as seen from the lives of others, I understand the inevitable confusion, grief, harm caused, and the seriousness of such a violation of God's moral standards. His laws are purposed to protect us from predators and ourselves – those sinful inclinations that each of us possesses. We should want to please our Father, but even so, that we may find protection from those destructive forces – even our fleshly appetites that war against us. Where left unchecked and not guarded against, will undoubtedly seek means to destroy or render us useless. This is why much-needed Biblical study and discussion are needed on the topics of sex, divorce, and other practical issues toward living a godly or sanctified life.

I want to give more attention to this matter of Covenant. A Believer identifying as a Christian acknowledges and accepts the salvific work of Jesus and our New Covenant established in His blood.

Jesus' predetermined journey to Calvary's Cross would be met with immense agony and tremendous suffering resulting from the torture inflicted by the Roman soldiers. He was severely punched, whipped, and a thorned crown was forced upon His head, causing blood to flow. However, the height of His suffering came from the unimaginable suffering and cruelty He experienced as He hung upon the cross. Hanging there by His nail-pierced hands and feet, He struggled to breathe … this was the climax of His selfless act of suffering and bodily sacrifice for you and for me. Jesus then responded … It is finished; bowing His head, Jesus gave up His Spirit (John 19:30).

While Jesus's lifeless body hung upon the cross, a Roman soldier who was in disbelief that Jesus had so soon died pierced Jesus's side with his spear. This was to confirm that Jesus was, in fact, dead. The account from Scripture further tells us that from the side of Jesus poured forth both blood and water. Here the water can be perhaps understood - amongst other spiritual illustrations, as symbolically cleansing man from sin, *Living Water*, or even our baptism into Jesus and, therefore, our death to self. One final thought regarding the water and blood. The water: Jesus' Spirit leaving His body. And the blood: The life of the body poured out indicating the body's cessation.

The reference to blood throughout Scripture should be understood as the central theme coursing through the Bible. Not only is blood the life of the body. But only the blood of Jesus provides mankind access into the New Covenant with Jesus and eternal life with the Father.

As previously stated, under the Old Covenant, the blood and sacrifice of animals merely covered the sins of God's people. God graciously and mercifully preserved the Israelites by the shed blood of animals. Unlike in the days of Noah, and God's judgment upon a sinful race of people, by flooding the world before the sacrificial system was inaugurated. God's following and final judgment of this sinful world or its people will be with fire (Genesis chapter 7 and 2 Peter chapter 3)!

It is through the salvific work of Jesus, our Redeemer, that we Believers or Christians have been cleansed from our sins, and God's death penalty of fiery judgment rendered against humanity satisfied. Indeed, the blood of Jesus has saved all from death and the wrath of God for those who have put their trust in Him! It is Jesus' very blood by which we, once afar off, have entered into covenant with the very Son of God (Ephesians 2:13).

In Jesus, we (the Bride, His Church) have become one with our Perfect and Holy Bridegroom. We do not have to bleed to receive Him. Instead, He has chosen to bleed and die for us! So that He may receive and restore us to our Father as we have entered into a *better covenant* with Him, which will last for eternity! Truly, Jesus has borne our griefs and carried our sorrows. Through the covenant of His blood, Jesus became humanity's substitutionary atonement and even the Church's Bridegroom (Isaiah Ch. 53).

Although we remain clothed within our weakened earthen vessels, we have been made the righteousness of God. As children of God, we make up the *body of Christ*. As a body of Believers, being as it is, the very Church of the Living God, even so, the bride of Christ. Rest assured that Jesus is coming back for us so that He may present us before His Father – clothed anew, as His spotless bride (Ephesians 5: 25-27; 1 Thessalonians chapter 5; Matthew 24:43; Revelation 16:15)!

Marriage as Foreshadowing that More Perfect Union in Christ

It has always been the objective of our God and Father that His lost and wayward children would be returned and presented before Him undefiled. That is to say - found blameless, holy, unblemished, chaste, or without sin.

Before man's restoration with the Father, God, in His infinite wisdom, purposed for man and woman to unite in holy matrimony, thereby becoming one, under and in Him, that they may not otherwise become defiled through prohibited sexual unions (Leviticus chapter 18). Man and woman as one, having consummated their union by entering their secret chambers. Thereunto, intimately, experiencing one another in purity and the beauty of sexual holiness; their marriage consecrated for and by God, and even consummated before Him, is to be to His praise and glory and our enjoyment. This established marital union of man and woman alone is honorable and received or recognized by the Creator.

Sexual relations expressed otherwise are considered a sin against one's body, even so, a sin against God, because His command for sexual purity has been violated (1 Corinthians 6: 14-18). Sexual unions of the forbidden sort, being out of God's ordering. This disobedience of the perpetrators or disorder can only beget of its kind – more chaos and confusion for those who commit sexual sin.

One of the challenges that many marriages or relationships face and even fall apart over is due to sexual relations that occurred either before marriage or unfaithfulness occurring while dating. And without question, where there has been infidelity. The issues of trust and insecurities often arise or become more apparent when a committed dating union is established or after marrying.

One thing is sure; for those troubled over their companion's or spouse's past relationships, this thing will persist as an agitator of their soul and union. Even though you may not have given your significant other a reason to feel insecure or not trust you. They will likely agitate the relationship because of their past or way of thinking. This disorder or way of thinking can only beget of its kind – relational disorder. Order or right thinking has to be restored, and healing brought about for the agitation to cease.

People, it's a huge mistake to believe that sex will lead to a committed relationship, let alone marriage. The problem that often goes unforeseen, and definitely with our youth who choose to engage in sexual activities, is the emotional or psychological injury due to forbidden sexual relations. For certain, other problems arise from premarital sex: sexually transmitted diseases, unwanted pregnancy, and even relational non-commitment.

Though our youth are most vulnerable, anyone can be overtaken by the intense emotional and psychological - and, lest we forget, the physical stronghold resulting from partaking in illicit sex. Is there any wonder why so many are broken, messed up, or confused regarding developing healthy, romantic, and loving relationships? Sex will only complicate matters where misused, or there is abuse. And more illicit sex only creates more complications; we are seeing it, though you may not realize it or want to acknowledge the fact that prohibited sex opens a pandora's box.

As it already is - developing and maintaining a relationship within an ideal arrangement is challenging and pressure-filled for those who really desire to be in a healthy relationship. Illicit sex only exacerbates matters.

Too many are allowing their sexual passions to get the best of them. Even where they know better, only to raise their level of anxiety in hopes that the relationship will lead to marriage if they give in to having sexual relations. And when things don't go as intended … we all know the outcome; it is accompanied by those debilitating emotions of hurt, rejection, and betrayal.

So, how can one prevent themselves from being party to such a predicament? It's simple – make God everything you need! Truly fall in love with God and yourself; learn how to live your life according to our Father's plan and His purpose for you! We all would be so much better off, if only we were taught and encouraged by our Christian parents to develop our *personal relationship* with God while we were yet little ones. Deuteronomy 4:9 and chapter 11:19, Proverbs 22:6, and Ephesians 6:4 speaks to a child's training. Therein these passages of the sacred text, they learn to develop a *personal relationship* with God!

God's ultimate desire is for man to become one with Him. That we, His beautifully adorned bride, may walk and live in this world before Him in holiness or sanctification as virgins who are no longer defiled by the practice of sin. Jesus has made this possible; He has betrothed us to Himself and left us with His indwelling Spirit.

Tragically, many believe that the Bible's teachings are antiquated, or they deny the God that I have come to know … Are you such a one? If so, I pray that your heart is being agitated by the Spirit of God, that you may come to know the love of my Father. Know this, God, whom I have come to know personally and who is constantly revealing Himself to me as I remain one with Him, has assured me through Scripture that His ways are unchanging. He is the same yesterday, today, and forever ... He is God! (Numbers 23:19; Malachi 2:6; Hebrews 13:8; James 1:17).

Here is something I urge you to contemplate regarding God's plans for you. This is a matter where many are challenged, even others losing faith, where God's plan for you, based on your expectations of things, has seemingly failed or come up short. For starters, God never fails at anything! I encourage you to consider these two things when you feel God has let you down: 1) Was there something you did or did not do which may have caused your path to take an unsuspected detour? 2) It may have been God who was behind the detour. He may be saying to you through the detour or delay ... "Not now. Not this or that way, or not with that one."

For sure, God's purpose and plan, no matter how things appear, is always intended for our good and certainly when we are walking according to His will and have permitted Him to have complete control over our lives. For He has said, "For I know the plans I have for you, declares the Lord, plans to prosper you and not to harm you, plans to give you hope and a future" (Jeremiah 29:11). During such times of uncertainty in your life, you must learn to trust God and/or the process! We are called to *walk by faith and not by sight* or our expectations, even as we keep eternity before our thoughts as our final destination (1 Corinthians 5:7).

True Love Will Keep You

When a relationship ends, and it is at the other's doing or even it being the will of God, although you may not recognize it as so, there is an array of emotions one is likely to feel, not the least of which is – rejection or abandonment. But know and hold fast to this truth - the love of God is steadfast towards you! To know the surpassing and unfailing love of God ... to really know and to be in love with God will keep you no matter what you are going through ... *Oh, to know your unfailing Love O' God!*

The understanding of love from man's layered positions on the subject is fickle. And therefore falls miserably short of God's perfect Love. Man's love can be on today and off tomorrow, meaning one thing for the moment and changing the next. Man, apart from God, misguided thoughts on love are often conditional, circumstantial, transactional, or situational. And therefore is inconsistent and even confusing. Apart from God, mankind defines love as we see fit. Or how it benefits one's self.

Case and point: Love, or being in love, understood or presented by the misguided, means one thing while pursuing another ... Or perhaps it was you that was being sought after. And once the flag was captured: meaning the person got what they wanted from the other person. Or, again, you. Love's meaning may be redefined or reduced to something less meaningful than what the one being pursued was led to believe. "Running Game," it is called. And the game has been played or run on many. Such a one giving themselves to sexual intercourse, only to realize that the person came at them under the guise of love. But in fact, they were really after one thing – sex, and perhaps what more they could get from you through additional manipulation! They had you believing their lies. Or what they presented to you as their warped meaning of love. Having gotten what they wanted, subsequently, you became disposable or less favorable to your pursuer. They may say, I've lost interest in you, or my love for you has diminished or perhaps is gone. As if they sincerely had a love for you at any point ... Certainly not, I will say!

Looking back at the situation, what an emotional roller coaster this person had you on. Sadly, this is the current state of many: a ride of emotional highs and lows, twists and turns this person with whom one has made themselves vulnerable and even invested time and effort with. Now, emotionally the individual or you are on edge because of the uncertainty of the person's intentions with whom you have joined yourself. People, this is not love where emotionally you are being led here and there!

Godly or agape-love is purpose-driven; its aim and intentions are precise, upward building, and sure about what it sees and wants for a future to be shared with its Beloved. Such love is to lead to that very good ... that good God desires to bring forth in your life as you and your Beloved build a godly relationship. Such a relationship is established as the two of you set your hearts or minds heaven-ward, looking to God, who is *Love*, and your help in getting to know Him, *The Master Builder* of everything sure and steadfast.

People, true love does not operate in deception! Love does not have one jumping through hoops and taking paths of uncertainty! Love does not demand its own! Love does not isolate you from family and friends! Love is not envious! Love is not manipulative! Love does not divide or create confusion!

Instead, godly love is activated or regenerated in the Believer. The child of God then seeks to infuse him or herself with their Beloved and all of God's people.

Upon the one with whom you are espoused or married to, your love is to be continually poured into them that you two become and remain one! Love gives of itself! Love is to be recognized as life-begetting and giving, building, healing, edifying, enhancing, and life-preserving. Love is forever and never fails! Love is steadfast as it manifests itself in the life of its Beloved, even as it helps to cultivate its attribute of love within the one of its affections. Beautiful and amazing is the love of God! It is this love – *True Love* that He desires for man to intimately know from Him and through Him.

The Bible declares that – *God is love* (1 John 4:7-9,12). Love is His very quintessence! Our *Divine Lover* is the source and key to our moving forward victoriously in marriages. Even so, as Christians, we are to leave a godly impression upon others with whom our lives will divinely intersect.

Transformation A Conscious And Continual Process

As self-determined creatures of habit, mankind is born and bent toward self-will. As Christians, we must therefore come to a faithful surrender of self to the Spirit of God. This is necessary for the ongoing work or change we desperately need within our self-centered and spiritually blind souls. As Christians, no matter how long one has been a Believer, it is incumbent to understand that this transformation is not due to our efforts alone. Instead, our total surrender and reliance upon God's indwelling Spirit actuate and perpetuate this change. He alone brings about our maturation, transformation, and sanctification. Even so, causing us to be victors or overcomers against this present evil and loveless world. However, we are responsible for regularly studying God's Word as we seek to know *His truth and will for our lives.*

However, the process of maturing in the Lord or receiving *the mind of Christ* is where many Christians come up dismally and gravely short. The cause? Far too many professing Christians are not abiding in the *Vine – Jesus, the very Word of God.* They are, therefore, ignorant of Christ's teachings, as found within the Holy Bible. This is also the cause for their vulnerability to demonic or worldly assaults, influences, and trappings leading to a Believer's subsequent defeat, even though they are children of God.

And so, the problem is rather obvious. Too many Christians are yet babes in Christ, even though they may have been baptized years or even decades earlier in their lives. This being the case. Is there any wonder why many struggle and tumble like toddlers in relationships and other areas of their life? And why many are often defeated. Children of God, it's time to grow up! It is past time for you to live as the victors you are - in and through Jesus!

By you taking the time to read this book, this is precisely what you are undertaking to do as you feed your inward man or spirit toward maturity. Continue to grow up, even rise up, as conquerors over the strongholds of sin and the evil influences within this Satanic, driven, or ruled world. Such a study, as provided in this book, assists you with renewing your mind as you mature towards the things or mind of God *"… that you may prove what is that good and acceptable, and perfect, will of God"* (Romans 12:2).

Furthermore, there is something vitally important that you must also attain; your spiritual success depends upon this truth. You see, it is one thing to read *The Good Book* or a good Christian book, thereby acquiring cognitive information. What I mean by acquiring cognitive knowledge is simply this … information retained in memory, which can be recited.

However, when a Christian reads Christian-related material or studies the Bible, which is not an ordinary book; instead, it is God's breath or God's inspired Word. One should therefore approach the study of God's Word prayerfully and humbly because it is God's body of Work – the Bible transcends mere human thoughts or reasoning. And so, neither is our Biblical understanding or the cognitive comprehension we attain of ourselves – rather, it's revelation from God. It is God's Spirit informing our minds while transforming or renewing our thinking. And we, therefore, discover or find agreement with His Truth or the Holy Spirit with our spirits. Bear in mind this matter of a renewed mind is a process. And it's continual!

The spiritual information received is not merely cognitive or head knowledge. Rather there is an ascending to God when one humbly sits and submits before God our Teacher, who is in heaven and yet indwells every true Believer through the Holy Spirit. Through God's indwelling presence, there has been a descending, where the Spirit of God has come to be with and within the Believer to teach us His will, among other things. He - the Holy Spirit, does a work not only within one's reasoning through transforming our minds, but He also performs a work upon our hearts, soul, or inward man through the Living Word of God.

When you approach your study of the Bible and related Biblical material, this is also by the Spirit's prompting. Nevertheless, one has to choose to act upon this nudging of God. Approaching your time of study or devotional period, be ever mindful that you are coming before the Almighty God! He is Spirit; His thoughts and ways transcend secular or humanistic understanding and reasoning. In humility and expectation, sit before your Father as a child who is eagerly waiting to receive instruction and guidance from your Abba–Daddy (Galatians 4:6). Prayerfully approach your study or time with the Father. Ask God to feed your spirit, lead, and guide you into His truth.

Prayer is about approaching God in sincerity with reverence and a contrite heart. With this approach, be assured that our Father hears you and eagerly desires to fulfill His purpose for your life.

In a prayerful approach to our Father, you may say something like this: "My God and Father, I need you and Love you! My total dependence is upon you; I can do nothing of myself. Therefore, work within me that which is pleasing in your sight; teach me and help me to surrender to You, even so, to do and live in Your will. Amen." Our Father is faithful; He will begin that work of transformation within you that you could never have imagined! This is the will of our Father to transform you into the likeness of His only begotten or Unique son - Jesus!

Hold Fast To Truth

God, the Father, and who is Spirit is *Truth* (John 14:6-11). Truth was embodied and expressed in the person of Jesus - the Son of God, who took on the form of man (Romans 8:3; Philippians 2:7). Jesus stated regarding Himself. "That He was the *Way, the Truth, and the Life*. He adds, "No one can come to the Father but through Him," Jesus, who is Truth and only Lord and Savior. If one desires to know the Truth, the Whole Truth, and nothing but the Truth, it is only through looking at Jesus and hearing His Words - the Truth as provided for us in the Holy Scriptures (John 1:1-18).

However, these Words of Jesus, that He was God in the flesh and He was holding or embodying or having absolute Truth, was and is a *Stumbling Stone* for many. Even so, Jesus was a *Stone of Offense* ... the very Stone that is now *The Chief Corner Stone* (1 Peter 2:8; Psalm 118:22,23; Mark 12:10).

Profound was the question of Pilate when he asked Jesus, "What is truth" (John 18:38)? Truth had come into the world; He had dwelt amongst His own. But they did not receive Him, neither did they recognize Him.

* * *

One accepting this glorious, eternal, or supernatural spiritual reality through human reasoning cannot be viewed or conceived through man's logic or deducement alone. Embracing Truth or our spiritual reality is not a fleshly undertaking. Rather it is by the Spirit of God that man comes to know the things of God as already stated. Additionally, consider the following as it pertains to intellect: our part in this process of spiritual maturity, and too, as led by the Spirit, is simply this: We are not mindless creatures void of volition or free will.

Therefore, regarding mankind's intellect: We are to consider and weigh the evidence or information Jesus has provided about Himself in Scripture, from both the Old and New Testament, including Biblical prophecy or text predicting the future. Resulting in the preponderance of biblically verifiable, credible, and historical evidence within God's Word, along with secular writings supporting Scripture. To include archeological or ancient discoveries which support a significant amount of what has been provided by Scripture. All things considered, no other religion or person can compare to Jesus and what He offers through Scripture, which is Salvation and eternal life! Considering what I have presented, I have chosen to covenant with and Trust Jesus! Will you? Will you consider the Goodness of Jesus and then make a choice to give yourself to Him? If you make Him your choice ... you will, as I have discovered that He is *Everything You Need!*

Though there may be times that doubt or questions about Jesus or even one's salvation invade their mind, the good news is our salvation is not based on the amount of assurance one has either in Jesus or their salvation. *Rather we are saved by grace through faith in Christ alone and not on the amount of faith or assurance one has.* And so, amidst the doubt that may assault your mind. All the more, hold fast to the Truth and the measure of faith you have been given. Hold on to the Word of God while praying to God the Father to increase your faith. Even still, for Him to increase your knowledge of Him, as you surrender and give yourself to the will of God, through study, prayer, worship of God, and fellowship with other believers. These practices are what draws one closer to God and into that deeper fellowship or intimacy with the Father.

A perpetual state of surrender or submission to God, and the life-long pursuit for Truth or God, must be the mindset and response of the one who has accepted Jesus as Savior. Submitting to God (Jesus) and coming under the authority of His truth is to make Him Lord over your life as one who is faithfully committed to following Him.

I raise this next point as I have noticed that many call Jesus Savior - and rightly so. They recognize their eternal salvation, which belongs to them due to Jesus conquering death. However, the challenging aspect for many Christians. Is allowing Jesus to also be Lord over their lives, even though many acknowledge (in word only) Him to be Lord. Meaning: to earnestly seek to be transformed daily by the Word of God, learning to surrender unconditionally to His will and/or the full authority He has over us. In other words, we should have the mind or be developing a mind and posture of total surrender to our Lord and Savior. If we grasp this indispensable relational undertaking – Jesus as Lord, while remaining faithful and committed to *Truth,* it will be Truth that holds on to us even as we lovingly cling to Him.

Designed to Be Seekers

We are designed to be Seekers. With varying degrees of enthusiasm, we explore the unknown or seek after that which has seized our attention. We seek after understanding - for things pertaining to this life and for understanding when life as we know it ends. We seek for truth and even justice. Through science, philosophy, astrology, and various disciplines and mediums, we seek to gain insight and knowledge about things, their function, and purpose that we may somehow benefit from our explorative efforts.

Such expeditions and explorations are well and fine. Still, they are not enough to satisfy what our souls indeed long for - that is, absolute truth and perfect justice, meaning, and the purpose of life. And what about our need to belong, to be accepted, and be loved. Man's exploits, although serving to benefit man. Our quests and disciplines cannot perfectly satisfy the longings our souls unknowingly yearn and yet desperately seek - that is, a perfect relationship with God!

Apart from God, these internal or spiritual longings we all have cannot be understood, let alone satisfied. We, therefore, must seek after and surrender to the loving care of God - the lover of our souls. He is the only One who can satisfy our soul's longings! Only when we seek to know God can we come to know Him and even know ourselves. This understanding and guidance elevate us above and beyond the plain of that which is earthly. And unto the spiritual or heavenly realm, that man lost sight of due to sin - the fall or Adam's rebellion. In and through God, our attention and focus are now being engaged through spiritual lenses. We now look up that we may learn how to live out our lives down here on earth. We hear this in the model prayer provided to us by Jesus: "Father, your will be done on earth as it is in heaven (Matthew 6:10).

Even so, there has been and continues to be the tender beckoning of God, nudging the soul of His Seekers, saying, "come unto Me; seek after Me, and you shall find what your soul longs for" (Matthew 7:7,8; Matthew 11:28-30). God longs for a relationship with you, even the entirety of humanity. Still, many often misidentify or disregard the call or loving beckoning of their Creator. This is because of our self-interest takes precedence over God. Or as it was for the child Samuel, they don't recognize or are unable to recognize God's tender nudging or pleading for one to covenant or become one with Him (1 Samuel 3:1-11).

That Great Shepherd of the sheep is always calling to His children, even so, those lost in this world, and at this very moment, He is calling. Will you heed and respond to the Spirit's voice by giving Him permission to reign over your life as Lord and Savior? Will you accept the invitation to enter His fold; will you choose to covenant with Him that you may receive the care and guidance and know the love He yearns to satisfy you with?

Love is standing at the door of your heart, knocking. Will you let Him in? And will you accept His invitation to join Him for fine dining? ... A meal prepared by *The Bread of Life* that will satisfy your soul's deepest longings.

CHAPTER 9

What Does Love Have to Do with It - And the Matter of Sex

I see the Bible as God's love letter to His people. Within its pages, God's love for humanity is on display. Upon these pages of the Bible, by a few, love and devotion are shown towards God. Love is presented among individuals and also within heterosexual marriages. In a world where the expression or term love has been so perverted, misunderstood, and misrepresented. It is needful that I direct your attention to perhaps the most referenced Scripture contained within the Bible regarding the matter of *love, 1* Corinthians chapter thirteen.

Though this Scripture speaks to the love that we as Christians should display, its operation or exercise also includes the relationship shared between a husband and his wife. As well as to be seen operating within a godly dating relationship.

God ordained the institution of marriage. He purposed that it be shared between a man and a woman to be experienced and that they may express the true love of God through their joining as one. Within this sanctified union, where true *love* is understood and embraced and observed at work in the relationship as purposed by God, who is Love, love is then to be freely expressed towards others. Love, as presented here, is not sexual. The true love of God begets Life (Zoe) – it is spiritual and eternal. Therefore, this union is for the purpose of expressing God's love and His glory to the world - that eternal life may be made known. Indeed, Christians are created to express the love of God for the world to see, that God's name may be made glorious! It can be said that such a union is a match made and affirmed in heaven.

A couple's undergirding being established upon Love - God Himself. Therefore, by acquiring some understanding of Love's truth as they build their union and continue to grow, then and only then, a couple is empowered to sustain their heavenly-ordained marriage. A couple grasping Love and even battling at times to maintain and walk in the love of God is nonetheless equipped to develop a healthy partnership and achieve a victorious and joyous union shared with their Beloved. But how often do we see couples seemingly *in love* but over time, the relationship fizzles? For this reason, the idea of being *in love and getting married* is catching a bad rap, not taken seriously, and for others, Love ... a concept to be feared and avoided altogether.

Look, your victory relationally can be made sure or guaranteed! How can I say this? Because the Almighty and All-Powerful God is on your side (Romans 8:31; 1 John 4:4; Philippians 4:13)! If only we, the children of God, will remain in Love or *in* Jesus, are we then assured victory! Sadly, this is where too many Christians fall short – we don't remain in Love or one with Jesus. Too often, we leave or fail to cleave to Him, making the mistake of thinking we are self-sufficient. We underestimate the ease with which we can turn to self-reliance. Or all together, denying a relationship with God, going it alone in this ruthless world, while depending upon our insufficient reasoning and finite understanding. Under these conditions, Satan has you where he wants you – defenseless if not defeated! Many have and will fail to see their defeat until things really get bad and blow up in their faces! And then, for many – it will be too late!

Yes, marriages can be victorious and joyous ... mine is! Now, I didn't say perfect, nor am I saying my marriage to my beloved Lisa is absent of moments of misunderstanding or disagreements. All marriages consist of flawed people; therefore, things will not always be in sync. However, it is a proper understanding of Love that sees a relationship through such times. We all are a work in progress. But the enemy of our soul seeks to halt that progress and even the process of us becoming more like Jesus in love and unity.

That said, if you haven't understood or haven't gotten it by now - marriages are and have been under attack since the beginning of time as we know it. I recall your attention to Adam and the defeat and division of his home. Yes! Satan wants your house and relationship too! Especially those unions where God is being honored through the institution of a holy marriage!

Let the warning trumpet blow! Readers beware! There is a concerted effort by the enemy of God – formerly known as Lucifer, the Morning Star. But now, Satan, that fallen angel, aims to wage war against God and man! Yes, Satan despises God and His image-bearers – you and me! However, he knows he can't touch God. But through our suffering and defeat, he causes our Father to grieve over His children, His imagers … The *Saved* and unsaved alike.

Where marital defenses (spiritual safeguards), if there were any in place, have been overrun by opposing spiritually wicked or demonic forces, whether through one's own doing or not. If there is to be hope for rescuing a marriage that is under siege or overtaken, or to just preserve and protect your marriage. If a healthy marriage is to be regained, sustained, or remain steadfast against such assaults, well then, my friends, you had better put up and keep up your spiritual dukes – arm yourselves, for we are in a very real battle! War has been declared against us (Ephesians 6:12)! We must constantly be in a state of readiness to do battle for the sake of our marriages and our family at all times! Keep in mind that our enemy may deploy various tactics and degrees of bombardment to come at us. But fret not … in Christ, we are *Overcomers* and *Victors* already if we abide in love – remain one with Christ and one with another through love.

Where any holy union (God-ordained marriage) has weathered adversity, know for certain that a battle was waged; spiritual warfare was occurring. Perhaps playing out with little to no spiritual armament, or even knowledge that the couple was actually engaged in spiritual warfare. Nonetheless, by the grace of God, they made it through! But know this, that it was not by their efforts alone that they remain standing; somebody prayed for them when they couldn't, or didn't know to pray for themselves, or even knew quite what to do. Oh, for God's grace and mercy and those praying Saints!

Listen. It may have been as the couple, or you were engaged in battle – and not knowing what to do, that someone was praying for you. Or it may have been the intercession of some caring and loving soul praying beforehand, which God honored on your behalf. Nevertheless, where victory was achieved, prayers were answered as heaven engaged in the battle that you may be victorious!

It is utterly important that we surround ourselves with those who put their faith in God – other Believers. It's vitally important to have believing parents and other faith-filled members covering us in prayer. *The effectual fervent prayer of the righteous avails much* (James 5:16).

Marriages, especially those established before God and witnessed by angels. And all in attendance during the wedding ceremony have been marked by God's archenemy – Satan, our foe, who is to be withstood when our marriages are under siege regardless of the cause.

All of the faithful attendees are targets of Satan by your mere association with that holy assembly – The Marriage Ceremony. Satan's aim, knowing that he is condemned and has little time remaining, seeks to oppose and attempt to inflict disruption of whatever sort upon all who are righteous. And he desires to turn you against the institution of holy marriage. And if you are married, divide your home and turn you against your spouse … Satan lusts to destroy the family structure as established by God!

Satan's mission is to distort, dilute, and even destroy all that has been ordained or established by God. Or that which has the potential of bringing Him glory and praise. Holy marriages are such institutions, as they are established by our Father to represent the *Triune Family of God* (Father, Son, Spirit) here on earth. If marriages are weakened, distorted, or destroyed by Satan, and where children are born through this union, it creates an environment or community of certain uncertainty, confusion, and brokenness of far-reaching consequences!

Many good marriages and well-intended couples have succumbed to the onslaught of the forces of evil. Even so, the evil or lovelessness arising from within our souls being a detriment to relationships if not kept in check … this evil within man results from our self-serving sin-nature. But we are called to be victorious: *as greater is He who is in us than he who is of the world.* To such battles and victory, I can personally testify. Who has not had to do battle? I have done battle; some I lost, but yet I stand as a Victor! With the help of the Spirit who lives within me, I stand as an Overcomer and can no longer be hoodwinked or defeated by Satan. With greater ease, I overcome and withstand the evils of this world. This is only possible because of my dependence on and relationship with God. I have chosen to remain one with Him. Why? Because of the love and care Jesus has shown to me!

I have a question for you. Have you ever written a love letter to someone, or perhaps had one written to you? They can be some kind of special! If you have not had someone invest the time and thoughtfulness required to write one to you, I present to you your first -The Bible. It is from God, your Father, who loves you beyond measure!

As I read the Bible. It is unquestionably the most incredible Love letter and story ever told. Its pages share God's Words, His love toward His fallen and lost people, those who missed the mark, and those who will miss the mark. This includes both you and me. To miss the mark: That is, fall short (to sin or practice sinning) of God's requirements for righteous or holy living.

God's love for fallen humanity is the reason behind this Holy Writ, His inspired writings, namely the Holy Bible, and our love letter from the Father. It is God's Word – the Bible, written to His beloved children and imagers that we come to know our Father personally or intimately. Having accepted His invitation to salvation and eternal life through Jesus - the *Living Word,* we are welcomed into the Kingdom of God.

If not beforehand … perhaps you can now see the Bible as God's love letter to man. A love letter informing you personally of the redemptive work of a loving and merciful God and Father. Even so, the beautiful attributes of God are shown throughout the pages of the Bible so that we may get to know Him better. Of His many marvelous attributes: the greatest of them would be the endless Love He has and extends to all! It is a love that continuously summons all who will; To come unto Him. To come to the One who is the Lover of our souls, our Rescuer from this present evil world! And lest we forget, though God's love is endless, there is also the matter of His justice and judgment, which is sure – it will not be delayed much longer! Though God's love never ends, one day soon, it will give way to His justice, judgment, and condemnation because of sin and the rejection of Jesus! God's love is sure, and so is His judgment for those who reject and refuse His love; His Beloved Son – Jesus.

Because of the love of the Father, He earnestly desires all to receive His love; so that we may covenant and become one with our True Lover, who also wants to pardon us from sin and condemnation. Now, give a moment to think about the suffering and humiliation that the Father allowed His Beloved Son to be subjected to; this agony He endured was for you and for me (John 3:16). Such suffering and selfless sacrifice I cannot fully comprehend. However, a recent movie depicting Jesus' suffering or passion is provided from Scripture, and historical writings detailing the manner and describing the whip used to rip open his flesh. Jesus endured hell on earth for you and for me! As if that was not enough torture, and it was not. He endured merciless cruelty as He was crucified by nailing His hands and feet to a wooden cross. What a horrible image to behold. Even so, we cannot fully fathom His suffering. And yet, this was a necessary evil that was predetermined by God our Father on our behalf because of the Father's love for you and for me (1 Peter 1:20; Acts 2:23; Hebrews 2:14).

The Father permitted the suffering of His Son. It was to this suffering and His destination with death and the cross for which Jesus came into this world. *Jesus facing off with Death and giving Himself over to it was the capstone of his display of love through suffering – He did this for you and for me! Greater love hath no man than this that He would lay down His life for a friend* (John 15:13).

Through Jesus's life, the service He offered, and the miracles of healing He performed. His love and care for man were openly shown, not only in His living but also through His sacrificial death.

The Bible unquestionably points to God's unceasing and patient love, which must be willfully received so that He may then impart Love - Himself to all who see the *need* for Him. It is not merely a cliché; the saying, *What the world needs is more love.* However, it is the love of God, imparted by His Spirit, into the hearts of man that the people of this world need. This Love is not sexual. It is not physical; instead, it is intimacy with God, our hearts connecting with His, thus leading to the transformation or renewal of one's soul. A conversion from acts and actions unto death. To a work or labor of love and service, even sacrifice to self, that life may be gained by others. This is Love!

The Apostle Paul provides for us in 1 Corinthians 13:4 - 8 the nature and outpouring of godly love. This is not an act of self or the so-called good that we may do. This display of godly love can only be achieved by the Spirit's regeneration and His perpetual infilling within the souls of man – which is to our sanctification. Even so, Jesus, while clothed in *flesh,* had to daily depend upon the empowering and/or provision of the Spirit of God (Philippians 2:7). For this reason, He prayed or remained in touch with His Father and our Father continuously. Should we do any less?

Saul, aka the Apostle Paul, and the penman of this letter to the church at Corinth. After his encounter with Jesus, he gave his life over to loving service and even sacrifice for the cause of Christ. This was a radical change in Paul's life toward Jesus. It occurred because of the love and mercy Jesus had for Paul, who was enabled to perceive that Jesus was, in fact, his Lord, Savior, and the King of kings!

On this matter of Love, let us now consider Paul's powerful and eternal words revealed to him by Jesus: *"Love (Jesus) is patient and kind; love (Jesus) does not envy or boast; it (Jesus) is not arrogant or rude. It (Jesus) does not insist on its (His) own way (rather the will of His Father); it (Jesus) is not irritable or resentful; it (Jesus) does not rejoice at wrongdoing but rejoices with the truth. Love bears all things, believes all things, hopes all things, and endures all things. Love never ends"* (1 Corinthians 13:4-8).

Now, feel free to insert your name within the brackets alongside Jesus' name. How well are you measuring up? I am there with you - a work in progress. And therefore, in need of the Spirit's fresh anointing daily, convicting me, comforting me, and enabling me so that I may live out my sanctification or separation from this present evil world.

Step One, Love

You have undoubtedly seen where product manufacturers have provided instructions for their merchandise's assembly or intended use. Provided are the necessary steps, as needed, to put together or utilize the product to maximize its effectiveness so that one may acquire full benefits from the product's designed usage. There may also be included in the instructions, prohibitions, and warnings to be heeded when using the product. This ordering is provided and written out that the end result of the intended purpose and usage of the product may not only yield the Maker's envisioned or purposed outcome. But also bring about for the beneficiary of the product; the ultimate satisfaction and fulfillment as the desired result of the product's purpose was achieved.

This positive and productive outcome could only be accomplished due to the instructions provided, read, and adhered to. On the other hand, a misstep, or for one to proceed without the product's instructions or with willful disregard for the steps or misuse of the product, will inevitably lead to a less favorable outcome; an inoperative or faulty product, the product's destruction or worst, harm occurring to the user or some other(s).

If man, God's creation, has recognized the need and understands the benefit of providing carefully written instructions. Whereby enabling the user to profit from the product of their making, thereby achieving the product's ultimate performance to everyone's benefit and delight. All the more, God, our loving Father and Omniscient Creator, who had you and me in His mind before the creation of heaven and earth, in His absence, would provide mankind with written instructions by which to live. For the Church, this is the Bible, our Father's love letter to His Creation.

This Manual is given to us by God to maximize our enjoyment - benefit, and safety while we dwell here on this earth. Adhering to this Manual, God's commands therein, and man getting things right … not necessarily perfect, is to the delight of our Father and Creator. However, before the Bible was written. God, in His wisdom, sent His only begotten or *Unique* Son to show us how to live out His ordinances and holy instructions unto righteousness. This shows how much the Father loves us, in that He sent His only begotten Son to demonstrate to us not only how we are to live as His Beloved in this sinful world but also how to die to sin and to be willing to die for some other, in order to display the greatest act of love - self-sacrifice!

When Love (God) is firmly established within a God-purposed and ordained union, with relative ease, notwithstanding disagreements and various challenges at times. Nevertheless, a godly relationship will prosper and be victorious! And so it is, in order for a godly relationship to be established and for it to attain its highest achievement or fulfillment – Love must be the first and main ingredient.

Why is it that we see what appear to be loving couples' relationships dissolve? The answer is simple ... Either *Love* was never established. Meaning ... What was experienced by the couple. And observed by others was merely a fondness the two shared for one another. Or perhaps it was lust for one another or some other motivation giving an outward appearance and inward deception or misunderstanding of love. However, *true love* was not understood by the two involved. Neither did those who observed what they believed to have been a loving relationship, was that which it appeared to be. That said, either one of them or neither of them had hearts that were converted through a true, life-changing, and loving relationship with God. Another reason some ideal couple's relationship comes apart is that they fail to remain connected to Love – Jesus the Vine and their Life source. *A branch cannot bear fruit unless it abides in the Vine* (John 15:4). Love is the fruit of the Spirit.

For a couple to attain their highest achievement or fulfillment, both individuals must be and even intently persistent in remaining one in Christ - the Vine. If only one person is committed to Christ, the relationship has, at best - a fifty-fifty chance at success. If, by chance, the couple remains together. And although things may be okay within the union. The relationship cannot achieve its optimum purpose since one individual has not united with or become one or committed to Jesus. Where Christ is not the center of a marital union and the fortress surrounding the couple, the union is vulnerable to the assault of the forces of evil. The evidence of those who have succumbed to demonic attacks is all around us. The casualties of Satan's spiritual warfare against marriages are apparent, as seen in the many marriages ending in divorce, even so, from those fearful of marital commitment - Gamophobia. And, enough cannot be said about the spiritually wounded and those who are spiritually broken or devastated as a result of horrific relationships they encountered within or outside of marriages.

Beloved of God, here is something you must grasp: No matter how sincere one may be presenting his/herself to you. They may be saying and doing the right things to win your affection - this being perceived as a good thing. However, godly or agape love (more on this later) cannot be conceived within the carnal mind or one who is unregenerate. Neither can a union be expected to remain solid where one breaks fellowship with Christ no matter how sincere they appear. Besides … a person who may be saying and doing the right things with what may seem like sincerity may only be a ruse to win your affection.

I caution you! If one's heart is not in tune with the heartbeat of Christ, they are merely motivated by their passions. They are speaking and acting or doing things for you due to their feelings, which can, and most likely will, fade away over time. At which time, they will be directed by their passion towards some other who has aroused them. This motivation is the operation of the flesh. And so, desires, passions, or feelings will fade when feelings are motivated by the flesh. True or godly love does not – it's a matter of a converted heart or renewed spirit and not fleshly desires alone!

Even within a godly relationship, a couple will not remain on cloud nine - that is, have intense feelings for one another perpetually. Instead, there are moments throughout a marriage, or there should be when there are heightened feelings and not merely sexual or fleshly interest that a spouse will have toward the other. However, this does not just happen. One has to pursue the mountain-top experiences within one's marriage! This requires putting forth the effort resulting from *Love* to achieve these moments of great delight or even ecstasy with your Beloved - your spouse. And even with God! Yes, with God also! God desires for you to have mountain-top experiences with your spouse and with Him as well! You didn't see the God part coming - did you?

We must grasp Love, God our *Chief Corner Stone,* which binds and holds godly relationships together. Jesus is the foundation upon which all things relational are built and made sure! There is no alternative! Even at our best efforts and intentions towards establishing a relationship, man is fickle apart from God. Where Love is understood and activated in one's life as described in the text of 1 Corinthians 13, blessings await the emerging couple! Victory is theirs!

Stay in the fight! Stay in Christ! Stay in Love!

America Is Shaking

Where there is an absence or rejection of *Love* - God Himself. A misunderstanding of love arises, and one will inevitably dream up and embrace a perverted form of love, which isn't love. Where *Love* has been lost or dismissed, immorality of all sorts will embed itself within the culture! We are currently witnessing this evil become a stronghold upon this nation!

No doubt, you have witnessed with some other, perhaps have even experienced yourself, an unsettling within your soul because of the absence of *Love*. Naively, maybe you embraced, or maybe you know or knew someone who was duped by the perverted version of love. The effects of the misuse, the misunderstanding, and the embracing of perverted love and/or sex are leading to all sorts of deviant behaviors and twisted reasoning. What pains me: many cannot see the mess they are creating for themselves and others because of their lack of godly understanding of love and sex.

It has been noted that Christian values are the foundation upon which this morally flawed nation (USA) was founded. Christian values ... Really!? Some may rightly scratch their heads when hearing this. This will then suggest that the outward working of love was in effect when this land was seized or stolen from its native people and this nation was founded. Far from it! Many people, and rightly so ... will beg the differ that love was extended by European settlers to the indigenous people of North America. Let alone love shown to Africans who were brought to the shores of North America against their will on slave ships.

Regardless of how you feel about this nation's beginnings or how much is questionable regarding its history. Or who this Country's primary beneficiaries were and are. The Christian values. Whatever they were, which established and helped to shape this country. They are being systematically disregarded and dismantled. America's moral foundation is currently the shakiest it has been in my lifetime and is worsening. We are even seeing this decline of morality amongst or within our local and national leadership.

Within their ranks, immorality is becoming pervasive, invasive, and an acceptable "new norm." All of which significantly affect the condition of families, individuals, and even the world. Humanity is one people, regardless of our different ethnicities or the land boundaries and waters that separate us. We are a global community. Things do not happen in a vacuum. There is always causality that affects our relationships with others, both near and far. In one way or another, we all are affected by the actions of others ... the good, the bad, and the ugly, simply because we are, in fact, one! We all are one – the human race, whether we like it or not!

America's influence - its good, bad, and even its ugliness cannot be underestimated. Nor its bad and ugliness excused when it is on display before the world to see! The world has seen America at its best when "she" is generous through her humanitarian efforts and the pursuit of liberation for the oppressed. Some may even describe this kind of regard or benevolence shown toward a fellow man as an act of love! These acts of kindness and the pursuit of justice by this nation on behalf of others are Biblical principles.

How is it, then, that one can associate such actions as benevolent ... a good, kind, or loving thing which is to be commended and even imitated? And yet, many fail at displaying love or having the same understanding while involved with another here at home. In our culture - the matter of love relating to heterosexual or monogamous relationships often seems to be viewed through a different and even flawed lens.

Why is it ... many have such sordid or perverted views on love and sex? And, without giving it a second thought, they readily interchange these two words when discussing or expressing sexual intimacy. Thus far, much has been stated regarding love. Biblically speaking, nothing suggests that it has anything to do with sex or sexual desires. Love is clearly demonstrated as being associated with man's heart or spirit, what we do or strive to display as children of God, Who is love. While sex is a matter of man's biology, his flesh or bodily passion - that which is one with this world.

This misunderstanding of love and sex. Satanic perversion of man's reasoning on the subjects is seen in operation through demonically influenced media, including all who oppose the Word of God, who thereby promote false doctrines or teachings contrary to the Bible. These messages received from the demonic spirit world by those of this world are tragically and sadly redefining America's cultural values and the worldview of many. But this should not and must not be the case for those of us who are Children of God! *We are in this world but not of it or one with it* (1 John 4:4-6)!

Unfortunately, countless men and women, even those of the faith, have fallen prey to the Seductress – this World's enticing or Satan's influence over it. As for those of us who are faithful Christians, though we abide in this world for a time. We are not to be like those of this world. Or become one with them, such people whose minds have been overtaken by selfish desires or the demonic world's influence over them. Therefore, they believe the lies of mortal man and their own lies. And, therefore, are aligned and even allies with Satan, with such people we are not to be yoked with.

Children of God. Worldly and idolatrous living. Being dragged along by the passions of our flesh must be a thing of your past. For we are now citizens of a Heavenly Kingdom! Our souls quickened (revived, made alive) having been sanctified (set apart, made holy) unto God our Father; our minds being transformed and/or renewed, we are no longer to conform to the dictates of this world. Instead, we are to live a life pleasing to our God and Father. Now that we have been consecrated (set apart, made holy) for and by Him, we are now one with God and are to live for Him alone.

As it had been for America's beginnings, Christian values significantly directed the mores of African Americans, even before we were brought to these shores. However, it appears to me that in the mid-1960s and 1970s, a rather noticeable deviation and decline from Biblical or Christian values began to overtake this country. Continuing there afterward, a hastening of this nation's moral decay, with the trend continuing and even picking up momentum with no deviation from this disastrous course. Because of this downward turn, godly relationships are being met with various challenges. Daily, the evidence of this Nation's increasing decadence is presented for the world to see. Neither has this debauchery gone unnoticed by God!

Let's take another glance at 1 Corinthians 13: 4 - 8. This portion of Scripture unquestionably underscores the fact that we have missed the mark or that many have a flawed understanding of the meaning and the matter of Love's method of operation. Look at what God declares: *"Love is patient and kind; love does not envy or boast; it is not arrogant or rude. It does not insist on its own way; it is not irritable or resentful; it does not rejoice at wrongdoing but rejoices with the truth. Love bears all things, believes all things, hopes all things, and endures all things. Love never ends."*

People, this is the Word of God! His love letter to you! It would serve all of us well if only we would receive and honor it; meditate upon it, thereby allowing God's Truth to saturate our hearts and minds. That it may redefine our reason for existing: Which is to receive God's redemptive love and share His love with the world!

Perhaps some of you may be thinking … "God is asking too much of me. Or I have said much about love, which I now know is separate from sex. Well, where does sex come into the picture … what does God have to say on the subject?" How soon we forget. On the matter of God asking too much of you: Look, and I remind you. What God wants you to become and do has nothing to do with your self-sufficiency or effort. I remind you. The inward working of your transformation or your new way of thinking. And acting is the procedure that God, through his Spirit, performs in - and works through those who belong to Him. So, you are absolutely right. *Love,* and all *It* encompasses, is asking too much for us to attain and perform. Apart from the Spirit of God, no good is in us, nor can we do the good such as He desires and requires from us.

Through His Life-giving and empowering Spirit, it is God who performs the work in us. He alone enables or empowers us to spiritually mature so that we may grow or come to know Love – God the Father. As a result of our relationship with *Love*, we are then enabled to show and share *Love* with others.

And yet, it is "Not by our might neither by our strength or effort" (Zechariah 4:6). Instead, it is God working in us those spiritual attributes of His. Or the fruit of the Spirit, which in and of ourselves, we are incapable of achieving or producing apart from Him.

Where Does Sex Come Into The Picture

Hopefully, you now see Love as diametrically opposed to the world's view of love. After all the talk on Love, a handful of you may be wondering about sexual relations. And when sex can be explored with your Beloved. It's not like I haven't addressed the subject. However, perhaps just a few of you need a reminder, or you missed what 1 Corinthians 13 had to say on the matter. I believe there is more said on the topic than a casual read through the text may provide. You shall see what I am talking about shortly.

It is embraced by the world's view that sexual intercourse is associated with one "being in love" … or not. And sexual intercourse is the act of "making love." Is there really such a thing as making love? My position on the idea is rather apparent: it is this world's view. And the people of this world have gotten the matter twisted or perverted. This is not new. This is what Satan is good at – perverting God's design and His purpose within the minds of His creation.

Because of this fallacy, "Making love." Commonly it is with men when our sexual feelings, lust, or passion diminishes; this often begins after the first sexual encounter with their naïve and eager participant. The so-called notion of lovemaking being only passion induced - the thought they had or what they felt toward the other person diminishes or becomes nonexistent. And so, what was considered or thought to be love through worldly or perverted reasoning and feelings. That which they had considered or mistaken as love. Instead becomes a mere fleeting moment enthralled in fleshly fervor or lust satisfied. And therefore, their feelings pass away in the night or whenever, and with whomever, immediately or shortly after sexual relations.

Do we dare call this love... let alone love-making? As a result of this confusion, the true meaning of love is tragically misrepresented. Therefore, what could otherwise be a healthy, meaningful, and lovingly committed relationship, is being fearfully entered into, if not avoided altogether. And why? Because true and real love has been cast by this world as something different from what God intended. Which is wrong thinking where love has to do with or is associated with one's feelings or fleshly longing. And so, we should understand by now. The true meaning of love and even sexual relations is so egregiously misunderstood or willfully perverted that we have before us relational dysfunction in the likes of a global endemic.

As for being in love, we now know it is not synonymous with sexual intercourse, as per this world's view. However, being in godly love teaches one how to care for their Beloved through righteous conduct. Even so, how to approach and even engage in the gift and the wonder and delight of sexual intercourse. When one is brought to completion or understanding of being in godly love, one's sexual relations with their Beloved will be more meaningful and delightful! After more than three decades of marriage, I speak from what I know to be the case.

1 Corinthians 13: 4-8. From this text, we have heard what God has to say on the matter of love. Paul presents to us what godly character should look like or how we, as children of God, are to conduct ourselves toward others. Will you take heed? Is there a need for you to ask God to transform your heart so that your character and conduct may reflect His image? Yes, daily!

Now for the matter of sexual relations. What does the Biblical text speak to us about the topic? I will now elaborate on the matter of sexual relations, also utilizing the aforementioned Scripture. I don't think it to be a stretch to read my sanctified perspective into the text. It was God's idea and His alone to give us sexual intercourse to be enjoyed between a husband and his wife. He established this incredible joining when God gave Eve to Adam as his bride.

1 Corinthians chapter 13 informs us of the following:

Love is patient and kind: Therefore, will one dare pressure their Beloved to engage in sexual relations before marriage? Or how about making them feel guilty about choosing to wait?

On the other hand, when married, one must consider their spouse's sexual desires and duty to minister to their spouse's needs. However, whatever the desire(s) may be, it must be mutually agreed upon. Only then can the sexual union between a husband and wife be spoken of as being expressed in the beauty of holiness or the two becoming one sexually in mutual fulfillment and harmony.

Also, bear in mind that there are times when sexual relations may have to be put on hold. During such time, love is expressed through prayerful patience and kindness until the two can unite sexually (1 Corinthians 7:5).

Love does not envy or boast: Whatever one's sexual experience may be resulting from their sinful past, be sure to keep this in your past! Your Beloved does not want to hear about how good you may have been to some other or what someone may have done to meet your desires. Therefore, be careful that you do not cause your spouse to become insecure or envious of a person with whom you practiced sinning.

Love is not arrogant or rude: If you are more aware or experienced sexually than your spouse. With humility, patience, and kindness, present yourself before your spouse with calming reassurance and understanding that they will be at ease within your loving embrace and guidance. Where sexual confidence may be lacking with your Beloved, be considerate and encouraging, and let them know that they can do no wrong. Through the holy expression of sexual intimacy, you two will grow together. And your bond will be strengthened when tender love and care are shown toward your spouse. Sexual relation is God's design and gift to freely give to your spouse. What enjoyment is to be anticipated and experienced when a married couple is joined together sexually in a sanctified union where humility, kindness, and understanding are practiced.

Love does not insist on its own way: A selfish spouse is not operating in love when it is all about them … and this is all the time. Sexual intimacy at times requires compromising, but not to the point of offending your spouse's conscience or conviction. It is not; neither can it always be about what you want from your spouse. But neither is a spouse to simply disregard the reasonable desires of their spouse. What is reasonable? In whatever manner and how often you two agree to freely give of yourself for the enjoyment of one another sexually.

Love is not irritable or resentful: If you are an unforgiving, irritable, and moody person, can you really expect your Beloved to freely and desirously give themselves to you? If you are a resentful and unforgiven person, a heart of love has been kept from you, making it difficult for intimacy and even love to flow freely and be expressed to you from your Beloved.

Love does not rejoice at wrongdoing: A heart that has been hurt or wronged may need time for healing. Intimacy, sexual or otherwise, will most definitely be affected by one who is emotionally hurting or whose heart has suffered a wound. Understand something. If you caused pain or the wounding of your Beloved's heart. You can't always expect an apology; your words, "I'm sorry," to necessarily bring about immediate healing or soothing. Yes, it depends on what occurred. However, there may come a time when you have to restore the confidence of your Beloved towards you. You must be willing to do your part to help facilitate this healing. Again, this may not occur overnight, nor over dinner and a movie – but it's a start. Love is patient and kind … where love prevails in a godly relationship - restoration will follow.

Love rejoices with the truth: Where truth is never compromised, a trusting heart will freely and confidently give of itself - it knows no limits! A faithful and trusting companion is a wall of protection and comfort for the soul of their Beloved. But where trust has been broken, and depending on how it was breached, restoring that wall can be challenging. Therefore, I encourage you to always walk faithfully and be led by truth.

Love bears all things, believes all things, hopes all things, and endures all things. Love never ends: Where Love is understood and lived out, bearing, believing, hoping, and enduring all things without end, the entire experience shared between you and your spouse will be victorious and rewarding in every aspect.

As I see it, 1 Corinthians 13 also addresses the question of sexual intimacy that is to be shared between a husband and his wife. While also providing guidance for couples who are dating or engaged to marry.

One of the many problems with defining and viewing sex and/or love from the culture's lens or this world's view. It falsely leads one to think they can decide what they want or need relationally based on their reasoning or desires. "Love is love," some say, wrongfully permitting or justifying homosexual relations or other perversions. For some, sex is all they want. And that is all they pursue from a relationship … be it from a committed relationship or not. Others want "love" with the benefit of sex but without marital commitment. The great mistake which is occurring too often: is that of sexual engagement or entanglement before there is an understanding of godly love. Tragically many don't realize nor comprehend that there is such a thing as godly love that a person can possess. Resulting from this ignorance of the Person who is Love – God Himself, significant harm spiritually and otherwise has occurred to individuals and countless families.

Those entering or engaging in these unholy unions are confused. The offspring or fruit of these unions, regardless of how good they may seem, turn out or produces more confusion and even greater spiritual depravity. Many are just confused by this world's messaging … they are spiritually blind. Others believe deep feelings for someone or deep sexual longings for someone are associated with being in love. More often than not, these relational situations or scenarios lead to disastrous outcomes. I am primarily speaking of the spiritual (mental or emotional) toll that these unholy unions have on a soul. The only remedy is first to know the love of God.

Within every soul, there is a natural longing to belong - to be wanted and to be loved. Where there is confusion and/or wrong messaging on how to acquire these innate longings, we will have the aforementioned relational scenarios and disastrous outcomes. Until one understands their longings are foremost spiritual, man will continue to make choices that appeal to their flesh or their own reasoning.

Until mankind enters that right relationship, his or her spirit quickened or made alive and one with God the Holy Spirit, man's thoughts toward sex in the perverted sense will remain corrupt. And on the matter of love... it being what man makes it to be. Where the two – love and sex, are misunderstood, this makes for a dangerous and even deadly cocktail.

At best (loosely speaking), emotions in the given scenarios will be all over the place. Listen carefully. The evidence is all around us. Inevitable hurt and confusion will be the likely outcome for those who join themselves sexually outside of the plan of God. In the unlikely event that a marriage is established from one of the unholy scenarios. Because the union's foundation was not found upon Love but something else. Let's say sex: when the marriage faces challenges of whatever sort. Let's say the thrill of sex is gone. Because the marriage was established upon that which is of this world or fleshly, it cannot stand or be victorious. Because it was devoid of Love.

Clearly, sex and "love" are not mutually inclusive as defined by this world. Two can engage sexually, and Love is nowhere to be found. They are simply acting upon their sexual impulse or flesh's longing. Often it is merely the appetite of the flesh or lust which is the reason for one to engage in sex apart from marriage. Or even commit adultery. No feelings involved - no Love, just lust, the craving of one's flesh! The absence of Love in the world and the lack of true understanding of Love are why the 1 Corinthian text and the entire Bible must be embraced as the very Word of God. God is our only help and hope for clarity on matters of Life and Love!

A person can have what is generally called "love" for someone. However, it really is intense *feelings*, which may also involve physical attraction, yet, without unnatural sexual longings for the person. I experienced this while courting my wife. However, regarding godly love, my understanding of the subject was greatly lacking.

A person who has feelings towards some other. From within that person is felt a stirring or excitement, care for the person or their wellbeing is heightened. One undergoing this experience can't get enough of the person; the person is constantly on their mind. So much is the attraction toward the person - one may dream about them. Or perhaps, not being able to sleep or eat because the person is overwhelmed by their feelings. This experience can often be mistaken for one "being in love."

Many have had this overwhelming feeling for someone, and perhaps the feelings were mutual. But for whatever the reason, the flame which once burned - one towards another, fizzled. No question those feelings were real. Just the same - what was felt can be easily misinterpreted for what it is not or ever was - Love. This misunderstanding - those who have recently entered into romance or a married couple. The length of time the two have been married or dating is of no consequence; their marriage or the relationship is nevertheless based upon feelings and not love. Simply because God is not one with the union.

And so, at the dwindling of one's feelings or affections. This, then is misunderstood or perceived as one "falling out of love." Is this really possible … can one "fall out of love?" If love is only based on how one feels towards someone, one can reason - yes. However, we have learned from the Word of God that godly love has nothing to do with how one feels affectionately about another. And besides, Love, as described in 1 Corinthians 13:8, is never failing and without end.

This misunderstanding of love. It being based upon affections or feelings alone is quite problematic for the person who gauges their feelings or attraction toward another as the indicator of their standing or love for another, at the inkling of there being any waning of attraction or emotions. The relationship at that moment is then put in jeopardy. Concern, discouragement of whatever the sort, and even unreasonable judgment of the person with whom they had strong feelings will begin to invade the relationship. Following, doubt is cast upon one's decision to have entered into the relationship. Often-time, the person's solution to their perceived dilemma, which is of their own making, is to cut ties with the person. Or unknowingly or perhaps knowingly sabotage the relationship.

The words love and sex, which has been minimized, maligned, and misrepresented by our culture, has lost their sacred and spiritual significance. Where attempts are made to apply these words or understand their meaning apart from God, the outcome for the couple or individual will be heartache and confusion, disappointment, and continual relational break-ups.

From my observation, there is more confusion with the usage of the word love than the word sex and what it implies. Sex, simple enough: speaks to a male and female engaging in sexual activity. On the other hand, the word love is often used to express one's great delight in *whatever* a person is highly satisfied by or with. The pleasure or satisfaction that one experiences through their sensory receptors can be so rapturous or gratifying that many do not think twice about expressing their "love" for or toward whatever has aroused them or brought them a high degree of fulfillment and pleasure.

We will now take a moment to look at - or into the word love. A proper understanding and application of the word *love* can prove quite beneficial. Its various meanings should enable one to better understand and appreciate other Biblical applications and ancient usage of this dynamic and provoking word. Therefore, one, gaining a broader and more precise understanding and the true sense of this word - love, should hereafter no longer carelessly or thoughtlessly apply the word love to whatever one delights in, resulting from their sensory receptors (flesh) having been stimulated. But instead. Embrace and elevate the beauty and sacredness that the word *love* was intended by God to capture and express.

In no particular order, let us discover the broader meaning of the word *love* and, to a lesser degree, sex as expressed within the Bible:

Agape (love): From this Greek word meaning love, it encapsulates the words benevolent, selfless, and unconditional. Agape is not stagnant; it is active and is recognized by what it does for the benefit of others, regardless of one's feelings or relationship toward another. This is love in its most perfect sense: unprompted love in action toward someone, producing positive results by demonstrating hospitality, sympathy, contentment, and faithfulness towards others. These things or occurrences just are.

Agape is demonstrated as simply doing the right thing, no matter what – no questions asked! This is the unconditional love of God – it is Agape.

Phileo (love) is the Greek word associated with tender affection and fondness toward another. This person is held in high regard by you. Their character and personality are most favorable. But the connecting with them measures shy of a deep emotional connection. This is highly valued friendship or brotherly love.

Ahav and ***Racham*** and ***Storge'*** (love): These three words have similar meanings. It is the love of a parent towards a child, a dear friend, or between spouses – there is a deep, heartfelt, emotional, or soul connection, and rarely related to sexual intimacy. Also, it is used for lusting, even for the love of certain things.

Yada (to have sexual relation): This expression is to *know* another sexually. A knowing through sensory perception or knowledge acquired of another as a result of sexual intimacy. This was expressed between Adam and Eve when he had sexual relations or *knew* (Yada) his wife, Eve.

Eros (love): The Greek word eros *does not* appear in the Biblical text. Nonetheless, the meaning is romantic, sexual expression, or passionate. From eros, we get the English word erotic. However, romantic and sexual expressions are clearly expressed throughout the Bible ... simply read Song of Solomon.

*As for sex, we have the word **Shakhav*.** This word usage is for the expressed purpose of lying down with, for copulation that is unfettered sex, no strings attached – in other words, fornication or sexual sin. Or the word can be used to indicate one resting. This word best describes what is occurring with many – sexual sins. The word love, as utilized in the Bible, clearly is not its equivalent.

We now see through a quick study of the words meaning love and their varying usage. Resulting from this study, you now have a better understanding and appreciation of the Biblical meanings of love. What are you to take from this insight? Perhaps, the word love being no longer carelessly mistreated and misapplied.

Love is to be viewed unequivocally as relational: Human interaction or expression toward one another. And with the boundaries of love (Phileo) either expanding or retracting. Depending upon the association of those you are involved with. However, as demonstrated to the church in Corinthians, Agape is to remain faithful at all times. Godly love knows no limits; it is to be extended to all, just as God has faithfully shown His Agape to you and to me. God's love is free to all… one must choose with whom one will partner. Will it be with this world's god (Satan), as was the case with Adam and Eve? Or will you partner with the *Only Eternal and Wise God* – The One Who Is Love and who loves you beyond measure?

On The Matter of Sex

As for sexual relations … without question, this is an essential aspect of every healthy marriage. And so, we must have clarity on this topic as well. It is by God's design that we are created as sexual beings. The pleasure experienced therein is a gift to be shared and expressed in the bond and beauty of marriage (1 Corinthians 7:9). Consequently, there should not be hesitancy in discussing this subject of sexual intimacy with your Beloved.

However, sexual relations between spouses should not be *the be-all-and-end-all* or the highest priority to be attained or given attention to. But no doubt, a matter of importance that must not be taken for granted, even as I realize the subject of sex and its significance may vary between spouses and other couples who are dating and discussing the matter of sexual relations. As the evidence before us also suggests, I am inclined to believe that there is hyper or extreme importance given to sexual gratification or sensuality throughout our society. My observation informs me this is also outside of the construct of marriage and not just within the marital union.

Now, I do not see sexual expression being a problem where a couple's sexual desires and frequency are equivalent. Or, where not, the *ins and outs* (pun intended) of sexual engagement are mutually agreed upon. It is when the two are not in agreement about sex that relational concerns or problems can emerge. Here is one such example: Where one's spouse desires unusual or even unnatural means of sexual gratification or extracurricular activities to be introduced into the sexual experience that is not welcomed by their companion. This may be a strong indicator that something ... some outside *influence* has brought about a change in the thinking and behavior of your Beloved about sex. Or even their behavior or thoughts towards the one with whom they are to love, honor, and protect.

When a spouse feels pressure and reluctantly gives in to their companion's desires or fantasies ... this becomes a problem. When in the view of the Beloved, sex is no longer loving or agreeable, but rather, it has become inordinate and selfishly motivated; the harmony and the beauty of sexual freedom and expression have been robbed from the union. This will result in the reluctant spouse feeling less valued or the object of their spouse's sexual desires. Or even a stand-in for some sordid fantasy their spouse may be mentally in bondage to. Which can lead to the beginning of the end of what was a healthy relationship because it became corrupted by means of wrong actions or thinking towards sex for their Beloved.

Here is another relational concern and problem that can arise. Utilizing the same scenario: A spouse introduces into the sexual experience that *extra what-have-yous*. However, these *extras* brought into the bed - to so call, bring excitement or enhance sexual stimulation. Instead, they became the *replacement objects* for one's now perverted desires. Those *what-have-yous* have effectively robbed you of the natural affection and pleasure to be enjoyed and experienced between spouses.

I have mentioned how media and its users intentionally promote their and/or even Satan's weaponized sexual agenda. They are performing his tactics of sensualizing the world at hyper-speeds through mass media. Many are indulging in various methods of sexual perversion. The expression of sexuality and sensuality is, in fact, being worshiped. And is thereby controlling and ruining the lives of many. Although such ones are unable to see it for what it is. Regarding sex being worshiped, more will be said about this shortly.

Daily, in steady successions, we see or hear the media blitz or this rapid-fire of sexualization. That is not only shown on many television shows or other platforms for so-called entertainment but also in the barrage of commercials that utilize sensuality to promote their goods. Not to mention ... advertisements promoting products to spice up ... get up ... or keep up one's sexual arousal.

And if this isn't bad enough, many of the so-called "children's shows" and even cartoons are not without their sexual suggestions and deviations. Some are subtle, while others are right in our children's faces. Is there any wonder we must work - and, in many cases, work extra hard at being relationally correct or upright to maintain and keep a healthy relationship? Can you now see why so many are struggling relationally? The purpose of sex has been misused and misunderstood. Many have been led to believe Satan's lies about sex. And as a result, he has made sex lethal – physically and spiritually. Sex weaponized is unquestionably leading to the destruction of the Father's ordained family structure through which our God and Creator is to be glorified! This gift from God – sex, has become one of Satan's tools and tactics, causing debilitation, divisiveness, and destruction through our unregulated passions to undermine God's purpose for sex to do us in relationally and render mankind ineffective.

Sex (Shakhav) Gone Wild

Shakhav (**sex**): *This is a word meaning for the expressed purpose to lie down with, for copulation that is unfettered sex, no strings attached.* In the Bible, the word we often see to describe sexual sin is fornication. Keeping the discussion of sex real. I want to look at this disturbing subject that I am calling *Sex Gone Wild!* Metaphorically, sex is an animal that needs taming!

Once again, the expression of sexual relations is a gift from God. That is to be experienced in the beauty of holiness between a husband (male) and his wife (female). Inversely, the purpose of sex and the understanding of its engagement has been perverted and corrupted to destroy the lives of man. Thereby Satan is accomplishing his mission – the destruction of man and families. If not man's complete destruction, Satan is quite satisfied when he can corrupt man's thinking, making man ineffective for the building of God's kingdom.

Look here ... especially those of you who are chaste. You can't miss something - here, the something is sex if you have never experienced it. I firmly believe that if only one (including myself) had remained a virgin until marriage, the overpowering urge to have or desire sexual fulfillment before marriage or extramarital affairs would not be so overpowering or at all enticing. The standards of God have been put in place for our protection! Where we violate God's standards that have been set before us, there will be consequences. And more so than not – at our own making! We will reap what we sow!

Sadly, man has become increasingly and more openly a people desiring inordinate pleasures. Many have bought into the lie that they can "Love who they want to love." Or express themselves sexually, however, or with whomever they choose. They actually believe the lie "That they are not hurting anyone." Such ones are in spiritual darkness, the very place where Satan wants to keep them. Therefore, they cannot see the harm they are creating for themselves nor for the one with whom they have chosen to practice sexual sin. Satan is cunning! Listen, young people. If there is no practice of unnatural sexual arousal or self-gratification. Or sex before marriage, one trying to determine if a partner measures up sexually would be a non-issue. And too, the ravenous appetite for sex- sex- sex, or finding the right sexual partner being non-existent.

Furthermore, this twisted idea of one measuring up or being compatible sexually is a method of deception by which to lure the gullible into having sex. After that, cast the naïve ones aside because they didn't so call – "measure up." If man would simply keep themselves pure or undefiled. The issue of sex or *Shakhav Gone Wild* would not be the ravenous animal it has become for far too many who have been consumed by their sexual cravings.

Society's rabid and ravenous appetite for sex can also be seen in the ninety billion dollars plus pornographic industry. We see it as well in the highly sexually charged "dancing" of whatever sort which has become acceptable and is commonplace throughout society. We see or hear about the increase in brothels, massage parlors, and, sadly, within organized crime - sex trafficking. Relationally, this world has its full of broken people!

If only there was sexual restraint among God's creation. However, apart from God lovingly convicting man of his sinfulness … as well, the restraining power of the Spirit, for many sexual restraint and fidelity, is all but impossible. However, if this wild animal (sexual unrestraint) were to be brought into subjection. That is, under the power and authority of the Spirit of God. Man could then fulfill his purpose as designed and for which our Creator created us … To marry and procreate.

Sadly, many have thoughtlessly given away their virginity, their bodily treasure before marriage, and to their loss! And for others, also to their regret! Even still, to the grief of our God and Creator. Though some sincerely regret engaging in premarital sex. I am convinced the number of those continuing to practice sexual sin and with more than one person far exceeds the ones who have had regret.

The more sexual partners, aka "body count," one has had, undoubtedly more will be the relational challenges stemming from emotional letdowns due to multiple sexual partners. Or the unreasonable expectations that one may have of their companion due to being with multiple people sexually. Where this is the case (multiple sexual partners), it is likely that this individual has begun to develop specifics regarding what they have come to expect or desire sexually. This can also pave the way for unforeseen challenges for Christians and nonbelievers alike when this person chooses to settle down. This only makes sense – right?

Adding to relational challenges is the availability of misinformation and just bad information regarding questionable "sex education" that can be readily accessed through one's devices. In their much learning or self-proclaimed wisdom, many foolishly believe that the more we are informed or educated, the better we can become as a people. The problem with this notion is that the wisdom of this world cannot effectuate positive moral character nor bring about a change of one's heart toward righteousness. On topics of morality or matters of the heart, being informed does not translate to a change of character and certainly not the transformation of one's heart that is truly needed. Only God can transform the hearts and minds of His creation! He is our Designer! He is the Potter; we are His clay vessels.

I'm not saying that there are not good resources of material to help one in their personal development. However, if God is not the foundation upon which one fine and defines themselves, nor His principles upon which one is to be led. That which one hopes to build for themselves or to become cannot stand victorious apart from God.

Returning to the matter of sex gone wild. Those same devices we hold in our hands by which to be informed. Has also given rise to the concern known as "Sexting," which is occurring among our youth. But also, grown folks are caught up in this so-called harmless and "fun" way of being sexually aroused or entertained.

Look, people! In case you do not see it for what it is ... this is participation in pornography (Job 31:1; Matthew 5:28; 1 John 2:16). One's payment is the arousal that sinful misconduct brings. The Bible makes it clear that *the wages of sin is death* (Romans 6:23). Sinfulness separates us from God. When immoral behavior becomes a matter of practice, we are spiritually weakened and lose or have lost our orientation towards God or proper *Life* perspective.

Clearly, this behavior is not in line with the will of God – hence sinful. What does the world say about the matter of Sexting? "Well, this sort of thing is harmless and fun; besides, it occurs between consenting individuals." When involving minors, some, for conscious sake, may reconsider the matter and take exception to this behavior when children are involved.

However, what those who are one with this world cannot see ... is the emotional and spiritual consequences of such actions, regardless of one's age. Neither can they understand that our youth are being robbed of their innocence because of this perversion.

Make no mistake about it. This pains our loving God and Father, who created us in His image. And not in the likes of wild animals who are without reasoning. Neither have the capability to analyze, conceptualize, theorize, hold conversations, or debate matters of appropriateness.

Beasts are not governed by moral law; they lack intellect. Instead, they are governed by their basic instincts or animalistic nature. Man alone is made after the likeness of their Creator, *who is Creative, Rational, Intelligent, and who alone is All-Knowing!* However, because of sin and its dominance over the lives of many, it can be said of man that many have degraded themselves to animal behavior. Or even worse than animals because man has volition.

The Bible tells us that *there is nothing new under the sun*; simply, the methods of operation or delivery of things change in a so-called *advancing* society (Ecclesiastes 1:9). So, today we call it "Sexting." However, on a personal note, when I was a boy of elementary school age, it was called … *Show me yours, and I will show you mine.*

This occurrence actually took place with a childhood friend and me. She was a couple of years older and likely in junior high school. I was, at the latest, in the fifth grade and was attending Merrick Moore Elementary School.

As the story goes, my family was residing in Cheek Road Apartments. I was standing in our sub-ground kitchen. Meanwhile, the girl was outside our kitchen window. We talked, or perhaps a better way of putting things; she attempted to entice me to *show her mine.* She said along these lines, *"I'll show you mine if you show me yours."*

Something about this just didn't sit right with me. I don't know how much it had to do with me thinking of getting in trouble or wanting the girl to show me hers first. Neither of us showed any parts of ourselves; nonetheless, there was anticipation that I might see hers! To that end … nothing is new under the sun. Satan has been and continues to weaponize sex by perverting the mind of all he can regarding sex – God's gift to man. And yet, more proof of the need for intentional and careful parental oversight to safeguard children from themselves, from wrongfully and woefully exploring their sensual inclination. While adults and their sexual proclivities need taming or brought under control or subjection to the will and purpose of God (1 Corinthians 9: 27).

Strange Going Ons In The Bedroom

I will submit that there are a variety of acceptable means by which pleasure can be experienced and enjoyed between spouses. Your spouse's canvass - their body, is for the enjoyment and pleasure of all your sense's stimulation: touch, taste, visual, smell, and even hearing. How you two choose to enjoy one another by arousing your bodily senses is between you two. And really… it is nobody else's business how you two decide to enjoy one another sexually. Unless someone sees the delight you and your spouse have for one another. And they want to know … "What is your secret." Then you can tell them what I just said: "How you two choose to enjoy one another sexually is between you two."

My personal conviction is as follows. There are no prohibitions in marriage regarding *holy sexual expression*, but what a married couple establishes as led by their agreement or conviction when joined together to enjoy one another sexually. A read through the book, Song of Solomon, seems to me to say the same thing … A husband and wife are to completely enjoy one another sexually!"

Unfortunately, and yet I feel confident saying what I am about to say. Many are taking the matter of sexual expression, variety, experimentation, or the utilization of things to so-call enhance one's sexual experience way too far! Hence, *Strange Going Ons In The Bedroom!* Marriage and the marital bed are to be honored – highly regarded, undefiled, and kept pure. Both treasures – marriage and the marital bed are to be protected. A couple, therefore, is to consciously safeguard their union in the bedroom. And their public union kept protected from all or whatever may try to intrude upon the sanctity and purity of their union to disrupt it.

I am concerned that many have been deceived by this world's trickery. Well-intended couples have allowed *extra what-have-yous* to enter their holy sexual union or sacred space. The end result … inordinate affections have crept into the minds and bodies of couples who have taken matters too far regarding their sexual liberties and expressions. Sexual bonding between a husband and wife is a gift from God. It is to be exercised or experienced in the beauty of holiness as a husband and wife freely give themselves to one another *bodily* without inhibitions. When there is a violation of the union through improper sexual entanglement of whatever sort, the intimate and loving marital bond shared between a husband and wife can begin to slowly dissolve or devolve.

Clarifying the matter: I am not saying that a couple cannot spice up the bedroom atmosphere or set the mood. Whereby making for a romantic and fun time to be shared with one's spouse ... Not at all! Neither am I against such *extras:* let's say, fruits, oil, or even whipped cream if that's your thing. My point ... You two are creating that romantic mood of intimacy, thereby bringing forth pleasure to be enjoyed together - bodily in erotic (Eros) purity. I see no harm in such extras to spice up or to change things up from time to time. Yes, keep the fire burning! Bring excitement or change into your bed chambers if you and your Beloved desire to do so! However, keep things holy and pure!

To underscore and make my point clear. Regarding abstaining from using these *extra what have yous* – so-called "sex toys," instruments, etc., were utilized for vaginal or other means of pleasure or bodily stimulation. As well - some doll or robotic or whatever invention or method by which one seeks to be physically or sexually stimulated. I submit ... A couple who practices such means of sexual arousal and deviation, and most certainly those who *need* this kind of inordinate pleasure, has entered into idol worship. And that natural intimacy or affection for your spouse has become secondary or altogether lost.

The "toys" or the instruments or *what-have-yous* have become one's idol. These objects have taken the place of how God our Creator intended the sexual experience to be engaged and understood. That is a sexual holy union, this gift from God to be honored and kept undefiled. I will also submit ... Where one has entered into unnatural sexual excess and all its trappings. One has even allowed sexuality or sensuality to become their god by choosing to please their abnormal sexual appetite above pleasing God and His idea and purpose for sexual enjoyment. In so doing, one has become a god unto themselves. Meaning – my body wants what it wants! Therefore, I am going to indulge its longing however I see fit!

Such things and actions corrupt the union shared between spouses. Can a union continue to stand or remain strong and faithfully committed after such a violation of the sacred has occurred?

Through sexual intimacy, each of our senses can be fully engaged, unlike anything else that man can experience apart from sex. One should be able to sincerely thank God for such a wonderful experience. I do! God is truly Good! And thoughtful! He has set all things - even the sexual experience to be for our good when experienced according to the order and purpose He intended. But, apart from God, left to his own devices and whims, man is inclined to pervert themselves - we can't help ourselves.

And so, regarding those *"Strange Going Ons"* in the bedroom. For you, godly husbands and wives do not allow the so-called innocently inviting usage of "sex toys" or devices to ensnare you. Learn to work with what God has given you!

These devices, or *what-have-yous* … I am confident saying. Have managed to take the place of *natural affections* and *natural bodily stimulation* as purposed by God to be experienced between a husband and wife. Such inordinate practices weaken the marital bond, thereby causing the marriage union to become superficial, an insubstantial union void of true love and intimacy. And consequently, a spouse who is without these instruments - been unfulfilled or dissatisfied through normal sexual means. Where this has occurred. A spouse who once genuinely desired only the sexual pleasure, from direct or personal contact from their mate, has now, and perhaps to include their spouse, has unsuspectingly come up against a rival - some "sex toy." Or whatever it may be, to be satisfied by, or with, in place of their Beloved's, caress, touch, kiss, and their loving embrace and engagement (Romans 6:12-14).

Again, this is idolatrous behavior … desiring an imitation or some inanimate tool used for the purpose of receiving sexual pleasure; instead of the *real, authentic, only, and right thing – one's spouse!* People. There's nothing like the real thing (one's spouse) and doing the right things to honor God! What God has purposed for us can't be duplicated nor improved upon by some highly sexualized and perverted idea that man has invented.

Trust me, when you experience and know God's best for you, even your spouse, nothing else or no one else matters concerning your needs being met! God's best happens to and for us and manifests itself *over and over* when we, as a couple, enter into an intimate and holy covenant relationship with Him.

Let me remind you that it deeply grieves our God and Father... He absolutely abhors the ideas and actions of His people who give themselves over to idol worship. Which is to bow or become subject to people, and even things made from wood, plastic, glass, or whatever the sort, that has been fashioned by man's hands. God desires you to Himself, and He is well pleased when He sees His children – you and me, conforming and conducting ourselves in the manner in which He created us.

Perhaps you are responding, "Man, get out of my bedroom and my business ... who are you to say what I can and can't do sexually!" Look. I understand your position regarding your business and, yes, your choices. However, I cannot agree with your decision to live outside of the will of God. And you need to get this... there will always be a price to pay to one's detriment for illicit behavior. This is one of the tactics of Satan: with seemingly meaningless feel-good moments of pleasure, he has many believing their conduct is harmless. Then you wake up to a spiritual reality that your soul has been bankrupted. The good thing is that you woke up – many don't. There have been countless who have fallen victim to this tension ... *how can something so wrong feel so right?* This is sin (Satan) doing what it does – deceiving and manipulating those who are led by their carnality or own reasoning.

My brothers and sisters, look. For this very moment in your life, God has appointed me to share His truth with you. Now hear these words as well, "... for *the wicked, those whose practices are perverse, whoever they are - to repent and turn from your perverted and wicked ways! Know this... that your evil ways, though done under the cloak of darkness or in secret, are not hidden from Me - God* (Proverbs 5:21; 15:3).

God has given each of us free will by which to freely express ourselves. And yet this liberty has not been granted to man to express unilaterally. Or apart from the wisdom and counsel of our loving Creator and Father. Consider these

Words of God spoken through the apostle Paul on Christian liberty. *"I have the right to do anything," you say—but not everything is beneficial. "I have the right to do anything"—but not everything is constructive"* (1 Corinthians 10:23).

The takeaway from this passage. There are parameters to our liberty by which every born-again Believer is required to operate or live within. As Christians, though we have been granted free will, we can't just live any kind of way or do whatever we desire. The Word of God must be our guide and counsel on right living.

Though it may be that Scripture does not speak directly to a particular matter – like, "sex toys." The actual problem is with man and we being without clarity regarding what God has purposed for man as revealed through the entirety of Scripture. Through the complete revelation and understanding of Scripture, beginning with the book of Genesis to Revelation, and even lessons learned from the created order, we can learn or come to know the mind or will of Christ for mankind. This is what our Father desires that we may grow to comprehend His true nature, His character through a refined grasp of Biblical understanding and even that which we glean from creation. In God's Imago Dei or image are we made, that we may conduct ourselves after His attributes that we may reflect His glory.

As Christians, we have a responsibility to conduct ourselves before God honorably. And even in the bedroom. In such a way that develops and honors the union of husband and wife as designed by God. Where conformity to the will of God is established within a child of God, this honors Him, thereby bringing blessings to the marital union – stability and longevity.

Where understanding is lacking regarding sanctified or holy living, I now encourage you to seek the truth of God as found in the Bible. Until you develop spiritual maturity regarding some issues, allow your prayerful conscious conviction to guide you.

Also, prayerfully consider what nature shows us. Listen carefully to what the Apostle Paul received from God regarding the created order. *"The wrath of God is being revealed from heaven against all the godlessness and wickedness of people, who suppress the truth by their wickedness since what may be known about God is plain to them because God has made it plain to them. For since the creation of the world, God's invisible qualities—his eternal power and divine nature—have been clearly seen, being understood from what has been made, so that people are without excuse.*

For although they knew God, they neither glorified him as God nor gave thanks to Him, but their thinking became futile, and their foolish hearts were darkened. Although they claimed to be wise, they became fools and exchanged the glory of the immortal God for images made to look like mortal human beings and birds and animals and reptiles.

Therefore, God gave them over in the sinful desires of their hearts to sexual impurity for the degrading of their bodies with one another. They exchanged the truth about God for a lie and worshiped and served created things rather than the Creator— who is forever praised. Amen.

Because of this, God gave them over to shameful lusts. Even their women exchanged natural sexual relations for unnatural ones. In the same way, the men also abandoned natural relations with women and were inflamed with lust for one another. Men committed shameful acts with other men and received in themselves the due penalty for their error (Romans 1:18-27).

Sexual expression and the pleasure shared between spouses are priceless treasures and gifts from God. For those of us sharing in our Father's intimate embrace and union, consider the following: He is very much one with us in our most intimate moments with our spouses. Not in some perverted sense, but rather as our Enabler, as we experience sexual enjoyment with our spouses. Even so, as our souls engage as one, not only physically but also spiritually. Resulting from this glorious union of husband and wife, God delights in our joy and the pleasure we experience and partake with our Beloved. No doubt, God is well pleased that the man and woman He created have chosen to join together as he ordained, thus representing marriage's true and only meaning. And thereby discovering marital fulfillment (Proverbs 18:22).

The very God who enables all, who became one with Believers when we first believed, is one with you and your spouse in all aspects of your union. Our Omniscient (all-knowing) and Omnipresent (everywhere at one time) God should be understood as not being blinded by the darkness when or if you turn off the lights to your bedroom. Neither is He left outside your bedroom door when it is closed. No, He's right there, in your moment of intimacy with your spouse. I will say, cheering you two on when you're honoring Him through sanctified sexual expression.

For this reason, think it not strange to be thankful to God as you anticipate sexual relations with your spouse. Or during sexual engagement and after you have reached the joy of sexual ecstasy shared with your spouse. Scripture says, *"Every good and perfect gift comes from God."* Therefore, give Him thanks and praise for the good things you experience daily, not the least of which sexual enjoyment with your spouse.

On the other hand, where things are not done honorably as intended by God, He looks upon those situations you've chosen to enter into with great sorrow and disappointment. Yes, we can grieve the Spirit of God (Ephesians 4:30).

The Father's Love - Our Father's Grief

If you are a loving parent who has raised a child to the age of understanding or accountability. When that child willfully disobeyed or disregarded your guiding counsel and protective wisdom. In such a case, you are undoubtedly familiar with the disappointment or grief caused by your child's rebellion. The reason for your displeasure is apparent. It has everything to do with the relationship, your deep love, and the concern you have for your child's well-being.

As a parent, although you may have been pained by your child's rebellion or lapse in judgment. This in no way diminishes the love you have for your child, or the love you will always have for your child or children. However, the disappointment that was experienced as a result of their disobedience is nonetheless felt. And because you are a loving parent, your hand has been forced by your child's behavior to bring forth some measure and corrective method of rebuke and/or discipline. This correction or discipline of whatever sort… is prompted by love. Love is often associated with pleasure, but corrective love can also bring about momentary pain or discomfort that works towards your child's benefit.

Consider the unsurpassed love and mercy of God; that He daily withholds his retribution toward sinful man and pardons the sins of those who are washed by the blood of Jesus. However, such pardoning is not a license for man to keep sinning. Rather, one must recognize the grace of forgiveness, even God's love and mercy toward us. Seeing God's gracious forbearance should keep one from willingly partaking in the practice of rebellion or willful disobedience, as we consider the Father's patient love and the cost of the cross, for which Jesus paid with His bodily sacrifice, for the sinfulness of man.

Consider the lyrics of the songwriter:

"How deep the Father's love for us,
How vast beyond all measure
That He should give His only Son
To make a wretch His treasure

How great the pain of searing loss,
The Father turns His face away
As wounds which mar the chosen One,
Bring many sons to glory

Behold the Man upon a cross,
My sin upon His shoulders
Ashamed, I hear my mocking voice,
Call out among the scoffers

It was my sin that left Him there
Until it was accomplished
His dying breath has brought me life
I know that it is finished

I will not boast in anything
No gifts, no power, no wisdom
But I will boast in Jesus Christ
His death and resurrection

Why should I gain from His reward?
I cannot give an answer
But this I know with all my heart
His wounds have paid my ransom."

~ Stuart Townend ~

The sooner a child of God can truly grasp the cost of their sins and even the Father's love for them. Less likely will be one's return to willful sin, which causes grief to our loving Father and God.

As with a child, that is naturally born. So it is with those reborn spiritually of God regarding the process by which one matures both physically and spiritually. Regarding our natural birth ... It is that which God has provided through the created order that we must partake or ingest for our physical well-being and growth. On the other hand ... God has given unto man Himself for the benefit of our spiritual health and maturity. That we may always have what or Who we need for our spiritual development and nourishment. This includes a steady intake of the Word and time with God in prayer and worship, individually and corporately or with other members of your church home.

The development process, for both our physical and spiritual maturity, is not flawless. Along the way, there will be stumbles and falls. There will be growing pains, heartaches, and disappointments. This should be expected. However, a parent's hope and even prayer is that - as their child matures, mishaps and mistakes will significantly diminish.

However, when a child fails to meet their parent's reasonable expectations during their maturation process, this being based upon the child's age and/or understanding will determine the parent's measure of disappointment during their child's failings or shortcomings. The greater or weightier the expectation of their child. More significant will be the parent's disappointment when their child does not meet their reasonable expectations.

We reason when one knows better, they are expected to do or be better. But life has taught me, and perhaps yourself … that knowing *the better* doesn't always lead to one doing the right thing or becoming better.

Howbeit, overcoming challenges or conflicts for an individual who is expected to do or become better after being told *the better*. It is not always as simple as choosing or becoming *the better* after being informed. I remind you of the spiritual warfare that we are all in. Some are engaged in spiritual conflict, inwardly or outwardly, deeper or with greater intensity than others. Therefore, it may not be as easy as one simply willing themselves, choosing *the better,* or doing what is socially acceptable. And of more significance, that which is biblically honorable or right.

Though some believe that their lives are *predestined* – already charted out. The truth of the matter is that we all have *free will.* And yes, we will be judged by God according to our choices. Therefore, what will matter when all is said and done: Was your heart set towards doing that which pleases our Father; did you choose Him and rely upon God for your help and strength (Joshua 24:15)?

This certainly was not always the case with me about doing things God's way or choosing *the better.* Before I was born again, I knew nothing of a personal and loving relationship with the God who first loved me. I was not raised in the church, and neither was I taught anything about God. Though I came to accept Jesus as my Savior at eighteen, spiritually, I would remain a babe in the knowledge of Christ for some time to come. I have found this to be the case with far too many Christians. Even those who are *good and grown folk.* As babes in Christ or remaining babes in Christ, we are not only ineffective in building others up for God's Kingdom … we are yet vulnerable to sin's assaults - from without and from within.

Still un-churched and without spiritual or Biblical guidance from within a structured church setting. I nevertheless began slowly gaining some understanding of the Bible as I occasionally read it. However, years later and yet a babe or, at best, a toddler in Christ. It would still be some time down the road before I would begin learning to submit to the Lordship of Jesus. Savior, He was - hence, my sin debt was paid in full, and heaven awaited me. But Jesus was not my Lord … I had not entered into a personal or lovingly obedient relationship with Him. I had not totally surrendered myself to Him. I had not set my heart to follow Him nor given Him a continued place in my heart and thoughts. He was just my Savior, not *The All* my soul longed for and needed - Jesus, my Lord, and my Savior!

Jesus, not having all of me – mind, body, and spirit, I was therefore incapable of being effective towards living a committed life to and for Christ, yet alone for some other. Because I was immature or a babe in the things of God, I, therefore, unknowingly was extremely vulnerable to sin's assault - those of my own making or that which the world assailed me with.

Let me make myself clear. We are fully responsible for the sin(s) we engage in. Know excuse that we dream up for our sinful misconduct can be deemed acceptable to God – not one! Even if we have no knowledge of Christ or are mere babes in Him, we have to own our actions – our sinfulness.

That said, here is one sinful instance of my many. I had not taken Lisa as my wife; nonetheless, we chose to engage sexually. Our actions and choice, without question, caused hurt and heartache to our loving Father and Creator. I understand this better today than I could have ever imagined then. Our decision to engage in sexual relations was far from the will of our Father and the expectation He had for us, His children.

And so, it is to be expected that any infraction of God's commands or purpose for which He has designed his people to conduct themselves, where those boundaries are unknowingly overrun or where blatantly disregarded, we grieve the heart of our Father. Yes, the creature – man, can cause our Creator and Father to feel sorrow and pain. It is because He loves us so much! And He wants to protect us, even from ourselves, that it grieves Him greatly when we choose sin or enter into harm's way, knowingly or not.

Now, we reason, what a person knows or the degree of information they hold, they are accountable for their actions based on their knowledge. Again, this suggests that when a person knows better, they are expected to do better. And where there is disregard for doing what is known to be the better, corrective consequences may follow (Luke 12: 47, 48). The correction or discipline may directly result from one's actions – one reaping what one sowed (Galatians 6: 7-8). Or God may choose to lovingly intervene in some manner to bring you to understanding or right mind pertaining to His will (Hebrews 12: 6 -11). His preferred method for our learning and correction is for His children to read and heed what He speaks to us from the Bible – His Word.

There is a great deal of responsibility that God has placed upon those who are parents. To bear children is indeed a gift from God. He has allowed man to be co-under agents with Him in bringing forth life into the world, but we are also responsible for their training or learning unto holiness.

However, there are those in their ignorance who have dared to say, "There is no manual provided regarding rearing a child." My retort – yes, there is! It's called the Bible - The Living Word of God … it's our operational manual on how we are to live our lives while here on this earth.

God did not create man to be self-sufficient or self-reliant, though to our harm we try, wherein determining our own rules by which we are to be governed. *To assume self-reliance is for one to become a god unto themselves.* Instead, as intelligent beings - like unto our God and Father, nevertheless, we are to be totally reliant upon Him - our Life-Giver and Sustainer. While utilizing our manual – His Word, from which we are to receive our operational instructions as we are taught and enabled by the Spirit of God. For our physical well-being, do we forego the nourishment that comes forth from this earth? No! Neither should we ignore the nutrition of our spirits that comes from remaining one with the Spirit of God and relying on His Word for our spiritual wellness or provision and maturity.

And so, it is. We all, whether we have our Bibles in hand or never opened one, will be held accountable based on God's Word for how we conduct ourselves. As well as how we gave care to things and the individuals under our care more importantly. It is a parent's responsibility to train their offspring in the ways of God and for them to also teach them to have reverence for God. Bringing a child into this world is a matter not to be taken lightly. However, it does appear that far too many Christian households. And most assuredly, those lost to the world. Have fallen short of God's expectation on this most important responsibility: To raise and educate our children in the reverence and knowledge of God!

People, God's Word has been given to be *a lamp for our feet, a light on our path.* The Father's instructions are to keep us from harm and danger – the path of sin and folly. I now raise a question. "How well is the job that we who are Christian parents are actually doing?" Answering that question. I'll respond – overall, not well enough. Looking throughout our society and within Christian homes, this seems quite evident.

As adolescents, neither Lisa nor I received anything about godly instructions from our parents regarding sex. Or much of anything, biblically speaking. Lisa's instructions from her mother on sex were simply to use contraceptives to avoid pregnancy. As for me, the instruction from my mother, "Don't be bringing any babies up in my house." And from my dad, "Don't be gay." At the time, his statement did not quite register with me. I don't think I'd become a teenager when he offered this meaningless counsel.

From what I know about our parent's upbringing, times were challenging for them. As a child, my mother experienced corporate worship within a church or physical building. As for my dad, I am inclined to believe he had none. Lisa's parent's experience attending church mirrored that of my parents. And also her parents encountered challenging times as children and young adults, this being more the case for her father. The answer to our relational woes can only be answered by establishing a *personal relationship* with our Heavenly Father. Merely going to church or attending worship service is not the answer. This is simply going through the motion or merely being religious.

After becoming a Christian as a young adult of eighteen or nineteen, I recall reading the Bible in my barracks while at Fort Bragg, North Carolina. I discovered what the Word of God had to say about sexual relations. It became apparent to me that the matter of sex is not given due diligence within Christian homes concerning discussing this extremely sensitive and vital topic from a Biblical perspective. Because of humanity's failure to study and apply the Word of God: is there any wonder why many are reaping the harvest of unwanted pregnancies, abortions, and venereal diseases. And to the breakup of marriages and all that's associated with illicit sex. Sexual relations performed outside of the boundaries established by God have become perhaps Satan's most lethal weapon against humanity.

I am certain that as our Father looks upon His self-destructive and wayward children, it is with heaviness of heart as He sees how His arch-enemy – Satan; is using the very thing(s) God has given for man's good to destroy the lives of many. *Sex has become a weapon of mass destruction! Both spiritually and physically! Illicit sex is gunning down or doing relationships in!*

Sexual relations have been perverted; this is the work and intent of Satan. He perverts; he counterfeits the things of God, at times sprinkling in enough truth that one may fall for his lies and deception. He causes many to think as a result of their fallen condition that if something feels good to them - it must be good for them! Many have fallen for the *Okie-Doke,* lies, tricks, and schemes of Satan. While others readily embrace his lies. And still, others who simply do not know the *Way* and *Truth* of God ... these being unchurched folk. Either way, none here described have entered into a *personal relationship* with Jesus. Nor have made Him Lord, such ones who readily *practice* immorality or who experience no conviction for their immoral conduct (Matthew 7:16). I am now talking to church folk. It is imperative that God's creation see Jesus as the One they need - their Lord!

Lisa nor I had deep, heartfelt convictions regarding following God's moral law. Because there was not an intimate or *personal relationship* with Jesus. It was easy for Lisa and me to choose to wrongly consummate our dating relationship sexually. However, I did have enough Biblical understanding to know that sex outside marriage was wrong. I was not in the dark about the Bible's prohibition of premarital sex, but this was not so with Lisa. Although we were consenting adults, we were both immature and babes in the ways of the Lord. In other words, we were babies having sex. Yes, this sounds messed up to me as well. From the Bible's standpoint, we were indeed messed up and mixed up! Babes in Christ, lacking in spiritual maturity.

Regarding the inappropriateness of things ... I did have a clearer understanding of the wrongness of premarital sex than Lisa. In the eyes of God, my knowledge being as it was, more aware than Lisa's. I would therefore be held more responsible or accountable for not doing the better or right thing(s) before God.

We are all responsible for what we know and do with the knowledge acquired. However, don't allow yourself to feel comfortable in your ignorance of Biblical truth. You see. As Christians, ignorance of Biblical truth will not be an acceptable excuse before God. God has revealed and made plain His Truth to those who belong to Him. It is up to you, the saved and unsaved alike, to get understanding, knowledge, and wisdom from God. The only way we can receive the things of God we must see our need for Him and then be willing to make Him Lord as we seek out His precepts from His Holy Word. And then purpose in our hearts. To be led and strengthened by the Spirit as we submit and come under the Lordship of Jesus.

Immorality's Freefall - Immorality Free For All

Unknown the number of people who've engaged in premarital sex. I suppose the motivation for some centers on the idea that if they had sex with the person with whom they are interested, the person wouldn't leave them. If they could just perform skillfully in their sexual endeavor, they could lock their partner down because of "good sex."

No doubt, the act of illicit sex can be an enjoyable experience and, at the same time, a spiritually incapacitating encounter. There is something powerfully seductive about the perceived pleasure and the actual pleasure of the forbidden. For example: when a child has been told to keep their hand out of the cookie jar. When the cookies have been prohibited, the child desires the cookie all the more! This is the nature and lure of sin at work within man ... I want what I want. And when told no ... many desire the forbidden all the more!

It's the lust for the forbidden ... remember Eve? Or the pleasure one has convinced themselves they are being denied and deprived of. Therefore stirring many to long for the prohibited even more! Again, remember Eve? Sin, the prohibited, and the pursuit of the forbidden can arouse a stirring within some that sets them in motion to pursue after the illicit – whereby experiencing the thrill, pursuit, and conquest of the forbidden. When they come down from their

physical and even emotional high, their soul yet remains on empty. They are in pursuit of what they think and even have been made to believe what will fulfill them, but it is only temporary pleasure – and even worst, forbidden. What their souls need, this world can't provide. What or Who we all need is Jesus!

Sin has a way of making one feel good! Even if it's fleeting, just a "little sin," whatever that means, or even when it is criminal in nature. The enticement to pursue after sin's poisonous and satisfying stimulation can be highly intoxicating and/or overwhelming. Many well-intended spouses have slowly been walked down by sin and found themselves caught up in the forbidden. In other words, they were not prayerful and watchful. What they thought was fun and innocent enough behavior. Or their interaction with some other to be of no consequence. However, this thing or person became a snare and a trap by which they were slowly lured by and subsequently became unnaturally excited and entangled with. The act of sin can be likened to a subtle addictive substance. Whereby bringing both the flesh and mind under its influence because of the euphoria of the experience. Therefore, one can become strung out on sex or others of sin's enticements.

Bear this in mind: *You can't miss something you never had.* That said ... where delight and the rapture of sexual relations are first experienced within the context of marriage. This beautiful and joyous experience between husband and wife, with no competition or comparing their sexual experience to some other from a past relationship. Because of their mutually exclusive satisfying sexual experience, known only within the framework of marriage. I am therefore convinced that the likelihood of either spouse venturing outside of their union to seek "greener pastures" or a so-called "better sexual experience" is highly unlikely. I base my premise on the idea: *That you can't miss something you never had.* Therefore, the temptation to venture outside their marriage for merely sexual pleasure is significantly reduced.

Nonetheless, one cannot be ignorant of temptation, those forces which seek to destroy even the best of marriages. Just the same, I am convinced when sex has been refrained from until marriage. Or not ... but where the pleasure of sex is not the driving force of a relationship, less likely there will be marital unfaithfulness or sex the cause of marital challenges. Again, you cannot miss what you have not had. However, when sex or other relational issues are not effectively dealt with by spouses, marital challenges of various sorts can lead to infidelity. Or perhaps even marital failure.

On the other hand, those including myself. Who practiced little to no sexual restraint before marrying. This type of lifestyle feeds the fleshly appetite ... and for many, their flesh left to itself is never satisfied. Or where the hunger or grumbling seems quieted, when least expected, its rumbling and stirring can be felt within, again longing to indulge in the forbidden. And yes! Even though one is married! And even happily married at that.

As it is with a struggling addict or substance abuser, the unrestrained sinful body craves for more-and-more, sexual or fleshly gratification! Like the substance abuser, who may not be aware that they have fallen entrapped to some substance, a person given to unbridled sex may not be aware that they have become enslaved to sex. But sex addicts they are, with the degree of the addiction, varying from person to person. For a new convert to Christianity, it may not be until they attempt to abstain sexually or become monogamous that they discover the sexual stronghold to which they have become ensnared or in bondage to.

Where natural pleasure goes unchecked, becomes lustful, and violates God's design. When one's sexual prerogative exceeds its natural limitation, thereby violating God's moral law. Concupiscence – that is, strong sexual desire or inordinate affection is sure to find its way at work in one's life. Unwittingly, one can become entrapped by their fleshly passion(s). Or led astray by their unrestrained flesh's cravings. Thereby fulfilling Satan's will or purpose -

weaponizing sex and even being pimped and prostituted by their master -Satan! It is not a stretch to say that such ones are being trafficked as sex slaves. And yes, Satan is the master ringleader. Nevertheless, we are accountable for our actions.

Man who has given themselves over to sin is not guiltless for what they (we) do to or with their bodies. The unrepentant stands indicted before God regarding this matter of unbridled sex. However, God has not yet condemned man to eternal damnation. Instead, He grieves and weeps as sin produces fruit for His creation unto destruction, chaos, and confusion of all sorts of their making. Those committing sin, in other words, have brought forth judgment of their own making and against themselves. Look at the staggering number of failed marriages, not the least of which those failures occurring because of a cheating spouse ... "sexting" can undoubtedly be included in this matter of cheating. Then there is the trapping of pornography - for spouses who have given their affection and time to embrace this alluring trash. Including giving their family's money over to some business for an image portrayed on paper. Or that which is viewed electronically. And I dare not fail to mention places of so-called adult entertainment. And even sex for sale. Such things and practices are sinful; they are sin's (Satan's) fruit or even God's judgment against man's wickedness. The offspring or judgment of such practices creates destruction, chaos, and confusion of all sorts – *the hallmark of death* - Satan himself!

Now, consider each of the sexual mediums by which sexual improprieties can be experienced. Add whatever sexual perversion of your choosing, not that it is necessary. Bring this person, the unchurched, new convert, or immature Christian with their past consisting of engaging in such activities for so-called - fun, or whatever it may be called, into what they hope to be a meaningful relationship. Now, is there any wonder why the unchurched, the babes - or new converts in Christ and those who are supposed to be mature in Christ fail to sustain healthy and meaningful relationships? The challenges that are before and/or against establishing a godly relationship are real and ever-present for those who have engaged in such gross sexual misconduct! In far too many cases, this sexual corruption of an individual began when they were mere teenage boys and girls. And tragically, many become victims of sexual perversion when they are just children.

Immorality's free-for-all or sexual perversion engaged in by the masses has caused a debilitating and even deterioration of the family. This immoral free fall and rapid descent toward base living can only be diverted when one becomes a Believer and lover of God. And no longer a lover of themselves and the things of this world. Through the enabling power of the Spirit of God, one must learn to subdue our flesh (1 Corinthians 9:27). And set our affections on our Lord and Savior or that which is eternal (Colossians 3:1-10).

We have the problems mentioned because of ignorance or spiritual blindness regarding the holy manner for which sexual relations have been purposed by our Creator.

Now open your Bible to 1 Corinthians 6: 9-20. Read the text. You will find in this Scripture the Apostle Paul sharing God's instructions for man on how we are to conduct ourselves in our bodies, particularly regarding sex.

My brothers and sisters in Christ. *"We have been bought with a price: therefore, let us glorify God in your body."*

The "price" … *the torture and Blood of Jesus!*

CHAPTER 10

Caught Up: To Get the Man of The House, Is for The Enemy to Get the House

Regretfully, I got *caught up!* Sadly, one of far too many who cheated on and cheapened their relationship with their spouse through sexual unfaithfulness. Whether this act results from willful or premeditative participation in such destructive behavior. Or a spouse being naive and therefore getting *caught up* … as was the case for me. Just the same, the violation of trust, devastating hurt, and unparallel betrayal are the same for the spouse, who put their total trust in their husband or wife to be faithful.

The willful cheater versus the naïve cheater. They are the same … Cheaters! This they must own unequivocally! The Bible is clear! Marital unfaithfulness is unquestionable grounds for divorce. Or where reconciliation or trust can't be reestablished in the union - divorce is allowable. Or it may be that the betrayed spouse is simply done with the marriage! This is their right. However, I want you to consider the difference between what I have chosen to call the *Willful or Wanton Cheater* as opposed to the spouse who *Got Caught Up*. Take a moment to read Psalm chapter *Thirty-seven, verses Twenty-three and Twenty-four*, I saw my former self in these verses. Yes, I was a good man who had fallen. And I also failed my wife! But God kept me! He also kept my wife and my marriage.

Keeping this simple: The willful cheater's heart has turned from their spouse; their actions might be malicious, void of heartfelt conviction for their wrong.

Their care, consciousness, and consideration for their spouse are gone or greatly diminished. These conditions can very well be in the spouse's heart before they actually decide to betray their vows of faithfulness.

As for the naïve cheater: An ostensibly harmless situation, and perhaps, not of their own making, begins with one seemingly small matter or interaction involving inappropriate associations, realized or not, with some other or with something. The activity or interaction not halted or effectively dealt with ... Therefore, the gullible continuing to flirt with or be entertained by the forbidden or threatening interaction knowingly or not, the mind at some point gives way to active entanglement or engagement with the forbidden. In other words, one is slowly brought to consciously participate in the prohibited. Consequently, far too many – here the ignorant or foolish one, hence *getting caught up* therein committing the worst or gross mistake ever – marital unfaithfulness! After the fact, there is regret! Or, as things were wrongly progressing, they felt and knew they were on a dangerous course. Nevertheless, they chose to follow after their sinful thoughts and passion or thrill for the moment.

For those who ignorantly and foolishly betray their spouse, the progression toward marital unfaithfulness can be slow and subtle. This was my personal experience. Before I betrayed my God and wife, all was well with me and my marriage. I had no thought of betraying my wife. However, there was a slow and steady chiseling away of my marital integrity, thereby slowly muting my sense of wrong and dulling *my* soundness of mind.

As for the willful and wanton cheater: This person is aware of what they are doing or considering. Their home or relationship with their spouse has already been met with challenges that have not been resolved. Therefore, the mind or heart of this person has begun to harden. They have turned from their loving care for their spouse. However, this is not the mind of the naïve and foolish person. Just the same, marital faithfulness was betrayed.

But there may be hope for this betrayer! There was for me. First, it concerns the heart of the spouse who *got caught up,* who is sorrowful for the hurt and betrayal they caused their Beloved. This marriage can recover from the betrayal; this union can be made whole and even better! Through the grace of God, the betrayed spouse who, nevertheless, loves and knows the good in their spouse. And who has not lost hope and confidence in their Beloved who jeopardized their marriage. This union can overcome and stand in victory! This I know for myself. It was because of the grace of God! And the love my wife maintained for me that my union with my wife was kept and even strengthened!

However, the husband or wife who willfully cheats on their spouse. Sadly, their heart beforehand, for a number of possibilities, had begun to turn from their spouse. This unfortunate and tragic reality leads to countless failed marriages. Where one spouse has turned from loving the partner – if they ever truly loved or cared for them, the hurting and betrayed spouse must be prepared to let the betrayer go. For the spouse betrayed. You can't be the only one hoping to save or keep your marriage – it takes all three of you to restore your marriage, the Spirit of God, and you and your *repented* spouse desiring the same thing – the restoration and healing of your union.

If you determine to part ways with your spouse. It must be through prayer, comfort sought after through God's Word and other Believers' support that will get you through this difficult time. It may take some time to heal from your hurt; however, the Spirit of God will renew your joy and strength in the Lord. God will bring healing to your hurting soul!

Here is something else to consider: Though one may not have had sexual relations outside of their marriage, has there been an alienation of affection? Have you neglected the emotional and/or physical needs of your Beloved? A husband or wife's first ministry is to their spouse … how well are you serving them? Are you meeting both their spiritual (emotional) and physical needs? Or has it been? That you have been cheating on your spouse by giving your time and attention to someone else? Or anything that makes your spouse feel like they are not your priority?

If your Beloved feels neglected, as though they are an afterthought. Or secondary to whatever has claimed your attention above them. This can be perceived as a significant problem beginning to fester within your marriage. It just may be that sin has crept its way into your union and is the reason for your absenteeism.

If this is experienced in your relationship with your spouse or while you are dating. In this case, I highly recommend you critically evaluate what's happening within yourself or the union and work to resolve the issue(s) before it is too late.

Regretfully! I sinned against my wife, myself, and even against my loving and merciful God. The thing about it; my wife was not neglected or left feeling that she was secondary or an afterthought. The fact that my wife never thought that her husband would cheat on her, this being her very words. And if I did anything to raise her suspicion ... which I was careful not to do. And apparently didn't; I was, therefore, free and clear – figuratively speaking, from my wrongdoings before my wife only. That said, roughly nine years later, I willingly disclosed to my wife that I had been unfaithful. Because I had managed to conceal my lie and unfaithfulness so well. When I did disclose my unfaithfulness to my wife, she was in total shock and disbelief that her husband could do such a thing!

Satan Places Hooks to Ensnare Man and Hold Captive Our Thoughts

Here is a brief look, but full disclosure is soon to follow regarding how *I got caught up*, hooked by sexual sin, and the ultimate betrayal of my wife and God. You will also come to understand better why I phrased the matter as – "*Caught up.*" Due to my ignorance or spiritual immaturity, I was at an establishment I should not have been. While there, I was approached by this person who had "eyed" or targeted me and then seized my thoughts with their words. I would become stunned, utterly surprised, and even intrigued as the person's intentions left me without question regarding what they desired from me. This spiritual assault or *hook-and-bait,* although at the time I didn't understand things as so, led my thoughts to briefly entertain - and wrongly, the ideal of my so-called "machismo," manliness, or sinful nature.

Sometime later, perhaps a couple of months had passed since my first and unusual introduction or encounter with these agents of Satan. Yes, agents! And be mindful … any of us, if we are not prayerful and watchful, can be used by Satan to do his evil or dirty work! This assault incited and excited my mind or thoughts to entertain a dark place of spiritual wickedness in the likes of which I'd not considered, at least not while married.

This encounter and breach of my mind prepared the way for the satanic or spiritual battle to control or hook my mind and body for Satan's work unto evil. However, I was unaware of this kind of diabolical tactic at this early stage of my Christian life, nor what I was up against. Yet I had a clear or conscious sense of right and wrong. At this stage of my life, the demonic spiritual realm and force behind the entertaining of wicked thoughts; and one's actions or the consequences, which could follow by giving in or submitting to evil or immorality, were beyond my comprehension. And so, neither was I spiritually equipped nor had the "willpower" or "self-fortitude" to withstand this assault. I was, therefore, easy prey, a victim, and yet, very much responsible for my behavior.

I would occasionally return to Satan's establishment after the initial assault upon my mind, ignorantly and ill-prepared, while not fully comprehending the death trap or hook that awaited me. Like Eve, that which was spoken to me by the enemy agent, I allowed to seize and influence my thoughts and conduct.

Satan is often subtle in his methods of ensnaring the vulnerable. This is the persistent danger before us all – the spiritually mature and, for certain, those who are babes in Christ or ignorant of Satan's wiles and devices. For this reason, we must be constantly vigilant, prayerful, and always abiding in the Word of God! Not realizing the clear and present danger that was before me, at some point, I began to nibble on the deadly hook and bait that was prepared and presented to me by this individual.

This is a good time to address a matter that nags me. Too often, Satan is given more credit or power for our shortcomings and failings. The saying, "The Devil made or caused me to do it." It is seldom, if ever, the case. For many, this statement is used as an excuse for their wrongdoing. While others actually believe that Satan is constantly on their trail and in pursuit of them.

Satan - his name means Adversary, opposes God at every turn, and he bloodthirstily desires to destroy God's crowning glory – you and me! He is quite lethal through his lies and deceit, whereby keeping or leading many into spiritual darkness, which is unto death eternal! However, Satan is neither omnipotent - all-powerful, omnipresent - everywhere at once, nor omniscient - all-knowing. Only *The Most High God* possesses these attributes! Satan's reach is no further than what God allows. Satan, aka the Devil, formerly known as Lucifer, is merely one condemned rebellious and fallen Angel. His days are numbered! Only God is Eternal!

My brothers and sisters, many unpleasurable things occur because of merely living in this broken or sin-sick world … this is a part of life – period! Nevertheless, there are some occurrences orchestrated or allowed by God to get our attention or even, to lovingly discipline us when we stray from Him (Hebrews 12: 4 - 11). And still, there are things that God permits Satan or his demonic agents to do, which will ultimately bring about God's purpose for His Beloved – His children, this world, and those belonging to it – the children of Satan.

And so, as for Satan specifically targeting you or me, it is highly unlikely. However, demons influencing us is another matter and reality that we must guard ourselves against. Instead, Satan's attention or relational ties are given to persuading and manipulating those in positions of power and authority. Those who have a platform to make decisions or control the masses' thinking. Therefore, we must not attribute every ill, misfortune, or unfortunate occurrence to Satan's doing. If the truth is told, a lot of the mess we find ourselves in is because of our own doing or bad choices.

Since Satan is not God, stop hyping him up to be something he's not! Stop buying into his lies of whatever sort! Satan is, in fact, a deceptive and yet, defeated foe. Satan, this ultimate villain, while he waits for his day of final judgment - imprisonment to eternal hellfire is attempting to take down and even out others along with him. This place of eternal torment (Hellfire) was arranged for him and his demon followers in particular. And subsequently, as a result of the *Edenic Fall*, all people who remain one with him. Who are these people? … All who reject Jesus as Redeemer and refuse to follow His teachings.

Satan, aka Lucifer, meaning Angel of Light, before his deconsecration and expulsion from heaven, nevertheless, had limitations imposed upon him by his Creator – God. Though Satan is unlike God, whose honor, authority, and power he lusted for. Nevertheless, his influence is felt and seen operating globally and most assuredly through his fallen angels (demons). They are a vast number who take their orders from Satan – *the prince of the power of the air* (Ephesians 2:2).

Though we are not to fear these demons or overly concern ourselves with these wicked and vile creatures. They are, in fact, the agents of Satan that can and do have a tremendous influence upon man – the Saved and unsaved alike. These unclean spirits perpetually dangle or present before us, in various manners, times, and degrees - wickedness, that which God has forbidden man to partake or partner with. The temptations or opportunities by which we can engage in sin – the forbidden, are ever-present and significantly increasing!

As for my situation, the forbidden fruit was presented and dangled itself before me. Before continuing, I believe it will be beneficial to briefly revisit my past and fast-track forward to when *sin* stood before me to offer to give itself to me: And so, I was not brought up in the church, so I had no vital or intimate relationship with the Father – God, my Creator.

People … what I now know is - that it's about one's personal, committed, and loving relationship with God that will keep you and get you through life victoriously. Our union with God does not make us perfect. But instead keeps the child of God from making costly decisions that would have been made because we did not know and have a relationship with the Father. It is not enough to know about God; one must come to know His love for themselves – the matter is personal! And in return, they choose to love and commit their life to Him. God must not be an afterthought or secondary in one's life. He must be revered as Lord and Savior, the Almighty God!

It wasn't until the summer of 1983 that I recall first opening a Bible to read it. I was stationed in El Paso, Texas, going through the U.S. Army's boot camp. There, I encountered racism unlike anything I'd ever experienced ... there was no escaping it! I was eighteen years old, far away from home, and my first time on my own.

Angered by the experience of racism, I called home to my mother, who now had five children by three different men. My youngest sibling was around three years of age. My mother was a praying woman; I learned this as an adult. She was a motherless and fatherless child. My mother did not know her father, who was killed in New Jersey when she was a child. The New Jersey newspaper article said my grandfather's killing was gang-style. His name was Lonnie Thomas. My mother's mother passed away in her early thirties when my mother was just thirteen years old. As a child, saying things were challenging for my mother would be an understatement. She experienced some hellish times! But God showed her favor!

Here's the short of the conversation I had with my mother when I called her. Me: "Ma, I'm going to hurt somebody!" Her response to me went something like this "You need to find Jesus for yourself ... turn it over to Him."

Now on my own, I opened the pages of the Bible for the first time. I also recall attending at least one church service during my months of military training. I do not remember reading my Bible consistently during my active, two years, and seven months of service. However, I am confident that I was influenced by what I read. Neither during this time did I have much of a prayer life ... and there definitely was no personal or *intimate relationship with God* - I knew of no such thing. He was just out there – somewhere in heaven.

Nevertheless, my Christian journey to spiritual maturity was underway. God would watch over me as I trodden – this journey alone for most of my adult life. Even to this very day, for the most part, I stand alone.

After completing my military training, somewhere around the spring or summer of nineteen eighty-four, I was baptized at Greater Saint Paul Missionary Baptist

Church, where my mother had been attending. I was taken to the pool for baptism by the late W.T. Bigelow, the pastor at the time.

My attention given to Bible reading was hit and miss or without consistency. Nevertheless, I was getting something from those periods I gave to reading ... this I now know! I was not involved in organized corporate study or worship during this period of my military life. However, looking back, I can clearly see how God had His hands on me, showing Himself to be merciful and faithful in keeping His own.

As a teenager and before entering the military, I knew I wanted to get married someday. I didn't receive counsel from my parents on being a godly husband or father. Besides, I was quite young when my dad left his home. My mother was then left to hold down the fort and her family's uncertain situation on her own.

When my dad divorced the family - I was somewhere around eleven years of age. I recall there being only good times within our home. The way my dad and mother interacted with one another was loving. And a time of fun and laughter as a family. Those moments certainly left a positive impression on me, giving me some idea of what marriage should look like or be about.

As a young man thinking about marriage, I felt confident regarding marital victory. Somehow, I just knew I would be a good husband and father. The thought of having a failed marriage never entered my mind. Divorce was not something I gave any thought to. There were fewer divorces in my family and neighborhood than I see today. Besides, unlike many children today, adult situations or problems going on within homes or marriages, my siblings and I were guarded against experiencing the fallout. My mother protected us from what she thought to be harmful as best she could. For this, I am grateful!

My tour in the military came to completion in April 1986. Within the same week of my return home ... a day or two later, at best, I was introduced to Lisa. Just shy of two years later, she would become my wife. After a mere six months of dating her, I married this extraordinary woman. Noticing the great qualities she possessed, I wanted her as my wife. However, at the time, I could not comprehend that she was God's gift to me and the answer to my prayer.

While serving in Germany, I clearly remember in prayer asking God for a wife, amongst a few other things. God has since and continues to show himself faithful! Where God is faithful, and He always is! Know, for a certainty, when He blesses His children, in whatever manner He chooses to do so. That His archenemy, Satan, desires to come against it or the child of God ... for this is the very nature of Satan - to oppose God and anything God has His hands on. Satan nor his demon followers can stop God from blessing us. However, after the blessing has been given, Satan, through his agents, can undoubtedly get to messing things up if we allow him to or give him a foothold through our own failings or involvement with that which God has forbidden (Ephesians 4:27).

Approximately six months after completing my military service, I became a Mount Level Missionary Baptist church member. Leading up to joining this church, this difficult period of my life was unlike anything I'd experienced – this being from an emotional and spiritual standpoint. Such was the uncertainty of life before me, with the accompanying void and loneliness that I was experiencing - to the church I was drawn. A mere babe in Christ. But by the world's standard, a man of the age of twenty-one. For the first time in my life, I will be exposed to the spiritual feeding my soul longed for and cried out for.

God, through His Spirit ... His Word and my fellowship with other Believers had begun a work or change in me. Slow it was, there was no fault in God ... just the same, the process of my spiritual development had begun. My brothers and sisters, spiritual nurturing and maturation must be understood as a lifelong process ... It's akin to sanctification. To suspend this process or the feeding of our spirit-man or body. And certainly, for a prolonged period can and likely will be very costly to one spiritual and even one's physical well-being. I would come to learn the spiritual cost of neglecting my spiritual nurturing and refinement first-hand.

Here we go ... *I got Caught Up!* The enemy of God and my enemy wanted my blessings or what God had done for me! Yes, he wanted my family and me. To get the man of the house is for the enemy to get the house – the family! And still - at this very moment, right now, over thirty years later; nothing, absolutely nothing regarding God's enemy and my enemy has changed this fact! But as for me ... I am no longer a babe in Christ; I far better understand the tactics and evil of Satan and my nature ... One who is born of corrupted flesh!

Early in my marriage - the infant stage, I will call it. And even before I had married Lisa. As an immature, self-confident, and self-reliant Christian, I remember thinking and even saying. "If a woman stepped up to me to have illicit sex, I was going to put her in her place." In other words, I would honor my marriage and respect my wife. And I really meant it!

I now know that my words got back to Satan or, better yet, were intercepted by Satan's demon representation ... really!

Some three years later, and faithfully committed to my wife, I reconnected with some friends of my youth. My wife had no opposition to this; neither was there a reason for there to be. My friends and I picked up where we had left off before I got married, which was a return to the club scene - *The forbidden!* It was not that these brothers were a bad influence, not at all. We hung out at these spots; what my friends may have done or were up to had no bearing on me. No, the problem wasn't my brothers. The problem was with where I chose to hang out. At the time, this was not obvious to me.

Very much in need of more seasoning on spiritual matters and therefore lacking in spiritual maturity and insight. I couldn't foresee the problem that hanging out at the clubs could bring to our home, and neither could my wife. At this time in our life, our sons were young. The wifey and I didn't go out often, but this was a nonissue. However, Lisa didn't mind me going out or doing whatever. I had been a responsible and loving husband and father.

However, I began to enjoy going out a little too much. This was a problem in the making – which, at the time, neither of us could see. I started going out to the clubs by myself to shoot pool. I wasn't scheming or being up to no good – I was simply out to shoot pool. However, I'm certain that the night's activities - the *Eye Candy* had become a major part of the club's appeal – considering I was in my mid to late twenties. But of course, it was!

But I was good! It wasn't like I was plotting to do wrong, no ... not at all. However, the enemy of my God, hence my enemy Satan or his demon buddies, were. Like a fish, I was navigating dangerous waters during idea fishing season, where there were baited hooks that I could not perceive. Like a fish navigating the dark and murky water, with the hook being undetectable, my spiritual eyes were not keen on discerning the danger before me. But I was good and self-reliant, so I couldn't see the trouble I had put myself and my family in. I was blind and undiscerning of Evil's wiles! This is just where Satan wants us!

The fresh and frisky bait was placed strategically in the water (club scene) before me. This fish (me) was out of place and in depths too deep and dark for my safety; the moment was now ideal for me to get *Caught Up, Hooked Up,* and *Reeled In.* People, things were fine at home. There had been no problems within my marriage. And neither had there been agents of Satan or demon influences to get me to this point and predicament in which I would find myself. Ignorantly, carelessly and with a lack of knowledge, foresight, and wisdom, my choice landed me in the club, thereby putting my family and myself in grave danger! I was easy prey because I was out of place! A place I had no business being as a babe in Christ or without my wife with me. This club scene was a problem waiting to happen!

Now things were about to take a turn for the worst. The situation's unfolding would be sinister, even with potential lethality ... either or both spiritual and physical death. Satan, I am convinced through his dark underworld, his host of demon allies and people agents were poised to take me down and even out. My brothers and sisters ... God has made it known that Satan's mission is to *kill, steal and destroy* whomever he can (John 10:10)! And the people Satan has recruited, whether they knew it or not, have been mightily effective in carrying out Satan's plan of destruction upon God's people.

It was time for Satan to strike! I had made myself and my family an easy target for him. The hook and bait would be dangled before me. Just like Eve, I would be enticed to partake of that which God had forbidden. Remember, Satan does not possess the *Omnis* of the Almighty God. However, as an intelligent fallen angel, as with his numerous demon cohorts, they see our activities and hear what we speak. Not only do they report back to Satan, but I am also convinced they are given the green light to harm us or to take us out whenever the opportunity presents itself. But be it known ... we also have the host of heaven and our God, who is on our side! The spiritual battle is real! In the unseen spiritual realm, this battle is fought daily! And we see how it is also manifested through people agents, those on the Lord's side. Or those, knowingly or not, who have aligned themselves with the forces of Satan.

Now bringing back to your attention the thought and comment I made about standing to defend my marriage. I said rather boldly. "If some woman ever stepped up to me to want to have illicit sexual relations with me, I was going to put her in her place!" Do you know who heard this ... in addition to whomever I spoke to? Demons who move about throughout our atmosphere. And who I am convinced gave special attention to the words I uttered at that moment. You are about to see why I am confident that demonic forces were at work to bring me down. They know all too well ... to destroy the man of the house is for them to seize the house. They may not entirely destroy the family. But to bring enough chaos and confusion into the home is sufficient to render the members of the home ineffective for kingdom living or displaying the best that God has for them.

The Spiritual Assault

While alone at this club – *The Forbidden Place.* I sat on the sofa while I waited to shoot a round of pool. Sitting there, I was minding my own business. However, unknowingly my business was being minded or observed by another individual. I occasionally provided security at this club; I was a police officer. I, therefore, was acquainted with the club's staff. While I waited for my next at the pool table, a guy who worked at the club approached me.

He was provided an inappropriate message to deliver to me. Upon hearing the message, I was somewhat stunned or surprised by the momentary disorienting effect of what was said to me. This message served as the initial assault against my mind. I will liken this assault to a stun grenade! The assault having been initiated, this strategic strike would become a life-altering moment, with the potential of devastating the blessings that God had entrusted to me - my family.

But look ... can you believe what happened!? The forces of evil knew what they had to do to bring me down. A guy was tasked to lead the assault against me; instead of the female from whom he received the message! It was, therefore, a male that would be led to approach me and not a woman to come against me! Consequently, I'd not anticipated this tactic and was unprepared, exposed, and left with my guard down. As for the mess(age) that he was assigned to toss my way from this woman was as follows: He pointing to the woman standing not too far across from where I sat. He said to me. "Do you see that woman over there?" I followed his guidance as he pointed in her direction. I was now looking at her. And she was invitingly staring at me while smiling. He continues with his assignment: "She wanted me to tell you that she is feeling you!"

As a result of this experience, I now know better than ever - we all must be mindful of our words. The forces of evil can and will use them against us if we give them the opportunity to do so through our careless or foolish talking. Here's an abbreviated story similar to mind regarding a brother who shared with me how he got caught up in adultery and the end result. In his self-confidence, he foolishly described in a conversation with someone the type of woman and qualities she must possess if he were to ever be unfaithful to his wife. Yes, this was foolish of him to open his mouth to say such a thing.

As a result of his job, he encountered a woman he had to interact with professionally. Initially, their interaction was merely work-related; she also knew he was married. He enjoyed conversations with her, and she with him. However, she turned out to be just the woman he had described that could possibly cause him to betray his wife.

Through the most unusual. And an unlikely series of events that had nothing to do with the woman. Rather a spiritual and physical challenge that he had faced and overcome. In his excitement! Instead of going home to share the story with his wife, who he knew would not understand or share in his delight. He found himself driving to the other woman's home instead. She would delight in his story and rejoice with him – this he knew! He stated that night, they engaged in passionate "protected sex." He says that this was the only time they had sexual relations. Several months later, he hears from her. She tells him, "It is only right that I let you know … you have a child." Other details I will leave out. Let me reiterate … We need to be mindful of the words we speak. The evil forces in the spiritual realm can and will, if at all possible, use our words against us!

As for my situation involving the woman at the club, I didn't know her. However, I may have acknowledged her while working at the club. Anyhow, eye contact was made between us. She cast a seductive smile, and I innocently acknowledged her with a return smile. I was flattered by what I heard but not threatened or offended. But neither was I moved or desirous of her or cared to know her name. To that extent, or from my standpoint, there was nothing more to make of what had occurred. I didn't go after the bait. But I smiled. The fact that I smiled obviously caused her to see things differently than I had. And no doubt, emboldening her to advance me in what would be both a spiritual and fleshly confrontation.

Though I was approached by this man and woman, another fact that God wants you and me to see and understand regarding our earthly conflicts is that they are, in fact, spiritual in essence. Our battles are not against flesh and blood. Now open your Bible to Ephesians 6:10 – 18. Read these words to better understand what you are truly up against.

Now … I don't recall the time that elapsed between the time she and I exchanged smiles. But it wasn't long afterward that she would present and dangle herself before me. I was still waiting for my next on the pool table while sitting on the sofa with my ring-bearing hand resting on the top of the couch in plain view. I did not advance toward her, nor did I indicate that I had an interest in her. Not following up on her invitation extended to me, I noticed ole girl sashaying my way as she cast a grandiose smile. She steps up to me. Stopping just behind the sofa and close enough to address and present herself in full view.

Her stay was brief, but her intention and desire were clear, destructive, and deadly! Now at close range, she laid before me herself and then exploded a second stun grenade as she released from her mouth the following words: "I know that you are married, but I don't care!" What she said beyond this, I really don't remember. All I recall was her smile as she confidently strutted away after propositioning me sexually.

I now sat on the sofa, contemplating what I had heard, as an idea rose within my mind that I had not considered. My mind had been targeted and effectively penetrated. The bait was within my grasp, but I didn't immediately go after her. Nevertheless, the battle for the takeover - the territory and claim of my mind was underway. The hook had begun to slowly sink into my thoughts, and grab hold of them. She stepping-up to me both times … yes, both times! As the guy was her and Satan's agent and messenger for her hope, through which to violate my marriage and conquer me sexually. And secondly, when she presented herself before me and disclosed her lust for me. Both of these individuals were used by Satan to do his dirty work. However, the woman was led by her sin-controlled nature and evil base passions. On the other hand, the man was used as a result of being ignorant and foolish. It would not be too far off in the future that I, too, would be recruited by Satan or excited by my passion for partnering with him and willingly participating in his dirty work of forbidden sexual relations with this woman.

At some point, this woman's words had begun to awaken within me, that sleeping giant, my unrestrained sexual inclination, which for the most part of my, just over three years of marriage had been quietly asleep.

For a while, but not an extended period of time, I had been visiting these noisy places of distraction, diversion, and entrapment – the club scene. Finally, the right bait and even the right *beat* and its thumping bass resounded, stirred, and moved me to dance with the Devil. This *beat*, symbolic of the woman, and her words reverberated throughout my mind, body, and spirit, causing me to move to her lyrics and melody. Her foolish and fiendish talk struck a chord within my sinful nature! Like the booming bass from the speakers within the club, I felt her words pulsing through my body. Her words penetrated my mind, causing vibrations within my sin-sick soul, thus stirring the sleeping Goliath within me. This giant - my unrestrained fleshly passion from within my soul, was awakening!

Other than working on minor things common in all youthful marriages, I was totally satisfied with the direction of how things were moving within my home. And I had been faithfully committed to my wife. However, now sitting on that sofa, I pondered a question that seemingly came out of nowhere. What I now know … is that when such an abrupt change in thought towards sinfulness, contemplating, or committing evil enters the mind, this is what the Word of God calls the *fiery arrows* of the enemy – Satan (Ephesians 6:16). I knew nothing of this at the time. And was, therefore, not equipped to guard my thoughts, let alone slay my Goliath, who was about to rise up to challenge and subsequently conquer me over what I knew to be wrong - Adultery!

That one question or fiery arrow would, in fact, incite and ignite a fire in my lower or base nature. For a season, my fleshly passion would become a raging inferno, a consuming fire capable of mass destruction! My actions could have easily set a trajectory for me that could have led to a devastating end if my merciful God had not intervened but instead left me in the way of destruction at my making!

As for that one question or fiery arrow that penetrated my thoughts? This was all there was to it, *"I wonder if I still got it?"* In other words … can I still pull a female for my sexual interest, even though I am married? Although I had this thought, it was not something I intended to pursue. Nevertheless, the battle for my mind had begun to give way to the ways of this world or the stronghold of Satan. I was a Christian…why had I easily succumbed to this battle for my mind? Here you are: even though the various answers have already been given. As for me: I was immature or a babe in Christ. I was somewhere that I had no business being. And what was not mentioned during this season of my life, I was not faithfully attending church or being spiritually nurtured. Unless you are thinking otherwise … I am not, and neither have I made excuses for my actions. Throughout this book, I have owned my wrongs. What I am sharing with you is to keep you from getting *caught up* as I did.

Listen to what the New Testament writer James has to say on these matters of temptation and sin … "Each person is tempted when he is lured and enticed by his own desire. Then desire when it has conceived gives birth to sin, and sin, when it is fully grown, brings forth death" (James 1:14, 15).

On that infamous night in the club, I did not make any effort to engage nor pursue this woman who had extended an open invitation to me to commit physical and spiritual whoredom with her. If I had had enough sense to remain away from the clubs, this book would not have been written, at least not as it has been presented. However, since I didn't have enough sense, God has seen to it personally that you may learn a thing or two from my foolishness and the error of my sinful ways.

Over the next several weeks or months, I occasionally visited and worked at the club. Though I can't recall the event's details, which were to unfold, I found myself nibbling at the bait even though it was not my intention to take hold of her. However, the fact remains … I foolishly engaged her under the known circumstances – that she desired me sexually.

I want you to consider the following Scriptures before taking you back into the club. I'm sure someone reading this book needs them. I wish I'd had them. I'm confident that if God and His Word had been richly abiding within my soul, His Truth would have prevented me from entertaining this *Seductress* and being reeled in by her - hook, line, and sinker.

Listen and learn:

1 Corinthians 10: 12 – 14 Therefore let anyone who thinks that he stands take heed lest he fall. No temptation has overtaken you that is not common to man. God is faithful, and he will not let you be tempted beyond your ability, but with the temptation, he will also provide the way of escape that you may be able to endure it. Therefore, my beloved, flee from idolatry.

Proverbs 5: 15 Drink water from your own cistern, flowing water from your own well. 16 Should your springs be scattered abroad, streams of water in the streets? 17 Let them be for yourself alone and not for strangers with you. 18 Let your fountain be blessed and rejoice in the wife of your youth, 19 a lovely deer, a graceful doe. Let her breasts fill you at all times with delight; be intoxicated always in her love. 20 Why should you be intoxicated, my son, with a forbidden woman and embrace the bosom of an adulteress? 21 for a man's ways are before the eyes of the Lord, and he ponders all his paths. 22 The iniquities of the wicked ensnare him, and he is held fast in the cords of his sin. 23 He dies for lack of discipline, and because of his great folly, he is led astray.

Proverbs 7: 1 Follow my advice, my son; always treasure my commands. 2 Obey my commands and live! Guard my instructions as you guard your own eyes. 3 Tie them on your fingers as a reminder. Write them deep within your heart. 4 Love wisdom like a sister; make insight a beloved member of your family. 5 Let them protect you from an affair with an immoral woman, from listening to the flattery of a promiscuous woman. 6 While I was at the window of my house, looking through the curtain, 7 I saw some naive young men, and one in particular who lacked common sense. 8 He was crossing the street near the house of an immoral woman, strolling down the path by her house. 9 It was at twilight, in the evening, as deep darkness fell. 10 The woman approached him, seductively dressed and sly of heart. 11 She was the brash, rebellious type, never content to stay at home. 12 She is often in the streets and markets, soliciting at every corner. 13 She threw her arms around him and kissed him, and with a brazen look, she said, 1 4" I've just made my peace offerings and fulfilled my vows. 15 You're the one I was looking for! I came out to find you, and here you are! 16 My bed is spread with beautiful blankets, with colored sheets of Egyptian linen. 17 I've perfumed my bed with myrrh, aloes, and cinnamon. 18 Come, let's drink our fill of love until morning. Let's enjoy each other's caresses, 19 for my husband is not home. He's away on a long trip. 20 He has taken a wallet full of money with him and won't return until later this month." 21 So, she seduced him with her pretty speech and enticed him with her flattery. 22 He followed her at once, like an ox going to the slaughter. He was like a stag caught in a trap, 23 awaiting the arrow that would pierce its heart. He was like a bird flying into a snare, little knowing it would cost him his life. 24 So listen to me, my sons, and pay attention to my words. 25 Don't let your hearts stray away toward her. Don't wander down her wayward path. 26 For she has been the ruin of many; many men have been her victims. 27 Her house is the road to the grave. Her bedroom is the den of death.

Clearly, you see why I wish I had known these Scriptures ... so it is, we live and learn. And from our mistakes, failures, and the resulting knowledge gained, we pass along what we've learned so that others do not duplicate our mistakes or wrongs. I know there will be those who will choose to make their beds hard. So be it ... they will have to lie there and face the consequences of whatever they may be.

Now that you have more Truth within you, let's return to the club. On this scandalous night, this woman and I were becoming better acquainted. I felt naively safe and comfortable, but neither was I in pursuit of her sexually. My first recall of the unfolding events from that night was she and I dancing. Yep, I had chosen to dance with the Devil! What was to follow accelerated the devious and, let me add, the diabolical plan this seductress had intended for me.

Leaving the dance floor, we returned to the table where we or one of us had been sitting before dancing. I was not threatened by this woman, although she would have been considered a relatively attractive female. However, I was safe because I was not overly physically attracted to her. Why did I sit with her? It is reasonable for you to ask this question … I am sure it was to have my ego stroked. Really, I was not answering yes to her offer or invitation to be involved with her. Just the same … my actions were saying something different to her, leading me deeper into a dangerous situation. What I couldn't foresee was that I was about to get more than my ego stroked.

We are now seated at the table. People, hear me! What happened next seems as if the matter was pre-arranged or even a setup by the forces of evil. I am just saying! Upon the table lay my cap and a glass of water. Somehow or another, the glass of water toppled. The glass incidentally fell directly towards me. I don't know if she hit the glass, the table was bumped, or what actually happened … things occurred swiftly! Or was this incident somehow directed by her sway, cunning, or craftiness? Accidentally occurring or contrived, things happened in such a way to benefit her perverted scheme and to fall right into her hand, and literally!

The glass fell in my direction; naturally, the water would flow towards me as well. The situation rapidly evolved, or one might say -devolved! The water makes its way to the edge of the table; the spillage of water flowing across the table has found me. Upon my lap, the water flowed. The water had barely begun to seep through my pants - and she was on *it*! I had not even had the opportunity to jump up! Or even attempt to move away from the water when she swiftly stroked my groin … as if she could really wipe away the water! People, I am not being dramatic … It was as if she anticipated this occurrence.

I was now in total disbelief regarding her action. Should I have been, considering how she initially came on to me? I was foolishly naïve, nonetheless, without saying one word. I quickly grabbed my cap - and all but ran from her and out of the club. Without looking back physically, I made my way back to the safety of my home. I did that night - what Scripture says to do under such circumstances, *"Flee from sin"* (1 Corinthians 6:18). Yes, God will make a way of escape. (1 Corinthians 10:13).

Here again, from the book of Proverbs, men are provided a warning and instruction regarding dealing with seductive women. Hear and heed these words of Solomon: *My son give me thine heart (listen intently to me he's employing) and let thine eyes observe my ways. For a whore is a deep ditch, and a strange woman is a narrow pit. She also lieth in wait as for prey and increases the transgressors among men* (Proverb 23: 26-28).

Physically, I had left the smell of the seductress' fragrance, the radiance of her smile, the enticing of her speech and eyes. And even the reach of her groping! I fled from my assailant and the scene of my physical assault and victimization ... loosely speaking. However, in truth, it was just that.

I had fled from the territory and the pursuit of my predator. Neither did I look back as I made my escape. However, my thoughts would take me back to the club while replaying and now beginning to entertain the seductress's offer to sexually rendezvous with her. My fleshly passion ignited; I would become a raging fire to consume and be consumed. Hooked and caught up by the seductress, I, the victim (not excusing my actions), would become a victimizer; embracing the diseased of sexual sin, I welcomed and looked for the opportunity to further transmit and spread the spirit-born pathogen – Sexual sin! I was assuredly headed toward certain defeat and the destruction of my family! That sleeping giant, my Goliath, which was slowly being raised from sleep, had now been awakened ... I would go forth to conquer and, too, be slain!

All that transpired from my first outing with friends to this moment of mere sexual pleasure with this woman occurred within a relatively short time – maybe, around six months or so. By being somewhere, I should not have been, and while entertaining company that was not beneficial for me, I began to set things in motion and even set myself up to get *caught up* before this woman ever approached me.

Scripture says, apart from actual sin: That "all things are lawful, but not all things are beneficial." The meaning is …We have the liberty to do certain things and go certain places. However, we must always consider the consequences or potential fall-out if we partake or participate in situations that we may be spiritually immature to handle. We must also consider how our decisions may affect others. How our choices may affect our witness, and not the least of which how our actions and thoughts affect our relationship with God.

Although I had departed this woman's physical presence, the trappings of this seductress – her words and action toward me had begun to lay a stronghold upon my mind that would arouse my fleshly passion. And so, it can very well be said that wherever the mind goes, the body will be willing to follow.

Only the Lord knows when and how what I am about to share actually came about. A short time, maybe a month or so after my rapid departure from the seductress on that fateful and regretful night. She accomplished her objective – her secret sexual rendezvous with me. Yes, I danced with the Devil; I took hold of the bait! As for my wondering, "If I still had it?" The Seductress didn't provide the answer. You see … she was merely the agent through which the thought was provoked. She was not a challenge of my choosing. And so the question yet remained … "Did I still have it?"

After my sexual encounter with her, but not before consuming a can of liquid courage, my involvement with her was that one time … *one-and-done*! Since then, and some three decades later, I've only seen this woman in public a few times. I have not cared to acknowledge her; however, I did make her known to my wife. She was the only female from my season of folly, except those I didn't encounter again, whom you will read about in the next chapter, that I have not spoken to, acknowledging my wrong, although they all were willing participants.

With each of the sexual encounters occurring in the following chapter, except for one female who I continued to engage with but not sexually, my sordid approach with these females was *one-and-done*. Whether I knew them beforehand or not, I only desired the sexual pleasure they willingly surrendered to me. After reading this, if you are bothered, you have every right to feel as you do. As I hear what I am sharing, my soul is also grieved. Looking at my behavior before I got married, *one-and-done* was my modus operandi. What a foolish boy and man I was. At that time in my life, I could not understand the sexual wickedness that I delightfully engaged in. Satan had me – to death, I belonged … an instrument of destruction I was.

* * *

Having gotten with the seductress heightened the appetite and screaming of my flesh. Understand that impure and corrupt desires arise from one's sinful nature (Matthew 5:28; Mark 7: 20-23; Galatians 5:19 -21). If that voice is not silenced, where one acts according to the voice or upon their flesh's lust, trouble awaits the one who gives in to its demands or who gives way to the fiery arrows of Satan. One being apart from the Spirit of God or failing to maintain a personal or *intimate relationship with the Father*. For such a one. The lure of sin from within or without. It will seek mastery over those it can. And it doesn't have to be through sex.

Listen to me closely! It is not enough to regularly attend church. It is not enough to sing or serve in some capacity in the church. It is not enough to know and to be able to quote Scripture. Until one seeks and even enters into a personal, loving relationship with our Father and God, we are prone to turn to sin's voice instead of listening to the voice of our Creator and Father. For this reason … Not having a *personal relationship* with God, many Christians struggle with regard to being committed to God's principles, teachings, or will. Only when one is genuinely committed to having a *personal relationship* with God our Father will one be able to live for Him through the honoring our bodies. And then, too, be enabled to commit oneself to another in a meaningful and victorious relationship through marriage.

CHAPTER 11

A Season of Folly and Decadence - It Was Inevitable (Proverbs 15: 21)

After my sexual encounter and ultimate defeat by the Seductress, my mind became fixed, even fixated sexually, with consuming and conquering such willing and unwise women sexually. I'd set my feet on a path to search out folly that I may see if "*I still had it.*" Although I was content and happy in my marriage to a terrific woman and mother, with whom I was raising our two sons, one who was around eight and the other seven years his junior.

Understandably, I realize that some of you, with raised eyebrows and perhaps with a few choice words, are saying, "If I was happily married, why didn't I keep my behind home!?" "If Lisa was that good to you, loving you, and you loving her, that should have kept you faithful!" Look, you already know the reason behind my foolishness.

Nonetheless, I will respond by saying. *Happy* won't keep you faithful! As for [L]ove – it or He not being understood or vaguely understood, this was the case for me. And so, a seemingly *good* or *happy* relationship or marriage is only as strong as the couple's depth of knowledge, understanding, and commitment to their union under God. Apart from God, the union is *self-sufficient*. Here the couple is hoping in their strength to be victorious maritally. However, true Love (Agape) does not exist within this union if there is little to no knowledge, understanding, or commitment to God. Therefore, the marriage is built upon and held together by one's feelings. And ideas of marriage and your efforts to remain committed to one another.

This union is vulnerable, even though you may be happy and things are seemingly well with the marriage. However, I am convinced neither of these things, being *happy* or *Powerless* love is enough to stake one's marital success upon. God must be one with the marriage. Both husband and wife must have a personal or loving relationship with their God and Father! When a couple's union with God is honored, relationally, they are assured marital victory!

While I was in my fiendish and foolish pursuit of flesh. This madness carried on for perhaps around a year or so. My wife, of unwavering integrity, suspected nothing of the sort. Initially, there was no reckless disregard in my behavior to alert and affect my wife. When I chose to share with her, nearly a decade later, that I had been unfaithful. The fact that my wife saw no indicators or suspected anything of the sort greatly perplexed her. I didn't want to hurt my wife, although I was doing just that. I was injuring and destroying myself – this included my wife because a husband and a wife are one. I belong to my wife and am one with her. My wife belongs to me and is one with me. As husband and wife, we become one. And so, my selfish action and thinking had an indirect effect and, after making my wrong known to my wife, had a direct and injurious impact on her emotionally.

During my rampage and season of great wickedness, as I look back at that sad and destructive period of my life, it's incredibly surprising the willingness of my participants. Spiritual darkness was at work … it was keeping us blind to the evil of our ways. I recall only one woman who initially displayed a measure of reservations about being with me - a married man. She was the only person I didn't connect with within a club setting. Apart from the seductress, there were four other women with whom I pursued and became sexually involved. But there was an exceptional encounter. The last woman I would be involved with – *The Game Changer;* I'll call her and our entanglement.

Regarding these other four women, details of our engagement are not relevant, but neither do I recall them as with the clarity of *The Game-Changer!* No disrespect intended towards any of these women; however, they disrespected themselves because the situation they willingly involved themselves in with me was done before we got started. Of course, they had to know this! In case you are wondering ... I did practice "safe sex." Now, if the truth is to be told, and it will be ... Biblically, there is no such thing as "safe sex" as this world defines the matter ... Oh, how the enemy of our soul seeks to deceive and destroy us. Satan wants us to believe his lies; sadly, many of us have fallen for them. On the other hand, God has approved "safe sex" as the sexual union between a husband (biological man) and his wife (biological woman). You can't be any safer than that!

It would be my final encounter or involvement with this woman, *The Game-Changer,* that I would come to realize that I would have to break free from my intense entanglement with her. I was eventually freed, permanently ending my season of folly, decadence, and wicked betrayal of my wife and God. The details of this forbidden encounter will be shared soon enough.

What I will say about my involvement with these other women is that I never took off my wedding ring; therefore, I never lied about or denigrated marriage. As a matter of fact, there was no deception of any kind towards these women. I recall talking about my family on at least one occasion, even showing pictures of them that I kept in my wallet.

Perhaps some of you are trying to figure out how I was able to do what I did without my wife suspecting anything. My wife was not naïve. Simple enough ... I had never given her a reason to question or doubt my faithfulness to her. When I did go a-whoring, neither did I disrupt the norms of my home. The bottom line - my loving wife trusted me unquestioningly, and I betrayed her trust!

As for the final woman – *The Game-Changer*, and our initial encounter, it would be that I was at a new club that had recently opened in the city where I lived. From across the dance floor, I saw this woman I'd first laid eyes on years earlier when she and I were kids, around eleven. Only as I now reflect on that brief encounter do I remember my instant attraction toward her! I had really forgotten about that moment. When my eyes first beheld her as a mere boy, I was immediately in awe and felt a boyish crush on her!

But that wouldn't be the last time I would see her before this chance night within the club ... if, in fact, it was chance. Remember, Satan's demons, though they are not omnipresent. However, they can show up, hear what we speak, get a sense of what we like, and learn our weaknesses. Now identifying our weaknesses and vulnerabilities, these evil forces use the information gained to derail and even destroy us!

It was some five years later; I am now in high school. Once again, I encounter *The Game-Changer*. I didn't think I had a chance with her relationally; I therefore never approached her to share my attraction for her. I don't think I ever said anything more than hello. Besides, she had a boyfriend. But then suddenly, so it seemed, she was gone. She had transferred to another high school. Nonetheless, the attraction I experienced when I first laid eyes on her had been rekindled!

Upon seeing her in the club, I will now refer to this woman by this fictional name, Cierra. Needless to say, my attraction towards her had not abated. I, just the same, remained reluctant to approach her. But it was good seeing her after all the time that had passed.

That which was to follow and take shape would be of uttermost surprise to me! A total game-changer! There's the saying: if you go looking for trouble, you are sure to find it! This was my time! Recognizing Cierra from across the dance floor, it simply being good seeing her; I decided to extend a kind gesture and a hello. With absolutely no ulterior motives, my spontaneous response was to buy her a drink. I'm sure I have never bought a drink for anyone before this evening. I did very little drinking; my wife didn't drink at all. Besides, I was tight with what little money I had.

Anyhow, this was my way of simply saying... hello. Summoning the waitress, I asked her to see what Cierra would like to drink. I told the waitress that the drink was on me. From where I stood, I watched this play out. I was only expecting from Cierra - a thank you or some meaningless form of acknowledgment.

However, Cierra was now looking my way as the waitress identified for her that I had purchased her drink. Then the unexpected happened! She immediately turned my way. Our eyes fastened on one another; Cierra was obviously pleasantly taken aback at my drink offering. With her head slightly tilted, as she cast a radiant and inviting smile, she made her way towards me and stood directly in front of me to say thank you and *Yesss*! At least, this was my take on things. She looking up at me and into my eyes. Everything about her gaze and body language was excitedly and curiously asking me, "What's up with you and this kind gesture of a drink offering?"

Interestingly, as I stood there with Cierra, it was no longer about seeing if *I still got it*. I had been on the prowl, looking for the next woman who would be down with me sinfully or who I could spiritually victimize, even though this was not how I actually viewed things. Now, with Cierra, there was a significant shift in my disposition, unlike what I had with the other women. The attraction and chemistry seemed instantaneous as we stood there, engaged in small talk. Needless to say, my boyhood crush on Cierra had not diminished!

My thinking had been ... whoever I was down with sexually, there would be no strings attached. They were not to have any expectations of me. The thought of leaving my wife or defecting from my family ... there had never been such thinking, not the slightest. *I wanted my cake and to eat it too, the cow and the milk.*

Now, standing before me, Cierra, my grade school, my high school, and now, even as a married man, this woman with whom I still had a strong attraction. As we talked that evening, Cierra came to know my marital status and that I had sons. However, this didn't seem to deter or give her reservation as we continued conversing, even in the days and weeks following.

Under the circumstances, we hit it off too well! I know better; I don't hardly believe what I am about to say ... it was like things were meant to be, but under the circumstances – certainly not the case! The ease with which we traveled down this forbidden, uncertain, and dangerous path seemed to be of no consequence. How could something... ever so wrong feel so right? Such is the nature of sin! It will blind and disorient you ... It will cause you to lose your way! Sin is utterly deceitful and can be captivating, leading to one's demise or loss of what they once valued!

[Of necessity, I digress to make a correction. Concluding my writing for the day. As I did from time to time, I shared with my wife where I was with my writing. She listened to my account of the five women I had been entangled with that I mentioned earlier. My wife said to me, "When you initially shared with me the number of women you'd been with, the count was six and not five." After considering the matter, I recalled my involvement with this other woman that made the count six. I'm glad that my wife could provide this detail. Further details she would also help me to recall.

I could have made this numerical correction without you knowing the difference. However, I want you to see how my wife has been able to move forward after the hurt and my ultimate betrayal. She actually did better with moving on than me. Also, by bringing this matter to your attention, I want you to see the openness we share in communicating on this matter and in every area of our life.

While I'm at it, let me throw this in: I don't think I had any other sexual relations other than those mentioned, but it wasn't because I lacked the effort. I had become a roaring lion, seeking that which I could devour.

Months followed from adding this addendum, keeping things one hundred, or maintaining my transparency and honesty. I recalled that the number of women I'd been entangled with was seven, not six.]

He's An On Time God

Over the days and weeks that followed, Cierra and my chance meeting ... If it was actually that. The magnetism which was experienced on that regretful night had not eased. If anything, the situation had become heightened. Maybe it was just me; however, I don't think so.

In addition to my physical attraction for Cierra. Which had persisted for over a decade. As I came to know her better. I also saw that she possessed a suaveness that was equally appealing. She was unlike any woman that I had met. Physically she appealed to me; her mannerism appealed to me, and she even appealed to me intellectually. This was trouble! She was the complete package! *The Game-Changer!* So, it was ... I set out looking for trouble. However, I would unexpectedly get into a situation with a woman I had not anticipated when I set out as a foolish man to dance with the Devil.

As I now consider the situation involving Cierra, I must admit that I didn't know her intentions or thoughts on where she may have seen this forbidden relationship heading. She just seemed content following my lead. With those other situations I was in ... there was no mistaking my end game – illicit sex. I assumed those women knew this; I never thought about them considering anything different. We had a mutual understanding of my making and imagination. However, sex was not the end game for me with Cierra. This connection involved more, and therefore, more would be at stake!

Led by my passion, I was entering into a greater stronghold and new dimension of captivity with Cierra from which I would have to break free. Stronghold ... because the situation had me on a mental lockdown, I began to succumb to the first night as we stood, face to face talking. Experiencing a sexual connection or physical attraction was not foreign to me. However, this situation and her intellectual appeal were new territories ... Cierra was the complete package! Meaning - she was equipped with every adornment and attribute I didn't realize that was appealing to me. Hereto, even arsenal by which to bring my family and me to ruin!

Over the course of time with Cierra, she never made any request of me or required anything from me, not that she could or really needed to ... I was all in! There were no demands, stipulations, etcetera; we just flowed with things. She followed my lead, not disturbing the fluid and smoothly moving situation we were in. Our situation was unpredictable, yet there was the unspoken and eager anticipation of what was next. A perfect storm was taking shape between the two of us ... sinfully beautiful, if I may be allowed to put those two words together. Yet, an ominous and potentially lethal situation was before me, capable of doing me and my family in.

I had become intoxicated with the situation I was involved in with Cierra. As far as I knew, she was single. And I assumed, arrogantly, that she was not seeing anyone. However, I figured that I would make sure this remained the case. Listen to my self-serving absurdity that came about at some point during our unspoken, undetermined, and unnamed situation. I expressed to Cierra that I didn't want her to see anyone. I actually felt that I could ask this of her. I also felt confident that she would honor my one request. I did not expect her come-back! Her response went something like this, "You are married?" With a smile, she's now looking at me as if to say, "What? Really?" She says, "You don't want me to see anyone?" while smiling and slightly chuckling. My read into this was, "Man, please!" I don't remember the conversation going any further. Recalling this moment, I am also laughing at myself. I was rather self-centered and full of myself, wouldn't you say?

My judgment involving Cierra became more skewed over time. I began carrying on with her as if I had nothing to lose. And still, leaving my wife .... was not a thought. It was like Cierra had become *the other woman* ... not that I supported her or did extravagant things for her. This was not the case. Instead, it had to do with me desiring to see her and talk to her whenever possible. I could not get enough of her, even venturing out in public view with Cierra on a few occasions. Somehow or another, I thought I would be safe. Or I didn't care because I was so caught up! What was I thinking? That's the point ... I was incapable of rational thinking! My desires had the best of me! But it was not sexually motivated.

On one of our in public occasions, Cierra asked about my seeming lack of concern about others seeing us together. Me, downplaying the question. She responded – "Alright, cool with me." We were really into one another, and yet, the matter of sex was not my focus or motivation. I do not recall expressing to Cierra any form of physical intimacy or sexual attraction toward her. However, our time together, or when communicating via telephone, was no less intimate, though non-sexual. This kind of involvement with one who is off-limits has led many to sin sexually. You are only fooling or lying to yourself or your significant other when you make light of this kind of conversation with someone you are strongly attracted to.

Certain aspects of my season of folly have long left my memory. However, I have been able to recall the unnatural attraction or affection toward Cierra in more detail. This is something to remember regarding any relationship one may enter into, and certainly where the relationship was sexual: Though the details of a relationship may dissipate, the feelings experienced sexually or otherwise don't easily go away – and for some people, they never will. This is one of the dangers of experiencing sex before marriage; are one's past experiences being brought into your new relationship.

Though time and space may have separated you two, the emotional and even the physical attachment may still be with you. And one may not even be mindful of the matter. This can undoubtedly create major hindrances, if not detrimental to subsequent relationships one may attempt to pursue.

I am convinced that many people, if not most (married or not), are or can become visually or even physically attracted to others. However, the measure of their attraction and that which attracts them to others varies from person to person. Utilizing a perfect stranger: The appeal may result from some feature of the person that was found alluring. This is acknowledged within your soul by the instantaneous feeling of approval or delight experienced as you beheld the person. Or the thought of the complete stranger unsuspectingly surfacing in your mind because something attracted you to them. Whether you showed your approval or not is irrelevant; nonetheless, delight was the resulting experience regarding that person, if not an actual and captivating attraction.

However, it may very well be that in the few moments it took for that person to pass from your presence, it did not take much longer for them to depart from your thoughts.

On the other hand, where several qualities or a strong standout about a person resonates with you. Although they are nowhere to be seen and perhaps never seen again. Nonetheless, you find yourself having thoughts of that person. My point. Being attracted to someone should not be viewed as problematic. Whether you're dating or not, this is a natural occurrence, and it doesn't end when one marries. It is unreasonable to think that one can only be attracted to one person. This should eliminate the erroneous idea of one moving from person to person in hopes of finding their so-called "soulmate."

However, it is undoubtedly a problem when you're married or are in a committed relationship, and your thoughts toward another person have become unhealthy or inordinate. Meaning your thoughts are lustful or sexual towards someone you are naturally attracted to. The Bible's judgment on one's thoughts has this to say, *You've already committed adultery in your heart* (Matthew 5:28). And when not married, such thoughts are identified as committing fornication. Fornication is the catch-all for all sexual impurities or sex acts, whether held in one's thoughts or engaged upon. So it is. Our thoughts and the process by which we willfully engage in such wanton contemplation are inappropriate. And even hazardous to our relationship with all others, not the least of which our Creator and God.

Lustful sexual thinking being played out in my mind was not my issue with the other women, including Cierra. With the other women, I wanted what my flesh wanted – sex, period! Regarding Cierra, a boyhood crush evolved into an unhealthy adult attraction. And now, over a decade later, since first laying eyes on her. Developing into a forbidden infatuation and attraction with her. Whereby ultimately leading me to unlawfully render unto her my time, emotions, physical affection, and anything else you may think of. Such things belonged to my wife! And to her alone!

As mentioned, the time that Cierra and I shared was not about some casual hookup or some meaningless sexual encounter and gratification. And when consummated, we simply move on – with no questions asked. Although I can only speak for myself regarding our situation, I also believe it to be the case for Cierra; we saw no end in sight regarding our evolving and/or devolving and descending situation. Things progressing with us as they were. It would only be a matter of time before we would find ourselves coming together sexually, thereby completing the ultimate violation of my marriage.

With the chemistry Cierra and I had from the jump. Unless we made the decision to stop seeing each other, our coming together sexually would only be a matter of ... When!? The day did arrive that we engaged sexually. Before this, now, regretful evening. The details leading to our sexual rendezvous are gone from my memory. All I can recall was the surprise element of wait and see, as I had no involvement in planning this arrangement other than making it known to Cierra beforehand when my wife would be out of town. Knowing the date, Cierra went into action, planning for the night we were to share together.

Cierra had arranged for our sexual rendezvous at a very nice Inn. It was by no means some low-end stopover for a "quickie." This arrangement was so like Cierra, a step above the rest. Thereby adding to her natural appeal and her being capable of reeling me in more.

Upon entering the suite, I noticed how well she had things arranged – this was to be her (our) night! But God would intervene! He may not show up when you want Him to, but He is an on-time God! It has only been after looking back on this situation. That I came to this place in my thinking regarding the event to follow. And that God had shown up in a timely fashion!

I don't know how long I had been in the suite; it wasn't long when the unexpected happened. I can't even recall getting comfortable or sitting before my phone rang – what timing!

I am of the mind that things don't just happen by chance or by coincidence. And certainly, when you are a child of God, whether walking in obedience or not. God is always watching over those who are the apple of His eye. God desires for those who belong to Him not to be ensnared by sin; therefore, He will always make a way of escape or send out a warning.

Nevertheless, it's against His character to force our hand. Even so ... God allows certain things to play out in our lives that we may learn from the experience, as they ultimately work toward our good and His praise. I see this resulting from this book - my story you're now reading about.

It is also a fact that God will also dispatch His angels to get our attention in an attempt to lead us away from certain harm. That said, God will not override our free will. *Love* does not operate in that manner. *Love* does not force *Itself*. Whether we take heed to His angelic messengers, His Word, or even our conviction of impending sinfulness, stirred within by His Spirit, to guide us to safety is up to our choosing. And where one has become desensitized to the voice of God or refuses His compelling ... well, they are left to reap what they sow.

As for how God showed up on time for me? I am now standing in the living room area of the suite, looking at my ringing phone. It was my wife calling me! There was absolutely no way that I would avoid answering the call. Although apprehensive, everything in me said, "Don't answer the phone." Including my thoughts about what Cierra might say, even what I was going to say to my wife, had me, "Shook!" I felt that I was in between a rock and a hard place!

This was my wife! There was nothing right about where I was mentally and physically! And the activity in which I was preparing to engage sexually! And yet, I was not that far gone in mind that my wife calling out for me would go unanswered. She was my wife, whom I cared for, and, as best as I knew how at the time – loved, though my actions were far from showing this to be so.

Being true to form - caring and loving, my wife was merely checking in and checking on me. Although I had been and was about to check out, yet again on her with another woman. Nevertheless, I knew my wife's call for me would not go unanswered.

I seem to recall that Cierra was sitting when I answered the call from my wife. I did not attempt to leave her presence while talking to my wife ... although I felt an impulse to do so. I think I was, somehow or another, now trying to man up as if I had something to prove to Cierra. I didn't go into observable panic mode when I answered the phone. But my insides felt different about the predicament I was faced with. The telephone conversation with my wife, if I dare call it a conversation, was short and hurried. This is one of two times I recall blatantly lying to my wife. The other time also involved Cierra. One late night I was on the phone with her; my wife waking from sleep, asked who I was talking to. My response, I believe, was, "It was work-related or a co-worker that I was talking to."

Ending talks with my wife, my nerves on edge, I attempted to hurry the night away with Cierra. However, she wasn't having this at all! In true Cierra form, she had me to *Slow my roll.* She may have even put it in those very words. The call from my wife had altered my mental and physical disposition, thereby disturbing my groove. The call from my wife was water to my flame! What was sure to have been a night where Cierra and I were to fully or entirely engage and give ourselves one to the other passionately and physically. Instead, for me, it became merely another stolen night for the physical exchange of diminished and now extinguished sinful sexual pleasure.

I cannot fully explain the workings of God; no man can. However, I am convinced my wife was *angelically prompted* to call me at the time she did. This strategically placed call was coordinated from the command center on high. My God certainly prevented me from entering into the felonious larcenous night with Cierra with the passion, focus, and even dedication I had upon arriving.

Though I physically engaged Cierra, the intoxicating infatuation and the emotions that had begun developing towards her were extinguished by the heavenly disruption and the passion-quenching call at hearing my wife's considerate and loving voice.

Following this night, nothing seemed to change between Cierra and me. However, this would be the only time we engaged in sexual relations; my Deliverer and God would see to it; He would again mightily intervene and disrupt my night with Cierra!

The Ultimate Divine Game-Changer

Cierra and I continued with the same enthusiasm toward seeing and talking with one another. Sometime later, not much later, Cierra and I made plans for a night out. This time my wife and our sons were in town. Because I'd been going out to the club scene for some time. An evening out without my wife wasn't a concern for her. However, my intentions and the frequency of going out made my guilty conscious somewhat wonder if my wife was becoming suspicious of my behavior. Doing wrong will certainly have you in the state of mind that I was in. That is ... if you still have a conscience that has not been totally given over to sin.

During this entire season of pursuing folly and decadence, I was in a bad place mentally and spiritually. Additionally, I had been estranged from the church. I did not have it in me to be able to practice the way of a sinner, then show up in church like I was living right when I knew I was living foul. Neither would my conscious allow me to attend church when I knew my intentions were to do wrong as soon as I could find the opportunity to do so.

However, I am aware that some can do just that ... willfully engage in sin without remorse or regret. And not only go to church but also participate in the various services and functions of the church ... This includes church leaders! Unless they repent! Unless they turn to Jesus, they will have to answer to God! Hellfire will be their end – the eternal condemnation of God for those who live foul and refuse His saving grace!

Although I was acting like a fool, I didn't have it in me to be that sort of brazen fool. This can be recognized as a blessing. In that, God had not given me entirely over to my carnal self wherein my heart had been hardened, without conviction, and unreachable. I was His child. He mercifully would not let me go nor give me what I deserved – His stern rebuke or even His sentence of death! I was not a mere Christian in name only. However, I was quite immature in the Lord. That is to say, neither had I developed a *personal or intimate relationship with my God and Father.* Those who remain in sin or practice sin without conviction or the rebuke of God ... the Bible declares, are not God's children (Hebrews 12:6; Romans 1:24; 1 John 3:9; Revelation 3:19).

On this particular night, Cierra was driving. We were headed to a club somewhere in Raleigh, North Carolina. I remember nothing of our outing. However, God would not let me forget the moment He divinely intervened! The *Ultimate Divine Game-Changer* would occur! God wrecked or ran interference regarding my situation with Cierra. He got my attention, thereby setting my thinking on the right path. When listening to music, I'm a beat person first, then attention might be given to the lyrics. Anyhow, a song began playing over the radio. It had a mid-tempo R&B flow. The vibe was soulful, and the brother singing had smooth-sounding vocals.

Surprisingly the song and its message arrested my attention. I began intently, listening to the lyrics. Unbeknownst to me, God had showed-up! There was no question about it ... I felt this right away after hearing a few lines of the lyrics! Through this secular song, God was rendering the right beat, the soulfulness of the music, and even the right lyrics sung by a gifted brother. That would grab hold of me, unlike any song I'd ever heard. God had finally gotten my attention! And it would be through a secular song heard over a car radio. Things with Cierra and I would never be the same.

Like sheep that are prone to wander, I had strayed from the sheepfold; the Church, the people of God, and God Himself. But as that Great Shepherd of the sheep, my Father came looking for me! He had not given up on me! I had not ventured beyond His reach. He knew my heart and my struggle and therefore sought after me that He may lead me home – to my wife and family! And back to Himself that He may care and watch over me!

Thinking back to that night in the car, I find it interesting that Cierra and I were not actively talking as this song played. Maybe, she, too, had been pulled in by the lyrics of the late and great Rhythm and Blues Artist George Duke.

Read these words that spoke to me that night, or listen to the song yourself. You will hear and see why the song arrested my attention, stirred my consciousness, and pricked at my heart, thereby causing me to hear from God ... And yes, from a song you will never hear sung by a Church's choir or vocalist.

Song title: *"No Rhyme, No Reason"*

"Girl, just take some time
Let me try to find the words I want to say to you

I've been searchin' my mind
I got to find the reasons I feel the way I do

Let me emphasize that I recognize
What I should and should not do

And though I know it's wrong
Every now and then I phone
Just to talk to you

Sometimes love
Has no rhyme, and no reason
Even if we try to be cool

At the strangest times
Love can make a connection
If you trust your heart to choose

Sometimes you cross my mind
And I don't know why
But I hear from you

And though I want to stay close
I realize the most we'll ever be is good friends
I got kids at home
I can't leave them alone
This I'm telling you

I've got another life
Cause I still love my wife
Though I still want you

Sometimes love
Has no rhyme, and no reason
Even if we try to be cool ...

Enough said! I will end the song here.

The lyrics mesmerized me like the power of a lightning bolt and struck a nerve deep within my soul, thereby jolting my conscious! The ballad spoke dead on to my debilitating and lifeless dilemma. I knew God was speaking to me through this secular song that had profound moral implications.

When George said, *"I got kids at home ... I can't leave them alone ... This I'm telling you. I've got another life ... Cause I still love my wife ... Though I still want you."* It was a wrap ... this done me in and did it for me! After hearing these words, I knew what I had to do! I had to get my act together; the voice of the secular prophet -though George was unaware, had spoken on God's behalf! Yes, God had spoken ... If He could open the mouth of an Ass (donkey) to speak to Balaam (Numbers 22:28). He can surly use George Duke to speak to me!

When the song ended, I looked over to Cierra and asked her, "Did you hear what the song was saying?" She calmly responded while remaining true to form, "What are you trying to say?" I knew what I was trying to say, although I didn't respond ... The song said it for me!

Continuing onward with our plans. Nevertheless, I knew with unquestionable certainty that it was now time for me to break free from this stronghold and those chains of my choosing that had me bound for the past several months.

While listening to the song's lyrics, I traveled to my home in my mind's eye. While I was yet out in the streets playing the fool. I saw my sons comfortably tucked away safely in their beds where I had left them. I then traveled across the hall to my bedroom. There lying in her bed was my beautiful wife. She was quietly and peacefully asleep without a care at all.

My thinking at that moment: How can I do this to them? My wife does not deserve this. Not that there is ever a time that such a wrong can be seen as deserving - no, not at all! Even if your spouse cheated on you first (Proverb 20: 22; 1Thessalonians 5:15; 1 Peter 3: 9).

If not the following day, shortly afterward. I made up my mind to permanently distance myself from Cierra. I scheduled a meetup with her; it was now time to confront her with my decision to end whatever we had. I don't believe she was expecting to hear this from me.

Other than me asking her if she had heard what the song said. I had remained quiet regarding how I was now feeling about things.

Our meeting place was at a park. I don't remember there being much conversation if there was at all. For my sake, I had to firmly and forthrightly express to Cierra that she was no longer to call me! I also said to her that I would not be calling her! The look that she gave me seemed to be of surprise and bewilderment. I really don't think she saw this coming, and certainly not how I felt I needed to handle the matter – this being for my good. Her eyes seemed to beg the question … Why? … What's going on? … And why are you coming off so strong? However, when she did speak, her response was simply, "Okay."

Being brought back to my right mind, I'd decided I needed to get it together for the sake of my family, myself, and my relationship with God and Father. Little did I know just how difficult it would be getting Cierra out of my mind. I had to consciously war against myself to keep from calling her or trying to see her. I had to force her phone number from my memory! I had no idea of the challenge before me! Nonetheless, I stood firm with a strong resolve to be free from the snare I'd been entangled in.

With each passing day, Cierra's pull and grip were loosening. Eventually, she would be purged from my mind, and the stronghold upon me broken. I would no longer have the intense attraction that had drawn me to her while I was a boy and now a married man.

Where one has purposed in their heart to repent from evil and do good – this is honorable and righteous before God. No matter the wrongs of your past, if Jesus is confessed as your Lord and Savior, if you in truth have turned from your history and the practice of sinning, God no longer condemns you, nor should you condemn yourself. This does not excuse our wrongs or the consequences of our actions that may follow. However, before God, you now stand sinless and guilt-free!

Unless we forget. Only God can bring true deliverance. God gives us the will and the power to seek to be free from whatever holds us in bondage. He is the Power and Strength that will deliver us. And He alone who gives us victory over sin when we acknowledge our sin and humbly submit to His Word and will (Psalms 32:5; 51:2; Jeremiah 3:13; 1 John 1:9).

To be led by God is to be taken into His care and pastures that we may find rest, peace, and protection from the troubles of our own making, as well as the troubles that this world will often dangle before us or tempt us with that we may become ensnared by sin.

The Psalmist, King David, was appointed and anointed by God. He, too, committed adultery. After discovering the woman was pregnant, he had her husband killed (2 Samuel chapters 11 and 12). There would be consequences for David's actions even though he became heartbroken for his sins against Uriah's house and his sins against his God.

Because of David's brokenness and contrite heart, God said of him that he was a man after His own Heart. This was not because David did everything right. Far from it! But instead, because David knew God for himself … he had a *personal relationship* with God. The relationship and the love he had for God, and the love that he understood that God first had for him, would not allow David to remain in sin and unrepentant or to continue to wonder from his God and Shepherd.

Hear and meditate on these familiar words of David:
Psalms 23

The Lord is my shepherd;
I shall not want.
He makes me to lie down in green pastures;
He leads me beside the still waters.
He restores my soul;
He leads me in the paths of righteousness
For His name's sake.
Yea, though I walk through the valley of the shadow of death,
I will fear no evil;
For You are with me;
Your rod and Your staff, they comfort me.

You prepare a table before me in the presence of my enemies;
You anoint my head with oil;
My cup runs over.

Surely goodness and mercy shall follow me
All the days of my life;
And I will dwell in the house of the Lord
Forever.

God, at this very moment, is looking for His lost sheep. He desires to lead the lost ... the wondering sheep and unsaved alike, into His care and protection. The invitation from God is now being extended ... He is asking, "*Will you follow Me?*"

CHAPTER 12

Time To Get Right
Easier Said Than Done

A difficult road was before my wife and me that I could not have imagined or believed if I had been told beforehand. Years following my infidelity, somewhere between eight to ten years, I chose to share with my wife that I had been unfaithful. I didn't expect much, if any, fallout or lingering effects from my decision to share this with her. She was not the kind of person who would "Go off!" Besides, she honored me as her husband. And the head of our home. Even though I had brought before her that I had failed to honor her and our marriage.

However, we would encounter more of a challenge, even a spiritual battle, than I ever could have given thought to. What awaited us, yes us, tested our marriage, so I felt at the time concerning my marriage. However, it was the level of stress that my wife endured during this season in our marriage that greatly grieved me. This stress and assault battled against and battered her well-being – mind, body, and spirit! I only came to recognize this fact or full impact and what my wife suffered not until I consulted with her as I wrote this chapter of the book. The struggle that my wife and I were up against. It was not as much for our marriage as I thought. Instead, it was for her mind! ... *Oh, for God's grace!* My wife made a comment to me that led to me making this assertion. You will understand how I arrived at this statement in later chapters.

Before unveiling what occurred in that chapter of our life, I will share my on-and-off or inconsistent Christian journey leading up to that climactic chapter and season of our marriage. I am convinced that this kind of inconsistency in a Christian's life, whether they are new converts (babes in Christ) or are viewed as mature Christians, can cause one to go astray and wander - as it was for me, from the care and guidance of our *Great Shepherd.*

By God's sure grace and mercy, I had returned to my right (not perfect or mature) mind, having ended my dreadful season of folly and decadence. I'd been ashamedly unfaithful! Now the time had come for me to move beyond the madness, to do right by my incredible wife. Also, get back in right standing with my loving Father!

What this meant for me: Asking my Father for forgiveness, returning to church, as well as becoming actively involved in the life or ministry of the church. This would also entail me giving sufficient time to reading and studying the Word of God, attending Sunday school and other activities and personal necessities, becoming one calling himself a Christian. This is a good start; however, these measures alone are not sufficient … One must have a *personal relationship* with God. Additionally, trust His sufficiency for all that we need so that we may mature as children of God and thereby consciously seek to live for Him, honoring and glorifying our Father through our living!

During this period of my turn-around, as previously mentioned. My wife was oblivious to my wretched actions approximately a decade prior. At this point in our marriage, I didn't feel the need to inform her, as I had not arrived at a level of spiritual maturity and confidence that would allow me to see the need and the benefit of doing so. Therefore, as far as I was concerned, and especially during this period of my life, there was nothing to tell. You see … my clandestine life of gross indiscretion was just that … my secret. As for the saying: "What one doesn't know won't hurt them." This seemed to apply just well to my situation for a time.

Now, I didn't consider my position to be an easy way out. Nor was I intentionally deceitful and avoiding acknowledging my wrong. Sometimes, your wrongdoing or sinful behavior only needs to be brought before God. Or brought to Him first. However, afterward, He may further direct your course of action. This is what He did for me, later, rather than sooner, to acknowledge and confess my wrong openly before my wife. *Confession is extremely beneficial for the soul!*

On the other hand, when one knowingly wrongs someone. Or the person wronged indicates as much. One then has a moral obligation to make things right. If you are a Christian, seeking and desiring to do right before God. It may be that you do not initially see where your actions or words may have caused offense. However, with your walk with God and growing spiritually and even closer to Him, you will gain spiritual insight or sensitivity. This will cause you to want to right your wrongs, which is to be attributed to God, the Spirit within you, Who gives understanding and guidance to your *quickened* or renewed spirit.

With this new awareness or sensitivity regarding matters of the Spirit, you will discover that you just can't say or treat people, let alone your spouse, in any kind of way. And neither can you readily leave unresolved matters unsettled. If you try … there will be a troubling or stirring within your soul that will compel you to set the issue right, for conscious sake. Or your peace of mind, or the fact that it's the right thing to do that you will very likely respond accordingly, although it just might be later than sooner. Or one can choose to woefully resist the Spirit altogether. This will always hinder or work against the one born anew by God the Spirit.

My coming forth to right or confess to the wrong I committed against my wife would occur some eight to ten years later. Although these years had distanced me from my sinful past and dark and dreadful secrets. I wrongly concluded: that my admission after all these years had passed would somehow make things easier for my wife. Just the same, my initial confession, and not even my full disclosure of my past, would be far more painful for my wife than anything I could have considered!

Later, and in more detail, I will unveil this matter. As for now, I want to share one thing my wife told me that left me stunned and speechless. Not only that, but at the time, I was also unable to immediately fathom or empathize with her enormous hurt and the depth of the grief she was experiencing. Here's my wife responding to my shocking revelation that I had been unfaithful. With a puzzled and disturbing look of shock and disbelief. She said, "It feels like what you did just happened!" The time and distance that gave me a sense of comfort and relief, however, for my wife, provided no such thing! My wife hearing of my infidelity was an immediate shock to her very being! It would be some three years or so later. That I would come to understand the magnitude of my wife's hurt and suffering.

Without question, God wanted me to know that I may inform others of the hurt I caused His daughter, whom He'd given and entrusted to me as a wife; to honor, to have, and to hold … to protect, etcetera, etcetera. I failed miserably! At this point in my early Christian walk, my family and I needed to be reunited with an Empowered or Spirit-filled Church of the Living God! I needed to know not just about God. I needed to know Him for myself, on that personal or intimate level. Over time and my failures would make this truth become my reality!

The Church A Home For The Homeless

After I had completed my military obligation in the Spring of 1986, life before me was uncertain. Unable to find in anyone what I needed. Neither in what this world had to offer to satisfy my soul's longings. This led my unsheltered, empty, and lonely soul to the *House of God*. Some six months after getting out of the Army, broken and with tears streaming from my eyes, I sat before the pastor of Mount Level Missionary Baptist Church, Dr. Reverend Leonzo Lynch.

I said to him, "I'm tired." My life was empty and meaningless. Having come to know a little about my mother's faith. And I having a shallow relationship with God that began while in the military. I felt it within my soul. That I needed to unite with a local church. This feeling and/or prompting I had was from the leading of the Spirit of God. God was also desiring to reel me in.

Becoming committed to Mt. Level ended my season in the summer of *1986* of trying to find fulfillment in club hopping, even hoping to find some willing female to be with sexually. Both the club and female companionship had been my elixir, intoxicant, or numbing agent to take my mind away from my worries and concerns. During this period in my life, I didn't have a meaningful job. I worked two jobs, but this wasn't what I desired. Besides, these jobs did not offer me the benefits and financial security I felt needed to have a meaningful relationship and then start a family.

After the meeting with Pastor Lynch, Mount Level would become my first church home. Though I'd turn twenty-one the year after joining myself to this family of Believers, spiritually, I was a mere babe in Christ.

As mentioned. Writing this book has been revelatory and even therapeutic, enhancing my spiritual growth. What is it for you, that unhealthy thing, person, or place of temporary solace and gratification that you identify with and retreat to, when you experience unrest and troubling of your soul? I make mention of this as I now see how the club scene was a place for which I sought empty pleasure and even consoling.

I can see the ease it may be for one, who may have believed they left in their past, those quick fixes to numb or distract themselves from the stress and troubles of life. However, amid life's crises or experiencing some low or challenge in life, they stumble back to that quick fix, distraction, or diversion they thought they were dissociated and free from. But no, time and distance had not remedied or freed them from those unhealthy and lifeless associations or relations of their past. And neither can they!

Therefore, when confronted by a crisis or challenge with accompanying uncertainties. The event triggers a mental default or relapse caused by the situation. With their feelings and self-sufficiency leading them, they alone are inadequate to deal with the matter effectively. This reset to their fallen nature or natural inclination thereby causes the person to return to the familiar … that euphoric or pleasurable situation by which they could momentarily soothe and/or conceal that which ailed them in their past. Even though, in the past, their method was to their detriment.

There seemingly being no other outlet, recourse, or resource to deal with their stressful or challenging situation. They found themselves back in some unhealthy involvement.

Look, we are creatures of habit … whether for good or bad. This *bad* (spiritual sickness) is now woven within our fallen or corrupted nature. The mind of man can be swayed in one direction or another – either for good or bad. Where there are no strong competing good habits, those favorable situations, or environments. And of most importance! For a Christian, our place within God. We then, like a ship without a sail by which to be guided. Will be tossed and driven, pulled by our conscious to do right, but driven by the competing evil within each of us to override the good we know to do (Romans 7: 13-25).

Regarding one's involvement within the Church: Their activities being simply routine or religious, wherein displaying merely a form of godliness; where God is not first and foremost in all we do; where the Spirit of God is out there somewhere if considered at all. What you actually have taken place within yourself or the church is "good religion." But good religion won't sustain any of us in the time of a crisis. What will keep us in the time of trouble? It is having a *Personal Relationship With God!*

Here's an example of what I'm talking about. We can see this matter take shape in the lives of Mary and Martha. You see, Mary sat at the feet of Jesus while listening to Him teach. On the other hand, Martha was more concerned with the habit of serving - hence good religion. I encourage you to read this story for yourself so that you may get a better understanding of this event. Listen to Jesus' response to Martha. You can find the story in Luke 10: 38-42.

Good habits or practices in the Church must accompany a committed and *personal relationship* with God. Or else we will be powerless to withstand the troubles of this world or those rising from within. We will be "good religious folk" but powerless! It will only be a matter of time before the crisis pressing in and around us will cause one to abandon their pious acts of good because of defeat, resulting from being encumbered by life's troubles. Religion can't sustain anyone. Only a Good God, with whom we have a loving relationship, can we be kept and empowered through His Spirit.

And so, it would be God at work through the song of George Duke. That prompted me to return to the Church. But what was the cause for my straying away from the Church and God in the first place? What happened within me, causing my departure from my Father's house?

Why is it for many that after becoming a church member, they can leave and, for others, seldom show up to participate in worship service or at any other time? I would need to add a chapter to this book to answer these questions more thoroughly. But I will say ... sometimes the issue is with the individual member. And other times, it is the church itself or a particular member or members. This includes leadership or the lack thereof of adequate or capable leadership. And/or wherein leadership fails to understand its members' uniqueness and thereby fails to meet the various needs of the *Body of Believers*. Therefore, the door that welcomed new or potential members, through that same door, they made their exit and sometimes permanently, while others scarcely involved themselves with the affairs of the church.

What I have seen as being in common with failed relationships, no matter the sort. It is when a person or group of people are prone or geared to conduct themselves too much within their traditions or ways, their established norms or routines, habits, or expectations of their making, and primarily for their own benefit and self-interest. When concerted and intentional heartfelt effort is not given or provided for the benefit of both people or all involved. When there is little to no compromise that there may be balance and harmony amongst those who are in partnership or relationship. The inevitable will arise, conflict or even the parting of ways resulting from one feeling disregarded or seen as an afterthought rather than a welcomed and contributing member.

I am primarily speaking in terms of the church. But also, within a Christian home, inclusiveness applies. Without the loving aspect of inclusion, here meaning - being one with Christ and genuinely seeing others as part or members of the Body of Christ, we can't be as effective or even as empowered as God desires.

I officially joined the Church (my first church home) around the fall of 1986. Perhaps some two years later, my attendance would begin to waver from the good habit or religious practice of attending Church.

Giving thought to the time before my decline, I felt I needed a *relationship with the church*. The church but only in part would be the answer to my problems. I needed an inner change toward a pure and dedicated heart toward God. Change, no doubt, was occurring within me; I was a child of God, howbeit, a mere babe. However, what I actually had at the time was *good religion and not a good relationship with the God of the Bible.*

As for change: this necessitates a process, even a progression toward spiritual development or maturity. Unfortunately, my most meaningful change and spiritual growth included my grievous personal failures, which nonetheless assisted me with understanding spiritual matters, however, at the great expense of my wife's grief. Now, personal failures don't have to, as some claim, as a "necessary" part of the process through which understanding and spiritual growth occur. I am convinced that neither does God want His children to have to learn life's lessons the hard way. But many often attend the school of hard knocks to get their training! While many never learn of the better and *Perfect Way of God.*

Let it be known! God and His Word are sufficient to teach *man* in all matters of life, thereby preventing us from needless failures and heartaches that we, unfortunately, experience unnecessarily (2 Timothy 3: 16 - 17). Even so, if the unlearned would only listen to and heed the wise counsel of godly men and women, who perhaps had to lay in hard beds of their making. Or the lessons they can learn simply from living and observing the mistakes and failures of others. One can then avoid this life's unnecessary failures and heartaches.

Throughout my early years as a young man and my spiritual development, there would be other times, and for various reasons, I found myself separated from the church and God. However, this time here, some four years after joining the church. And now the father of two sons, a toddler and his brother, seven years older. Therefore my distance from the church would be of greater consequence.

It was during this season of my life. Now some three years into marriage, I ventured into the ways of darkness, folly, and decadence. Leading up to my season of whoredom, I was depressed and grieving the loss of a dear friend and mentor. Only as I write this book can I acknowledge and recognize the state of mind I was in at that time. My church home, Mount Level, was in the midst of a transition. My dear brother, friend, and Pastor was leaving me! He had answered the call to pastor another church. I felt significant loss and grief from his departure! What I only now realize is that I was dealing with the matter of abandonment or separation anxiety, resulting from my dear friend departing from me.

Reverend Lynch was my first Pastor and a dynamic leader who challenged the old norms of the church. He was my spiritual leader and, equally important, my friend. He saw something in me and took me under his wing. He invited me to be actively involved in the good work of the church. He assisted me in finding purpose and belonging within this traditional family-influenced Baptist Church. No slight intended on Baptist churches. Rather, my issues were with the ongoings, staunch habits, or traditions of some within this family-laden Church; this sort of family dynamic often works against the Spirit's best for the church.

Years later, I would grow to better understand this spiritual dynamic that was working against the church's effectiveness – God's best for Mount Level. The embrace and love that Reverend Lynch showed toward me aided in setting the foundation upon which I currently stand as a man of God. I truly appreciate the importance of that relationship God-ordained and the influence Dr. Lynch had upon me.

Initially, I was considered by some as an outsider. But my big brother and friend, Dr. Lynch, sheltered me from the opposition and gave me a place of belonging and purpose. Resulting from my work within the church. Additionally, the service I provided to my community as a Police Officer and viewed by many as a positive young husband and father. In 1989, I was nominated by Reverend Lynch and selected to be among the fraternity of *Outstanding Young Men of America*.

Although Mount Level called a new pastor, much remained the same for a while. Over time, the church's effectiveness and great potential for spiritual growth began to decline.

As I saw it, things were going well for the Church and me when we were under Pastor Lynch's leadership. I was enthusiastic about my newly found *purpose* within the church. And really, for the first time in my life, I had real and meaningful purpose. However, I must add this reminder. It is one thing to be active in the church – performing good works and habits. But it is something totally different to be involved in the Church, comprehending your service to be relational, as unto God; in this, He is well pleased! This is truly good work; when we do whatever, we do as unto God ... This is service, sacrifice, and even worship of God! In this, He is well pleased. This is one aspect of the *intimate relationship God* desires for us to understand and to have with Him!

As the result of God answering a particular prayer, I prayed in the military. Beginning in the Fall of 1986, and after uniting with Mount Level, the next four years of my life would be met with significant unfolding events. The first: A couple of months after joining the Mount Level family, I was offered a job to begin training to become a police officer from Chapel Hill, North Carolina, Duke University Public Safety, and Durham's Police Department, whose offer I accepted. I could now begin to see a potentially promising future. Just over a year later, God caused Lisa and me to cross paths for a second time. God, unbeknownst to me, was reintroducing me to Lisa at His appointed time. A mere eight months following our second introduction (the first through my brother Dexter), Lisa and I would be publicly united as husband and wife by my pastor and friend, Dr. Lynch. Two years and eight months later, we added to our family our first and only child conceived through our union. God had, in fact, answered my prayer! However, there was more He desired to do for, in, and through me.

A New Thing
The Calling Upon My Life

Before becoming a police trainee and marrying Lisa, I had been attending church. However, there were periods of irregularity. After marrying Lisa and embracing her child Mario, as my son, who three months earlier celebrated his fourth birthday, I continued to lead my family to church. Symbolically, Mario represented what Lisa and I were spiritually - mere children, immature in the knowledge of God. However, God had given me enough sense, though at times it was hit and miss, to bring my family to church, *the house of God.*

Needless to say, as the head of my home, God's designated spiritual leader, I lacked a firm understanding of the importance of *Life's* spiritual matters. Regarding practical issues of Biblical truths, I was gaining cerebral understanding. Additionally, there was change occurring in my life ... I could sense or feel this within my soul. I was, in fact, experiencing spiritual growth. At the time, I didn't fully grasp what was occurring. Therefore, I could not clearly evaluate nor value the change God was working within me. Therefore, instead of remaining faithful in His *Way,* unable to embrace His process that leads to spiritual growth. There would be occasions that I would get in His *Way* and even out from under His *Way* and the cultivating I needed to further my spiritual development. Regardless of our spiritual maturity, we must be intentional about remaining in God's *Way* ... we must keep Jesus before us at all times!

Approximately four to five years after joining Mount Level, some three years of marriage are behind us. And after my season of whoredom. There was a period of consistency regarding my involvement in the church and my pursuit of Biblical understanding. Occasionally and to my surprise, there were times when others brought to my attention the wisdom and the knowledge they saw operating through me. I was in my mid-twenties when this occurred.

However, the most sobering and unexpected revelation was yet to come! I don't recall what occurred on this particular Sunday while attending worship service. We stood in front of the sanctuary, where we gathered to pray. There had been times that I had been asked to pray or read Scripture during church service. I can recall occasionally delivering a presentation for one of the church's special occasions. Perhaps after one of those moments, Deacon Ronald Daye, being led by the Spirit, shared with me what God revealed to him regarding me. There was not a build-up to what he had to say. Perhaps he shared more with me on this day. However, I can only recall him saying, "I see the calling on your life to preach."

I was not brought up in the church, so I didn't quite grasp what he was expressing nor how this "*Calling*" would be answered. Nonetheless, I was intrigued by what I was hearing. I delightfully considered the matter. However, I was keenly aware of my feeling of inadequacy and even intimidated by the idea of standing before the church to preach God's Word.

Nonetheless, God was performing a change within me that I'd noticed. However, I was unable to comprehend the significance of the matter. My spiritual development was evolving. Just the same … the transformation He was working within me would be for my benefit, His Kingdom, His glory, and His praise! However, I lacked spiritual discernment regarding what God was doing in and through me.

I mentioned in a previous chapter that God has placed purpose in each of us. What I now know is that God was preparing me for my purpose. He was drawing me closer to Himself. And so. He was transforming my way of thinking in answer to my prayer. And His greater or my spiritual purpose He had intended for me. This was a specific prayer that I prayed in 1985. At the time, I was stationed in Wackernheim, Germany. This prayer was sincere, simple, and from my heart. Such speech that would come from the mouth of a dependent child who calls out to their parent to have their basic needs met.

Most importantly, my request to God was not unreasonable. It was in line with what I believed God desired for me. I call this prayer my *Infant Prayer*.

The prayer followed along these lines: *Lord, if you get me out of this man's Army … Give me a wife, a job, and a car; I'll serve you.* I was unknowingly enlisting to sign up to serve in *The Army of the Lord* if He would just do these things for me.

Now that I better understand God's ways, I know He is not moved by the stipulations or dictates of man. Rather, when we pray, we should first acknowledge God in His Wisdom, Knowledge, and Supremacy. In doing so, we are, in essence, saying as did Jesus, "Father, not my will be done but Yours. As our Father, God certainly knows what's best for His children and even the motives of our hearts. Regarding what He did for me. I'll say this: it was about His grace and proving Himself to me His faithfulness. That I may one day tell of His goodness and grace towards me. Also, we must understand that it is God's prerogative to operate in our lives, in answer to our prayer, how He sees fit. He is Father ... He alone knows what is best for us.

Another thing worth mentioning that my Father did in answer to my prayer: He opened a door that allowed me to depart from man's Army, my military service, six months earlier than my actual end of service date ... What timing! My early departure timed my return home to the United States perfectly. The Durham Police Department recently opened its application process for police recruits. God was clearly ordering my steps ... He was positioning me to walk in His purpose for my life.

The Divine's Set-up
The Right Place And His Timing

God was showing Himself faithful. And He wasn't through with me yet. Nearly a year and a half later, following my first introduction to Lisa, we would become acquainted again through God's divine set-up or providence. I know God delights in answering the desires of his children ... what parent doesn't. But keep in mind that this doesn't mean that things will necessarily unfold as you've planned or think they should be – simply because you prayed. When this occurs, the probability is high that it will. If you are not settled in your faith when things don't go as you hoped, this will be the time it shows. However, this time of your uncertainty can or should become the opportunity by which one learns to grow in faith and trust in God during times of uncertainty or when things don't pan out as you hoped or prayed they would.

Here's an example of what you are to do and pray when your life seems uncertain: *Continue to walk in obedience to the will of God. Let your response be to Him ... God, you got this; even so, Father, you are in control and are working things out for my good even though I can't see it as so. Thank you, Father, and amen.*

Know this as well: your faith, and it becoming established, is granted by God. It is He who is working to settle you in your faith towards Him. And so, God desires for us to grow in faith. It is through uncertainties and often life's challenges whereby we mature in faith, grow closer, or become more intimate with God (Hebrews 5:8). And as our faith increases, this leads us to our purpose, destiny, and the future God holds for us. *"For without faith, it is impossible to please God"* (Hebrews 11:6; Romans 10: 17; Ephesians 6:16). As Christians, we are called to *walk by faith and not by sight* (2 Corinthians 5: 7).

It was nearing the end of the summer of 1987 that I again saw Lisa. Admittedly, when I first saw her, I was not ready to receive her as my blessing ... this God knew. Nonetheless, He presented this gift – Lisa, beforehand so that I may receive her a short time later as my wife.

When I first met Lisa, *She Was Not What I Thought I Wanted*. On the other hand, God knew what I desired or needed in a woman, physically and, more importantly, what I would *need* in a wife to complement our union and His purpose. Though I was a work in process ... we all are, some worse than others; nevertheless, God was working things out for my good.

How about God's timing and even His setup! Even so, His providential hook-up! Here is how Lisa's and our second encounter played out. Returning home from a day's work as a rookie Police Officer, and making my way home to my first apartment, God, too, unexpectedly, opened this door for me. I would now meet with my defining moment and Divine crossroad, forever changing my life's course.

In His response to my infant prayer, God, not even a year after I became a Police Officer, would present before me my wife-to-be, Lisa. At that moment of our second encounter, I didn't regard Lisa as my future wife, but for certain, someone I wanted to get to know!

Anyhow. I was driving through the parking lot of my apartment complex – Morreene West. I notice this fine specimen of a woman to my front right, walking on the sidewalk. I thank God there was no obstruction from vehicles that typically lined this location, which would have blocked my view. What strategic alignment by God! It was evident that this fine specimen of a woman was leaving the apartment's pool. Yet again, what timing! Being that I'm visually motivated.

Having a little fun now. Lisa's version of the story slightly differs from mine. Instead of saying she's correct, I will simply give her side of the story too. Where our versions differ: Lisa recalls, "Walking in the parking lot. Hearing a car approaching her from behind, she moves out of the way. Looking in the car's direction as I pass her, she recognizes me and waves." We then hold a conversation. Less dramatic – right? However, regardless of whose version is correct, our paths crossing was a set-up, not chance … rather a development occurring by God's good and perfect will. I can't explain it … neither will I try. I will simply say our Father knows what's best for His children. And if our hearts are turned towards Him, He will work all things for our good and His glory!

My version of what happened: What caused Lisa to capture my eyes and arrest my attention was the fact that she was wearing a white t-shirt, length, about mid-thigh, that sparsely covered her. Extending below her shirt were the prettiest legs I'd seen. And they were complimenting her fine petite figure that the *Tee* did not fully conceal. As I drove adjacent to her, this fine woman, and gift to man, waved at me while I was still gazing her way. I immediately got excited about the attention she was expressing toward me … but I kept my cool.

With confidence, now that I had something meaningful to offer a woman – a career job with benefits and a promising future. I stopped my new car a short distance in front of her. I then backed up to acknowledge her, although I had absolutely no idea who she was.

With a smile on her face, she cordially greeted me. It quickly became apparent to her that I had no idea who she was. She, therefore, reminded me of our first meeting. Me giving the matter thought and finally recognizing her, exclaimed

… "Oh! Lisa!" The Lisa whom I'd met through my brother almost a year and a half earlier. The same Lisa who, at the time, was wearing those ugly brown polyester work pants that did nothing to display her cute petite figure. Now, this very Lisa. That I had given little attention to. Is shining before me, radiantly beautiful and so fine standing before me in all her glory at my passenger-side window! This was a Divine setup!

God, our Designer, knows what we need and even what we prefer. On the other hand, He knows best that person who matches or is to be partnered with our personalities so that we may learn and grow together. Even so, where there may seem to be a mismatch of our personalities because of our flaws. Or our way of viewing things and even our wants differing. God, through His Spirit, can transform our way of thinking relationally. Bringing alignment or harmony through love so that a relationship dependent upon Him can thrive as those involved seek and see what they truly need from God as they align themselves through His Word. Opposites can and do attract and can remain together victoriously, where God is the source that holds the two in a harmonious union, even though the joining of the two falls short of perfection. And so it is, as a heterosexual couple, no matter who they are, seeks to align themselves with the mind or will of God. They can be victorious in marriage to the glory of God! Therefore, do yourself a favor, and throw out the window man's concept of there being just one perfect and one and only "soulmate" for you on all the earth.

Considering my rotating work schedule, I was reasonably active in the Church when I met Lisa. Though Lisa obviously appealed to me physically, my intentions towards her were not sexually motivated, unlike it was with most, if not all, other females before her.

Lisa and I talked while I remained in the car. She shared with me that she, her three-year-old son Mario, and her sister, Sharon, had recently moved into the apartment complex. God's timing and plans are astonishing! Our challenge is learning to get out of His way while trusting *The Way* – God's plans unfolding for our lives. Additionally, and simple enough, those who are His children, with sincere hearts, need to put forth the effort to grow closer to God and even trust

Him and His process. He will then do the rest. He orders our steps according to his plan and purpose for our lives, no matter the outcome, as we remain faithful and dependent upon Him.

As my conversation with Lisa ended, I asked her to go on a date with me. I specifically asked her if she would like to go out for ice cream… she kindly accepted my invitation.

Shortly after that day, we went on our first date. However, it wasn't for ice cream. Lisa seems to remember that we went to a club – and why not? Over the next two months or so, I would pursue Lisa hoping to win her affection.

Lisa's son Mario, who would soon turn four years old, didn't cause me to have second thoughts about pursuing her. This was likely because Caswell Scott, who I knew as my dad, had legally adopted my sister and me, making us his own. I, therefore, welcomed the total package – Lisa and her son Mario.

While my dad was still a part of our home until I was around eleven years old, he and my mother, as husband and wife, left a positive, loving influence on me. Therefore, my pursuit of Lisa and my interest in being responsible for her son came naturally … the fact that she had a son did not concern me. I will acknowledge that I was naïve, embracing this not-so-ideal or understood family dynamic. Nonetheless, things would work out for us, however, not without a few challenges that we would have to overcome and work through early on in our relationship and marriage.

Before continuing with the story of Lisa and me, I want to leave this cautionary note or words of wisdom for you: One should not enter into a family orientation that I chose to embrace unadvisedly and without knowing the nuances of this sort of family dynamic. You must understand the involvement of other family members or participants who may have or feel they have some say because the child does not belong to you biologically.

That said. You and your spouse, or if dating, must agree on how the child will be raised and other matters concerning the child so that you may have harmony in your home. Otherwise, your union can suffer and even fail if you are indifferent towards taking this simple yet necessary measure to align yourself with your Beloved on this potentially delicate and divisive matter. What you must consider: others may feel or even have the right to involve themselves in the affairs of the child. You must know what you are up against where this is the case. This entire matter can be extremely sensitive or volatile and can take an emotional toll on all involved. Most importantly, you and your spouse or soon-to-be spouse must stand as one or in complete agreement regarding the rearing of the child and what input, if any, is welcomed from others who may equally care for and love the child with whom you are taking responsibility for.

During the next two months of getting to know Lisa, I grew fonder of her. I must say, my pursuit of Lisa was still of honorable intentions. My pursuit of her was non-sexual weeks into dating her. Things felt different with Lisa. No doubt, I was physically attracted to her. However, her character was also overwhelmingly attractive. I wanted a wife and not a fling or situation. I'm confident Lisa saw this as the case due to my openness and care toward her and Mario. She felt at ease and was growing fonder and confident in me.

Over the following weeks, Lisa and I would see each other often. However, I was far from where I needed to be spiritually to effectively care for a family in God's way. Nonetheless, my gentlemanly approach toward Lisa had to do with the fact that I was involved in the church and attempting to do right by her and the faith I'd confessed. I'm confident that my approach also had to do with how Lisa carried herself as a woman to be respected.

While writing this book, I occasionally relied on Lisa's memory to fill in details that escaped my thoughts or to help me understand her frame of mind at various stages of our relationship. At this point in my writing, I asked Lisa, "When did she recall having "feelings" for me?" Her response was, "She couldn't determine a decisive moment." However, as I give thought to our beginnings. I'm confident that it was a particular situation I will soon share, in conjunction with my consistent action of kindness towards her, during our short dating period, that she would begin to give herself to me emotionally.

As a single mother – hence extra protective, she likely listened to and held on to everything I said and did. My consistency in my thoughtful and caring words and action would lend way to the committed relationship we would shortly enter into. And what I will now call that decisive moment which allowed Lisa to see that I was *all in*. And she, too, becoming all in with me relationally.

I addressed this earlier, but it's worth repeating: One's actions towards the person with whom they've entered into a relationship can give a strong indication of the direction of the relationship, even so, insight into the mind and heart of the one you're establishing a relationship with. This will strongly indicate who you're dealing with... but by no means foolproof.

Remember what I said regarding *Running Game?* Let me remind you: This person's motive is getting what they can from you ... Period! Their motives are selfish or fleshly! They will say and do just enough or even go to church so that they may gain your trust to get what they can from you; from a person whose motives are not genuine, you must be prayerfully watchful. Even while you seek the counsel of trusted friends and family members. Or respected and tested members of the Christian faith. With a discerning spirit and prayer, ask God to reveal what this person is about. Or, if they are not the one God has for you, ask God to remove that person from your life.

Adding this caveat: Look, it is hard enough to get over those relationships where you've given your trust to someone who then takes advantage of you. However, when one gives over or submits themselves sexually to a liar and manipulating person, bouncing back from such betrayal can be challenging, even an extremely long road to recovery. Or even a far worst outcome! Ladies in particular! ... Guard your hearts and your treasure! And the hurt; if the person you were fond of chooses to part ways, their departure will not be nearly as painful.

A Look Back Before The Journey Forward - Can No Mean Yes, And No, She Didn't

Before continuing with Lisa's and my story, I want to share a couple of interesting relational situations I was in before meeting Lisa. This time would have been while I was training to become a police officer and there shortly afterward. Sexually, I was still doing my thing; however, my moral consciousness or compass was more engaged than ever before. I attribute this awareness to what was occurring within me spiritually. And too, I desired to have a wife and not just some meaningless sexual situation that only - and temporarily satisfied the flesh. Satan was at work; my flesh was at work. But my God was at work too!

There were two very interesting yet, bizarre relational situations that I found myself in. It became apparent that these two females, besides others - were particularly interested in establishing a relationship with me. However, I did not see in these women what I desired, which would cause me to want to enter into a committed relationship. Although I was living foul – engaging in sexual sin, I could not deceive or have a woman thinking that more would come of us relationally if they gave themselves to me sexually. I didn't have the heart to *use* or blatantly take advantage of a female for my selfish pleasure.

However, my method for managing the situation and having sexual relations went as follows: The less that was said or done by the female or me that did not suggest relational commitment, although she was aware of my motives, the better. It made it easy for me to move on after sexual relations.

And so, I countered these situations, thereby avoiding relational obligation and awkwardness from this angle: When it was apparent that a female wanted to be with me sexually and desired more from me relationally. I would say to her, whereby clearing my conscience regarding my intentions towards her, "Don't verbally express your feelings towards me unless I do so first." Neither was it acceptable for her to express care or interest for me, tangibly or in any other way unless I initiated this form of expression.

For me to allow her to do otherwise. Or to accept from her in word or any other manner, her affection towards me. I would be implicitly showing my acceptance of her beyond the physical, thereby giving her false expectations. I simply couldn't do this. Where the rules of our relationship are understood. And agreed upon, for our time, this sort of agreement is referred to as "Having a friend with benefits." *"There is a way that seems right unto a man, but the end thereof is destruction" (Proverbs 14:12).*

Ladies. Perhaps this will help you to better understand the mind of some boys … Yes, boys! And thereby, better guard your hearts. Brothers. I know that there are girls who are also running Game. You, too, must guard your heart!

Before marriage, with perhaps an exception or two, I viewed females solely as objects of my longings. However, I had a measure of respect for them, so I couldn't simply *Dog* a woman! However, a woman's immeasurable worth, her innate value, and even the honor that God has fixed upon them as one belonging to Him, a creature made in His image and even a gift to men, was far beyond my comprehension. We must learn to see one another as God sees and has created us … in His likeness and with unmeasurable worth. Otherwise, we will continue to misuse and abuse one another!

There were two women who will go unnamed that I will now applaud. They did not freely give in to their passions when tempted by sex and their want of me relationally. Nonetheless, the firmness of their stance had a loophole or seemingly one important stipulation if they were to have sexual relations with me. Though they were interested in establishing a relationship with me, there had been no confirmation on my part expressing mutual interest. In the heat of the moment, as we drew near to forbidden sex. Though falling short in their twisted reasoning regarding going all the way or having sex with me. Merely hinged solely upon my word acknowledging that we are in a committed relationship, I could then have them sexually. No ring! Only my word.

Almost verbatim, they asked me, "Where will things go between us if we have sexual relations?" If they received a "Yes" from me to us becoming committed as a couple, then sexual relations would be permitted. If my response was nothing beyond sex, such it was, their willingness to have sexual intercourse was off the table.

But I will give them some credit; they had enough self-respect and common sense, although twisted reasoning, to ask me what our relational status would be if they gave themself to me sexually. And to think, these females were willing to take me at my word. No doubt, countless women have made this mistake of their own making. Or are equally to blame as they gave themselves away sexually and merely at the word of some "horny" boy!

My response to these ladies and without giving it thought. "Nothing will become of us beyond sex." This quickly put the brakes on what we each desired at that moment because they wanted more of me than I was willing to give. Though I didn't get what I wanted, I genuinely respect and even appreciate the decisions of these two women.

By the way, these females were Christians. If only more women would shut it down, as they did, however, without offering a compromise. I believe many boys would learn to man up and cease using and treating women disrespectfully or as objects of their sexual desire.

There was another unique relational situation, a potentially costly one, that I faced. I had never encountered anything remotely close to this. I thank God for keeping me! Though I was ignorant on some matters and foolish on others, I was learning there was a line that a fool should not cross.

The woman in this situation was a couple of years older than me. She was a mature Christian, raised in the Church, and had a genuine heart toward God. Unbeknownst to me, she had me in her sights, even though I saw her as a valued friend. The friendship we shared was refreshing. I really valued it.

Though I saw her as only a friend, I eventually noticed her intentions beyond our friendship. Being a younger Christian, even a babe in Christ, she made herself available to me ... someone I could talk to. Because I saw her as a friend, I had no reservations about accepting her kindness or the little things she did for me. When I moved into my apartment, she freely purchased something for the apartment. And when I underwent surgery, she was there for me ... what a friend.

Call me naïve. But this I was. She was a mature Christian; surely, her intentions regarding our friendship were righteous – so I thought. However, she had other plans. On this particular visit, she made to my apartment; the details of that evening have passed from my memory. Nonetheless, things would turn in a direction that I had not anticipated.

What I can recall from that moment at my apartment, we were about to engage sexually. I was right there! Yes, right there! I could not have been any closer! But at that critical moment, she forced out from within her soul the words, "No ... No!" I will submit that her conscious conviction, aided by the Spirit of God within her, overrode her fleshly passion and that which she desired physically. Her simple words, "No ... No," immediately halted my actions. Spiritually I was not where she was. Nevertheless, I respected her utterance and disengaged from the moment.

My brothers, my simple message to you ... No means No. But, neither should we have been in that situation. This matter, and for the worst, could have easily gone in one direction or another. However, I made a choice to shut it down. What more was there to do or say? ... Really, nothing. I simply respected her utterance of, "No ... No!

After resetting, we began to talk about what had occurred. Details of the conversation I am unable to recollect. However, what I do remember, came as a total surprise when I heard what she had to say. Her response. "Though I was saying No, I really didn't want you to stop." My response to you, my readers. How disastrous this situation could have been for both of us if we'd continued or if I persisted beyond her ... "No!" God will sometimes do the inexplicable; He can show up when you least expect Him.

As for this woman, she put herself in a position of which she knew better ... more so than me. She gave Satan and/or her flesh a foothold. But God gave her and me a way of escape. This is *Grace*!

Satan really has many of us messed up and twisted concerning sex and relationships. Here is another situation that I was in. It is really quite bizarre and dark in nature – that is, Satanically influenced. Although this book is spotlighting my life, each person in this book has a story that can be told. We all are products of our upbringing. That said, I would really like to know the backstory of the person who did this unthinkable act I'm about to share. It was her intention and hope of hooking me relationally - no doubt in marriage. This person really wanted me … I'm not being arrogant. You will soon see how I arrived at this belief.

During this same period of my life, I occasionally had females over to my apartment. Two particular females were visiting me around the same time, one of which did this unthinkable thing I will share. Which one? I can only speculate. However, both of whom I called friends, one with whom I had a previous sexual encounter.

Nonetheless, at this point in my life, I wanted nothing more from these two ladies other than their friendship. They were educated and good people but not what I desired from a wife. This was also a time in my life that I wanted genuine companionship - a lady with whom I could see marrying.

I can say that being a part of the church was a positive change in my life - even though I was yet a work in progress. Here is why I say this now. I recall telling another female who had visited me. She, too, was older and a friend. After having one sexual encounter with her. I said to her that I could not do so again. She and her husband – yes, husband, were separated at the time, a marriage that had failed. However, my conscious would not allow me to continue with her sexually. I'd read in the Bible. That what had occurred between her and me was considered adultery. Which, for some reason, just didn't sit well with me – at all!

And yet, another female also visited with me; she was even older. She was more of an acquaintance through our adjoining professions than a friend. Because I did not make sexual advances toward her. This woman said to me, "I thought you were gay." I believe this was her way of trying to force the matter. I had shared my Christian faith with her; after this, she made that statement.

Now back to the initial two females. What I'm about to share, I'm convinced, occurred at the hands of one of them. They both had an interest in me, one seemingly more than the other. And they were from the same state where the activity I will share soon enough was known to be practiced. Make no mistake about it; what I am about to describe was Satanic. The matter involved the occult and some "Root Ritual!"

The wiles and attacks of Satan are all around. He will relentlessly continue performing all sorts of deceptions and tricks to ensnare us or keep us in bondage to sin – that is himself. Sexual perversion is one of the greatest tactics in his arsenal that keeps man from intimately embracing and coming to know God! But other satanic beliefs and idolatrous practices also hold man captive to sin and in spiritual darkness.

For those of you with soft stomachs, prepare yourself! This is your warning as you might just find this following situation of mine nauseating or just downright disgusting ... So brace yourself! Shortly after, these two females visited my apartment; they had stopped by at different times that week. I went to my refrigerator to retrieve something. Therein, I discovered the unimaginable! Upon opening the door to the fridge, I noticed something extremely odd and puzzling! Something was put into my bottle of red wine. Taking the bottle from the refrigerator to examine it closer. To my utter surprise, I discovered a tampon had been placed into the bottle!

Bewildered by this occurrence and not sure what to make of it, I called my mother in the hope of gaining any insight she might have on the matter. She told me that it was some ritual practice of "Roots." I will not attempt to go into detail about this ritual evil. However, my mother stated: that one belief had its dealings with a woman's menstrual blood. Women who engaged in this wickedness or Cultic practice believed they could trap or enrapture a man if they could get him to ingest her menstrual blood. Unbelievable!

People ... where proper knowledge of God and His influence in our lives are absent. Any of us can be swayed by the teachings and doctrines of the Devil. Or that of this world (1 Timothy 4:1, 2). To God, we must return, submit and commit to His *Way*; we must!

The Opportunity To Step-up

Picking up from where I left off regarding Lisa and me. I had mentioned: For the two months or so of getting to know Lisa, I was growing fonder of her. As a result of my openness and care towards her and Mario, I am confident she felt at ease and was growing fonder and more optimistic of me. My pursuit of Lisa was of honorable intentions. I also recognized; that within me, things felt different with Lisa. And though I was physically attracted to her, Lisa's character was also overwhelmingly attractive! I was desirous of having a wife; I am inclined to believe that Lisa knew or sensed this.

Unexpectedly, and what I again believe was God's providence at work. I would be provided the opportunity to *step up* and show myself faithful and even more caring towards Lisa. God would position me to put my feelings and concern for Lisa into action. I believe this was that pivotal moment between Lisa and me. Perhaps more so for her! Earlier, I mentioned that I had asked Lisa when her feelings for me began to develop? However, she was not able to identify that decisive moment. As a single mother, I believe Lisa was not too optimistic about being in a promising relationship. Therefore, she wasn't going to open up to me quickly or allow her emotions to be given to me too soon. At some point in our marriage, I remember Lisa commenting about being concerned only about taking care of herself and Mario before meeting me. She was determined to handle her business as a single mother; having some guy in her life was not a priority.

However, I am convinced that it was on this particular night that I will now share with you that she rather quickly submitted her heart to me: I was visiting with Lisa at the apartment she shared with her sister, Sharon. It was apparent that Lisa was ill! However, she was determined to go to work the following day. Even today, my wife will press her way to work when she doesn't feel well. Most of the time, I actually have to shut her down or insist that she remain home.

Though Lisa was clearly sick, her mind was made up … Not going to work was not an option. I was concerned for her and watched as she made preparation for work and was about to turn in for the night. Watching her determination to handle her business, I asked Lisa, "Why don't you remain home and rest." She responded, "If I don't go to work, I don't get paid."

My heart was sincerely grieved for Lisa, toward whom I'd begin having deeper feelings. Without giving the matter any measure of thought or hesitation, I knew what I had to do! I asked Lisa one question, "How much money would she lose if she did not go to work?" I had determined at that very moment what my response would be once I knew the amount ... Write her a check! Lisa had no way of knowing my intentions.

At the time, Lisa was holding down three jobs; I was only aware of two of them at the time. The following day she would have to report to two of her places of employment. Lisa calculated what her loss would be and shared it with me. The amount did not concern me; I simply needed to know what it was so that I may cover her loss. My desire was for her to remain home the next day and rest! After Lisa gave me the figure, I reached into my jacket pocket to obtain my checkbook. I joyfully wrote the check out to her. I experienced such delight in showing Lisa that I cared for her. And too that I had her back! I was put in a position to *step up*! Lisa was able to see my words further put into action!

For Lisa to say no to my gift was not an option. I'm sure she knew this. Lisa had heard me speak of my desires for the past two months or so. Now she had observed me in action at my finest hour! Me giving of myself financially and showing care for Lisa, I'm sure this was when she opened her heart to me! This moment had to be that turning point for her.

I don't remember there being an abundance of gratitude shown from Lisa. However, she was grateful! As a matter of fact, I don't recall much talk about anything, let alone the direction our relationship would take from that point on. I guess I can say - we just knew things would be - between us! But clearly, things were now different - and for the better, between us! And would continue to be!

Sometime after that night of writing the check, Lisa and I officially and exclusively began to date and saw ourselves as a couple. Neither of us can recall how or when it came about. Nonetheless, we would continue to grow closer, but not without some obstacles to overcome. Those obstacles mainly were at my making, partly due to my thoughtless actions and immaturity in carefully navigating the situation involving Lisa's sister Sharon and their parents.

CHAPTER 13

The Road to Proposal

Lisa and I becoming a couple was not initially embraced by her dear sister, Sharon. How my sister-in-law felt about me would eventually make its way to their parents, complicating things all the more for Lisa. She would feel the full weight of this unfortunate matter; I, too, would be impacted. This tension and family divide subsequently affected the home that I, a young man of twenty-two, was attempting to establish.

The reason for the opposition; is perhaps a combination of things: The ease with which Lisa embraced me, the short time it took for our relationship to be established, and Lisa's willingness to follow my lead, although we were not married. I believe my dear sister-in-law felt she was not just losing her roommate. But her ultra-reliable and caring sister and also her nephew, Mario.

Reflecting back, I now understand why she may have felt and responded as she did. I never considered how my sister, Sharon, was affected by things. I was operating in my, in charge - take-charge, strong male, military, and police-minded personality. I was operating to establish my house (dating relationship) without knowing or considering the family's history, the feelings of my sister, or how others in the family may be affected. I do not apologize for wanting to establish my home and headship while Lisa and I dated and after marrying. However, I clearly lacked wisdom and insight at the time to consider how others may have felt. That said, in due time, I would really give my sister-in-law a reason to take issue with me, as well as my beloved in-laws. But Lisa would experience the pain from it all; me, the frustration, even some months after we were married.

As Lisa and I continued to date, my visits to her apartment stopped; for the reasons stated. My apartment became the place where we would spend time together. However, one evening, Lisa came over to my apartment before I'd stopped visiting their apartment. I had prepared dinner ... this was the first meal I'd cooked for her. Lisa and I laugh now, but we can't recall when she first cooked for me. The meal I prepared was another decisive moment. I'm sure this drew Lisa even closer to me! If Lisa had cooked, we might not have gotten married – I now joke, and we laugh.

Though I don't recall discussions regarding our evening, Lisa and I knew how things would culminate. My relationship with Lisa was growing, but my Christian expectation, well ... I will describe it as not being as solid as it should be. Unfortunately, neither Lisa nor I had been instructed by our parents regarding the inappropriateness of sex before marriage. *"The practice of safe sex – yes."* Therefore, Lisa saw no wrong regarding sexual intimacy that was soon to be experienced between us. However, from my Biblical reading, I had discovered otherwise ... I knew better!

Things being as they were with Lisa and me ... our bond tightening. We would soon come to a place where we would be motivated by our fleshly desire for one another. From this book, you've been instructed on God's view on the matter of sex. Therefore, all precautions should be taken to avoid such situations that tempt you to engage in illicit sexual activity.

That said, if I had been the man, a godly and mature Christian man (not a perfect man) that I now am. If I had led as a godly man and suggested to Lisa while we were dating that we abstain from sex until we got married, no doubt, she would have willfully and graciously followed my lead on this matter. That's the kind of woman Lisa was, willing to follow my lead, and in this manner, she continues to be.

Dogsinitis - A Contagion Needing Retraining and Taming

Lisa and I choosing to express ourselves sexually had nothing to do with either of us proving ourselves. Or trying to measure up sexually. Neither was she nor I trying to secure our relationship through sex. Simple enough, we wanted what God had forbidden: sex before marriage. And why not? ... we cared for one another. This is perhaps the main reason many give to justify sexual sin – they care or have feelings for one another.

We had been establishing a trusting relationship. Even still, trust building is a continuous work of maintaining trustworthiness and unwavering commitment to the person they have chosen to partner with. Lisa did just this while we dated and has continued to prove herself flawlessly in this area. Me, on the other hand ... well, you know the story. Now, I am about to add to it.

Lisa and I cared for one another. However, I don't think she was in love with me, not this soon into our dating. Or was she? And now, I know far better how I fail miserably in the proper care and love (agape) I should have displayed toward Lisa. Clearly, I was not in love – meaning, committed, or Agape (*Love*) toward her. I knew nothing of agape love and therefore was incapable of relational commitment. Just the same, neither had we expressed verbally being in love. Nonetheless, we were to engage in sexual relations reserved for *Lovers* only – those who are sincerely one *in Love* and whose hearts have been united by the direction of the Holy Spirit through marriage.

"Good sex," neither good intentions will sustain or keep a relationship or marriage together. Unless one understands, respects, and honors God's purpose and instructions for establishing a relationship. And the lifetime bond of marriage, the sureness of the union, is lacking and is therefore in constant jeopardy. A marriage can't be sustained by man's good intentions or strength alone. The partnership must be built upon and girded by the *Truth and Power* of the Spirit of God.

After Lisa and I consummated our dating through illicit sex, it was a mere week or so later when I told Lisa that I no longer wanted to be in a relationship. In an attempt to do the honorable thing and to also contemplate my exit strategy, I first shared with Lisa's dad that I would no longer be seeing his daughter. However, like a boomerang, this would come back at me with Lisa's Dad and mom's disdain for me. This was a problem of my making to soon come. Lisa was unaware of my intentions and the conversation with her dad until after the fact. Wow, I suddenly recall … this was not the first time I'd told a dad, after having sex with his daughter, that I didn't see things working out. Neither of these fathers called me out on my mess! No, they did not know that I'd been sexually intimate with their daughters. But neither were they foolish enough to think things didn't *go down* with their daughters and me.

I want to believe. That if I had met these dads beforehand. If only they had taken the time to engage me in meaningful man-to-man conversation with their daughters, the ease with which their daughters willfully consented to my violation of them perhaps would not have occurred. Unfortunately, neither of these fathers were godly men. They, therefore, left their daughters untrained, unguarded, and vulnerable! Because they did not test and challenge me, I, like a wolf in sheep's clothing, made their princess my prey. Or, what about? If I had a dad to instill within me a woman's worth … how I am to value and respect her. What if he had raised me to *fear* or reverence God as well as encourage me and lived out before me, demonstrating how to have a *personal relationship* with God. Perhaps, just perhaps, I would not have this history and story of mine that I now share with you.

Why had I decided to call things off with Lisa? … What was it that I discovered about her? … Was it that she was sexually inexperienced and therefore had not measured up? … Had I decided I didn't want the responsibility of raising a child who wasn't my own? … Was it that she had little to offer - financially speaking? … Was it each of these things; some of these things … What was it?

People, it was one thing! And it had absolutely nothing to do with Lisa. The problem was me! My sinful and selfish disposition! It had to do with the fact that my mind or thinking had not been renewed, nor had I been empowered by God's *Word* and *Truth!* My intentions with Lisa had been honorable. Then, after experiencing sexual relations with her, I excited and awakened that which was dormant within me - that *Dog*! And therefore, I found my way to the exit in search of the next *Cat*.

That highly contagious flesh-born pathogen! ... I've given the designation – *Dogsinitis,* otherwise known as my sinful disposition or sinful nature. I have known this malady firsthand. When active, its effects can be rabid, volatile, vicious, widespread, and relentless! I see the evidence of its crazed symptoms and consequences throughout society. The famed songwriter George Clinton perhaps best described the nature of *Dogsinitis* when one has been taken over by this fleshly baseness or debauchery. He says: "Why must I feel like that? ... Why must I chase the *Cat*? ... Nothing but the *Dog* in me!"

Sex had not been the means or tactic by which Lisa hoped to secure our relationship. Throughout our short time of dating, she presented herself as an ideal woman to partner with in life. However, because of where I was mentally – a powerless babe in Christ. Being spiritually, mentally, and physically inept and powerless, I was vulnerable and at a high risk of being overtaken or given to the practice of sin. Having not brought into subjection my *Dog* or as the Bible explains – *brought my flesh under subjection* (1 Corinthians 9:27), my *Dog* within me reared up and displayed its viciousness! And so it was, after sinfully indulging in sexual relations with Lisa, I ended our relationship shortly afterward. That I may have the encumbered freedom to chase after the next *Cat*.

Listen, my sisters. Although you may not have it all together ... who does? Where you find yourself alone following a break-up, consider the following, as I am inclined to believe, based on my experiences, that the break-up often has little, if anything, to do with you. The issue is *Dogsinitis*!

That said, take this alone time as an opportunity to perform a critical analysis of yourself. If you are serious about where you are in life and where you want to be in the future ... I am now primarily talking about your emotional and/or spiritual well-being. You must allow the Word of God to examine and assess your state of well-being. If you are willing, God will show you where you are and even where He desires you to be, spiritually and otherwise.

I can't over-emphasize this: Lisa had presented herself as an ideal partner. However, because my mind had not been transformed and my passion or flesh dealt with. Even though we were only dating, just the same, I failed Lisa and her son, Mario, to be a man, leader, and protector for them, though my intentions were well intended toward Lisa. Nonetheless, after having sexual relations with her, I became a feral animal, operating from my base instinct. My *Beast* not brought under subjection, my *Dog* not under control – so I would be prone to wander! My *Dog* had been roused from sleep!

We are creatures of habit and are born with evil inclinations! Therefore, our bad habits must be broken, as it is with taming a wild animal, before it can be domesticated and deemed beneficial for the service of its master.

The takeaway: It matters not how good a person's intentions are, how good they seem, or how incredible the sinful pleasure of the illicit sexual experience is. Relationally, they guarantee no stability or assurance for a meaningful and enduring relationship. If a person's mind has not been renewed, their heart turned to depend or trust entirely on God; no relationship apart from Him can receive the favor or blessing that He desires to cover and protect it with.

God's restraint or hold upon us is to protect His children and to demonstrate His love for those made in His likeness. Contrast the tethering utilized by a master to keep his untamed and untrained beast under his control. God, our Master desires rather that we see His love for us through Jesus. And then decide to love Him in kind and submit to the transforming work of His Word and indwelling Spirit. Our Master's teachings or disciplining and enabling through the Spirit lovingly breaks or domesticates us so that we may be effective or beneficial within His Kingdom and toward its expansion.

To comprehend that God's longing and embrace of us are based upon the long leash or reach and outstretched arms of His unconditional love towards mankind. To grasp *This* love displayed through the suffering and humiliation of *His Only Begotten Son – Jesus* ... Is to know our Father and understand how much He loves us. To apprehend the cost of our salvation and the unceasing love of Jesus, should move all to willingly attach themselves to the compassionate tether of God our Master. And therein seek to be tamed or made obedient to Him, in and through love by His life-altering Spirit. Within his care, not only will He lead us. He will also meet our spiritual needs; even so, provide for us, His counsel and understanding needed to live out a meaningful and purposed-filled life in and through Him.

Dogsinitis - The Relationship Destroyer

Before writing this section, I shared my limited recall following my breakup with Lisa to her. I asked my wife what did she recall about what resulted. Lisa mentioned that she had come to my apartment hoping to find out what she had "done wrong or the reason for me calling things off." However, I didn't come to the door, she stated. It was roughly a week or so after calling things off with Lisa that I saw her and her sister at the mall. I was there hanging out with a friend, Kelvin.

My encounter and conversation with Lisa were brief. Lisa recalls that I appeared apprehensive or uncomfortable. When Lisa stopped by my apartment. I don't know if I was merely avoiding her or if I had a *Cat* over. Nevertheless, I had done her wrong! And my conscious convicted me as much and was getting at me!

At the time, I'd never considered what effect the break-up had on Lisa ... Do guys ever? Neither had I thought about how this matter affected her family, but I would soon find out. I now realize my action was thoughtless, selfish, and hurtful!

Shortly after the breakup, I paid my mother a visit. She knew Lisa, and I was dating. However, she was unaware that I had called things off, or so I thought. Lisa had been to my mother's house before me and informed her of my decision to call things off. What my mother had to say to me after discovering my breakup with Lisa would be life-changing for Lisa and me. Sitting in the kitchen with my mother, she asked me, "How was Lisa doing?" I responded, "I am no longer seeing her." My mother simply responded. "Lisa is a good girl ... That girl hasn't done anything to you."

My mother was absolutely right! Her comeback caused me to immediately go into thought. I don't know if it was the same day or shortly afterward; I reconciled with Lisa, and we were a couple again. I'm sure I apologized; however, neither of us can recall how things came about. Nonetheless, our transition back together as a couple was seamless. My sight was restored to see the good in Lisa, as well, Lisa yet beholding the good in me.

However, Lisa's sister, Sharon, and their parents would not take too kindly to her being back with me. Withholding the details for now. This would be a most challenging season for Lisa. Her heart would be pulled in two directions as she would be forced to choose between her family and me. Having chosen me, Lisa would have to pay the painful cost of being ostracized by these members of her family, whom she loved dearly. Lisa followed her heart! ... She chose to follow me. Although I don't recall Lisa saying she loved me, she clearly expressed it when she chose me over her much-loved family. Unfortunately, I could not fully grasp Lisa's love for me. Or the sacrifice she had made for me! Only now, as I write about this experience and consider the matter, have I come to fully understand the sacrifice she made and the love she had for me when she chose me over her family.

Understand something, being led by your heart or the Spirit's conviction, doesn't mean that the road traveled will be one of ease ... but stay the course, you must! If God is for you, nothing can stand against you! Stay the course when you know that God has set your feet on the path you are to follow. Even though it may mean you will have to go it alone without the ones you thought would be by your side. Remember, God is the one who will, *Never leave nor forsake you* ... you are, therefore, never alone!

Whatever apprehension the family initially had towards me, I further exacerbated things with the breakup and Lisa then deciding to reunite with me. Though I'd met Lisa's family, we didn't know one another well. What would become apparent to them was that I was the man of my house. And the difficult part for them, Lisa, their go-to, reliable, thoughtful, caring, and loving daughter, would willingly submit to my headship and my leading of our relationship. What made things worse was that Lisa also entrusted Mario, her son, to my care, even though we were not married. Though Mario was not my biological child, he was never referred to as my stepson; the thought of doing so just didn't sit well with me. I saw Lisa as my lady and complete responsibility. I'd even embraced Mario as my responsibility as well.

Lisa's choosing me was difficult for her family to accept. Her decision went against her parent's heartfelt and passionate desire. They likely could not fathom how she could so quickly and totally give herself back over to me, considering that I'd already shown myself to be unreliable ... I now get it. However, Lisa had seen my potential to do good by her. She had heard my words. She believed and hoped I would continue faithfully demonstrating my commitment to her and Mario from that point on. However, it has been well documented how I miserably failed Lisa and my family regarding marital fidelity.

Dogsinitis is an ever-present pandemic! This spiritual contagion, disease and stronghold, and battle for the flesh must be acknowledged by all Christians as a crisis and spiritual evil that must be eradicated! Or spiritual battle which must be warred against effectively or inoculated from as often as needed! My story is an example: that this contagion, our *Dogs* of whatever sort, must be put down or adequately dealt with with the help of God before a meaningful relationship can begin, as well as have any hope of not being fatally infected *by Dogsinitis* or any manner of sin that can destroy a family or us individually. My friends, this spiritual warfare is undeniable! Looking at the way things currently are in our society. I can say the spread of *Dogsinitis*, in particular, sexual sin is more pervasive than in any period over my half-century-plus years of life (I am considered a gen. "X-er)."

Ending the twentieth century and gaining momentum in the twenty-first century, sexual sin became more endemic and evident. Modesty, decency, and morality, God's ordering or decrees that once in some measure provided oversight and *light* for this Country, have been disregarded. The world is taking notice and is too influenced by our morality or the lack thereof. Sadly, in this country, when there is public mention of the name God. It's done so for convenience's sake or the benefit of some politician. God has shown throughout His Word that this downward moral spiraling will only continue. Corruption within fallen man is the cause. Individually, we, children of God and followers of Christ, must understand the seriousness of sexual sin in particular and combat it at every turn.

I didn't understand this spiritual warfare or the matter of overcoming my flesh when I broke things off with Lisa and broke her family's trust in me. Therefore, my pattern, habit, or sinful inclination easily had its way. But I now recognize *Dogsinitis* as an evil within! Even so, the spiritual wickedness at work within this world, whose mission is to keep us separated and at odds with God, one another, and even with ourselves.

Therefore, relational matters, particularly intimate ones, are a serious undertaking. Pursuing and embracing such a union cannot be taken for granted nor entered into lightly. Hoping for a relationship or establishing a loving and lasting one is by God's design. Inherently, we desire relationships, whether good or bad ones. We have been made in the image of God; he is a person – a relational Being, and so are we. Essential to establishing and maintaining any healthy relationship is trust. It's in our nature to trust. It is not until our trust is betrayed that we become guarded or leery of others. Even then, we desire to trust again; however, it's problematic for many. After one's trust has been betrayed, it does not have to be regarding a significant matter, nor the person who disappointed them in this area.

Nevertheless, when one desires to give their trust over to someone, it can be a struggle to do so. Confidence or trust in some other isn't a given; it has to be earned or established over time. And for the betrayer of trust, they must be willing to put in the work to reestablish trust.

To make my point on our trusting nature, before it is corrupted, let's look at an innocent child. Unless taught or conditioned otherwise, most children are not only curious; they know no strangers. How precious and innocent are these little ones. Where a child has not been taught to fear or their trust betrayed. A child will wander up to anybody who catches their attention or excites their curiosity. This is innocence or naivete, but it is also trust. Rob or betray a child of their innocence. They will undoubtedly become less likely to trust. And too, they can become fearful or wary of others.

Where trust has been violated, emotional distress and conflict within result from the betrayal. Not only does trust in others become difficult, but those who know what you have been dealing with or are going through are also inadvertently affected by your trust issues. After one has been betrayed, whether they are mindful of their counter response or not, they often put up a protective barrier to prevent themselves from experiencing betrayal again and the subsequent hurt. Where that protective barrier has been erected to isolate or insulate oneself from being hurt again. What often goes unrecognized. Is that the person inadvertently places before themselves a barrier that will handicap them, thereby keeping them from effectively connecting socially or relationally.

Those who are aware of the hurt of their beloved and can empathize with their pain naturally want to bring comfort and assurance to their beloved. But not only that. They, too, may also instinctively become a protector of the one who has been hurt. While the empathizer(s) may also be inclined to become the avenger for the one wronged! Because we are social beings, our actions and reactions do not occur in a vacuum ... what we say and do, has a ripple effect upon others, even the unsuspected.

My betrayal of trust against Lisa through my unwarranted breakup; and the fact that she accepted me back in opposition to her Dad and Mother brought about relational conflict and emotional distress between Lisa and her parents that was far more severe than I thought or could have imagined things would be. As for me and Lisa's parents, I wasn't concerned or perhaps incapable of being concerned about what they thought or felt about me. My concern was for me and my house that I was attempting to establish.

As for what occurred: Lisa went to her parent's home to visit them and bring in the New Year - *1988*. I arrived on New Year's Day to pick Lisa up. She was preparing to leave with me. Her parents made their disapproval abundantly and demonstratively clear! Lisa's parents even threatened to cut ties with their daughter if she left with me. That day a great chasm was successfully established between my house and my in-laws' house. *Successfully established, indeed!* Remember people! We are in spiritual warfare! Lest we forget! Satan wants to keep us divided and ignorant of our power when we, as a family, come together as one under God! Though Lisa's parents may not have been able to provide godly guidance for my home, they were family. Families may fight and disagree. But Satan wins; he is the victor when he divides a family and keeps it divided!

The mutual support and encouragement both homes needed one from the other were now cut off. Lisa and her (our) home were immediately and indefinitely cut off from the family she loved … simply because she'd chosen to follow me.

A couple of weeks before *the great family divide*, I had proposed to Lisa … she accepted! This became the decisive root cause of our fractured families. These occurrences mentioned thus far unfolded within the first three months of Lisa and me dating. Shortly thereafter, Lisa and I begin cohabitating at my apartment. She received a letter from her mother. The letter read in part, "If you (Lisa) have a child by him (me), I (Lisa's mother) would not have anything to do with the child." Lisa did not give in to this tremendous pressure. I can only imagine the pain and feeling of abandonment and confusion that Lisa was experiencing. Her mother occasionally called our apartment to dissuade Lisa from being with me. In order for the distractions which disrupted my home and disturbed Lisa's peace would be halted. I now demanded Lisa, "Tell your mother to quit contacting you." Or else, sternly assuring Lisa, "I would end our relationship." I had allowed the disruptions by Lisa's mother and had seen Lisa's anguish from this long enough! This predicament greatly grieved Lisa! She loved her parents tremendously, but she had chosen to show her love for me by following me. And now, I had decided that enough was enough! She had to tell her mother as much.

* * *

No doubt, now looking back, things could have been done differently by each of us. Just the same, I am inclined to believe that we still would have met with some challenges, primarily because their grandchild, Mario, was involved. And I was the man I was and who their daughter had chosen to follow.

There's Going To Be A Marriage

Because God had purposed the union between Lisa and me, as well as with her family ... but not the chaos and confusion which was at our making. Without a word ever spoken regarding all that occurred, twenty months later, our difference would be reconciled or at least put to the side; for unto us a child was born, unto us a son was given!

Lisa and I, through marriage, brought forth one child - Desmond. God gifting us with a son actually united our families. After Lisa had given birth to our son, Des, my beloved and late mother-in-law, Elsie Goddard Land, came to town. She stayed in our apartment for some two weeks as she tended to the needs of her daughter and grandson.

I will now enlarge the picture one final time leading to our family's dysfunction ... apart from the fact that we all are broken people in need of God's restoration and Lisa and my marriage. And so it was, approximately a week after breaking up with Lisa, our relationship was restored. Shortly afterward, a month or a few days beyond, I proposed to Lisa to become my wife.

Leaving out the details of the proposal: Leading to the proposal, Lisa had no idea I was going to *put a ring on it!* Including our short breakup, we had only been dating for approximately three months. No doubt a concern for her parents. My proposal to Lisa was a total surprise for her! However, she immediately responded, "Yes," as tears began to flow from her eyes. Lisa was clearly all in with me!

Lisa's aunt, who was visiting Lisa and Sharon at their apartment, witnessed my proposal to Lisa. I remember seeing her aunt smile ... at least, that's what I thought it was. Lisa's sister was also present; however, I don't remember her response. During this time, she was at odds with me ... I believe she felt like she was losing her sister and nephew to me. As I now write and reflect on that moment, I asked Lisa if she recalled her sister's response. Lisa said her sister seemed happy for her. However, Lisa added that they never talked about the proposal. Not only was my dear sister-in-law not too fond of me during this time, but neither were her parents. Needless to say, for the moment, Lisa was full of delight! But things would quickly go downhill from here.

Unfortunately, this season, which should have been a joyous occasion for all, especially Lisa, would be met with great disappointment and heartache. After the proposal, my influence and assertion as Lisa's head, which she wholeheartedly embraced, were clearly established. Lisa did and continues to embrace and submit to my lead or authority that God has set for the man in a *Christ-led home*. At that time, I did not fully grasp what I now share. Nevertheless, I felt that Lisa, as well as Mario, were my responsibility.

Perhaps this language or description I am presenting is difficult for some to embrace. Nevertheless, I remind you that this is God's order for a Christian home. Things being as they were with Lisa's family and me, the tension would become heightened as I established my house. Push-back and tension would mount up quickly as I clearly and decisively assumed my role as Lisa's and Mario's under-shepherd.

As a result of my assertion, another pivotal and cataclysmic moment with my in-laws came to a head when I made a decision regarding Mario that his grandparents, particularly my beloved and late father-in-law, William Land, disagreed with. I was clearly establishing before Mario, who was now 4 years old, and his grandparents that I had the final say over him and that of my home.

Visiting with Lisa at her and her sister's apartment following the incident at Lisa's parent's home. And things not being harmonious between Sharon and me. I, therefore, invited Lisa to move in with me. I felt this was best. Our decision to move in together can be debated - I know. This was not an ideal situation. Neither do I recommend cohabitating. However, under the circumstances, this was what I thought was best for Lisa and me. Let me emphasize! Lisa and I were not "shacking" for the sake of shacking. We were not together for mere convenience's sake. *I had put a ring on it!* There was absolutely no doubt about it. I was going to marry Lisa ... Period! And it would be sooner for sure and not later that she would become my wife.

Our decision to live together, as you can imagine, did not help the situation with Lisa's family. In the month or two following Lisa and Mario moving in with me, she would be subjected to her parent's efforts to derail our intentions to marry. Lisa's parents were not bad people ... not at all. They absolutely loved their daughter and grandson immensely! They just did not know me or my intentions. Again I did not help things. Neither could they understand how Lisa could give herself over to me in such a short time. I am sure that misunderstandings on their part, my breaking up with their daughter, and my approach to things made for the toasty environment we encountered. I never harbored bad feelings towards Lisa's family. Nevertheless, I was persuaded to run my home as I saw fit.

Lisa and I were going to get married! After all that she went through, she never wavered in her commitment to me. Or her desire to carry and be recognized by my name and not that of her father. Lisa endured her testing. What perseverance she displayed and continues to have over 3 decades later! This is praiseworthy!

A mere three months after proposing to Lisa Marie Land, approximately six months in all of dating, we now stood before God, His angels, my family members, and church members to become husband and wife. Our wedding ceremony immediately followed a Sunday morning worship service. In addition to my family and members of the church who stayed for the wedding, only two of Lisa's friends were present. Things happened rather quickly for Lisa and me; as for other family members not being in attendance, perhaps this was the reason. And the fact that communication was now broken between Lisa, her parents and her sister.

Lisa's parents had previously told her that they would not attend the ceremony if she married me. Nonetheless, in due time, God brought us together as a family. He is faithful!

Now allow me to share this bit about our beautiful wedding. It was a simple, quaint, and inexpensive wedding ... actually, there was no overhead cost. Lisa and I did not have extra money for a showy wedding. Besides, if we did have money, it was not likely that an enormous cost would have gone towards a wedding. I said to my Pastor and friend, Dr. Lorenzo Lynch, that Lisa and I wanted to get married and that I did not want the Court to perform it. I told him I would be fine standing in his office with our witnesses while marrying Lisa. My brother then suggested holding the wedding following a Sunday service.

He said, "I will announce to the congregation the Sunday before your wedding that you and Lisa are getting married. And on the Sunday of your wedding day. I will announce, Immediately following the service, the wedding ceremony will be held. And all wishing to remain for the service were welcome to remain."

Several of the members stayed over. A friend of mine took pictures. I had my best man and Lisa, her maid of honor. A couple of the ladies from the church sang a song or two. My friend and Pastor, Reverend Lynch, presided over the blessed and wonderful ceremony. At its conclusion, my bride and I stood before the congregation as husband and wife. There was no reception. There were no bells and whistles, rice throwing, or confetti. There were no decorative ornaments, no jumping over the broom or a limousine driver to whisk us off.

But know this certainty! Our hearts were exceedingly joyful, as we now stood as one! There was great rejoicing in the heavens; also, between Lisa and I, and all who sincerely prayed for Lisa and me, and who wished us well.

CHAPTER 14

Marital Vows - Not Mere Words
Life Beyond And God's Process

As newlyweds, Lisa and I flowed along quite well. The first year or so of marriage was carried away swiftly by the excitement and newness of things. I will say that around year two, we had begun to settle into our roles; we were learning about ourselves and one another. Things were moving along quite well. Beyond year two, we were in sync, with the honeymoon phase long passed. I believe that you and your spouse should be operating as one at this point in a marriage. Apart from dealing with everyday concerns and the usual mishaps of life, you two should have it together. If not, you two need to figure out the problem and fix it. Or get help to set your house in order before it is too late.

Before marriage, a couple must have some sense of what they want for their future. They should then set out a plan to achieve those goals and desires. However, this was not the case for Lisa and me. I believe this simple matter is overlooked or not even considered by many. It's not enough to just want to get married. Marriage is honorable; it must be understood as so from the mind or will of God for a couple to maintain a victorious marriage. However, far too many welcome the idea of marriage; enter a marriage but are ill-equipped to stay married or to have a healthy and victorious union. They say, "Yes," ... "I do," ... and "I will" to marriage. However, when marrying, they have not *truly* considered what they are embracing and agreeing to.

There was a time, and not that long ago when the understanding of marriage and the spouse's role was understood by most. However, times have changed … God has been expelled from being a Teacher of morality and our personal Tutor of truth unto acceptable or righteous living.

Instead, man has chosen foolishly to school himself or follow the instructions of this world. And there we have it; the esteem for marriage and godly family values have greatly diminished. The covenant *vows* expressed at weddings, inaugurating a lifetime union, seem a mere formality and thereby hold no significance or consequences. They have become empty words spoken during a lifeless ritual that is put on for show. This is the kind of wedding Satan enjoys – a lifeless one. It's already doomed! Even so, Satan rejoices when the marriage fails – ending in divorce and ripping a family apart. When this happens, others desiring to one day marry become doubtful or fearful of entering a marital and lifelong relationship. As for those already married: some begin to question and doubt the strength of their union or even the integrity of their spouse. Satan also rejoices at this!

Make no mistake about it! In every marriage, and certainly, those established under God, Satan's aim is to attack and destroy that union. Or to keep a God-ordained marriage from being pursued and established: "Let's just shack up" … "Let's be friends with benefits," these are the vows written by Satan, which are in the hearts of many … are you subscribing to them?

Look, my brothers and sisters, I know firsthand that the enemy of our soul wants our marriages defeated. I have made this plain for you to see. Therefore, you must arm and guard yourself and/or your marriage against the attacks of the Evil one! In chapter seventeen, I will share how Satan used another individual to attack my marriage in the most vivid, detailed, and unbelievable way. This spiritually depraved, demon-possessed person, or greatly influenced by demons, targeted my wife in an attempt to destroy my marriage and home! The assault from this person was relentless, vicious, and potentially lethal. This assault could have ruined my wife mentally!

People, whether the attacks are from forces without or those struggles from within, you must be aware of them. You must be watchful and prayerful! You must be steadfast and unmovable when engaged in this spiritual battle that desires to overthrow you and take your marriage from you!

If you had a Christian wedding ... such union has been deemed established under God. The vows made to your spouse while standing before God, witnessed by the heavenly host (angels) and all in attendance, should stand as a reminder of the covenant you freely entered into with your spouse. Reflecting on your vows from time to time will serve to be a most valuable source of strengthening when you or your marriage is under spiritual attack. However, before the power of your vow or words can be activated or empowering for your life. They must hold significant and heartfelt meaning to you; before, during, and after you have married. You must embrace the spiritual reality of God presiding over your union! Also, He who is giving you - one to the other, as you two agree to enter the holy union of matrimony. Whereby, your oath to one another confirms that you understand the marital arrangement, wherein, the life-long commitment and responsibility you have towards caring for one another. As well as living to honor God through your union. And being a witness to others unto your faithfulness to God and your spouse. Marriage is a serious matter. It takes three: the Spirit, you, and your spouse to have marital victory!

Though individuals may be allowed by the officiating minister to write their own vows. Nevertheless, the heart and central theme for the Christian Marital Ceremony is, and must always be – God! It is He who has established the union of marriage. And He alone! Who has set before man what a *Holy Union* looks like! And how it should be lived well before all to see!

Let's examine a condensed version and the wording of the execution of a Marriage Ceremony. I want you to closely and carefully consider the weighty words spoken by the presiding minister and the vows freely spoken by the couple to be wedded:

MINISTERIAL CHARGE:

I now charge you both, Tony, and Lisa, as you stand in the presence of God, to remember that true love and the faithful observance of your marriage vows are required as the foundation of a victorious marriage and the establishment of a healthy and enduring Christian home. Without this understanding, there can be no faithful or godly marriage, and the home in which you will endeavor to establish will be a vain effort. Keep the solemn vows you are about to make. Live with tender consideration for each other. Conduct your lives in honesty and in truth. And your marriage will last. Your home will endure. The marriage bond will be a blessing to you, and you will be a blessing to others. This should always be remembered as each of you now declare your desire to be wed.

MARRIAGE VOWS:

The Minister: (to the man)
(Name) _____, Do you take this woman to be your wedded wife? And do you solemnly promise, before God and these witnesses: That you will love her, comfort her, honor and keep her in sickness and in health; and that, forsaking all others for her alone, you will perform unto her all the duties that a husband owes to his wife, until God, by death, shall separate you?

The Man: I do.

The Minister: (to the woman)
(Name) _____, Do you take this man to be your wedded husband? And do you solemnly promise, before God and these witnesses: That you will love him, comfort him, honor and keep him in sickness and in health; and that, forsaking all others for him alone, you will perform unto him all the duties that a wife owes to her husband, until God, by death, shall separate you?

The Woman: I do.

The Minister: (to the Man and the Woman)
Since it is your desire to take each other as husband and wife, please join hands, and repeat after me, before God and these witnesses, the marriage vow.

The Man:
I, (Name) _____, take thee, (Name) _____, to be my wedded wife, to have and to hold from this day forward, for better or for worse, for richer or for poorer, in sickness and in health, to love and to cherish, till death do us part, according to God's holy ordinance; and, thereto, I plight thee my faith.

The Woman:
I, (Name) _____, take thee, (Name) _____, to be my wedded husband, to have and to hold from this day forward, for better or for worse, for richer or for poorer, in sickness and in health, to love and to cherish, till death do us part, according to God's holy ordinance; and, thereto, I plight thee my faith.

THE RING SERVICE:

The Minister: (holding up the rings)
The wedding ring is an outward and visible sign of an inward and spiritual bond that unites two loyal hearts in endless Love (Agape).

Woman and the Man in turn:
(Name)_____, will you receive this ring from (Name) _____ as a token of his/her affection, sincerity, and fidelity toward you, and will you wear it as a symbol of your affection, sincerity, and fidelity toward him/her?

Each shall answer in turn: I will.

DECLARATION OF MARRIAGE:

The Minister: (to the People)
For as much as (Name) _____and (Name) _____ have consented together in holy marriage vows. And have witnessed the same before God and this company. And thereto have given and pledged their faith to the other. And declared the same by joining their right hands and by giving and receiving a ring. I declare, by the authority committed unto me as a Minister of the Gospel. That they are Husband and Wife, according to the ordinance of God and the law of the State, in the Name of the Father, and of the Son, and of the Holy Spirit. Amen

The Husband and Wife kneel and remain kneeling through the blessing, humbly submitting before God, acknowledging His Sovereignty over all things.

The Minister:
Those whom God hath joined together, let not man put asunder.

PRAYER:

O gracious and merciful God, our heavenly Father, of whom the whole family in heaven and earth is named: Be Thou pleased to seal the vows which these Thy servants have taken with Thine approval. And grant to this Husband and Wife all spiritual grace and willingness to keep the vow and covenant between them made. Defend them amidst all temptation and save them from indifference and a love grown cold. In the midst of adversity or discord in their home, be Thou their stay, O heavenly Father; and lighten their burdens by strengthening their spirits. May they live each for the other in peace and with growing *true* affection that their home may be a haven of rest and a place of Thy abode, through Jesus Christ our Lord. Amen.

[Minister's Service Book – For Pulpit and Parish; Jesse Jai McNeil. Pages 46 – 50]

The wedding ceremony is unmistakably consecrated unto our Holy God. And the couple's vows rendered - *no ordinary or lifeless words or mere recitation! Their words are weighty! They are legally binding, both on Earth and in Heaven!* And where the importance of the wedding vows is understood; faithfully acted upon, it serves the good of all; the union brings honor to God and incurs his favor upon the marriage and home.

It would benefit every engaged couple to give time to read and contemplate the spoken words of the wedding ceremony. Afterward, a copy is given to the married couple to reflect upon from time to time, to be reminded of the vows made and the sacredness of the institution of the marital union both agreed upon.

I don't know where this is practiced. Neither Lisa nor I have the benefit of what I'm recommending. I'm sure it would have been to my advantage if such instructions had accompanied our premarital counseling, which I scarcely recall. However, my wife recalls better than I do the one brief session we had with pastor Lynch. In his defense, I believe my friend was 26 when he married my wife and me. He was merely 3 years my senior if I'm not mistaken, and single. What did he really understand about marriage?

Who Giveth Thee Away

Who giveth thee away?... is also one of the questions asked by the officiating minister. This matter or question is not to be taken lightly! Therefore, I want to give some attention to this question, as I see the matter of a woman (daughter) and her literally being given by her father to the care of another man. I am convinced Scripture supports this view.

Traditionally and ideally, the bride's father gives her away. After he has escorted his princess down the aisle, the two stand arm in arm before the officiating minister. While the soon-to-be husband stands feet away, waiting to receive his gift from God – his bride, from the bride's father. The officiating minister then asks the question. *"Who giveth this woman to be married to this man?"* The question is directed to both the father and his daughter ... but the father responds, "I do."

Now consider this: These two words, "I do," containing only three letters, are not mere empty words expressed by the father or stated by the role player or stand in, in the absence of the woman's father, as some meager formality or ritual!

This is to be a proud and emotionally filled moment for the father of the bride! However, much more is involved than emotions ... at least it should be. Now, hear me carefully on this matter! A Christian father is actually giving his precious daughter and gift from God as a gift to another man. This man, her husband, is to honor and care for her. As they now dwell together as one under God! And without the unwanted influence or opinion of the father or anyone else for that matter! However, newlyweds. Don't forsake the knowledge and wisdom that can come from those who love God and you both!

I do not have a daughter. However, I can imagine the powerful bond between a father and his daughter. And yet he is entrusting his Christian daughter to the care of another man who should also be a follower of Jesus (1 Corinthians 7:39; 2 Corinthians).

A girl's father is to be her first example of what a godly husband and loving father should be. Her Daddy would have demonstrated himself as a provider and protector; he would have been a nurturer and a caring person before her eyes. Though not perfect, his loving demeanor is his guide, therefore overshadowing his minor faults. Each of these positive characteristics aids in forging a lasting and loving bond between the father and his daughter and sets the standard to which the husband she hopes to have one day must measure up.

Depending upon the daughter's age, the subject of boys and men should be discussed between the father and his daughter. As she comes of age, yet, still under Daddy's care, although she may no longer be under his roof. Because of her admiration and love for her Daddy, she values and perhaps longs for her father's input as she learns to navigate life. Therefore, when she takes a liking to some young man, she can't help but think about her Daddy. She knows he will be there to assist her, if needed, with determining whether the young man possesses the character of godliness, even though she may already have a good indicator of his character.

Daddy's approval of the young man suggests to his daughter that he, too, sees potential (or not) in her person of interest. Therefore, the father, who now is serving as his daughter's protector and wise counselor, will give her male friend time to prove himself worthy of his daughter's time and attention. And perhaps even her hand in marriage.

Within these interactive norms between a father and his maturing daughter, her self-esteem and worth are established. Her strength, confidence, and limitless potential will result from her father telling her who and *Whose* she is. This will cause her to truly see how special, even wonderfully, God has made her. Where this loving bond between father and daughter exists, her self-esteem will not be an issue. It will not be an issue because her Daddy has already esteemed her as his. And a child of God! A godly Daddy, from the time his daughter was born, she was dear to his heart, the apple of his eye, and God's wonderful creation!

The love a father must display before his daughter is never to be called into question by her. The daughter, having been assured of her father's love time and time again, will know that no matter what, her father will always have her best interest at heart. This is agape (Love)! As the daughter becomes more independent, she will undoubtedly have her own views on some matters. However, she will always reflect upon the values her Daddy taught her.

Giving his daughter away. The father can now stand proudly and confidently because he knows his daughter is prepared for the life that awaits her. The father's daughter heeding his godly counsel, the godly man who is now to receive his daughter being adequately vetted and found worthy of his daughter. Only now, unto this man's care, can the father, with a clear conscience, give his daughter over to marry this man who has proven himself worthy. Such a man is not only after his daughter's heart but the father's heart as well.

Where a person sincerely desires to fulfill the will of God for their life and seeks to display the character of God. This person cannot treat a child of God, or any person for that matter, with contempt. Or in any kind of way! The Spirit of God within the person will convict a child of God of inappropriate conduct every time. When one becomes aware that they've offended their spouse (or some other), forgiveness must be sought. This act points to a contrite and repentant heart, thereby leading to reconciliation. This is the heart and will of God.

For a Christian couple who is to marry, the prescribed traditional wedding ceremony that I presented or a similar one is the manner that should be sought. The wedding ceremony must see or hold God as its focus; He is the Originator and the Sustainer of a holy marriage. I, therefore, submit as a must; ministerial counseling, or professional wedding counsel, from a Christ-honoring practitioner before one marries. I would like to believe that all officiating ministers offer premarital counseling. If not, seek out godly counsel before marrying. And indeed, seek counsel first if you are a Christian and, for whatever reason, you are being married by a government representative.

It will be from one of these godly counselors, including those closest or dearest to the both of you, who will or should assist you two in determining if you are prepared for marriage.

In the absence of godly fathers ... this being the case for far too many homes. We are witnessing this major dilemma and even a crisis among many who lack fatherly oversight. As for the fatherless daughters ... *Who will give them away?* There is no protector, no one to model for her, the acceptable character for a godly husband and Daddy. Daddy is not present to help her to see that she is royalty - one inherently holding immeasurable worth. Who will help to build within her - her self-worth and confidence? And instill the belief that she can do anything she sets her mind to. The dilemma and crisis before far too many daughters: There is no father! No man to model God before them! No Daddy to screen and hold accountable her suitor and potential husband.

A child first understands love, having seen and experienced it freely and sacrificially given and offered by their daddy and mother. This paves the way for the child to know and welcome the love of *The Heavenly Father.* The two go hand in hand ... to know their Daddy's love is for the child to know the love of The Father – God, their Creator!

It matters not what the world has to say ... God has established the Father as the head and leader of his home. The husband is to imitate the love of Jesus! He is to set the course for his home ... the husband and father, however, is yet, under Christ, as he seeks to model Christ before his family. Just as Jesus – the Bridegroom, is Lord or Head over the Church, He even laying down His life or sacrifices Himself for us - His bride, the Church. So must a husband and father be willing to do the same! This means what it says, he dying or giving himself to care for and to preserve the life of his spouse, but also by making sure his bride's spiritual needs and that of his offspring are met.

Let's look briefly at this matter of *Giving Away* from a broader Biblical lens: God the Father gave us Jesus, His Son. In turn, we are given or presented back to the Father through Jesus. God gave Adam Eve to be his wife, who gave him sons, who were to be given back (dedicated) to God, their Creator and the Giver of *Life*. And so, a man is to be given a wife by her father and even *The Father*. That they may bear (be given) sons and daughters through their union. Who, like Adam and Eve's offspring, should be dedicated back to the Father. As for a son, it is said in the Bible that a man who *finds* a good wife has a good thing. She is already *wifey material* because she is one with her Father – God. In this, God the Father provides or gives a woman of God to a man of God. I remind you, God gave Eve to Adam as a *help mete*. From the Bible's account, a good woman is *given* to a man. Rebekah's father gave her to Isaac (Genesis chapter 14). The father of both Rachel and Leah gave his daughters to Jacob to marry (Genesis chapter 29). And the father of Zipporah, Jethro, the priest, gave his daughter to Moses for marriage (Exodus chapter 2).

I believe the Bible has established and set before us the pattern to follow: A father is to give his daughter to the care of another man, a worthy man of God to marry. I will also submit that Numbers chapter 30: 3-5 clearly speaks to the father's authority over his daughter. I recognize that in our western culture, a woman may be "self-sufficient," she, therefore, makes her own decisions about who to marry ... among other things. Just the same, I believe the Bible – God's Word has set the better way before us to follow. That a father is to give his daughter to the care of another godly man. *However, there is a dilemma and crisis in both areas; godly men and women!*

I Can't Give You Away

My dear sister, Wendy, welcomed me to share this portion of her life. As I, and she too, believed, sharing her experience may be beneficial for others.

Approximately fourteen years ago, I was then in my early forties. I was more mature in Biblical faith, as well as my understanding of the will of God. Embracing my role as the oldest of my siblings. In this season of my life, I began to view myself as one who sits at the city's gate. In the Old Testament of the

Bible, they were the wise elders of the city, from whom the people embraced and gained knowledge and wisdom. As it was then and remains true today, wise counsel can be received or rejected. As it stands, godly counsel and wisdom from God have been widely disregarded. As a result, I have found in this generation that elders, wise men of God who are to maintain the city's gate (figuratively speaking), are few and far between.

My sister considered that she was doing the honorable thing when she reached out to me, her elder preacher-brother, to meet a need of hers. At the time, she, and the individual she was dating, had come to a decision to get married. When she called me and asked that I pay her a visit, I was unaware of this.

Before my visit to her apartment, I can only recall an introduction to her companion, which occurred at a family gathering she hosted. That said, I did not know this person. Upon arriving at the apartment, the purpose of my invitation was made known, *to give my sister away in marriage to this individual.* Among other matters discussed with them in which we did not see eye-to-eye. My response was clear and straightforward, *"I can't give you away… I do not know him."*

My decision and other oppositions regarding their thoughts on things did not sit well with either of them. They responded in like manner - countering my position or the counsel I offered.

From my Biblical insight, life experiences, and wisdom, I fully understood the gravity and significance of what was being asked of me. I knew that my words "I do" to give my sister away were not empty words to be uttered when prompted to respond. Surrendering my sister over to this person I did not know caused me to think about our dad, Wendy's biological father. He had already divorced the family when she was conceived by our mother. And he died in a vehicle accident when she was seven years of age and me nineteen.

As a result of Wendy's request of me, I saw myself standing in his stead – as my sister's protector and wise advisor … I wondered about what position he would have taken. More importantly, I knew my Heavenly Father's perspective regarding this matter before me.

I'm convinced, and so is my sister, that things would have been different for her if our Dad was present. Just the same, my Abba – my God and Father, was present in my life. Therefore, I knew something about His will for marriage. And was learning all the more about His will for mankind. I also knew that a couple not knowing the will of God for marriage would likely face insurmountable challenges that would lead to a house becoming divided.

My refusal to participate in their wedding did not deter their decision to get married. Neither was this my intention. I simply wanted my sister to understand why I couldn't be her role player. That which she desired from me and what I would say … "I do" to giving her away was not some mere formality and inconsequential! They did get married, and I was in attendance. But it was her uncle who gave her away. Not even a year after they married, they had a son - my sister's first and only child.

Now, I don't know when their marriage began to deteriorate. However, two years following the birth of their child, the marriage came to a sad and tragic end - that of divorce. I say tragic because a child was born from this union. I've already discussed this matter of a broken marriage and its overall effects, so I will not elaborate again. Nevertheless, I will say this. The impact of a house divided when a parent, particularly the father, is absent. The consequences or collateral damage to a child is evident.

Over a decade has passed since that sit-down with my sister and her companion. However, as I worked on writing this book, some six or more years after their divorce. There were two distinct but general conversations that I recall having with my sister regarding her life as a married woman and her subsequent divorce. In each conversation, Wendy shared her frustration with her former husband and their divorce. I was taken by surprise by what she was so freely sharing with me.

On one of those occasions as she expressed her past frustration and difficulties resulting from her former husband and failed marriage. As well as the challenges of raising her son. She spontaneously said, "I wish somebody would have told me." I took this to mean that she would have known what to expect from a marriage. Or to have been better prepared for it. Or even not to have married at all. I immediately responded, "I tried to tell you." Without missing a beat, my sister replied, "You did ... You did!" As she gave a slight chuckle, no doubt recalling that day in her thoughts.

In a much later conversation – years later with Wendy, I was again surprised by something she would say to me. She shared, "I had a grudge with you for not giving me away!" This was somewhat of a surprise. However, it was the length of time that she held the grudge that truly profound my thoughts. I asked her, "When did you get over it?" She responded, "About two years ago." I had no idea! This meant that my sister held that grudge for nine years, including some two years following the conversations I previously mentioned.

Relationally, there had been a slight rift between us. Only looking back can I now see brief periods of this. I asked my sister, "How did you get over how you'd felt towards me?" She responded. "A few things had been bothering me over the years. Finally, I had to take a look at myself." *Did you all hear that?!* "When I did, I realized I had to face the truth about what I saw about myself. I then had to take responsibility for my actions." One of those things was the grudge she wrongly had against me.

Only after she shared this with me that I remember something else she said to me a few months before this conversation. In light of this last conversation ... why and what she had previously spoken to me became clear. In that conversation, my sister expressed her "appreciation for me." And the fact that she doesn't have to "try to figure me out or second guess me ... a rare quality she said that is in people today." She continued. "You are going to say what you mean and mean what you say. And also give counsel worth lending an ear to, although I may not totally agree with you."

She had to drop the grudge against me when she realized that some of her problems were of her own making. People, that's wisdom! We must be willing to conduct a self-examination from time to time. My sister and I are good to go! Relationally, we are solid! However, this is not always the case amongst families. Even within our immediate families, Satan works to divide us. But we also do a great job of this ourselves, all because we fail to take a look at ourselves and take responsibility for our actions. We must identify and acknowledge our brokenness, which has created a divide between those with whom we should be close to. Together, we are stronger!

Here is something else worth mentioning: Further elaborating, Wendy added that *she got married for all of the wrong reasons!* She shared three or four wrong reasons for marrying, although I don't recall what they were. However, I remember agreeing with her that her motives were wrong.

I asked my sister. Did she love her former husband at the time of their marriage? She responded, "Yes." However, I didn't ask her about her understanding of the matter of love. And I think it is accurate for me to state that neither she nor her husband had a godly foundation upon which to establish a marriage. Though both of their intentions were *good* before and after marrying. As I shared in a previous chapter, *good intentions* regarding marrying are not enough to build and sustain a marriage. One must know God for themselves … *That personal and intimate relationship to be held with Him.* That one is then more likely than not to have a healthy and enduring marital union.

To further assist you. I asked my sister what advice she could provide my readers from her experience. Her response followed these lines: "What you see in the person before the, "I do`s" and "I will`s" before the wedding is the person you are going to get. Take off your blinders of lies and deception you're telling yourself about the person you feel you must be with. You've heard the tale … If it looks like a duck, sounds like a duck, and quacks like a duck, it must be a duck!"

Significant Occurrences

Approaching the third year of my marriage to Lisa, three significant events occurred regarding me, helping to direct my life's story and shaping me personally. The first of these occurrences caused me to pause as I considered the possible spiritual significance and the unique timing of my encounter with Ms. Rosa Parks, "The Mother of The Civil Rights Movement."

One of the sayings expressed within the two professions that I worked, "Never volunteer for anything." Well, when my supervisor asked my squad, about seven of us, for a volunteer, I spoke up. I volunteered without knowing what the assignment was. My supervisor, the late Durham Police Sgt. C.R. Thompson said, "Your assignment is to provide an escort and security for Ms. Rosa Parks. He provided me with her hotel information and the time of her speaking engagement that was to be held at North Carolina Central University - Eagle Pride! I was off to this assignment with excitement! It was a surreal moment, greeting Ms. Parks and standing face-to-face with her in her hotel room.

Something about that moment invigorated me! Reflecting upon the occasion, I felt God was moving me toward more significant work for his Kingdom. What could it be? I really didn't know. But I felt there was more He wanted me to do.

Nine days after meeting Ms. Parks, Lisa and I became parents of our first child together, adding to our family unit - four. The birth of Desmond was the second significant occurrence in my life! During this period in Lisa's and my life, we were simply living as best we knew how … things were moving along rather well.

Before our son's birth, we attended church services as my work schedule permitted. This was twice a month. Though I felt what I will now call a spiritual nudging after meeting Ms. Parks, including the arrival of my son, my perspective on life was shifting; a broader awareness about life was overcoming me. However, our church attendance would wane after Desmond's birth. It didn't help that Reverend Lynch was no longer the pastor of Mount Level. I've noted: Irregular church attendance is never a good thing, especially for a young couple or an individual who is a babe in Christ.

It was a short time before the birth of Desmond that my pastor and dear friend Leonzo Lynch answered the call to pastor another church. As I mentioned, this greatly affected me … I felt abandoned. No doubt I felt this way because my dad had deserted me – and his family. One dad was deceased, and the other (who, at the time, I thought was my biological father) was nowhere to be found. I needed my father! I needed a relationship that only a dad could provide. But I also needed my friend!

There was another time that I felt abandoned. I experienced this feeling of desertion when my dear friend, Lawrence Smith, from Detroit, was headed back to the "States" after completing his military tour of duty in Germany. Lawrence, aka "Sweets," aka "Smitty," had embraced me as a brother upon my arrival to Germany. He was one real and cool friend! However, beforehand, God allowed our paths to cross a year or so earlier while we were both going through basic training in El Paso, Texas.

We were assigned to different platoons; therefore, we didn't know each other. At the time of our paths crossing, "Smitty" was on a *Corrective Attitude Adjustment Detail,* I will call it. He was picking up cigarette butts from around the barracks. Funny enough, when I arrived at my new duty assignment in Germany, there was Smitty. He was in the Headquarters building, buffing the floor. This was also a measure utilized to adjust his attitude. Smitty was from – DETROIT! Somewhat funny and unbelievable, Lawrence Smith is now a veteran Police Officer in Detroit.

For reasons unknown to me ... maybe because I was in the minority, as I stood in the haircut line with dozens of white soldiers, I caught brother Smitty's attention. Smitty was standing a short distance from me. No doubt he had no business doing what came next. Being defiant towards his superiors and breaking his mandate to remain silent, Lawrence called out to me to get my attention. In that brief encounter, he shared insight that helped me elevate my status through boot camp. Unaware of the fact at the moment, I had forged a brotherly bond with Smitty. Good relationships matter!

God has a plan for His own ... To work things out for our good and for His praise! Until we come to know the Father, it is impossible to see such significant occurrences that He's working out for our benefit and His glory. When we come to know Him, only then can we learn to trust or put our confidence in Him!

Being rejected or abandoned by the man I thought was my biological father, the dad who adopted me, whose last name I bear ... Yes, indeed, had a negative effect on me. As it would be, Leonzo had become that significant brother in my young adult life, more than I gave thought to at the time. And now, he, too, had left me! My friend, Leonzo's departure, made staying away from the church

– the place of worship a thing of ease. I now know this was my way of coping with the fact that my friend was gone. However, my being away from the church left me exposed and vulnerable to sin or the ways of this world.

Committed To Family – The Called Of God

After marrying, while focused on being a husband and father, I drifted apart from my few childhood friends. They were all single. Spiritually speaking, neither could they offer support. It was these same friends that I reconnected with prior to *my season of folly.*

Anyhow, during this time of my life. I was more purpose-oriented with my season of whoredom now a year or so behind me. I could feel the Spirit's gentle pull that was occurring within my soul, although I could not understand this realignment or orientation that He desired to bring about in me. Not fully grasping the significance of prayer, worship, reading the Bible, and implementing other Christian disciplines ... just the same, a change within me was occurring because my heart and intentions were in the right place. People, this is part of the process by which we grow spiritually. When one sincerely engages in such practices or disciplines that lead to spiritual growth ... grow you will. This growth at various times can be seen by others and even felt or discerned by you. I was experiencing spiritual growth; however, I did not fully comprehend what was occurring at the time.

It was during this season in my life that Deacon Ronald Daye said, "I see the call of God upon you to preach." I had felt a change occurring within me, but Ronald Daye saw, acknowledged, and spoke forth what the Spirit of God had revealed to Him.

However, me ... standing at a lectern to preach? Me proclaiming the Word of God was an intimidating thought! I saw no chance of this happening! Having been requested to do the following a couple of times. Write a five-minute message to be delivered before the church for some special occasion. In addition to this ... participate as the worship-service Presider, Scripture reader, or leading the congregation in prayer. I could not envision boldly and effectively preaching the Word of God. But God knew otherwise! He would teach me – *"that it is not by might nor by strength* (mere man's effort) *but by His Spirit" (Zechariah 4:5-7)* that man will be able to accomplish things worthy of God's approval.

During this time of my life - as a husband and father, I managed and handled the business of my home quite well. My wife was also holding things down impeccably as a working woman and mother of two sons. Our growing together was not met with significant challenges, as is often associated with newlyweds. What a magnificent wife I had in Lisa; she has made being married to her of relative ease. However, with my lack of spiritual maturity. I did not recognize the jewel I truly had in my wife early on in our marriage. I, therefore, was incapable of appreciating or valuing my wife as much as I now do.

Lisa loved me unconditionally. She saw and respected that I viewed the care of our home as my responsibility. Because of the care and attention given to her, it was with ease that my wife willingly submitted to me, her husband, and the one she loved. *Lisa was everything I needed and more!* And to think ... I could have lost this extraordinary woman because of my foolishness.

There are other factors to consider, but more importantly, God, who knows our hearts, will work with us and even within us so that we may fulfill His purpose for our lives. Now, God will not and cannot force His will upon us ... *Love* does not operate in this manner. However, according to our heart's desires and one attempting to align with God's purpose, He will then set the path that brings Him honor and our ultimate victory. But we must say "Yes" or surrender to His way that has been set before us. It's as simple as one stating through faith, "Lord, let Your will be done." And then trusting the process or His guidance no matter how things may be unfolding.

Even while we are in our mess, God can yet call us or have His purpose for us to fulfill. For whatever reason ... either at one's own making or God's delay. It may be that it is not time for the move to take place. It might just be that God is setting the stage. Or preparing you and the events that you may move into and within His purpose according to His timing. Or, it could be that through a series of events, one must first travel before getting to the place to acknowledge and answer the call or fulfilling God's plans for you.

It's also possible that one must first learn to hear or come to know when God has an assignment for you. Or as it was for me, some man or woman of God, being divinely put in place to reveal to you what they see or have seen God doing in your life. Thereby that person bringing forth a witness or confirming what you felt was occurring but could not make sense of things. Or it might be one simply responding "Yes" to God because they already know His voice or how God deals with them personally.

So, I came to say "Yes" to God. I answered His "*Call*" and agreed to enter into this unique relationship with Him as His spokesman or Prophet. However, I could not remotely conceive all that my " Yes " response to God would encompass! In November of 1992, I preached my initial sermon. Beforehand, and months earlier, Pastor Dr. William C. Turner Jr. presented me with a few questions to satisfy himself that I had been *Called* by God to preach. After I preached my initial sermon, the church agreed that I had been *Called*. I was then issued my license to proclaim the *Good News of Jesus*.

Shortly after preaching my initial sermon, I briefly talked with Pastor Turner. He is sincerely a decent man of God and a man of integrity. I often describe him as a gifted preacher and teacher to the preachers and a brother I love. He said to me, along these lines, "There will be challenges that await you as a preacher." And there has been! More so spiritually and/or emotionally!

However, at the time, I had no idea what he meant; additionally, his comment puzzled me and caused a small measure of uneasiness within my soul. Perhaps if he'd elaborated, I could have embraced his statement better. But also, from his leadership and that much-desired relationship I wanted and needed from him, I felt I could have significantly benefitted. But there was no such shepherding from him. I desired to be under his tutelage, to receive from my pastor the wisdom and guidance that I thought he could have provided. The relationship I had hoped for with my pastor never developed. I needed a friend! I longed for a father-type man to share their wisdom and insight with me.

No doubt, it would have served me well if pastor Turner explained his reason for sharing what he expressed to me. But even so, encouraging me as my pastor that he would be there to help guide me through whatever challenges I faced would have been reassuring. Reverend Lynch, on the other hand, had taken me under his wing. But, I did not receive such a relationship from this older pastor (approximately 17 years my senior). Sometime later, I respectfully expressed this, amongst other concerns I had with Reverend Turner's leadership or the lack thereof. I now realize that as gifted, caring, honorable, and much-loved person he was. He did not possess the *pastoral gifting needed* to lead God's people effectively.

I was twenty-seven when I was licensed to preach, a husband, and father of two sons. However, I longed for the wisdom, guidance, and relationship a strong African American brother or father figure could provide! I was one with the church yet separated from what I longed for, a godly relationship with some brother in Christ.

What was also apparent to me was the separation of others due to me being a police officer, especially those outside the church. Interestingly enough, living my life as a Christian brought about the same effect. And now that I had become a preacher, greater would be my isolation. My longing for true and faithful companionship was, at times, burdensome. I am now in my fifties, and that true and faithful godly fellowship with other brothers in Christ remains elusive. However, at this point in my life, I rather like the way things are. This time to myself has been just what God needed to bring me to where I am in life and that which I have accomplished through Him. I am glad about it! However, it would be so refreshing to occasionally meet with other godly and wisdom-filled brothers at the city's gate.

I would learn, far from it, that the life of a Christian, and certainly for pastors/preachers, to be a walk in the park. For those serious about the Word of God, your faith, and spiritual growth – various challenges may await you. For those who answer the call to preach, it will likely be multiple experiences of highs and lows that you will encounter and yet, be brought through stronger by God. It will be for the purpose of equipping you to become better servants in God's kingdom … this is within the will of God for you.

Me answering the call to preach, there would be much I would learn over the years ... my learning has not ceased. And though I wish that I had been better prepared through mentoring. Nonetheless, I now understand that we as Christians may need to go through some things to *become fit to fight the good fight of faith* (1 Corinthians 9: 25; Hebrews 12: 5-12; Timothy 4:7-11). As well as to become better equipped to help others along our Christian journey. And so, the fight continues!

Walking According To God's Purpose - The Silent Struggle

So, I'm now a preacher. I've been restored to a right mind in Jesus. I am leading my family as a man of God. And as one who is committed to the cause of Christ, things are moving along just fine.

There are songs we sing in the Church as we worship God and petition our Father *for more of Him.* And even that, we may *do more for Him.* Songs like "Closer to Thee," "I am Thine Oh Lord," and "Have Thine Own Way." Little is it realized by many new converts to Christianity, and some not so new. When we set our hearts and minds to enter into a closer relationship with our Father through prayer and song, there is the inevitable and often uncomfortable process of pruning and purging that our souls must undergo (John 15:2).

This process is that through which God will show His Redeemed – His children what we consist of, that which internally in-lives or inhabits us (like a virus) resulting from our fallen nature or unredeemed flesh. Resulting in the process of the pruning of our souls. There sprouts forth a change within Believers, a renewal or transformation of our minds. And subsequently, the fruit of the Spirit. This renewal, made possible by the Holy Spirit, enables one to overcome the practice of sinning.

When the pruning or purging discomfort is upon you, a process occurring in different ways or through different life experiences. Don't look at your challenging situation as if God is angry with you and, therefore, is punishing you for some sin you committed. This is not the case at all! Rather, such times should be embraced or understood as an occasion to be strengthened in our faith. These seasons should move us to call all the more on God as we put our total trust in Him. Though it may not seem like it at the time, this time of testing or disciplining is permitted because of God's love for us. Even so, to bring his children into a deeper, more dependent, loving relationship with Him. Make no mistake about it; our Father knows our pain and sorrow. He even hurts along with us (Hebrews 2:18 and 4:15,16).

Who goes through what training ... yes, even training, and for how long is the prerogative of the Father. *He knows just what we need and how much we can handle.* During our season of training, our responsibility is to put and keep our trust in our Father; trust the process while holding fast to such words as found in Scripture: *"God will put no more on you than you can bare."* Trust the process we must, as God will, *"Cause all things to work out for the good of those who love Him, who are the called according to His purpose."* Even so, *"To count it as joy as we go through trials of all sorts."*

These truths and instructions of God, and a significant amount of His teaching, I did not know or fully understand beforehand ... Before saying, "I will" to the proclamation of the Gospel of Jesus. Thereby adding to my lonely journey that of silent struggles. At the time, I did not realize just how much I did not know about Scripture or God, for that matter. As for me, I would have to go through seasons of training. And I'm not the only one before that greater understanding of God and His Word becoming real, alive or active, and relational within the soul of a Believer. God's Word quickening or becoming alive within me also resulted from looking back over my life as I consider what God had brought me through and where He had brought me to. With my rearward perspective, I could better see and have confidence in what God was doing in my life ... in my right now! And to trust Him all the more for my future. Because He alone holds my future and charts my course in this life.

I will admit, there were times, not as much, since I have matured in the Lord. I was troubled beyond what I cared to be at various testing and trials as a younger child of God. But now I can say even though I may not have initially responded to life's challenges the way I should have or hoped to. However, having matured in the Lord, I handle matters better. I've learned to trust my Father and give whatever the situation more quickly over to Him! He reigns Supreme and is Lord over everything!

I remember this one particular thought I had as I considered the idea of preaching. "If I'm to preach, I want to know what I'm talking about." Giving thought to that period in my life, I thought I knew a little something about the Bible. What little I did know was not sufficient for where God wanted to take me. And the work/ministry He desired to do through me.

It's correct for me to say that a bit of pride and/or self-sufficiency needed to be purged from within me. I remember thinking how my understanding of some Biblical matters had surpassed many who had grown up in the church or were long-standing members. I was soon to be humbled. That which I thought I knew, and my limited understanding or shallow rooting would be tested, even so, that I may become rooted deeper in my knowledge regarding the things or the mind of God. Now, just over three decades after saying "Yes" to the *Call*. I know that this deepening unto God or training offered by God is a lifelong process. However, the process is not nearly as challenging these days, although reaping the same spiritual benefit or growth.

I remind you that the remedy for not growing faint or becoming weary during testing or pruning is to find solace in the Word of God. Let me share this Word again: *"ALL things work together for good to them that love God, to those who are the called according to his purpose"* (Romans 8:28).

Also, consider and meditate on the following Scriptures: *"Count it all joy, my brothers (and sisters), when you meet trials of various kinds, for you know that the testing of your faith produces steadfastness. And let steadfastness have its full effect, that you may be perfect and lacking in nothing"* (James 1:2- 4).

"My child, don't reject the Lord's discipline, and don't be upset when he corrects you. For the Lord corrects those he loves, just as a father corrects a child in whom he delights (Proverbs 3:11, 12).

The refining work of our Father, His disciplining of His own, resulting from His love for us, may cause discomfort for a season. Nevertheless, seek God and trust His process. See the Father's loving care through what He is attempting to get us to see about ourselves. Having been pruned, purged, and/or disciplined, God has, in turn, equipped us and made us effective through our deepened faith and spiritual understanding to share His Good News of Jesus. And to stand against the wiles and assaults of Satan and life's challenges.

Too often, as Christians, we are unable or unwilling to see God at work in our lives, especially when the situation is one of suffering. Our pride or self-sufficiency may be the culprit behind this. Or there could be a lack of understanding pertaining to the will of God and how He accomplishes His purpose for the world and even for His children, not just through the good times but even so through the difficult times – our time of testing that we are deepened or grow closer to our Father.

Perhaps, you may have been taught to believe that God is punishing you or, better yet, getting back at you during your time of difficulty. Wrong thinking and struggling in isolation is where Satan wants to keep you. While in this state, he can weaken you or keep you from being effective for the Kingdom of God. For this reason, wrong thinking, including pride or even shame, some struggle and even suffer in silence and isolation when faced with life's challenges. This is where Satan wants you! Alone where you are most vulnerable to his attacks!

My first encounter with God's pruning and purging to mature me, although I didn't see it then, my rear perspective brought this into view. Wherein, He drawing me in deeper or closer unto Him was a season met with mental anguish and me suffering alone and in silence!

This experience was unlike anything I'd encountered since becoming a Christian. I attempted to but was unsuccessful in dismissing a thought and question that put me in this highly distressing state of mind. In my previous few experiences, when God provided or was trying to give me guidance, I could feel what I would describe as His urging or nudging within me. I also liken my experience with God directing me as a stirring, the lack of ease or even calm or peace about a matter I was considering.

This time the experience was quite different; it was unusual in that it created an intense unsettling within my soul! And I didn't like what I was being tested on! I was presented with an internal question on the day of the occurrence. I felt uncomfortable and challenged by the question. My immediate reaction was to dismiss or avoid addressing the matter. This question came from out of nowhere … It caught me off-guard, thereby causing me to be exposed, vulnerable, and troubled by the question!

Before this experience, perhaps a year or so prior. Although I felt that I knew a little about the Bible, I certainly thought that I knew more or at least had a better spiritual grasp of the Bible than many with whom I attended church. Just the same, I remember saying to myself, "If I'm going to preach, I want to know what I'm talking about.

Our Father knows our hearts; He intimately knows everything about us. He hears our prayers, even those not articulated but only given vague or subliminal mental recognition. Even so, the Spirit of God knows those deeper needs or longings of our soul. Though we may not have words to express our wants or are even aware of these needs, having entered into an agreement or covenant with God, He then answers these prayers or attends to our needs according to His purpose. And, too, that which works towards our spiritual benefit. In response to our heart's desires or spiritual needs, God will position us to receive what He knows is best for us. Surely God knows the plans He has for us (Jeremiah 29:11). They will be fulfilled when our hearts or set on Him.

On one beautiful spring morning, perhaps, as soon as the following spring or the year after preaching my initial sermon in December. I was sitting in my backyard studying the Word of God. And that troublesome question, like an uninvited guest, just showed up! I'd never considered this question. And yet it originated and resonated from within my soul. The question that shook me, thereby revealing my lack of faith and depth in God or that which exposed my shallow rooting, was, *"Why do you believe what you believe?"*

Initially, I was somewhat annoyed by the question. And therefore, I dismissed it, as it was not relevant to me - the preacher, a man who had been called of

God. As the minutes wore on, the question returned. *"Why do you believe what you believe?"* Maybe after being presented with the question for the third time, I was compelled to contemplate the matter.

After giving thought to the question, I discovered that I did not have a satisfactory response. Now, I'm really troubled within my soul! This question left me in doubt about my faith. I could not raise a good enough argument or apologetic reply to satisfy why *I had chosen* the Christian faith. And that *One - Jesus the Christ*, which I believed I was called to proclaim. I was troubled and deeply disturbed, realizing I did not have a sufficient answer.

My mother had embraced the Christian faith as a child. However, as a family, we had never attended church. My mother told me while I was in the military and going through a tough time dealing with racism that I needed to find Jesus for myself. Interestingly, I can recall attending a Wednesday night Bible study. At the time, I was not a preacher. I don't remember saying "Yes" to the Call of God. I don't think this was the case. However, I clearly remember saying during Bible study, "I don't want to believe in the Christian faith simply because my mother did." Perhaps I remember this moment, as I can recall the mystified look on Pastor Turner's face when I said this.

I spoke those words from my heart, although I had no idea or expected any outcome from my utterance. Within the Christian community, you may hear, "Be careful about what you ask for or the words you speak." And if, in fact, we are mindful of what we are asking God for. We must then trust Him and welcome the process as He answers our prayer while providing for us what we need according to His plans for those who are His. As a result of our prayers, we may not get exactly what we want, but God will certainly give us what we need!

* * *

My Christian faith and foundation not solidly laid, or my roots deep within my Christian belief; the question, "Why do I believe what I believed," caused me to waver in my faith. My automatic counter to the question and as for the way I was made to feel, I attribute this dreadful experience to an attack from Satan.

He was, in fact, and remains, the author of confusion! Even so, that one or through his demonic agents is capable of causing doubt in the minds of Christians. Surely, he had infiltrated my thoughts; his influence of evil had come against me. He somehow got into my head and was now waging war with my mind. Make no mistake about it; he is waging war for the influence over our minds! The fiery arrow of Satan had hit its target - my mind.

Here I was, a young preacher; I found myself silently struggling to hold on to the faith I was called to proclaim. The question exposed my roots and lack of depth in my Christian faith. My emotions ranged from embarrassment to anxiety and confusion. This could have ended tragically for me because I had no one I could confidentially share what an emotional wreck I'd become. Secretly and in silence, I was suffering.

This deep troubling within my spirit ... the isolation and mental anguish I underwent lasted better than a year. The only thing I knew to do. And what proved to be the right thing and the only thing that I may get the help I needed was to remain in the Word of God in order to counter this opposition! I toiled, digging and mining through Scripture to get answers. I would find the answer to one question through searching, and another question would arise.

I endured this process of searching and digging, knocking, and getting answers, while silently suffering in isolation, without anyone knowing - not even my wife. I didn't want anyone to know what I was dealing with. Because I couldn't help myself, neither did I want anyone else to potentially experience what I was going through.

I now know that having doubts or questions that can only be resolved through exploring the Bible is perfectly fine. However, it was quite later that I realized that this may very well be the process that God might set before those who belong to Him; this is what relational building with God is all about...getting answers to questions.

I finally arrived at a place in my seeking Biblical understanding that my faith and knowledge were deepening. My roots, having dug deeper into God's truths. The peace and comfort I had lost were beginning to be restored. Through a firm or better understanding of Scripture, I was becoming equipped to be a stronger Christian. As well, my personal or intimate relationship with God was slowly developing. So it is … *"Faith comes by hearing and hearing by the Word of God"* (Romans 10:17).

Beloved of God. It is normal that questions or even doubt may be a part of your Christian journey… so don't be hard on yourself. Just keep digging into the Word of God! As stated, I thought the *question* originated from a demonic assault on my mind. However, as I've matured in the Lord or have also come to this place in my understanding. I wholeheartedly embrace this truth: That God was asking me the *question*. He wanted me to get closer to Him. He wanted our relationship to be strengthened, leading to me having a stronger faith as a Christian and spiritually strengthened and mature as His son.

From this experience, I have learned to never again suggest that Satan has this kind of leverage or influence over me. As a child of God, spiritual wickedness does not have the kind of control over me that I attributed to it; unless I yield to his influence and evil ways! Yes, the fiery arrows of Satan may come our way. But here is the most critical thing and fact to remember. God may test His own; however, spiritual wickedness always tempts us or floods our thoughts to do evil … this is never the case with God!

As for the question, *"Why do you believe what you believe?"* What loving parent doesn't question their child occasionally to ensure that they fully understand their expectations or their will for their child? Or by presenting this testing or questioning to ensure that a child knows what they are supposed to know and that no one trips their child up or leads their Beloved astray. This is how a loving and caring parent ensures their child has at work within themselves, their mind, or guidance. And this being for the child's good! A protective parent preps their child for life, testing them beforehand as they prepare to send them out with the right thinking and deep rooting to survive in this cruel and dangerous world. They want to make sure that their child is adequately equipped. This is love. This establishes a trusting and enduring relationship between a parent and their child. This questioning equips or causes the child to become strengthened for life's challenges, although a child may be slow to grasp this kind of love coming from a parent. This was just what God did for me!

The question I now see was God's way of showing and/or causing me to see things about Him and myself that I had not considered. Even so, this line of questioning being the only way for me to draw closer and dependent upon Him.

This final note: Never should a child of God have to experience going through a trying or difficult time alone! And certainly, if they belong to an organized assembly of God's people. That is a Church where the love and compassion of Jesus are preached. And where care and love for one another through the Holy Spirit are supposed to be demonstrated. And in so doing, abounding to the praise and glory of the Father. There you have it ... A child of God should never suffer secretly, silently, and alone!

If you are not part of a body of Believers, therefore, having no godly brother or sister in your life who can offer you support. Then do as I did, remain in God through his Word. *My God will never forsake or leave you (Hebrews 13:5).* Additionally, find other good Christian resources to read. Maintain your faith; remain in a constant relationship with the Father. Until such time, He unites you with a faithful body of Believers – those who follow after Jesus that His will may be performed in you and through you!

CHAPTER 15

Darkened Days - The Light Overcomes the Night

For all outside of the Salvific Grace of Jesus, the Bible declares they are spiritually dead. And therefore, the *children of Darkness* - their father, Satan. However, to receive Jesus as Lord and Savior is for one to embrace and become one with the *Light of The World - Jesus!*

And thereby becoming *children of the Day* (1 Thessalonians 5:5).

As children of *Light* and *Life*, we are to be representatives of Jesus while dwelling here on earth. Just as it was for Jesus, who was opposed by evil-influenced people or spiritual darkness (Satan) of this world. Don't be surprised – though I believe it is rare when the direct forces of evil come against you in an attempt to put out your light. Or to destroy you or your family! In chapter seventeen, I will share how my wife and I had evil or spiritual darkness come against us, unlike anything I had previously encountered!

We must always keep before us that our warfare is not against man – that is, against flesh and blood, some other person who Satan may be utilizing. Rather, our battles are spiritual (Ephesians 6:12). It is rightly stated that we (Christians) have dual citizenship ... our temporary sojourn here on earth (as spirit beings clothed with flesh) where we encounter satanic spiritual resistance. And our permanent residence (we are patiently anticipating) when Jesus makes all things new, and then our spiritual self clothed anew with a sinless body.

As the Word of God informs us, the heaven that encompasses this earth as we currently know it *"Will one day be rolled up like a scroll."* Afterward, the children of Light will be settled within our new bodies. And given unto us our new earthly and heavenly home.

Children of the Day, we must comprehend our spiritual reality – our true identity. Only then can we clearly see and understand the spiritual darkness or the forces of evil that oppose us as children of the Light.

My sisters and brothers, if we hope to be victorious in this bleak world and not overcome by darkness … we must then walk in the Light. This is our only hope from being ensnared or engulfed by spiritual darkness.

Where light is cut off, as with a light switch; where *Power* is interrupted even momentarily, in rushes the dark! As children of the Day, we cannot take for granted the necessity of abiding in Jesus, *the Light of the world,* and relying on the *empowering* that comes from the Holy Spirit! Indeed we must be careful not to turn off the *Switch* and our *Power from on High* by our actions or inaction!

As I think things over, I see how God preserved my soul from darkness' grip! I was indeed a child of Satan, as are all the unsaved. But the love and mercy of God kept me from sudden destruction. Immediately upon accepting Jesus as my Lord and Savior, my contract or covenant with Satan and/or Death were annulled … Our breakup occurred during the Spring of nineteen eighty-four. I was, therefore, no longer one with Darkness or Death. Jesus' death had freed me from Satan! At that moment, I became a child of the *Day.* However, my candle only flickered - and on more occasions than I care to give thought to, did not put forth light at all. It was those times when I chose to consciously partake of sin before I matured in the Lord and remained in the Light, whereby my candle emitted a steady radiance.

I learned some things as I faithfully studied the Word of God or remained in the Light. The most significant spiritual insight I acquired was regarding the prophetic Word of God – His foretelling the future. What was fascinating about my God and Faithful Companion was seeing that when He said something was going to happen or come to pass (the prophetic word) … it did! Indeed, my God is trustworthy! At this point, my silent struggle with doubt, resulting from the question, "Why do you believe what you believe" was a thing of my past.

My faith had been restored, and my candle was once again flickering. But I did not have displaying from within my soul a steady and consistent radiance needed to be a strong and victorious Christian, let alone a preacher in this darkened world!

Also, behind me, but not that far (a year or two at best), was my season of adultery, again of which my wife had no idea I'd engaged. It wasn't until about a decade later that I told her of my unfaithfulness. I was now free from those dark days of sexual immorality and doubt. I had purposed in my heart to live in obedience to God and to be that beacon of light He *Called* me to be. My purpose towards doing right was in reverence for my God, but not fully understanding that I had also enlisted into a God-ordained marital commitment of sorts with Him, nor all that this union's development would entail. However, I was not spiritually equipped; I remained ignorant of the Holy and sacred institution of marriage or oneness with my Father; therefore, spiritual darkness would make another approach at hindering me or even destroying me. Our destruction is Satan's endgame! However, I would conquer darkness as I learned to dwell in the Light of God and His Truth!

I don't believe anything unusual was occurring in my life when this assault upon my mind came. Perhaps, there was some residual effect from my season of whoredom that brought on this new conflict. Whatever it may have been, I knew that I was highly vulnerable to, once again, being overtaken by sexual sin. And again, in silence, I would suffer and struggle.

Previously, I had gotten caught up in sexual sin; now, I found myself contemplating how I would return to it. I tell you, what I was dealing with was unlike anything I'd encountered. Here I was, about two years in, as a preacher of the Gospel. Therefore, my union with Him being more significant and/or consequential if I fail to remain faithful! There would be more at stake, towards the hurt of my brothers and sisters in Christ, and others, if I failed to remain faithful to Jesus. I have told you, "Satan wants your marriage!" He desires to destroy the union you share with your spouse, even so, the union you share with Jesus, to Whom all born-again Believers belong!

Once again, in silence and isolation. This time I was indeed struggling against spiritual darkness for mastery of my mind and, subsequently, my flesh. Pastor Turner had said, "There would be challenges that awaited me" as a young preacher. He didn't discuss what they might be; he didn't suggest how to handle or safeguard myself against them, and neither was he there for me as I struggled. I was all alone … But God knew my heart and my struggles! Therefore, He would be there for me and see to it that I came through as a Victor!

This spiritual warfare was unrelenting! That constant nemesis was beating at my mind and tormenting my thoughts! Urging and pressing upon me to return to sexual sin (Romans 7:21)! This time, there was no seductress. It was me against me - my mind or thoughts, contemplating how to go about committing sexual immorality. The struggle was real! My dark and evil thoughts were seemingly winning out; it was only a matter of time before I would surrender my mind and body to what Satan – the Prince, the Ruler of the darkness of this world wanted me to do.

I was a man in body but infantile and weak spiritually. My lack of understanding of the matters of spiritual maturity and spiritual attacks left me vulnerable! Even though I possessed a greater conscious and/or conviction of right and wrong (this results from the indwelling Holy Spirit), I was being worn down daily so that I might give in to the temptation of sin.

True it is, one can wrongly justify their wrong or sinful behavior if they desire to do so … I had arrived at this place of perverted reasoning! Although I had not committed sexual sin in my thoughts. Or actions (Matthew 5:28; James 1:15). Nevertheless, I was considering what women would be in play and how things must take shape that I may be able to justify, in my twisted and evil logic, engaging them sexually.

What's crazy about all this ... I had a clearer sense of right and wrong than I had previously. However, not being well versed in Scripture, I did not have the *Power of the Word of God* to counter my evil thinking or the assault that was coming against me. Consequently, I was attempting to do battle under my own strength and was desperately struggling ... and at the brink of falling! However, the Spirit of God within me did not leave me alone or give me over to sin. In other words, my renewed spirit or awakened consciousness was troubled by what I was considering. This is one sign; there are others that indicate the Spirit's indwelling one who is a child of God. My brothers and sisters in Christ. This is precisely what you want to occur if you are considering or even ignorantly walking into sin; this uneasiness or troubling of your spirit! This is the convicting work of the indwelling Holy Spirit. Even so, the very real battle or conflict we face that's either prompted from without or from within ourselves. That one may not enter into sin! This was what I was faced with. And yet, I came forth victorious! O' for the grace of God!

People, I want you to understand what I experienced was different from merely having a passing or momentary sinful thought. Satan wanted me back! ... The struggle weighed me down and pressed against me daily. He wanted my mind and my body! When I was whoring around, I didn't feel what I was now experiencing! I tell you, my battle against this spiritual darkness wanted to take hold of me!

The Apostle Paul no doubt knew what I and each of us would go through while in this body of flesh. He said in Romans 7:24, "*Oh, what a miserable person I am. Who will free me from this life that is dominated by sin and death?*" Paul gives the answer in the following verse ... It would be Jesus - our *Help and Strength!* However, one remains powerless when they don't know Him in His power and/or the efficacy of His Word. When you don't have or are not armed with the sword of the Spirit, which is the Word of God, you can't fight against the wiles of Satan.

By the grace of God, I did not give in to sin ... I was therefore victorious! I was able, but not easily, to rid Satan, powerless over me. I cannot recount how it all came about. But the pivotal moment was when I, by the aid of the Holy Spirit, realized that thought alone or being tempted to sin isn't sinful within itself. Not until the act of sin is either carried out in one's mind. Or the sinful misconduct engaged outwardly has sin been committed. What I do know … is that there was an opposition that I was waging against. And if conquered or having succumbed to the temptation, I would have given myself over to sin! This one thing was clear to me!

A look again at how the force of wickedness came against me. Whether it was from within my fallen self (sin-nature). Or it was the fiery arrows of Satan, I'm unsure. Just the same, Satan is the root of all evil. As mentioned, I had been considering committing sin … but I didn't.

At some point, I realized, thereby loosening Satan's grip on my mind: *Though a thought or Satan's fiery dart may momentarily find its way into one's thinking, this is not necessarily sinful.* However, even if one inadvertently finds themselves entertaining a wicked thought. Once you shut the thought down … repent due to entertaining evil. The matter of sin has effectively been dealt with. The issue of sin is over and forgotten by God! And so should it be over and forgotten by you!

But Satan doesn't want you to know that dealing with him can be that easy. He would rather have you condemn and beat yourself up. And run somewhere and cower! But, our Father has told us. *There is, therefore, now no condemnation for those who are in Christ Jesus. For the law of the Spirit of life has set you free in Christ Jesus from the law of sin and death* (Romans 8:1, 2). I recommend that you open your Bible and read the entire chapter. You will find it liberating, encouraging, and strength for your soul!

What I had to learn about temptation before I could be freed from its power over me: 1) Don't condemn or beat yourself up when tempted. 2) To be tempted is not equivalent to committing sin. 3) When you are tempted, it doesn't mean you are weak; instead, it's an opportunity to grow even stronger while in the fight against sin as you abide in the Power and the Light of God's Word. 4) To be tempted in some manner or another is a way of life. Just continue to allow your light to shine and be not overtaken by darkness. Therein you stand as the victor. 5) When tempted, tell God all about it. *Cast your cares before Him, for He cares about you* (1 Peter 5:7). It is also great to have someone to share your struggles with ... we all need this support. For me, it is my wife.

Confession Is Good For The Soul

As mentioned, there was that one time when I didn't freely discuss things with my wife ... That was when I was caught up in sin. When I finally decided to share the matter with my wife. Initially, I provided the story in part. It was a year or so later before I would give her the full account of my gross betrayal of our marriage.

I was then freed from the lie of my making and my conscious clear before my wife and our God! However, another disturbing and unique matter arose that I had not addressed with my wife. Nor did I even consider bringing forth my concern involving this other woman to her. Besides, I had not done anything wrong and had no intentions of doing so. Things were as they were; I would simply have to deal with it. However, I was clueless about how to deal with what I was faced with.

I really don't recall how long this interesting yet potentially problematic situation involving this other woman, who was also married, came to be. There is not much to say other than I was highly attracted to this woman the first time I saw her several years earlier. My attraction toward her was non-sexual. Our few times of interaction were only in passing ... a mere hello, a cordial acknowledgment, and a smile were all there ever was between us.

However, somehow or another, she, her husband, Lisa, and I became rather sociable when we saw one another while out and about. Whenever we all saw one another, which wasn't frequent, we stopped and engaged in friendly conversation. Meanwhile, my nerves were on edge – hence my problem! I am rather good at reading the body language of people. And so, I am uneasy, wondering if anyone is reading mine. My great concern: was my wife, this woman, or her husband, picking up on the fact that I was highly attracted to this woman?

While writing this chapter of my book, for the first time, I felt I should share with my wife what I was experiencing regarding this woman. What I came to realize, as I shared with my wife, what I had been experiencing is that she possessed similar physical characteristics that Cierra had. Not until then had I realized my natural inclination toward such women. One other woman possessing the same physical attributes whom I'd encountered before I got married also had such an effect on me. The takeaway from sharing this: is that I can freely express myself to my wife about anything. Secondly, when I shared with my wife what I had been feeling and the pressure I was under, the weight I had been carrying was immediately lifted. *Confession is good for the soul!*

Ironically, within a few days after this conversation with my wife, I saw this woman at the mall. She was not with her husband, and neither was Lisa with me. I felt so liberated, having shared things with my wife. I felt overwhelming freedom to share with this woman not only what I had felt about her. But also my talk with my wife regarding my attraction toward her. And how I was made to feel because of it. She simply listened, smiled, and we went on about our way. People, that was every bit six years ago. Interestingly, I have not seen her or her husband since.

If you are a child of the Day, let your light shine! Don't give way or place to darkness. Those evil forces are operating from without or that which is from within. Over darkness, we are to gain mastery. We can and will if we walk in and remain one with *the Light of the world – Jesus!*

I had now been set free from the grip of Satan, *the Prince of Darkness*! Sexual sin became a thing of my past. Therefore, *"This little light of mine, I'm going to let it shine … let it shine … let it shine … let it shine!"*

CHAPTER 16

A New Millennium
A Better Me - A Broken Her

I believe the year was two thousand, the dawn of a New Millennium. Approximately nine years had passed since I violated my marriage. For the next two or so years beginning in the twenty-first century, my wife would experience and endure the most distressing season of her life. Some sixteen years into this new era, while working on this book, I asked my wife when did I share with her that I had been unfaithful. On that day of partly disclosing the ultimate betrayal of marriage to my wife, this "took her breath away!" It caused "time to stand still" for her, and she said that her "body went numb!" This moment is forever etched in her memory. Without hesitation, she responded to my question, "July 4th, 11:15 am." The year, we are unclear, likely nineteen-ninety-eight or nine.

On that day, I only disclosed a portion of my truth of unfaithfulness. At that time, I only welcomed a brief discussion on the matter. As far as I was concerned, what I did was a thing of my distant past. Therefore, we were to simply put it behind us and move on. We did just that … so I thought. I said all I desired to say and answered only the questions I wanted to answer that my wife had for me. She did not push the matter. It was and is not in her nature to do so. I thank God for such a wife! We eventually moved beyond this moment, and all was well within the Scotts' home.

But roughly two years later, a slow resurrection of her hurt would begin in February of two thousand. This would come about due to an unimaginable succession of demonic assaults, targeting my wife in an attempt to destabilize and ultimately bring down my home … *The enemy wanted my marriage!* Yet again, he had working on his behalf, another human adversary and his agent! Along with this assault, my wife would have to also deal with life's challenges and crises that came her way.

As for me, spiritually, I'd arrived at a better place. I was a better me. For this reason, I wanted to set things right with my wife. I'd kept my infidelity a secret long enough. I'd always cherished the fact that I had been able to talk to my wife about anything. However, regarding my unfaithfulness, this had not been the case. Now, the time had arrived for me to come clean. I felt a strong conviction about this. I knew in my spirit that my marriage would not be moved or suffer due to my speaking the truth. Howbeit, at my first sharing with the wife of my folly, it would only be in part. I just knew Lisa would champion over this adverse situation of my making. Besides, what I did, occurred almost a decade earlier.

Totally oblivious to how this truth would affect my wife; nonetheless, I felt confident that she would be just fine simply because I had chosen to come forth with my lie and unfaithfulness. I thought she would commend my honesty and see in this my intentions to continue to do right by her. My assumption was correct in part. A year or so later, I was confident that my wife had dealt with my truth and betrayal rather well. But then, like a relentless cascade, Lisa would be pounded by life's happenings for the next three years or so. And, too, that demonic attack that I mentioned earlier! With these things coming at my wife, I became concerned about her well-being, and doubt about our marriage would arise for me. As I look back on that time, I say it was only by the grace of God that she came through as a Victor. And not just standing, but with her unwavering love for me still intact, and the strength and the impeccable character she's always displayed throughout our union, untainted.

Lisa will not hesitate to say that I have always been a good husband and father. Because I'd not given my wife a reason to think otherwise, my violating our marriage created a great challenge and conundrum for her. As we talked about my unfaithfulness years later, I discovered from my wife that she could not reason how her husband, who consistently did everything he should be doing as a husband and father, could have done such a thing! From the pain that my grief-stricken wife endured; the experiences we shared and persevered through, I emerged even a better man - enlightened and unwaveringly committed as a husband.

In chapter twelve and elsewhere, I mentioned that I was trying to live my life acceptable to God. Perhaps you had this question, "What about doing right by your wife by telling her what you had done at that time? As far as I was concerned, there was nothing to get right with my wife at this point in my life. You see, my secret life of indiscretion or whoredom, was just that – clandestine and safely concealed. My secret had not been discovered by my wife. I had not been so reckless, even uncaring in my actions and misdoings, to cause my wife to suspect I had betrayed her in the most horrible of ways.

Something is to be said about ... "What one doesn't know won't hurt them." And by no means am I saying this to give anyone this avenue as an out, and not accepting responsibility, nor to lie or to be deceitful or to avoid acknowledging the wrong you may have done to some other. However, there are times when your wrongdoing or sinful behavior initially or even only needs to be brought before God. On the other hand, when you knowingly have wronged someone or even think you have and certainly have been told as much. You must make your wrong right.

That said, when the wrong is brought to your attention, it is morally correct and your obligation to make things right with whomever you offended, even for your conscious sake. If you are a sincere Christian who desires to do right by God – trust me, though you may not initially see where your actions or words may have caused offense. Or not seeing the necessity to revisit some past, unresolved matter, or secret. Your walk with God, and your growing closer to Him, will cause your spiritual eyes to gain insight or understanding. In this, your heart is being fashioned after the likeness of our Father in heaven. Spiritual sensitivity and discernment are integrated within this renewal or maturation process. Therefore, you will be compelled to set right your wrong(s). This compulsion is the operation of the Spirit of God within you!

With this transformation occurring within your soul, you will find that you can't just say or treat people, let alone your spouse, in any kind of way and not be troubled in heart or convicted by the Holy Spirit. Such will be that troubling or stirring within your soul that you will be compelled to set the matter right with whomever you've wronged – for conscious sake, peace within, or just the mere fact that it's the right thing to do. Nevertheless, being free will imagers of God, we can resist the Spirit.

Though the matter of my whoredom was a thing of my past. Listen to what my wife said to me after my initial and partial confession … "It feels like what you did just happened." Later on, following some two years of peace and harmony in our marriage, circumstances would dictate my coming forth with full disclosure of my wrongdoings. And so … this was the onset of a time that would be the most challenging and devastating season ever encountered by my wife.

How I arrived at the place where I was initially – howbeit only in part, truthful with my wife was the result of my spiritual development. During the process of my spiritual maturity, I recall reading "*Loose That Man and Let Him Go,*" a book by T.D. Jakes. As well as a couple other books that interest me.

T.D. Jakes' book at that time in my life really spoke to me. It was informative and liberating … just what I needed! His book kindled a fire within my soul, which caused me to want to purge myself from the secret, and lie I'd kept from my wife for all this time.

Days before that 4th day of July, I had decided to reveal my wrongdoings (the partial story) to my wife. However, this went against my mother's concerned advisement … I had consulted with her. It was not that I wanted her advice; I simply wanted to inform her of my intentions. As with any loving parent, she offered her opinion; she thought this truth would be "too much for Lisa to handle." However, I was convinced that honesty was the best and only option for me and my house as I moved forward as a righteous but not perfect husband. This was before I came to know the following Proverb: *He that covers his sins shall not prosper, but whoso confess and forsake them shall have mercy* (Proverbs 28:13).

Furthermore, I was confident and had an inner peace that I attribute to the Spirit of God, that my wife would forgive me for the wrong I'd done because our marriage was as strong as it was. Moreover, I had not openly or discernably neglected my marital responsibilities during my season of folly and great crime of wickedness against my marriage.

On that most memorable day, July 4th, I lay across our bed, preparing to share my criminal act of sin with my wife. I had decided not to go into the details. I didn't see the need, as I couldn't see how full disclosure would be helpful, considering all I'd done. Not only did I think full disclosure would be counterproductive. I will also admit that I lacked complete confidence to address the questions she may have wanted answers to. My thinking ... Acknowledge that I had committed adultery. And make It clear that it was a thing of my past. Entertain a few questions, and we would then simply move on.

While preparing to write this section of my book, I asked my wife if she could remember the morning leading up to the bombshell I dropped on her. She responded, "We had just finished making love." Well then ... I guess I thought sexual intimacy would allow things to work in my favor. Just the same, I earnestly desired to come clean. Attempting to reassure my wife. She then added that I said, "You know that I love you? What I am about to say to you is not your fault." Lisa says, "She then sits up." I then proceeded to tell her that I'd been unfaithful and that it was about ten years ago. As I have mentioned, I thought this length of time would work in my favor and ease any hurt or uncertainty my wife might have.

In concluding my forthcoming summary of my foolishness, I felt relief and even good about confessing my wrong. It was my wife's right to ask me any questions she had of me. But again, I felt that responding to all of her questions would not have been beneficial, and assuredly not towards her mental well-being. I thought that I had said enough. Saying more at that time would have been too much for me to handle. And even more so for my wife.

My wife asked me, "How many women have I been with?" I answered – "Six." She wanted to know, "Who were the women?" I was unwilling to answer this question, as she was familiar with at least two of them. She also wanted to know, "How did this happen?" "Where and when did this occur?" I had said all that I wanted to say; I had voluntarily acknowledged my wrong; as far as I was concerned - it was time to move on. Knowing this, my wife had no choice but to cease with her questions. Well, she did for that day. My wife was noticeably hurt and perplexed as a result of everything she came to know. And even that, for which she did not receive an answer. Nevertheless, she maintained her composure and did not "go off," – meaning she did not become argumentative or combative.

My wife's calm and caring demeanor are just two of several attributes I've come to greatly appreciate about her ... a woman of God who He prepared just for me! She was not going to forcefully challenge or rise up against me. Her nature is that of a peaceable spirit. She is not given to conflict and confusion ... what a blessing my wife continues to be for me and others. Despite the tremendous hurt and grief I caused her, she still endeavored to honor me, care for our sons, and maintain her home.

I will say that being the man I am, my wife "going off" on me was not something I would have accepted. My response would have been to turn a deaf ear to her. We both are reasonable people; nasty and hurtful arguments are not something we engage in. Such outburst of emotions in times of marital or relational discord does not accomplish a thing. Instead, uncontrolled emotions in the time of relational tension create an environment that worsens things. If in a time of relational tension and conflict, where things are not managed reasonably and delicately, this can lead to the demise of what was a good and strong relationship. Therefore, don't weaponize your words due to unrestrained emotions and hurt. Like a bullet shot from a gun, a punch thrown, or a kick delivered.

It's imperative to be aware of rising relational tension. Then back off if you feel you are about to "go off" on the person you are to display love to. Your words can't be retracted! Don't let your flesh/tongue get the best of you ... don't give

Satan a foothold (Ephesians 4: 26, 27; 1 Peter 3:7). Your words and your action in times of conflict can have a devastating and long-lasting effect on your relationship.

If conflict resolution is not your strength, get help to improve in this area. Or find a qualified and/or mutually respected godly mediator to assist you with overcoming relational discord. At the same time, pray to God to release you from the hurt and anger due to betrayal. Or whatever it may be that is causing you to fail in this area of conflict resolution. Additionally, see what God has to say to you through His Word on the subjects of anger, hurt, and how to deal with problems and challenges ... God has an answer and the solution for you! It really is in *His Word*!

Beloved, even amidst your hurt and pain, you must guide and/or keep your tongue in subjection and conduct yourself in a godly manner. Beloved, you must also seek to understand the matter and the reason behind what has brought about this contention and your grief; then, be ready to forgive for the sake of all involved, even those indirectly impacted.

As for the offender, you must be patient or long-suffering, showing empathy and understanding towards the one you wronged. Understand that recovery or healing may take a little time. And so, conflict resolution is not about who wins the argument or gets in the last word ... instead, it's about reaching a godly outcome - bringing about healing and reconciliation.

* * *

Ending my brief discussion with my wife, she was obviously troubled. I didn't quite grasp the counsel I now provide you ... that of patience towards my wife's recovery, understanding, and empathy for her hurt. However, more than I could observe or even could have understood at the time, my meager consolation and partial truth offered no relief for my wife ... how could it? It was my hope and expectation. That this period of my wife's grief would be short-lived.

Although talks of the matter ended for the day, I had not considered that my wife would return with questions. Over the next few days, or a week or so, Lisa would periodically revisit the matter. She wanted answers, she needed answers - or so she thought. It's human nature to seek understanding for things we don't understand.

I greatly underestimated the injury that my actions brought upon my wife. I really thought Lisa would be able to move forward quicker than she did. I was wrong in thinking; time and distance from my season of sinful folly would minimize her hurt.

At one point, because she persisted with her questions, I wrongly assumed that my wife was attempting to stir things up. Or that she was looking for and out or an exit from our marriage. This was not the kind of person she was; she simply wanted answers. She wondered, "How could this happen to her?… And from the husband she loved? Who had done nothing to indicate that he had been acting in such an outrageous way?" The fact that I told her she'd done nothing wrong; made no sense to her. She could not reconcile this fact with her reasoning. She desperately needed an end and clarity for her unanswered questions. She was in need of peace of mind, which I had taken from her.

Beyond the two years after my partial disclosure of my wrong, neither following my full admission of my wickedness and the life challenges that came at my wife, I would grow to understand that the healing she desperately needed would not come in the answers to her questions alone nor *the healing of time*. However, her relief would come in time with me being patient, caring, understanding, and anything else within reason she needed from me. And certainly, not least of which, the comfort, guidance, and restorative work of her soul; this could only be provided by the Holy Spirit.

So there was that day of my partial confession, with my wife's brief questioning ending shortly thereafter. It would actually take a little longer than I'd anticipated before Lisa stopped pursuing questions from me. When she did, I, therefore, wrongly concluded that my wife was able to completely put behind her the injury I inflicted upon her and that her wound had healed when the questions stopped. In silence, I imagine she undoubtedly had her moments of wonder, perhaps even times of distress. Nevertheless, she championed forward, seamlessly from what I perceived doing what she always did as a wife and mother.

Lisa wanted her marriage to survive the storm of my making. Her love for me had never diminished ... this she later told me. Her way of coping and attempting to go on with life with some sense of normalcy, in Lisa's words, *"I block from my mind what you did."*

Punch After Punch and Staggered - But God Offered Reassurance and Consolation

Approximately two years had passed since I'd revealed to my wife my partial truth. Just the same, things were moving along quite well for us. There were no signs, at least not apparent, that she was bothered or remained hurt by the revelation of my abhorrent adulterous past. It was typical for my wife to portray herself as being "Ok" when this may not have been the case. Or for her to say that she was "Fine," and this not necessarily so. It was years after my wife's crisis (mine as well, but to a lesser degree) had passed before I realized this was her method of dealing or not dealing with things. As I write this book, she tells me she had "always been this way." When I learned this was her tendency, I informed my wife that this was not a good practice.

I shared with her that she was not being true to her feelings. And that this could give way to an eruption of emotions over something minor if she kept her feelings bottled up, adding she wasn't being true to our marriage. Now, let me ease your mind. In no way did I make this statement to be held in comparison to my lie. Not even remotely! Besides, what I had done was now years behind us.

Is it possible that one can be hurting emotionally and freely and willingly give of themselves entirely to the one who has caused them injury? I think not! Wherein the case of my wife or anyone dealing with relational hurt. In particular, where addressing the hurt has been neglected or disregarded altogether. Or where an apology has not been given, or forgiveness extended. For the hurting, I say they aren't operating from love and free will, but instead duty or obligation to their spouse. This is not good! Resentment can arise when matters of hurt are not adequately addressed. Slowly a relationship can erode when genuine love ceases to be exercised but instead spousal duty.

My wife is a woman of few words; she is just a down-to-earth person. Nevertheless, Lisa or anyone for that matter, and for whatever reason, not expressing their pain or feelings about things that truly matter or concerns they may have is counterproductive to a healthy marriage … where love, care, and affection are to be freely given and truly desired in return. And not merely some duty-bound response from the one who is hurting. This does not represent the love of God. No caring spouse should want their Beloved to perform, in whatever manner, out of duty or obligation!

As I mentioned, things were good with my wife and me for the first two years after my confession. We were indeed going forward with our lives quite well. There was no doubt in my mind that my marriage was steadfast and unmovable! However, a series of events, like punches … one occurrence, in particular, caused my wife to be spiritually or emotionally staggered! And for me to also believe, at the time, my marriage had also been severely stunned and on the brink of collapse. It was one event or punch after another, with one of those blows or assaults I am thoroughly convinced came from the influence of *Darkness* in an attempt to knock out my marriage permanently!

The first of these events: This one I will describe as the beginning of the buildup began when Mario, our oldest son, entered high school. Although this event or punch was delivered in 1998, this strike's delayed effect hit Lisa emotionally in 2002. Mario was soon to graduate from high school. This by itself was tough on Lisa. But adding to her heartache, Mario was headed off to the United States Marines – yet another punch! And, if that wasn't hard enough on her, the terrorist attacks on America had occurred on September 11, 2001, a mere 10 months or so before Mario would begin his active-duty status – this being a punch also! Lisa's love for her sons and their relationship is truly special! For my wife, the thought of harm coming to either of them is unbearable. Also, during this season, my wife had to undergo knee surgery. And, too, a punch!

Now, a daughter's love for her mother is also something special. Lisa's love for her mother was just that – special! The same year that Mario graduated from high school, Lisa's mother, Elsie Williams Goddard Land, health began to decline ... A breathtaking punch to my wife! The following year, on May 12, 2003, and two days following Mother's Day, Lisa's mother passed away in her hometown of Williamston, North Carolina. Lisa was devastated! This punch not only took my wife's breath away, but it was also a devastating blow that seized her physical and mental fortitude! These events or punches were wearing my wife down ... she had no doubt been stunned! To this very day, Lisa has what I've chosen to call her mommy moments.

The passing of Lisa's mother was indeed a devastating blow. While dazed, my wife nevertheless faithfully pressed on while maintaining her home and other responsibilities as a mother and wife. However, three months before Lisa's mother's death, my wife encountered a most sinister and even diabolical punch. Her mother's passing caused the effect of that *hellish strike or demonic assault* on my wife to be exacerbated! My wife was now staggering; my marriage was in jeopardy ... well, this is what I thought at the time. My wife couldn't do or say anything to make me feel any different. How could she? She was fighting desperately to stay upright and maintain her sanity.

If what you've heard thus far isn't enough for one person to have to bear. Now factor this in as well. My wife was also experiencing her own health issues regarding uterine fibroids. This matter had been causing Lisa varying degrees of pain and discomfort for years. To address her ailment, Lisa decided to have surgery in June 2003. This entailed her having a partial hysterectomy. The procedure occurred the month following her mother's transition.

As I consider that period from two-thousand-and-two to two-thousand-and-three, only now can I see the big picture as I reflect on and write about those occurrences that so drastically worked against my family's stability! During this time, I hadn't considered - not even remotely the accumulative toll these punches were taking on my wife emotionally and physically! My wife was, in fact, engaged in battle physically, mentally, and even spiritually! Just the same, by the grace of God, she continued to persevere! As well as our Father shielding our marriage as the battles waged on.

Needless to say, I was there for my wife, battling on her behalf. And also fighting for our marriage, which I believed at the time was in jeopardy, as best as I knew how. However, at the time, I did not comprehend what we were up against: these assaults on my wife, one being certainly spiritual in nature, which advanced from all fronts - against her mind, body, and spirit in order to ultimately destabilize our home. Just the same, we stood allied in this colossal struggle ... we never warred against one another.

Nevertheless, resulting from the strikes my wife and marriage incurred. There was a season I felt our union had been winded, staggered, and about to fall. While in the heat or heightened stress of things, my God gave me reassurance through a dream. I've only had such an encounter with God a few times. I received this message or dream from Him in the summer of 2003, I believe, there shortly after the passing of my mother-in-law and my wife's surgery. God, through the dream, gave me assurance that my marriage was going to be victorious! From the dream, God showed me that there was *new life* that He would bring forth through my wife and me.

Occasionally and perhaps more with others, God will communicate to us through our dreams. We see this throughout the Bible, in both the Old and the New Testament (Joel 2:28; Acts 2: 16, 17). I have had only five communications from God in this manner. His primary method by which to speak to us is through His Word. Now beware, even nonbelievers can have dreams that may come from evil spirits. That said, God may also choose to speak to a nonbeliever, the unsaved, through their dreams so that they may find their way to Him unto salvation. Or they may have been provided a message to deliver to a Believer. Think it not strange that God might just choose to communicate to you through a dream.

The dream of *assurance and consolation* my Father communicated to me: Lisa and I were in our bedroom. I was lying on my back on the bed. People, I was visibly pregnant! My legs and feet were positioned to give birth ... delivery was imminent! Meanwhile, my wife stood at my feet, facing me with her back towards our bedroom window. My wife, as she stood in front of the window, I saw what I will describe as rays of hope pouring through the window and illuminating the room and us! She was there with me to help deliver and receive that which I was about to birth into the world.

I immediately awakened from the dream! There was no sign of slumber upon me. Mentally and/or spiritually, I was fully alert! I was also full of excitement about the dream! Instantly, I understood the meaning of the dream! *For Believers, it is God alone who can give understanding to dreams* (Genesis 40:8: Daniel 2:28). When a Christian is met by God through a dream, the dreams neither add to nor take away from the Word of God. Our dreams from God may be to encourage us, give us direction or clarity regarding a matter, or provide a warning of some sort, either for ourselves or some other.

As for my dream, I recognized that God had spiritually impregnated me so that I may bring forth or birth something wonderful for His people, my wife, and me, and this being for His praise! My wife was not only present at my feet as I lay on the bed! But she was also going to be intimately involved in the process of delivering and receiving that which God was going to birth through me due to our union. And we being one as a result of remaining one with our Father!

Pregnancy and the delivery of a child, more often than not, bring discomfort and even tremendous pain. Face it! Like it or not ... as for me, "Not!" Pain and discomfort are part of the process that new life may come forth or be birthed! Spiritually speaking, Lisa and I were experiencing discomfort and pain. But that which God has purposed for us to birth together was soon to come to pass. Not only that, but our God would also be with us to see the delivery through. And also to comfort and reassure us in our time of need!

I mentioned in earlier chapters – speaking spiritually, we are capable of numerous pregnancies and births. This book or baby of mine, even so, my wife's book and baby that you have chosen to behold, is, no doubt, from my spiritual pregnancy shown to me in the dream! From that time and even beforehand, God has been doing a work in me! And I am convinced that He isn't through with my wife and me yet! And because you have chosen to read this book, He is not through with you either! Only if you submit and surrender yourself to Him, our Creator, will God impregnate you and birth through you something wonderful to His glory and the uplifting and building of His kingdom!

I was so excited about this revelation that I wanted to share it with my wife. It was around 3:00 in the morning, the same time I'd awakened from previous dreams, when God chose to visit me in such a manner. Yes, I woke her up! However, the dream didn't have the same impact on her as it did on me ... not in the slightest! It really didn't matter; I knew God had spoken to me, and in due time, all things were going to come to pass for our good and God's glory!

At the time of the dream, Lisa was far from the emotional healing and restoration she needed. Meantime, I, having been divinely encouraged, continued to lead and minister to the care of my wife the best I knew how.

As for how Lisa arrived at this place of brokenness and me thinking that our marriage was in jeopardy, the bottom line is that I failed to protect my wife and our home over a decade earlier! When the punches started coming and thereby weakening her, Satan seized upon the opportunity to try to either take out my wife or at least cause my marriage to be permanently "K.O'd," a boxing term meaning to be Knocked Out!

CHAPTER 17

From The Hand of My Enemy, Death Letters to My Wife - Her Soul Our Marriage He Wanted

Satan, through his human agent, was coordinating a decisive strike that was aimed at taking out my wife in an attempt to destroy my marriage and our home, and even our witness for God! I had failed as a husband to protect my wife and my Father's gift to me! Satan wanted my marriage, even if it meant taking my wife's sanity. Howbeit, it was my actions ... my marital unfaithfulness, that gave Satan this advantage over my house, a foothold by which he could take advantage of my Beloved and molest her mentally.

People ... Satan's assault against my wife through his human agent was relentless, ruthless, and downright evil! What my wife and I encountered was unimaginable! What kind of person could be so hellish!? The answer. One who does not know or have a personal relationship with God ... One who is one with Satan (demonically possessed). Or one who is demonically influenced! However, a true Believer in Christ can't be possessed. We have the Holy Spirit who has taken up residence within our earthen bodies. Just the same, we can undoubtedly be influenced by dark and wicked spiritual beings. And therefore, act in ways that are of the Devil – Satan himself! My season of whoredom was just that ... I, too, had become an agent of evil!

The dawn of a new era was before us; roughly two years had passed since I shared partly with my wife my season of unfaithfulness. As mentioned, my wife seemingly had gotten over the hurt and shock of what I had done. From my perspective, the two years after disclosing my horrible deeds were a thing of the past; we were now back in sync. All indicators from my wife suggested to me that our marriage was solid! However, unbeknownst to either of us, my wife's mental state had not been completely restored. The injury I caused her soul to undergo had not been entirely fortified.

During these two years, a few of the punches (life's occurrences) I mentioned in the previous chapter had landed. However, they were not disruptive – at least not noticeably, to my wife's well-being or our home. But consecutive blows will undoubtedly wear anyone down. In this chapter, you will see how these strikes or life occurrences and that one decisive demonic assault caused my wife and, seemingly as far as I was concerned, our marriage to be staggered! This process … the beatdown can be slow, steady, and methodical. Then comes that unexpected blow that can stagger one or even take them out.

These consecutive demonic attacks were violently and maliciously repeated upon my wife's mind. Satan wanted to devastate her; he wanted to break her mind or her will to stay in the fight. It was me who put my wife in this position! But it would be God, who would keep his daughter, and even work through me to bring healing and deliverance for my wife. But not only that … my God and Father also provided a shield for our marriage during this crisis!

The first punch at the hand of Satan's agent was delivered in February of 2003, three months before my mother-in-law's passing. The deadly force was executed in the form of eleven letters and two postcards. It has been said, "The pen is mightier than the sword." I clearly understand how one can arrive at this thinking. If you don't understand this meaning … you will soon see what I am talking about.

The messages from Satan's messenger were random. But consistently delivered over several months, striking my wife's mind with concussion force blows in an attempt to incapacitate her and render her useless! These letters were sent to her place of business. And put on the windshield of her car while she was at work. And even sent via mail to our home.

This battery and barrage of letters actually continued for over a year and a half! And then, one day, the punches simply stopped coming. There were at least two letters that Lisa nor I read. These two letters were sent to my wife's workplace. By now, I was over the foolishness and would no longer allow my wife to be subjected to this nonsense. I informed her to trash those letters, and she did just that. These letters did not make it to our home. While receiving the letters, I did everything I knew to identify the source of the letters ... Every avenue led to a dead end.

After a hiatus of about a year, a final punch (letter) was delivered to my wife. By now, the punches had lost their power over her. She received this final card in July 2005. God, our Healer, and Deliverer, had brought healing and restoration to my wife's soul. As I close out this chapter, I will address the circumstances regarding this final message from Satan's human agent.

Warning! As I open these grossly disturbing writings for your reading, be ready to be dumbfounded by the crude, explicit, devilish, and hurtful content contained therein. You will see and even feel the evil of Satan in these letters. More so in some of the letters than others. A second warning! Some of the content in these messages you will find disturbing!

You will now see how Satan, through his human agent, stalked my wife's mind to seize and utterly break it! To take away her sanity would have incapacitated her so severely that our marriage would have been devastated. Our witness through God's established union would have been lost ... But God! Let this be further proof that Satan desires to destroy all marriages, particularly those unions that God Presides over!

These messages are recorded as they were actually written ... they have not been edited. By the way, I still have them all.

My third and final warning regarding the vulgarity and evil contained within these letters! Now let the barrage of punches begin. On February 25th, 2003, my wife received the following letter at her place of business. This was the first of the demonic punches she incurred!

The letter reads as follows:

"Hello Mrs. Tony L. Scott

You don't know me, but I know who you are. You have two sons Mario and Desmond. I know where you work, live and I know what you drive. I know how long you and Tony been married. Tony and I have been seeing each other for quite some time now. I care a lot for Tony and willing to fight for him. I know Tony loves you, and he doesn't want to tell you about us, because he knows it will break your heart. My reason for writing you now is, I'm tired of being the other woman I have given Tony the chance to tell you about us, and if he doesn't I will. Again, I will fight for him.

Until later goodbye."

When Lisa returned home from work, I was in our bedroom. She greeted me and handed me this letter without saying a word; I had no idea what I was receiving. I remember that we were now standing at the door of our bedroom as I read the letter. Lisa stood quietly, watching and waiting for my response. When I finished reading the letter, I laughed as I looked at her.

I laughed because I knew there was no truth to this foolishness, as asserted by this unknown penman. Neither did this person provide a forwarding address. However, this was no laughing matter to Lisa. To my dismay, I saw that the letter obviously bothered my wife; this became abundantly clear. We were scheduled to attend the CIAA basketball game that evening; Lisa responded, "I do not want to go to the game. But you can go," she said to me.

I responded, "We are going to the game ... we are not going to allow this letter and whoever this person is to stop us from enjoying ourselves. This is what they are trying to do." I continued, "Don't let this letter get to you. If you are not careful, it can set you back." During this season of our marriage, Lisa was at a good place emotionally. But this letter, I now know, like an unsuspected jab, however, did manage to stun my wife, although I had cautioned her ... Not to allow it to happen.

Letter #2. The second punch! One month after Lisa's mother's passing. Here we go!

Postmarked 6/05/03 15:47 NC RTR 276 ISS4

"Mrs. Tony Scott

I'm sure you are surprise to hear from me again. You probably thought that my first note was a joke. Not so. I told you that I have given Tony a deadline, guess what the deadline has arrived.

In the beginning, I agreed with him to keep our affair quiet. We have tried several times to go out separated ways, but our friendship and love is so strong for each other we just can't. We see each other at least twice or three times a week. Ask Tony what happens every time you go out of town. Enclose you will find a key to one of our special places to let you know I'm not lying. We didn't go to the beach together this year, but we meet down there, I know he left early but we had fun before he left.

I'm trying to let you know I'm willing to fight for him. As you know Tony is a kind, special, sweet and loving person and I will do anything to keep him in my life.

Yours truly,
Ms. Washington
PS I mauled a copy to your home address just in cause this one get missing off your car.

[The keycard referenced in the letter was a white plastic swipe card. Printed on the card, "Onity Innovative Thinking"]

Postcard #1. The third punch! Mailed to the home. Lisa had recently returned home from the hospital following her Fibroid Tumor surgery.

Postmarked NC Research Triangle Region PM 276 19Jun2003

The front of the card has a picture of a wooden bench. The setting is a beautiful park. Printed on the front of the card, *"You're in My Thoughts"* Opening the card and printed on the left side reads: *"I remember you in my prayers at all times - Romans 1:9-10 (NIV)."*

This unknown sender wrote on the same side of the card: *"Hope your recovery is going well. I really enjoyed myself while you were hospitalized. Because every night Tony was with me not with you. You coming home on Friday early has put a small damper on things for us. But as soon as he returns to work thing will pick back up for us.*

Best wishes on your recovery until next time
Ms. D. Washington"

Printed on the right-hand side of the card read: *"May the prayers and friendly thoughts that daily come your way Bring you cheer and comfort and help brighten up each day."*

Well, this person didn't consider their lie … "the nights I was with her." That I was actually home with my son Desmond, who was twelve.

It was sometime following this letter when my wife was beginning to get beaten down and staggered emotionally from all she was dealing with. This was only a month or so following my wife's mother's death. And on top of this … here comes these two disturbing, disruptive, and devastating letters from Satan's agent! Satan is called the father of lies and that great deceiver! (John 8:44; Revelation 20:10). Satan, through his demonic and human agents, was clearly at work to destroy my marriage!

Letter #3. The fourth punch! Mailed to our home.

"August 19, 2003

I must say you looked very nice in your purple outfit. As you know Tony loves for his women to look good. Let me get to the point. I guess you didn't receive my letter I sent you because you didn't meet me on August 15, 2003. I guess I will have to come to you since you didn't meet me at the restaurant. I took it as if you were afraid to hear the truth and decided not to show up. As I stated in that letter, it's time for me to introduce myself to you. I have given Tony several months to do this in a orderly way. I guess he can't and he don't think I will. Yes, you have meant me on several occasions not knowing who I am or should I say not knowing what I mean to Tony. When we do meet I will tell you everything.

See you soon.
D. Washington"

Sometime after this letter, things really came to a head for Lisa! My wife couldn't bear any further the mental anguish she was under. She told me that she needed time apart from me. This came as a total, absolute, and unfathomable shock! There will be more said about this day later.

Letter #4. The fifth Punch! Mailed to the home.

Postmarked NC Research Triangle Region PM 276 25Oct2003

"Hi, Ms. Tony L. Scott

You were praying that you were not going to hear from me again. Yea right. I told you several times that I do exist, whether you believe it or not. I will keep you up to date with information about us. I didn't see Tony last week like I thought I would. I had to go out of town for my job and I know he hasn't told you. Tony is upset with me because I told you a little too much about us. Don't worry he will come around, I know how to make him come around. Bout of course you know I talk to him on the telephone every day whether I see him or not. Don't worry I will be back in town sooner than you think. He told me you cut your hair. I'm sure you did this against his wishes, you did that to piss Tony off. You know like playing in our hair especially the hair between our legs.

Write to you soon.

D. Washington"

What this person could not know … was that I actually cut my wife's hair. By the way, her hair was cut at my suggestion. Oh-well…

Letter #5. The sixth punch! Mailed to Lisa's workplace. Post Dated 10/25/03

"Oct 14, 2003

Dear Mrs. Scott:
I know you have been wondering what has happened to me. Tony and I met for lunch and had a great time, we talked things out. Tony wants this break up between you two to go as smooth as possible. Do I want this easy for you? (NO). Because I have been waiting for a long time to receive what should have been mine a long time ago. You know when you have a great thing and things are moving slower than you want them to move. You do crazy things. I just jumped the gun by letting you know about us to early. Now that you know about me don't fool yourself by believing that I don't exist. However, I told Tony that I was going to write you to remind you that I am still in the picture. Just ask Tony about the times we spend together, how hard it was for him to leave my presence. I have let him know on several occasions that I'm not giving up. Like I told you I will fight for him. One thing I do want you to remember and know is every time he kisses you, that you are kissing me (many parts of me).

Later, D. Washington"

Letter #6. The seventh punch! Placed on Lisa's car windshield while at work. Not dated.

"Ms. Tony L. Scott
Tony hasn't been in a good mood since you cut your hair. I told you that you pissed Tony off by cutting your hair. I don't appreciate Tony being in a bad mood because of your ass. Every since I returned from my trip I have to work hard at keeping him a great mood. The only way I can do that is by letting him come over to the house for a few hours during the day and letting him relax in my garden tub. When I get off work he will be waiting for me to rub his body down with warm oil and do what I do best. Then I let him go to you knowing that he is happy and he will be able to rest at night. Ask Tony what happens on Wednesday and Thursday night after 10:00 pm.

Later
D. Washington"

On page #2 in all caps: *"ASK YOUR HUSBAND DID HE HAVE FUN!!!!"*

Letter #7. The eighth punch! Mailed to the home. Post Dated 11/05/03

"Dear Ms. Scott

I writing to see why in the hell you drove Tony's truck last week, then you tried to park it in a different spot from where you normally park your car. I want you to know that you changed my plans for the last week. What plans, Tony and I have quickies in the truck, by you having the truck I didn't get one. If I don't get what I want I get very upset. I'm upset with Tony because he didn't tell me that you were going to drive the truck. Why don't we go to a hotel or my house? I only have one hour for lunch breaks and I live a little too far just for the quickies. On my days off if I am in town we would go to my house for more than just quickies. I want you to picture this. I would suck on his dick until he can't take it anymore, then he would stop me then start eating me until I start creaming then he would put his fingers (2 of them) in my pussy until I can't take it anymore. Then I would sit on him and ride him until we both climax together what a joy. That's how some of our quickies are, so think about the all day event. So every time you ride or drive the truck, I want you to think about how enjoyable my ride's are.

Later
D. Washington"

What this unknown person was unaware of and could not have known: From about the late part of October to perhaps the beginning of December, my wife and I were apart for about two weeks on two separate occasions. I had honored my wife's request of me that we spend some time away from each other. Yes, there is more to be said about this as well.

Postdate 11/13/03 Letter #8. The ninth punch! Mailed to the home.

"Dear Ms. Tony Scott

It's clear to me that Tony don't know about the letter I wrote last week. Tony didn't mention anything to me about you getting upset. It's O.K. that you are driving his truck this week. Why it's O.K.? This week I have my period and we don't have sex during that time and just being in his presence does wonders for me and he has been. But you best believe that next week its back on. Let me tell you how enjoyable the sex is after my period. Tony and I will take a long warm shower or bath together at my house. Keep in mind that this only happens once or twice a month. Sometimes we will make to the bed, sometimes we don't. He will play with my clit and I will play with his balls you can imagine the rest. If you can't remember what I wrote in the previous letters. So, I hope you enjoyed him this week because I am next week. I know next week is Thanksgiving that doesn't matter. We will see each other.

Later,
D. Washington"

I will continue to identify the remaining letters received throughout 2004 as punches. However, they no longer had power over my wife. Our God intervened mightily and brought complete restoration to the soul of my wife!

Letter #9. The tenth punch! Mailed to the home. Post Dated 03/17/04

"Hello Ms. Tony L. Scott,

I know you are surprise to hear from me. I've been out of town a couple of days. But I'm back. Tony and I having been keeping in contact with each other via telephone. I haven't had time to write, to keep you informed about Tony and I. Let me tell you a few things since I have time. We don't see each other like we use to, because Tony convinced me that you are moving out of town as soon as Desmond get out of school this year. He wants us to stay cool for a while. I have been waiting for more than sixteen years and I can wait a few more months. Hell, I see him like I want anyway. I know Tony went back home to you. He was feeling sorry for you, because you started looking sick and losing weight. Believe me, people that you think care about you is and were talking about you more than you can imagine. Sine you cut your hair and lost some much weight you've been looking bad. You need to buy close to fit you. You need to have hips and breast like mine ask Tony about the body. That's why he can't let me go completely.

You know Tony is stuck between hard place and a rock. You were just around when it was time to get married and you said yes, you surprised us all, the whole family.

Because him and I was still getting it on. You know I was in and out of relationships at the time so it was cool with me so he tried to keep us both happy. I know I've been happy with just the sex and small talk. You know he love to have sex and talk.

See you soon,
D. Washington"

Letter #10. The eleventh punch! Mailed to the home. Post Dated 05/12/04

"Hello Ms. Tony L. Scott

Time is getting near. I just want to remind you of some things. You have 18 to 20 days left before you move out and I move in. I hope you are packed and ready to go. Because when we return from the beach, I will be moving in on the 2nd of June. Tony said you have been taken this well, I'm glad because I don't want any drama from you. When Tony comes to pick up Desmond or when you two meet I will be with him. When you see me you will not be surprised. I have been in this family a long time. Like I said before the whole family was surprised that the marriage lasted as long as it did. Or should I say you stay as long as you could before you had enough. This is a warning, don't make this divorce last a long time, and I don't want any drama from you. You have been a good dealing with this matter. Oh, I will invite you to the wedding. Our wedding will be larger than yours.

Later
D. Washington

Letter #11. The twelfth punch! Left on Lisa's windshield while at work. Between June and August of 2004.

"Dear Ms. Tony Scott,

I know you are surprised to hear from me. Are you surprised that I didn't move in the first of June. Tony told me that you were sick and he could not let you move out. So, Tony and I decided that you will keep the house since you and Desmond are settled there. He doesn't want to have to pay any more money than he has to. I know you want everything. By September our apartment will be ready. That's the time Tony will move out. Desmond will be use to the idea of his father not there everyday and living with another woman and soon be his wife. You need start looking for someone to keep you company because your nights are going to be lonely and long. Ask your sister-in-law about the nights Tony and I had when he left you last year. Tony may tell you that I don't exist and nothing happened while he was gone but it did. I know Tony Love you and don't want to hurt you. Just remember I didn't give a fuck about your feelings. Again, the only reason why you don't know who I am is because of Tony. Tony doesn't want me to tell you or visit your office. Because he knows you can't take the pressure. That will prolong him and me. Because he's obligated to that care of you if you get sick.

Later,
D. Washington Scott"

Letter #12. The thirteenth punch! Mailed to the house. Post Dated 10/02/04

"September 30, 2004

Hope you enjoyed your last day with Tony. I'm sure you cried your eyes out don't be sad. That why you looked so bad on Thursday. It will be O.K. At least you got your hair done, that was the only thing looking good on Thursday. Your suit was too big get another one. I guess you have to get use to paying for your own hair dos and buy your clothes. Lisa, I know you are a sweet, kind person, stay that way, I would hate to see you pay if you start tripping. Desmond will be taken care of, so don't trip and try to get child support or extra money for Desmond. You buy his food we will buy his clothes. I know you will see Tony on days he brings Desmond home from school, don't try anything, again you will pay. I'm looking forward to meeting you face to face, or should I say you finally know who I am.

D. Washington"

The last of the letters! Wow! ... Right!? However, there would be one later and final communication just short of a year from this malefactor. One can only imagine just how these letters initially affected my wife.

People, it had been years since I'd read these letters that I have shared with you. Nevertheless, both Lisa and I are perplexed, and I am just short of being angry that someone could be so diabolical in their intent to hurt my wife in an attempt to destroy our marriage.

A brief recap leading to where we are now in this unfolding drama: In February 2003, the first letter was received by my wife. June of 2003, a month after the passing of my mother-in-law, my wife received letters two and three. These letters were concussion-causing blows that began to do my wife in! The effectiveness of the punches took a toll on my wife! Mentally she was on the brink of collapse! It was also around this time that God reassured me through my dream that my wife and I would be okay.

However, my wife was in great need of relief from her mental battering and suffering. Shortly after these letters, about 2 months, she would let me know that she desperately needed peace of mind! Though her solution to her presumed fix initially shocked me, I would quickly come around. I responded with the help of God to meet her at her point of need. I gave my wife the space she thought she needed to get better ... so I moved in with my sister. Doing this time, I did all I knew to do to aid in my wife's recovery.

Additionally, I encouraged my wife to receive professional assistance to deal with the grief of losing her mother. Afterward, we would receive marital counseling. Lisa hesitantly agreed to pursue this route. My wife was and is a very private person ... she doesn't want people in her business. And yet, she followed my lead on the matter. Although I recommended marital counseling, I wasn't really feeling this for myself. My reservation was for varied reasons. More on this shortly.

Satan's Dark Human - Agent Exposed

As for the culprit's identity behind the letters, during the time of the assaults, we could not determine who it could possibly be. Trust me ... It wasn't from a lack of effort! I conducted stakeouts at Lisa's place of employment, hoping that I would catch the person in the act of placing a letter on her car ... They were a no-show! I also went to the post office from where the letters were sent, but nothing helpful was provided. There was no method of tracking the identity of the sender. I also had a couple of the letters fingerprinted; no visible prints were found. Lisa and I were left to speculate, who could be so full of evil?

However, ten months from September 2004, when the succession of letters ceased, my wife would receive the final card (punch) from this demonically influenced person. By now, our God had taken the power from the punches. My wife was standing firm, and our marriage was solid. Now God would perform an amazing work, to expose this agent of evil who was behind the letters.

Watch God work! It was in July of 2005, I was on a work-related trip. I was in Lacrosse, Wisconsin, for two weeks, some 1077.5 miles from my home. Interestingly, I would befriend a co-worker who, before this trip, I did not know. However, he knew about me. This he told me, adding that he had respect for me. The brotherly bond we developed was unique; it was established instantaneously. This was a strange occurrence because I don't readily take to people quickly. However, it was God who was working things out. He wanted to reveal something to me. And it was going to be through this unlikely relationship and brotherly bond I had with my coworker.

There was such freedom within our friendship. That my brother opened up to me regarding the marital challenges before him and his wife. I began ministering to him while encouraging my brother to fight for his marriage. I even told him to send flowers to his wife … which he did. I told him my story of unfaithfulness and how Satan came at my wife and marriage through the letters. I really poured into him the ways of God and how Satan schemes to work against us … I now knew this all too well based on my past.

As I shared with him the content and language used in the letters. The most surprising thing occurred! He lit up or appeared astonished! He excitedly expressed himself by saying what I believe was, "Hot-toe-mighty!" This was a common expression of his. But it wasn't the nature of the letters alone that provoked his response … it was the verbiage used! My brother responded that he knew someone that talked in the manner expressed in the letters. My interest and excitement in what more he had to say were heightened!

My brother continued to share with me the peculiarities of this person he called a friend. He told me a few stories about some "strange things" this person had done regarding their professional and outside-of-the-job relationship. My friend also told me his wife had informed him that this person had been annoyingly calling their house to talk to him. And was also driving by their home to see if he was there.

I had heard enough! I was convinced from within my spirit that this person was the culprit behind the letters. My coworker was also confident of this as well!

Before I knew my coworker personally, he, this person, and I were YMCA members. He shared with me a time when we all passed one another. I was leaving the "Y" and was walking down the stairs, and they had just arrived. My friend stated that he acknowledged me and that I responded in kind. That was that. Interesting enough ... I actually remembered that brief encounter from what would have been approximately three years earlier. Why would God help me to retain in memory this insignificant event ... I will suggest, for this moment that is now before us!

After our passing, my coworker went on to say that he started speaking to the person who was with him about me. At that time, I was really into bodybuilding. This was one of the reasons my friend and coworker had noticed me and had "respect" for me. He mentioned my demeanor and how I carried myself had also gotten his attention. Continuing his conversation with the other person, he said he spoke highly of me. Now, based on everything my coworker shared in our conversation ... some details I left out. Not to mention my friend's admiration for me that was expressed to the other person. So, it seems to me. Howbeit, for reasons unknown, neither anything that could possibly make sense to me; just the same, I am convinced that it was this person who decided to assault my wife and come after our marriage.

Jealousy and envy have been known to cause people to do unbelievable things. Was this the bases for the war that was declared against my namesake? I may never know.

The person suspected of writing the letters did not know that our now mutual friend was together on job-related training. While my coworker was away for training, this person had asked his wife about her husband's whereabouts.

Resulting from my firm conviction regarding this person as the perpetrator behind the letters. I wanted to somehow confirm what I knew to be true in my spirit – that this person was the villain! And so, I asked my coworker to have his wife inform the person when they called his home again. To say to the person, "My husband is out of town. And that he and Tony were together for work-related training."

In a matter of a day or so, this person again called my coworker's house; his wife relayed the message as instructed. The conversation with this individual and my coworker's wife occurred on the weekend just before the week of July 17th or maybe that same week. What happened next was by no means a coincidence. Postmarked 7/xx/05, the day of my wife's birthday, she received that second and final postcard and now, powerless punch. It was mailed to our home. Yes! … The same week that this person called my friend's home. And they received word that we were together in training. Satan's dark agent had been exposed by the Light – God Himself!

Information from this final postcard:

Card #2. Powerless punch #13. On the outside of the card was a picture of a monkey. Also printed on the outside of the card: *"Let's see… add 4, divided by 7, take that times 3. So in monkey years you must be…"* I'm not sure what to make of this. Written on the left inside cover: *"Long time no hear, I guess you thought I had forgotten about you no such luck. Naw it's time for you to move on. Desmond is going to high school now and your ass is getting older. Tony doesn't need to stay with you any longer. It's time for Tony to move out and take care of his other Family!!*

Until Next time"

The opposite side of the card printed: *"Pretty dang Old. Signed, D. Washington"*

For over a year, these hellish letters came to us. Lisa and I were clueless as to who was behind these letters. Now, finally, and miles from home. Under the most unlikely of circumstances. I was led by God to the truth that had evaded Lisa and me for now almost two years.

As for the person's identity, I will not disclose their name. However, from the revelation provided by my Father, His agent, and my friend, my wife and I discovered that this person would have often visited her place of employment! They handled their affairs at the exact location of my wife's job that she had for two decades.

I'm sure that I had cordially greeted this person a few times. But not a time that I could recall. There was also a time when this person stopped in front of my residence to inquire about the Akita puppies I was selling. But here's the kicker … this individual was a neighbor. I could almost see their house from my yard. And could be on their door stoop by car or if I cut through my neighbor's yard in less than two minutes. This person would drive by my home daily and even multiple times. We associated with some of the same people. It would not have taken much effort for *him* to gather information regarding my home affairs. Yes! You heard it right! The person was a male! Satan utilized yet another man to get at me! Who would have thought?

Based on my conversation with my coworker-friend, he also mentioned this person was "unnaturally fixated" on him. Read into this as you choose … I have. This person was also married and had a young child, who has since passed away. Could this have been God's judgment for what this individual did to my wife and me? This is a valid question … I can't say if it actually was. But Scripture tells us that *God will fight our battles … that vengeance is His. Even so, He will discipline His own* (Romans 12: 19; Hebrews 12:4-11;1Corinthians 11:27-32). This may seem to be a stretch for some of you. However, God, at times, will clearly discipline His own to bring us to repentance. How He chooses to discipline us is at His discretion.

Because the child was not of the age of personal accountability at their death, they will certainly be with God for all eternity. What about the child's father?

Did he repent? Did he really know God as his personal Lord and Savior? I think not. Has he since accepted Jesus as Lord and Savior? I hope so! God also desires to have a relationship with him.

After returning home from Wisconsin, there, shortly afterward, I paid the person behind the letters somewhat of a reconciliatory visit. What I really wanted; was for him to acknowledge what he had done.

I took the less than two-minute drive to his house. I walked up to his front stoop. The front door to his home was open. This was great; it allowed me to see him and for him to see me as he approached his glass storm door. I either knocked on the door or rang the doorbell. His appearance when he noticed it was me can be likened to a deer staring at the headlights of an oncoming car. He was undoubtedly surprised by my visit. He opened the door to acknowledge me. I don't recall what he said - or if anything was said at all. My words were to the point. I said, "I know what you did." This was regarding the letters. He did not acknowledge his wrongdoings. Instead, he responded, "What are you talking about?" I responded. "You know what you did." I continued, "I know that you attend church. I forgive you."

He did not attempt to say anything further. He just looked at me. His lack of response confirmed what the Spirit of God had shown me. I then turned and walked away. I'm guessing my visit to his home occurred some 8 years ago at the time of initially writing this book. As of a year or so in passing, he remains a neighbor. He has not since reached out to me. Neither has he acknowledged me while driving by my home. Perhaps he has avoided coming my way; I have only seen him once or twice after visiting with him. And guess what …neither has there been any more letters or cards!

CHAPTER 18

God -
The Healer of Our Soul
The Restorer of the Breach

I only arrived at the point of fully understanding the hurt and grief that a
cheating spouse cause when I asked my wife to describe the experience of her
suffering that I had subjected her to. This question was presented after I had
been more forthcoming about my whoredom, and after her heart no longer
ached. This likely occurred in the spring of 2004 after the punches lost their
power over my wife. This was the season of my God's restoration of the breach
I had foolishly created when I committed whoredom. Because of my selfishness
and foolishness, and mainly those letters, a wedge of sorts had been presented
between my wife and me. Unbeknownst to me, this distancing or wedge had
been slowly forcing my wife apart from me emotionally; here, meaning,
emotionally, she was drained and overwhelmed by the weight of all that she was
under.

I sincerely desired to know what effects my actions had on her. My wife was and
is a woman of few words; therefore, the unforeseen word picture she would paint
for me enabled me to understand her pain … this would be profound! I will
finally get it! What I experienced and felt when she shared with me; her hurt
changed my view on sexual relations. I saw what I had done to my wife
emotionally for the first time! Yes, I got it! I saw the emotional damage I inflicted

upon my wife and this gift from God. And so will you! But not until a little later.

It was of necessity and the right thing to do when I initially shared with my wife that I'd been unfaithful. However, I was unaware and unprepared for the hurt this would bring her. Neither could I comprehend the depth of her agony, and therefore initially unable to adequately minister to her wounded soul. Again, I thought time and distance – roughly a decade had passed since my marital betrayal; and the fact that I had acknowledged my wrong would cause minimal, if any, hurt to my wife.

However, once the letters started, although Lisa put forth a valiant effort to press on in silence, she could only bear up for so long through the pain and weight of her mental anguish. Tired and battered from trying to withstand the blows on her own, she would inevitably seek out a means to try to find solace for her weary and wounded soul. At her point of immense confusion, conflict, desperation, and breaking point, she would present to me the only option she saw so that she could somehow experience some measure of relief.

The fact that she remained *in love* with me and maintained her trust in me through it all. However, because of the weight of her hurt! And the perplexity of mind she was under … she was desperately seeking relief! The only option that she saw to eliminate her pain would create a challenge for both of us. Here's one reason why this was so for my wife: While we were having a random conversation one day after all this drama of my making had passed. My wife provided me some insight into her thinking on the subject of love. She said, "There is a difference between *loving someone* and *being in love*." She had to explain to me what she meant by this.

This is what she said: "I can love you. However, I can live without you." On the other hand, *"Being in love* with you, my desire is to be with you."* I'd never heard this; however, I understood where she was coming from … this made sense. And now for the challenge before my wife!

My wife would arrive at a conflicting crossroads and difficult decision! My wife was *in love* with me! And therefore wanted to be with me. However, with her desperate need for peace of mind, as she tried to make sense of things. My wife saw no other way to arrive at this. Other than to seek to be apart from her husband, who she was *in love* with! Here is how things unfolded: It was the early fall of 2003; Lisa and I had been out on this gorgeous day for a joyous ride on the motorcycle. Upon returning home from what I'd assumed was a great outing that we shared together. Nevertheless, I would receive from my wife the most unexpected, stunning, and staggering words she could ever express to me! Just as it was for her nearly a decade earlier when I told her about my unfaithfulness.

I was sitting watching a football game; what happened next would show how desperate my wife had gotten. I'm sure she waited for a commercial break before approaching me ... my wife is just that considerate. When the time was right, she took hold of the footstool and positioned it directly in front of me; she took a seat there. She then placed her right hand on my right thigh. She then leaned toward me with her eyes fixed intently, sincerely, and earnestly upon my eyes. My wife calmly said, "I can't do this anymore."

My response, while being totally confused, "What are you talking about?" She responded, "I love you. But I can't keep acting like I'm okay when I'm not."

I was perplexed! With my questioning gaze, I looked at her. She continued, "What you did, I haven't been able to get over it." We were doing well, or so I thought. I would occasionally ask my wife how she was doing ... this question could be out of the blue or for no particular reason. Or maybe because I simply wanted to know where she was in her thoughts. You already know her response, "I'm ok ... I'm fine. Or I will be ok." And she really believed this. This was her method of coping. As I mentioned previously, there was no apparent reason for me to think otherwise regarding my wife's mental well-being.

And so, I was dismayed and confused as to how we'd arrived at this crossroad. At the time, I did not recognize the power of the letters or their influence on my wife. Even so ... why now? What was the cause of my wife saying this to me? Seeing my bewilderment, Lisa said, "You are a good husband and father, but I need some time apart." My immediate response was, "How can you say that I'm a good husband and father and that you love me? But you need some time apart!? ... That's hypocritical!"

People, I didn't get it at all! I was oblivious to what my wife was going through. She had not missed a beat regarding the care of her home and her loving care for me. I was left thinking, "Where is this coming from ... What was she up to?" I was truly blindsided by what I was hearing!

Her comment - I can liken to me turning the corner of a building and unexpectedly being punched square in the face. And then receiving a second blow to my gut! Now I was dazed and staggered from what my wife said to me! As far as I was concerned, my wife and I were doing well ... But she indeed wasn't!

The Beauty And Blessing In Sound Reasoning

It wouldn't take long for me to regain my senses from this shocking revelation my wife brought before me. I had shared with her two years earlier that I'd been unfaithful. I did so because I loved my wife; I had been able to talk about anything with her; I, therefore, no longer wanted to live with my lie. Ironically, though forced by her pain primarily at my making, my wife would have to stop living with her lie (loosely speaking) or hope better stated and share with me what she felt she needed. Because she, too, loved me and desired for her marriage to remain steady – although she wasn't steady mentally, she had to be forthcoming.

Scripture tells us, "Love bears all things, believes all things, hopes all things, endures all things" (1 Corinthians 13:7). My wife exemplified all of these things; however, her heart was weighed down. She had borne the weight of her pain by and within herself for too long! Now, and from the depth of her soul, mind, and heart ... My wife was crying out for the solace she desperately needed!

She desperately needed to express what was going on within her, but this was not something my wife readily did; such conversations were a challenge for her. Nevertheless, as her spouse, I am to become her strength and support where she is weak! And where I am weak, she is to become my strength and support. Marriage is always about supporting and building one another up! What you do to or for your spouse, you do to yourself! The Bible makes this clear that upon marriage, a husband and his wife are one (Ephesians 5: 25-33).

The Holy Spirit eased within me the shock of what my wife had expressed to me. He would now be at work within me so that I may be compassionate and sound in my reasoning to begin this journey of healing for my wife. My wife is ultimately my responsibility ... I knew this even when I was carrying on as a fool!

The Spirit of God enabled me to see that my wife was desperately hurting and in need of a remedy. However, her pain's magnitude and depth were beyond my complete comprehension. Now giving an attentive and sympathetic ear to hear my wife out. She told me she would find an apartment and take Desmond with her. In two months or so, Desmond would reach his thirteenth birthday; Mario was now in the Marines. My wife, desperately needing what she thought was time apart to get herself together, was willing to leave the comfort of her home. However, she had no idea where she was going, yet, her hope was to find peace and clarity for her soul wherever she went.

However, I wasn't in agreement with this ... the thought of my wife leaving the comfort of her home ... Never! And uprooting our son, too, would not be a matter of discussion. We reasoned together without arguing but with calm and collective thinking. This moment was numbingly taking shape for me; perhaps she was numb too. This ordeal felt unreal as we considered how to proceed with our separation. I could never have imagined that I would have been arranging a separation from my wife ... Never!

Lisa's and my son's well-being were at the forefront of my thoughts, so I told her I would find a place to stay. Maintaining the house's expenses was a concern for Lisa. To think; she had considered moving out of her home and doing whatever she needed to without asking for my assistance also speaks to the kind of person she is. Needless to say, I then set forth the financial arrangements so she would not be burdened with maintaining the household expenses and our son on her own.

My wife was in love with me! Leaving or us being apart was a tough decision that she'd come to. Although I decided to make the move, this agreement was difficult for both of us. Arriving at this unexpected place in our marriage, I knew I would do everything in my power to help my wife recover and get her the help she needed – she was my responsibility! I failed at this once; it was never going to happen again!

The wisdom and insight God endowed me with over this time leading to Lisa's recovery was amazing, a true blessing! Seeing God at work during our time of challenge brought comfort to me, although my wife was not at this place with me. But, there was one evening when I felt that I was on my way out – meaning possibly throwing in the towel on my marriage! Stay tuned for that moment.

Lisa and I were as one as we began on this road toward her healing. I'd not known anyone who had received professional counseling. This was our next step. Nevertheless, I was somewhat apprehensive about receiving marriage counseling. While on our journey to recovery. I'd begun to discern that there was more going on with my wife than her simply not being unable to cope with my unfaithfulness. I was keenly aware that her mother's passing could not be ignored; my wife was greatly affected by this. However, during this time, I had not considered the hellacious effects of the letters on my wife!

Regarding the matter of counseling for my wife, well, in addition to being a peacekeeper, she is also very private. Her business is her business! This is apparent about my wife when you get to know her. However, she has no problem letting it be known if need be. Although she may be easygoing, there are some things that can cause her to check or correct you if she has to ... she is not a pushover! As a matter of fact, she had to get to the place of accepting me telling our story through this book. I impressed upon her; that this is what God would have us do. I told her that our story can serve to minister to the needs of others. I knew what I was strongly feeling about writing this book before the first letter was typed: That this book could help many regarding relational matters. In this writing of our book, she would also follow my lead. My wife is - who she is, *Not What I Thought I Wanted But Everything I Need*. Although apprehensive regarding counseling, Lisa would follow my lead regarding receiving professional help.

As for my reluctance to speak with a counselor, well, it had to do with me not knowing what to expect. I was also thinking that I would be branded in an unfavorable light. Furthermore, what could a counselor offer me? I say this with humble sincerity. At this point, I had been a police officer for sixteen years and a minister for eleven years … I counseled people. I was gifted at doing this … therefore, I did not require this service … I was one who now sat at the *City's Gate*. Just the same, I was willing to do whatever was necessary to aid in the recovery of my wife's mental well-being or spiritual healing, as well as that which I thought was necessary to maintain our marriage.

Now that things had been sorted out between Lisa and me. That she would remain in our home and agree to see a counselor. I acknowledged to my wife yet again my wrong and took full responsibility for my actions. I reassured my wife that nothing about what I did, had anything to do with her. She had always carried herself as an exceptional woman and wife; I knew I needed to reassure her of this fact.

I wanted my wife's conscious absolutely clear of anything she thought she may have done to contribute to my wrong actions. My words were as follows: "I wronged you … I was the one who committed adultery, and you have every right to divorce me." I added, "The ball is in your court … "You have control over what happens next."

Things were now sorted out between my wife and me; our separation was now to take place. I hate saying that we separated! I like better, our time apart. Being perfectly honest with my wife, I said to her perhaps the most foolish thing, so some of you will undoubtedly think. However, at the time, I didn't see what I said as being so wrong … I was merely being honest. I told my wife, not knowing how long we would be apart, "I was going to date." I know, I know! … but hear me out.

Here is my explanation: Me going out on a date with whoever was solely for the purpose of non-physical socialization … Period! I enjoy good company with like-minded people; therefore, I wasn't ruling out the possibility of hanging out with someone, even if the person was of the opposite sex. I expressed this to my wife, thinking it was a non-issue. She just looked at me; her eyes said it all – REALLY!? People, I didn't get it! But my heart was in the right place ... this God knew.

Making the decision to leave our home, I reached out to my sister, Wendy, who, with open arms, allowed me to stay in her home. In the meantime, Lisa sought counseling that, at best, minimally aided her. [*There may be hurt or sickness in the soul of man that can only be remedied by God.*] My wife completed her grief counseling with a Christian Counselor, Dr. P. Davis; now, the time had arrived for Lisa and me to meet with Dr. Davis for marital counseling.

From the time of our voluntary separation leading to this meeting with Dr. Davis, I'd been relentlessly ministering to the emotional needs of my wife. My wife thought she needed questions answered from me regarding my season of folly; they were often the same questions. Nevertheless, I would now freely answer her questions. She needed answers, so she thought for her healing and peace of mind to be restored. However, my responses didn't offer any consolation for my wife. I remember talking and taking questions until my mouth was dry! I didn't mind; my wife desperately needed answers and healing. But her recovery would not come through my answers nor in what Dr. Davis had to say alone.

So it was; I was apprehensive about our first meeting with Dr. Davis. I had no idea what to expect and thus believed I would be negatively seen and portrayed by her as such to my wife. I entered the meeting guarded and emotionless. The fact that I was working and therefore was wearing my police uniform no doubt enhanced Dr. Davis's incorrect perception of me. As I observed Dr. Davis, I hung onto every word she said and responded to her questions stoically and direct. She then commented along these lines ... "You are hard and don't show emotions." She was ever so wrong, and I didn't care for her assumption, but this was the image I portrayed. Needless to say, I responded quickly, "I'm emotional, and I don't have a problem expressing them. I couldn't allow her to have the wrong assumption about me from the persona I aired.

Therefore, it's essential that when receiving counseling, transparency is a must!

Dr. Davis asked a series of questions from each of us. There was one question, in particular, that was asked of Lisa. My wife's response to the question weighed on me for quite some time. Dr. Davis asked Lisa, "If you had to *rank your marriage* on a scale from one to ten, regarding how you feel about your marriage … where would you rank it?"

My wife questioned Dr. Davis. "Which number reflects the worst – one or ten?" Dr. Davis responded, "One." My wife answered: "Zero." I could have crawled under my chair! I was hurt and embarrassed … Remember, I thought things in *my marriage were moving along smoothly.* I couldn't believe what I was hearing. I wondered, "How did things get to a "Zero" when I didn't see the evidence of this being the case? Amazingly, God would allow me to see into the reason for my wife's response months later.

Knowing that we had sons, Dr. Davis questioned me about how they were affected by things. However, Mario was now in the Marines. I had always shared truthfully with my sons regarding life matters. *[Desmond was never led to believe in the lie of a Santa, and Mario was freed from this lie.]* And this matter regarding their mother and I would be no different … I presented to them the truth of my failure as a dad and husband.

I shared with Dr. Davis that I'd brought my family together to talk about what I had done. Mario was in high school at the time. Desmond was around eleven years old. I went into more detail with my sons at that time than what I will now share. However, they knew the certainty of my sinfulness and actions and how I got *caught up.* I also took full responsibility for my wrong!

They understood that I had made a major *mistake*, for which I apologized. That I had caused hurt to their mother - my wife. And that my wrong decisions put my family in jeopardy. I assured them that this could never happen again! I made it plain to them … that a *mistake* of this sort can only happen once! And that if such an occurrence was to take place again, it would not be a mistake – rather something that I willingly did. Therefore, in my mind, any apology I would try to offer would have no credibility if I wronged my family again in like manner. This I also expressed to my family.

My family was to take from this gathering at the dinner table: That such foolishness from me would never occur again! That what I did was a *colossal mistake* ... And that I got *caught up!* Dr. Davis's response to what I said I shared with my family surprised me. She actually expressed to me that she thought that I had shared too much information with my sons. There was no debate regarding her position. However, I completely disagreed with her on this point. This was the only matter that I did not see eye-to-eye with her.

My next session was one-on-one with Dr. Davis. This was my only private meeting with her. This session resulted in discovering some things about myself and my past that I had not considered. Having shared my history with her, Dr. Davis presented her thoughts on what she heard from me when my wife and I had our final meeting. She said something along these lines. "Every man who held significance in your life disappointed you." I'll say it plainly and with more impact ... They failed me! The subject of abandonment was also considered in her analysis of things with me. I don't think I'd ever given much thought to what she observed. Those three men in my life and the fathers of my siblings. If the truth were to be told – and it will be, they were all failures as dads and husbands. *More on this in my next book if the Lord permits.*

During our time together, Dr. Davis had asked me questions about my infidelity; she wanted to hear about its unfolding. I shared with her how I got *caught up.* I clearly remember sharing with her the thought that I expressed chapters earlier regarding wondering, "If I still got it?" In case you have forgotten about this thought I had. It was after I was seduced by the woman while waiting to shoot pool.

A few days after meeting with Dr. Davis, Lisa and I came back together for our final session. I listened intently as Dr. Davis shared with my wife and me her evaluation of me, which I've already shared. She would now provide her closing assessment regarding our marriage. And her judgment of my wife and her recommendation for Lisa. I was taken aback by her conclusion and evaluation of things! That which she said regarding me ... and the fact that everything and some things verbatim that Dr. Davis said to my wife, I'd already administered or ministered said wisdom or counsel to my wife! What a relief! Seeing how God had been working through me on my wife's behalf was truly satisfying! And even confirming my *Calling* and purpose as a minister or servant of His. Not that I was in need of this. Just the same, it did my soul well!

I will only highlight these few remarks Dr. Davis shared with my wife. Her comment went along these lines: "What your husband did, is not who he is. His inappropriate behavior occurred years ago when he was a younger man." Now regarding my comment, "I wonder If I still got it." Dr. Davis told my wife this was a "male machismo thing" resulting from his past.

Dr. Davis added, "Lisa, you must forgive your husband." That statement would prove to be easier said than done. Our marriage counseling ended on that note. Later, God would pay me a visit on this matter of forgiveness. Nevertheless, I was delighted that I had not been vilified by Dr. Davis.

During the time my wife was receiving her eight sessions with Dr. Davis, two of them included me; I was staying at my sister's home. Sometime after the sessions had ended, my wife asked me to return home ... I gladly returned! However, I soon discovered that my wife was still struggling to let go of the past. It remained difficult for her to grasp how I could have sexual relations with these women without having emotional connections or feelings toward them. Again, relief from her struggle was not to be found in answers to her questions as she thought. Not even at this point had my wife been provided the complete details regarding Cierra. Besides, I had been freed from my attraction to her.

As if cheating isn't awful on its own! It's far more complicated and problematic when a cheating spouse gives their affections to some other! This really begins to raise questions and self-doubt within the spouse who has been betrayed! I'm sure this was what my wife was feeling and even wondering. Had her husband given all of himself to these women? Was she not enough to satisfy him? Also, bear in mind that giving of oneself doesn't have to be physical or sexual. One can also inappropriately give over their emotions or affections to another in other ways.

Recovery from this type of affair, where emotions are involved, is more challenging to move beyond for all involved than where "just having sex" occurs.

If this relationship is not severed, the home will suffer, be destroyed, or even worse, can be the outcome!

The notion or defense, "It's just sex," or any other foolish claim that a spouse may try to offer to diminish or downplay their wrong, is absurd! Sex outside marriage or adultery is never "Just sex!" It is a crime against marriage and God!" Or that sex is merely a biological urge to be satisfied, anytime and with whomever you shall choose is wicked and a lie from Satan! Sex outside marriage is a sin ... *it's* wrong, and there will always be consequences!

The Word Pictures From My Wife –
I Finally Got it

Fellows, as for that, something we don't seem to get or fully grasp ... I finally *got it!* It was the result of my wife helping me see and/or comprehend the hurt I put her through. I simply asked my wife to explain what she felt when I informed her of my adulterous activity. Listen to her words, my brothers; see these pictures she painted for me, my sons. Now, consider and take this matter to heart! Unfortunately, I had to learn what I am about to share with you at the expense of my wife and her pain and suffering! I now, through my book, share this invaluable knowledge. And much that I have learned over these many years through my life experiences. That I may keep you all from making the mistakes I made and steer you away from the snares that Satan will set before you.

Asking my wife to explain to me what she felt. Our God would give her a few words and the ability to express herself most powerfully and in a manner I could not have imagined! She shared two vivid and graphic word illustrations that would forever change me! The eyes of my soul would now see. And my ears would be opened to grasp and hear the depths of grief I caused my Beloved. And for all who have ears to hear and a heart that can empathize with my wife's agony resulting from my marital failure and infidelity. I pray that you also will be affected and changed as I have been regarding marital or relational infidelity.

Hear these profound words spoken from a gentlewoman - my reticent wife of few words. And yet her words surgically penetrated my *being* and brought light, truth, and conviction to my soul that I had not encountered to this depth beforehand! Hear *ye* her! "What you did to me - was like you put a dagger in my heart and twisted it!" Briefly pausing, she followed up. "It was as if you reached into my chest and ripped my heart out!" At that very moment, *I got it!* My heart sank when I considered what I had done and the torment I caused my wife to have to endure.

Not that I had any doubt of remaining faithful, as I'd indicated while sitting at the dinner table with my family a few years before my new perspective. But I knew with an eternal certainty! My wife would never again experience such pain from me, her husband ... the man who had vowed to protect her and to forsake all others! My brothers, my sons ... now you have it! I pray that you really *got it!* Now, how dare any of you, after hearing my story put your spouse through the same pain I caused my wife! How dare any of you to devalue your marriage and wife, God's gift to you! And for any of you to dishonor our Father and God! Now, knowing what you now know. I will submit that none of you can make the claim that you made a mistake or *got caught up!*

Listen. None of us can live for God under our own power, nor did God intend for us to try. And so, I remind you, by abiding in God, we are strengthened and enabled to gain victory over sin! *With God, all things are possible* (Matthew 19:26)!

My Cry For Divine Intervention

As for my wife and our time apart: My wife and I giving up on our marriage was not something that we were contemplating. I was confident in our victory! However, there was that one time I felt myself emotionally drifting apart from my wife. It was that evening that I spoke about earlier when I felt as if I was on the verge of throwing in the towel!

Though Lisa had asked me to return home shortly after receiving counsel from Dr. Davis, this period of our separation was perhaps two weeks; this was our first time apart. A second separation would soon occur. This was when I thought I was about to call it quits. After returning home from our first separation, my wife and I soon discovered that my past still weighed on her emotionally. This became apparent following a time we shared in sexual intimacy. I noticed my wife blankly staring at the ceiling as we lay on the bed. I knew what was going on in her mind before I asked her. Confirming my suspicion. I asked my wife what was wrong. Her reply, as tears flowed from her eyes, she was clearly saddened: "I can't get over what you did." She thought she had gotten over my past. It was for this reason that she asked me to return home. I responded, "I returned home too soon." As if my being away for a more extended period would really be the answer. No, time and distance would not and could not bring the healing and relief from the pain that my wife needed.

Nonetheless, this would result in me returning to my sister's home. As for me ... this time, things felt different; the duration of my stay seemed as if it would be indefinite. As a result, this began to affect me emotionally. The first time I was away from my home, as I mentioned, was perhaps two weeks. However, being away from home for a second time, just days after returning home. The reality and weight of our situation rested heavier upon me!

This time, the real uncertainty about things had me give greater thought to my marriage's outcome and that which was occurring with my wife. *My God is faithful!* He would allow meet to discern precisely what my wife would have to overcome. Having received or been reminded by God of the answer for that which would bring healing for my wife and our complete marital restoration, I asked her to meet me for dinner. I did not share with her the reason behind our date.

As we sat in the restaurant, I asked my wife two questions to confirm my belief regarding that which hindered her healing and our restoration. The first question I asked my wife was. "How would you respond if a co-worker wronged you and then came to you to extend an apology?" Lisa: "I will accept their apology." Me: "Would you forgive them?" My wife paused. After giving the question thought responded. "No. I won't forgive them, but I'll accept their apology."

As for the next question, I will not go into detail as this question pertains to our son Mario's biological father.

[For the record. Our families are on good terms. This has been the case since Mario was a child. I will admit … when I first appeared in Mario's life, an obstacle or two had to be worked out. Such matters I will address in my next book. I touched on this dynamic in chapter 12 of this book].

Having received my wife's answers to both questions, I confirmed what I knew to be my wife's challenge or spiritual ailment. Again my wife was oblivious to my motives behind the questions. However, now that I had spiritually identified the problem, I could present to her my spiritual conclusion.

I told my wife, "The issue hindering her soul's healing and the restoration of our marriage hinged on forgiveness." I continued, 'Until you are capable of forgiving me, our marriage will not be restored." Lisa simply heard me out. There was no response from her one way or another. I remember feeling optimistic about things. I felt if she would merely say at that very moment that she forgave me, all would be well! There was no such reply. Besides, getting to the point of forgiveness may take time. Even so, the matter of forgiveness or understanding it and how it can release one – the victim from the bondage of emotional hurt is not immediately understood, if ever, by some. Our dinner date concluded, and my wife returned home with something to think about.

This issue of forgiveness (there is a mystery and medicine behind it) was what Dr. Davis had told Lisa that she must do. We both heard Dr. Davis that day; however, the healing and deliverance that comes from sincere forgiveness, we did not grasp at the time. Nevertheless, when the Spirit of God visited me on this issue of forgiveness. It was as if I heard what He revealed to me on the subject was the first time. This can be understood as Spiritual revelation or a word from God. When I discerned God's message, I then, with certainty, knew that Lisa's healing and the restoration of our marriage depended upon her forgiving me.

Jesus spoke on forgiveness … it's His mandate that we forgive. Jesus is a God of healing, deliverance, restoration, and reconciliation; forgiveness allows these things to occur in a broken relationship (Matthew 6: 12 -15; Ephesians 4:32; Colossians 3:13).

Our second separation lasted for two or three weeks. The week that followed our date, I began to experience the weight and stress of being away from my family and the uncertainty of things about my wife and me! Not being able to attend to my responsibilities as the head of my home. The thought of being away from my wife and son, not being there to protect them, to secure the house at night, and other matters regarding my responsibilities, raced through my mind. What I felt … my helplessness from this separation pressed upon me tremendously!

To deal with what I was experiencing, I somehow began consciously detaching my emotions from my wife and even my home responsibilities. It didn't take long before I began to feel my emotional disconnect occurring. This was when I grabbed the proverbial towel! I was alarmed about what I was feeling! I knew if this divorce of my emotions regarding my marriage that I felt continued to widen, I would end it! In desperation, I cried out to God! I don't remember if it was audible or my desperate plea coming from within my soul.

Nevertheless, I cried out to my Father and God, saying, "You have got to move … You got to do it now! Or else I'm done!" I wasn't demanding God … my sincere plea was for His intervention. The towel was now raised in the air! My heart towards my wife was turning, and I had no way of reversing it! I was not at peace, and I desperately needed help! This was an earnest cry unto God for His involvement.

In such times as these, all situations for that matter. God wants us to call on Him and to wait for Him to move on our behalf. He knows how much we can bear, and He will show up to rescue us or enable us to endure whatever we are going through.

I now have a few questions: What are you learning and doing as you wait on God? Are you trusting Him through the process? Are you conducting yourself as a child of God? These things may also determine how long you may have to wait. As hard as it may be to embrace this training process, it is through difficulties that much can be learned about ourselves, others, and God Himself. It is during our seasons of waiting that God is trying to reach, teach, or that He is perhaps disciplining us. As His children, this training we must undergo should be understood as working toward our good and spiritual maturity.

For every challenging situation we encounter, at least these two things should take place: Our trust in the fact that God is with us no matter what. In this time of waiting, we truly learn to put our faith to work. And our question for God. "What do you want me to learn from this experience?"

I did all I could and knew to do as my wife, and I went through our spiritual healing and relational growth process. I was waiting and listening for God as best I could. But in the time of my desperation! For the first time, and after all that Lisa and I had experienced, I cried out to God in my hopeless plea! Soon after, He would show Himself faithful to me, yet again!

Within a few days, I received a call from my wife. She asked me if I could come by the house that upcoming Friday. There was no urgency or emotions of any sort displayed in her request. She didn't say why she wanted to see me, nor did I ask. However, I told her I couldn't because I had plans for that evening. I had a date planned with my friend Cierra. She had paid for an event that we were to attend that evening. You may not understand how I could do this. However, she was now only a friend. God totally freed me from the attraction I once had for her. Furthermore, I did not desire to be with anyone sexually.

Following the day of the date with Cierra, I had a role in my Church's Christmas play. I was playing the part of the angel Gabriel. I told my wife that I would be over to see her after the play.

On the evening of the play, minutes before my grand entrance, I stood behind the door that would open to signal my entry. I had a lengthy and significant part to recite as I gloriously walked into the sanctuary. However ... I was "Shook!" I had spent hours rehearsing and memorizing my lines. But now, I was all out of sorts; I could not remember my lines.

I remember thinking. "Was I going through this experience because I had gone out with Cierra the day before?" God had indeed removed from me the attraction that I had towards her. And by now, I was far removed from my season of whoredom … this was all of some thirteen years later. Cierra had been made aware of my situation with my wife. She even thought it was great that I had been honest with my wife. My reconnection with Cierra, or *date with her,* occurred during the second separation from my wife.

[For the record, all is well with the three of us; Cierra remains an infrequent acquaintance with whom my wife is cordial. People, this is what God can do if one's heart is willing].

As for how I was feeling and the fact I was unable to remember my lines, was I condemning myself, which is ultimately the result of Satan, for having gone out with Cierra? Perhaps, and if so, God was about to show up for me again! His story/play was not going to be derailed because of Satan! Flabbergasted and worried that I was unable to remember my part. I decided to read from my script. The doors were mere seconds from opening. But my pride wouldn't allow me to read from the paper I had in my hand. Besides, this was a Christmas play; a powerful story was to be told, and my role set the tone, even that of invoking the Spirit's anointing upon the event. At the time, I was not aware of this. My mind was blank! My nerves were stirring within! With the doors about to open, I would again appeal to my God and Father for help!

Walking down the aisle, I began to recite my lines. They flowed from my lips more fluently and with power than I experienced at any rehearsal or while practicing alone! The anointing of God had taken over. Before this experience, I'd never encountered such a take-over or *infilling* of the Holy Spirit. What a mighty move of God! But I was soon to discover that He'd been moving on my behalf all of that week.

I was on a cloud or feeling great from my performance of the evening, and God was about to lift me higher! Leaving the church, I went home to meet with my wife. Upon arrival, I first checked in on Desmond, who was asleep. I then went to the room and sat on the same chair during that unforgettable moment when my wife had said to me approximately two months earlier, "I need some time apart." I am now comfortably sitting and looking at my wife to find out why she wanted me to come over ... I really had no idea why she wanted me to pay her a visit.

Looking back at me, the first words my wife said to me were, "I am ready for you to come home." There was no excitement in her voice; however, without question, she was sincere about wanting her husband home ... I saw this in her eyes! I asked my wife what caused her to arrive at this decision. I had no idea what she was about to say.

My wife responded, "I had a dream ... my mother came to me in the dream. I could not see her face; I only heard her voice. She said to me, Tony is a good man. You need to forgive him." Lisa said, "I was then awakened from sleep." My wife described her dream as being crystal clear and also was her alertness after waking up. My wife knew it was time for me to come home! She had no doubt! God had made it plain through the dream He spoke to her through.

I actually expressed more excitement from hearing this than my wife. Her lack of emotion was more in line with her personality. It was late; therefore, I told my wife that I would return home in the morning ... she welcomed this.

This was the highest point of my day! However, God was not done yet; He wanted to further show off or prove Himself faithful! I was now preparing to leave and return to my sister's home; me standing, my wife and I embraced and kissed! To kiss one another had been our usual way of greeting. Or, when we were leaving one another's presence for an extended time ... To extend a kiss was our practice.

Warmly, we embraced and kissed one another; how wonderful this was. However, I became confused and quite surprised when my wife, with both of her hands on my chest, abruptly pushed back from me; as she did, she gasped! She is now looking at me wide-eyed and is obviously astonished. I asked her, "What is wrong!?" Her response would prove that our *God had mightily* intervened and that He had, in fact, healed my wife and restored the breach between my wife and me! My wife, now displaying excitement, exclaimed: "Our kiss felt like the very first time we kissed!" God showed my wife and me that He had brought new life and renewal to our marriage! The woman *I needed*, my God, had given back to me! My God, who at one point in my life I did know I needed ... did and continues to show Himself faithful and the *One I need!*

Some time having passed since that night, and I now sitting on my renowned chair in the comfort of my restored home. I found myself giving thought to what my wife and I had accomplished and overcome. With time removed from that transforming and glorious night of refreshing and renewal manifesting through the kiss. However, as I sat there, one matter continued to trouble my thoughts. It was the question that Dr. Davis asked my wife, "If you had to *rank your marriage* on a scale from one to ten, regarding how you feel about your marriage ... where would you rank it?" to which my wife responded, "Zero."

Replaying that moment in my mind and all that had transpired before meeting with Dr. Davis. I thought about the first letter or the punch that my wife received. I remembered what I had said to her, "Don't let this letter bother you." Then the epiphany or spiritual discernment was provided to me. "It was the letters! ... It was the letters!" My wife's response of "Zero" was regarding *how she felt at the time*. And not that our marriage was at a "Zero." Upon receiving this revelation, I went to my wife to ask her about her response that day. She confirmed for me what I had just discovered. That she understood Dr. Davis's question pertained to how she felt then. This gave me relief. Again our marriage, my wife's care for her boys, me, and her home was without interruption. She didn't miss a beat in those regards. And so it was; my marriage was fine, but my wife wasn't. My wife acknowledged that the letters had gotten to her.

Satan wanted my marriage! Through the foothold I gave him, He came at my wife! Just like he came at Eve, He went after my wife in an attempt to divide and even destroy my marriage and home!

But to God be the glory ... it would not be so!

He is the Mender of the breach!
He is The Restorer of our soul, Healer, and Reconciler!
He is our Exceeding and Great Reward!
He is everything I need!

476

And too, what you and this world need!

Thank you to my wife, Lisa! You are my gift from God! I need you!

Thank you to my God and Father, Our Healer and Defender! You gave yourself for me! You are the Greatest gift ever given … I need You!

"Now the God of peace, which brought again from the dead our
Lord Jesus, that great shepherd of the sheep, through the blood of the
everlasting covenant, Make you perfect in every good work to do his will,
working in you that which is well-pleasing in his sight, through Jesus
Christ; to whom be glory forever and ever. Amen."

Hebrews 13: 20,21.

Milton Keynes UK
Ingram Content Group UK Ltd.
UKHW020123030823
426203UK00016B/612

9 798988 593300